21 VOICES

The Art of Presenting
the Performing Arts

21 VOICES

The Art of Presenting the Performing Arts

Naomi Rhodes

Association of Performing Arts Presenters
Washington, D.C.

Copyright © 1990 The Association of Performing Arts Presenters

No part of this publication may be reproduced by any means without the written permission of the publisher. For information, contact the Association of Performing Arts Presenters, 1112 16th Street, NW, Suite 620, Washington, DC 20036.

Edited by Melinda Robins
Book and Jacket Design by Jane Tenenbaum

Typesetting by Impressions, a division of Edwards Brothers
Printed by Bookcrafters
Manufactured in the United States of America

This publication funded in part by the National Endowment for the Arts.

Library of Congress Catalog Card Number: 90-84768
ISBN: 0-926517-09-0

To my "silent partners,"
my mother, Martha
my brother, Samuel
my sister, Celeste
whose enduring support and encouragement sustained me
more than they can ever imagine.

And to my first mentor,
Fannie T. Taylor
who set me on my professional path in 1963
and now, as a friend, continues to inspire me.

Acknowledgements

It is impossible to undertake a project of this size and not have many people to thank. First, I must thank the Association of Performing Arts Presenters and its executive director, Susan Farr. Susie invited me to research and write this book. She had confidence that I would be able to embrace the project and take it where it led me.

When we first began talking about this book in 1986, neither of us knew it would be as big or involved, or take as long as it has. I thank her for her continuing commitment, for not losing her faith in me, and for her ability to adjust to a much-attenuated schedule. I also want to thank the Association for committing to the project and providing the resources that enabled me to write the book.

I am deeply indebted to my editors for helping make my words and ideas sing. Bill Keens worked with me at the commencement of the writing, when I had my greatest crises of confidence. He saw me through each of them and enabled me to go back to my computer to face the next chapter. Melinda Robins took over later and guided the revision and tightening process. Her journalistic expertise and editorial sensitivity to my own voice were always greatly appreciated. Project director Gayle Stamler, Director of Publications of the Association of Performing Arts Presenters, is the ultimate editor's editor. She was the glue that held the project together, and she provided the momentum that enabled it to reach its final culmination.

I am very grateful to my former associate, Beth Schenker, who worked with me shoulder to shoulder in the development and implementation of this project. In addition to doing much of the detail work in connection with this book, she ran my office during the long periods of time I was on the road, engaged in the research. Bruce Peyton transcribed the bulk of the interviews and, as a writer himself, always was ready to lend a sympathetic ear to me when the writing process bogged down. Peter Pennekamp was a willing and constant source of ideas and suggestions. He read drafts of several chapters, before I was sure I was on target, and kindly helped me find my own path.

I cannot thank them all by name, but there was an army of people who provided gracious hospitality to a travel-weary visitor in sixteen different cities. The friends, the family, the colleagues and their husbands and wives offered kindnesses that made life on the road that much more enjoyable; I appreciated them deeply.

Then there were my friends, who offered untold hours of support and expressions of confidence. My dear friend Toni Fountain Sikes willingly and patiently read a number of chapters in early drafts and offered comments and reactions that aided immeasurably in the revision process. Nancy Shear was constantly reassuring and kept pushing me to think beyond where I was at any given time. Martin I. Kagan provided crucial encouragement and support without which I would have faltered any number of times. I am more grateful to him than he can possibly know. Carl Larsen frequently offered indispensable guidance and advice. Then there were "les

Cinq," who were always there for me with kind and caring words. Sheenah Hankin and Dayna Blossom helped keep body and soul together throughout the final stages of the writing. I feel as if I never could have done it without them all.

Finally I must thank the organizations and people profiled. Their stories give voice to the ideas, achievements, hopes and potential of the field of presenting the performing arts. Without their stories, there would be no book. I am indebted to everyone in the twenty-one organizations who allowed me to interview them. They each sat with me and reflected on their organizations, themselves and the field. I am also grateful to those people beyond the staffs and boards of these organizations—the members of their communities, the funders, the critics, the artists, the scholars, the elected officials and members of their staffs—who took time from busy schedules to share their thoughts, ideas and feelings with me for the benefit of the book. I was greatly enriched by the words of everyone I interviewed, and constantly challenged by their ideas. Their views consistently pushed the limits of my own thinking and dramatically expanded the scope of the project.

If these profiles resonate, it is because of the richness and depth of the twenty-one presenting organizations and their people. If they do not, it is my own failing.

New York City, August 1990

21 VOICES

American Dance Festival	*Durham, North Carolina*
Appalshop	*Whitesburg, Kentucky*
Baltimore Theatre Project	*Baltimore, Maryland*
Brooklyn Academy of Music	*New York, New York*
Caribbean Cultural Center	*New York, New York*
Chamber Music Chicago	*Chicago, Illinois*
CITYFOLK	*Dayton, Ohio*
Dance Theater Workshop	*New York, New York*
Dartmouth College, Hopkins Center	*Hanover, New Hampshire*
Helena Film Society/Series for the Performing Arts	*Helena, Montana*
La Peña Cultural Center	*Berkeley, California*
Madison Civic Center	*Madison, Wisconsin*
92nd Street Y	*New York, New York*
On the Boards	*Seattle, Washington*
P.S. 122	*New York, New York*
Quantum Productions	*Atlanta, Georgia*
San Francisco Performances	*San Francisco, California*
Spoleto Festival USA	*Charleston, South Carolina*
University of Iowa, Hancher Auditorium	*Iowa City, Iowa*
Walker Art Center	*Minneapolis, Minnesota*
Yreka Community Theater	*Yreka, California*

Contents

Introduction

Presenting the performing arts is an art. In the best of all possible worlds, performing arts presenters are artists, and the organizations they run, works of art.

There is a distinction between the *act* of presenting the performing arts and the *art* of presenting the performing arts. The act of presenting is procedural: to introduce, demonstrate and offer to the public the highest quality work from a variety of disciplines. The art of presenting requires not only the ability to handle the procedural aspects of presenting with finesse, but to transcend the administrative role by investing vision, imagination and passion in the work.

As choreographer David Gordon put it, "A great presenter is an artist, a great manager is an artist, because they redefine a set of circumstances in a way that makes it newly functional, and that elevates the level of possibility for the artist and the public."

In the past three years, I have had the privilege of living in the best of all possible worlds. I have been on an odyssey that has taken me all over the United States, from New Hampshire to Georgia, from New York City to Seattle. It has been a journey of discovery, as I have become intimately acquainted with the 21 organizations profiled in this book, each of whom demonstrates in a unique way the art of presenting.

The conceptual point of departure of my journey was a firm conviction that this book should focus on the art of presenting the performing arts, rather than the act of doing so. The presenter who makes an art of his or her job will understand what the work is all about and how to present it in a context that illuminates it for the audience; what's more, he or she will know why a given work should be part of the presenting program.

The idea for *21 Voices* began to take shape early in 1987 when I was invited by the Association of Performing Arts Presenters to undertake the preliminary work on this project. This was to be a book about "exemplary presenters" of the performing arts. The hope was that by focusing on a number of organizations doing excellent and singular work, the entire field would benefit. In short, the idea was inspiration by example.

One of the first steps in setting up the framework for this book was to develop criteria that would help identify exemplary organizations. My goal was to find presenters whose content-based approach to their work would give rise to a discussion of the art of presenting. Although each presenting organization is unique, with certain traits more outstanding than others, all meet these criteria in large part. The presenters you will read about are:

• uniquely visionary, with the ability to imagine programs that others have not considered and to articulate singular ideas;

• single-mindedly dedicated to their vision, while at the same time able to see the big picture;

• imaginative and capable of seeing limitless possibilities. They derive inspiration, ideas and direction from a broad range of interests within and outside the arts field;

• ready to implement new ideas and nurture different approaches to the field; pathfinders;

• mission-driven, with a strong sense of what they are about and why. They meet unmet needs in their communities, while reflecting their own underlying philosophical ideals and principles;

• risk-takers who are open to challenging genres and events regardless of whether there is a proven market;

• passionate about excellence and willing to search for it. They recognize excellent work when they see it, and are comfortable making artistic decisions based on quality;

• partners in the creative process. They seek opportunities to provide the proper environment for meshing the artist's expression with the community's needs;

• active creators who see presenting as a form of artistic expression, and see institutional creativity as an intrinsic part of the process of presenting;

• entrepreneurial in spirit, tenaciously pursuing a chosen path and making it financially viable through innovative fundraising, marketing, promoting and packaging;

• capable of seeing change in a positive way. They meet obstacles constructively, rise to difficult challenges and create opportunities in the face of adversity;

• adaptive, carving out a place for themselves and their ideas while responding to community needs, all without compromising their artistic vision. They recognize that arts and cultural institutions die if they do not evolve over time;

• tenacious even in the face of stiff odds. They give developing programs the opportunity to establish themselves and flourish;

- central to community life. People's lives would be different if the organization ceased to exist;
- cognizant of their institutional responsibilities to the field. They promote and serve both presenting and the arts by using resources to explore pressing issues and advance important ideas;
- activists, and cultural leaders. They are proud to champion a cause and they interact with artistic and non-artistic communities to establish the arts as an integral part of the fabric of society.

These attributes are embodied in many activities: presenting new works; commissioning new work; incorporating new works or new groups into an established season; producing in conjunction with presenting; sponsoring outreach programs; preserving for audiences traditional programs such as instrumental and vocal recitals and chamber music; presenting work grounded in non-European-based cultural communities; participating in collaborative ventures with artists and communities; using space in an innovative way; and creating breakthrough projects that have changed the face of presenting.

In choosing to focus on these attributes I am not saying that organizations need not be well-managed or fiscally stable. Indeed, they must. But without an artistic mission and an understanding of how that mission serves the community, there is no reason to have an organizational structure, much less an organization.

I felt strongly that the final list of presenters should reflect the fact that the presenting field is not a monolithic entity representing a single style, discipline, kind of organization or point of view. Performances can be presented in any type of space, including theaters, concert halls, auditoriums, multi-purpose rooms, warehouses, lofts, lobbies, outdoor parks, tents—in short, anyplace where people gather. Events may be from around the corner or around the world; they may come from any era from ancient to contemporary. Some presenters focus on a single discipline while others offer a combination of presentations that span the entire range of performance.

That being the case, I wanted to include the widest possible range of organizational types in the consideration of exemplary work: festivals, performing arts centers, contemporary art centers, urban cultural centers, rural cultural centers, community presenters in both towns and rural areas, and colleges and universities, among others.

With all this in mind, I canvassed 150 people connected to the field, asking for recommendations about exemplary presenters. These people themselves represented a diverse cross-section of the field—directors and touring staff of state, local and regional arts agencies; directors of art service organizations; performing artists; artist managers; and the deputy chairmen, program directors and regional representatives of the National Endowment for the Arts. All were asked not only to recommend presenters, but to provide as much documentation as possible on their choices. In the end, I received 339 suggestions naming 195 organizations that we should consider. That list was eventually narrowed down to approximately 50 organizations.

Experts knowledgeable about the field, and committed to the principles that this book would advance, agreed to serve anonymously on the selection committee. The committee was asked to make the final choices from among the 50 organizations with which I presented them, as well as a few others that the committee members proposed.

The selection process utilized the 16 attributes listed above as a point of departure. The list provided a conceptual base that offered guidance, but was not used as an inflexible model to which all the groups had to conform. (And once the 21 presenters had been selected, I used the 16 attributes to create a philosophical basis for broad areas of exploration, not as a rigid yardstick providing a standard for measuring one against the other.)

It is important to state right here that the list of presenters finally chosen by the committee does not and was never meant to represent a "top 21" or "21 best" list of presenting organizations. The selection committee's discussion was spirited and wide-ranging. The decisions were difficult. Choices often hinged on the balance they would produce in the list itself, which was intended to illustrate the range of the field. Using the same list of attributes as a guide, any reader might have arrived at a different combination of organizations.

I began intensive research on each organization in November of 1987; information from the early phase of research was updated through August of 1990, as I wrote and revised each chapter. I visited every presenting organization, and attended at least one live performance each place. Where time and opportunity permitted, I attended more than one. In every case, I felt privileged to be afforded an inside view of the operation.

As each profile unfolds, it is important to remember that by and large it is a snapshot of the organization at a particular time. In a dynamic organization, things are changing all the time: staff members move on, new projects are initiated and new avenues explored.

Much of my research entailed interviews with the people who run these presenting organizations. They are the 21 voices.

I also interviewed members of the boards of directors from these organizations, as well as other staff members, artists who have been presented on their stages, members of their communities, critics from newspapers that cover their events, elected officials from the community, and funders from the public and private sector.

This process included some of the most memorable moments I have ever experienced in a lifetime of attending performing arts events: hearing Astor Piazzolla and his New Tango Quintet for the first time, thanks to Quantum Productions in Atlanta; being in the audience for the world premiere of Billy Taylor's *Homage*, which the Madison Civic Center commissioned for Taylor's trio and the Juilliard String Quartet; taking part in the Caribbean Cultural Center's tribute to Oya and Yemanja in New York; witnessing Minnie Black's Senior Citizen Gourd Band at Appalshop's Open Windows Festival; observing the California E.A.R Unit improvising a piece of music with the Capital High School orchestra at the Helena Film Society/Series for the Performing Arts.

I was moved by the American Dance Festival performances of Pearl Primus' solo works, recreated onstage by young dancers from Philadanco and introduced with poems recited by the choreographer herself. I was overwhelmed by the explosion of lights, music, costuming and energy that was *The Warrior Ant*, performed outdoors at the Spoleto Festival in a tree-filled college quadrangle. I was warmed by the rich beauty of Schubert's vocal and choral music in a February performance at the 92nd Street Y; sitting with fellow music lovers in the intimate theater, I felt almost as if I were in a Viennese salon.

Every place I visited presented me with something unique and compelling in performance.

I will never forget the people I interviewed. A few I had known previously, but most I was meeting for the first time. I was thrilled that so many of them opened their minds, hearts and souls to me, answering my questions thoughtfully and with surprising candor. They permitted me an intimate view of their organizations and communities.

I was also stirred that so many artists were willing to come forth and talk about how presenting organizations and presenters have made a difference in their lives. They were eloquent about this subject.

21 Voices was written as a sourcebook for inspiration. It is not meant to be a "how to" book. Rather, I hope that readers within and outside the field of presenting will see how presenters and their organizations can implement very personal visions; how they are empowered by artists and communities; and how they in turn empower the people they serve. If the field is enriched by the inspiration provided by the work of these men and women—our colleagues—then this book will have accomplished everything I might have hoped when I embarked on the project.

Chuck Davis African American Dance Ensemble

Photo by Jay Anderson

1 The Past, Present, and Future of Modern Dance

At first, it looked as though it would be a regular post-performance party, with the customary food and drink, and lots of people chit-chatting. Then, the voice of Chuck Davis—director of the Chuck Davis African American Dance Ensemble—rang out over the crowd, calling for attention.

What followed was a spontaneous and memorable scene, a West African-style traditional ceremony to honor the legendary Black choreographers showcased in "The Black Tradition in American Modern Dance," a three-year project established by the American Dance Festival and held at its home in Durham, North Carolina. Garth Tate—former public affairs director of Dance/USA—describes that memorable evening in June 1988, during the project's first year.

"Chuck told us it is very important to pay tribute to those who have gone before us, those people who paved the way for those of us creating now. He got people to chant with him in a very rhythmical, very African way, and to clap their hands. He came out to the middle of the floor and started dancing. Everyone understood that when they were pulled from the sidelines, they had to come into the center of the circle and do a solo dance of their own creation."

The impromptu dance started with the choreographers and performers of the evening and then went on to include some of the spectators, many of whom had been in the audience. "You had a variety of people who crossed racial lines and socio-economic lines who participated in this communal event," Tate recalls. "There have been few instances where I've experienced that feeling, that sense of happiness, of unity and mutual support."

Black modern dance continues to struggle for its rightful place in the arts world, just as modern dance once fought a battle for recognition. During its history, the efforts of the American Dance Festival have helped both gain a measure of credibility and acceptance.

"The Black Tradition in American Modern Dance" sought to explore and understand the intellectual and artistic contributions of Black choreographers and dancers by bringing together scholars, critics, choreographers and dancers to "make a new history of modern dance, restoring to collective memory the names of Black artists and the shaping role they have played."

With such projects, the American Dance Festival has earned an unrivaled spot on the modern dance scene, and has produced programs of singular interest and timeliness.

The ADF "Iceberg"

"I think the American Dance Festival is clearly one of two organizations in the country which are perceived as embodying the spirit of modern and related dance forms," says Richard Long, a dance scholar and poet who teaches at Emory University. "The other, of course, is Jacob's Pillow. I think that anything which transpires at the American Dance Festival has relevance, meaning, and significance for the entire dance field. For (the 'Black Tradition' project) to have happened at ADF means that it has entered into the consciousness and on the agenda of other dance organizations and people who are concerned with dance."

The arts-going public knows ADF mostly for its six-week summer series of performances. Works, choreographers, and companies both familiar and unknown have made their mark at the Festival since its inception in 1934 in Bennington, Vermont. To look at its list of premieres is to read the history of modern dance. In the 1930s, there were Martha Graham, Hanya Holm, Doris Humphrey, Charles Weidman. After World War II, Merce Cunningham, José Limón, Erick Hawkins, Alwin Nikolais, Paul Taylor, Alvin Ailey. Then, the dance rebels of the late 1960s: Meredith Monk, Twyla Tharp, Pilobolus, Laura Dean, Trisha Brown.

The ADF's 1988 events schedule included premieres from the Erick Hawkins Dance Company, Molissa Fenley, Anita Feldman Tap, and by international choreographers. Other performances were given by Pilobolus, Lar Lubovitch Dance Company, Merce Cunningham Dance Company, Bill T. Jones/Arnie Zane and Company, and others. These were in addition to performances from the "Black Tradition" project.

These performances and premieres are only the tip of the iceberg that is the American Dance Festival. Its school is an integral part of the institution, and in fact has been at the center of the Festival from the start.

"First there was the school, going back to the beginnings in 1934," says ADF Director Charles Reinhart. "The school was important because it gave the choreographers and artists money, because the students paid tuition. It also gave them a source of dancers to take into their company; it gave them a source of work. It served all the purposes of the choreographer. The school was the foundation of it all—and it still is."

ADF under the watchful eye of Dean Martha Myers offers an intensive six-week summer school with faculty members Betty Jones, Donald McKayle, Stuart Hodes, Chuck Davis, Linda Tarnay, Jose Meier, and many other outstanding professionals in the field of modern dance.

ADF considers itself a "producing service organization" rather than a festival or a presenting organization; it sees its role as broader than either of those classifications might indicate. As a result, its national and international professional services are extensive.

The range of activities in its 1990 Festival program illustrates the breadth and depth of services offered to the modern dance field:

—seven weeks of performances in two theaters on the Duke University campus;

—a six-week school offering courses in modern, ballet, and jazz techniques, composition, and improvisation;

—the "Black Tradition" project activities;

—the Young Choreographers and Composers in Residence Program;

—the International Choreographers Workshop;

—the International Choreographers Commissioning Program;

—the Center for the Study of Professional Dance Training and Education, which includes the programs "Body Therapies in the Art of Movement," and "Dance Update for Professional Dance Artists/Educators;"

> ADF presents and nurtures artists, continually commissioning new work and providing an environment in which collaborators can work together.

—the Institutional Linkages Program, which establishes and conducts exchange projects between ADF and select dance institutions abroad, including sites in China, Venezuela, Argentina, USSR, South Africa, and Zaire;

—two mini-ADFs in Seoul, South Korea; and Delhi and Madras, India;

—the Philadelphia Choreographers-in-Residence project;

—a teaching certification program;

—a community outreach program;

—summer internships;

—the Dance Critics Conference;

—the Young Dancers Workshop; and

—the Video Archival Project.

In addition to this ever-expanding activity, there is the $25,000 Scripps Award periodically bestowed upon a choreographer for lifetime achievement in the field.

In addition, the Humanities and Dance programs—which began in the late 1970s and are co-directed by Gerald Myers and Stephanie K. Reinhart—have focused on the art form's humanistic dimensions, which "make dance something more than simply entertainment or recreation, something more than simply physical technique," Myers writes. "Human beings have always danced, and the reasons for this include but extend beyond fun and games."

The programs have included series on "Dance, Culture and Humanities," and "Dance and Their Peoples," in which scholars, choreographers, and dancers showed how dance is a window on culture, and how it provides insights into a society or civilization. In 1984 ADF presented "The Aesthetic and Cultural Significance of Modern Dance," a program in conjunction with the Festival's 50th anniversary program. This was accompanied by a booklet of commissioned scholarly essays and a photographic exhibit tracing the history of modern dance.

This format became the model for "The Black Tradition in American Modern Dance," a three-year project that in 1989 and 1990 expanded beyond the six-week summer Festival. Humanities programs began in March, with speakers and demonstrations going out to 10 traditionally Black or under-served colleges in North Carolina. In addition, students from five of these colleges came into Durham to spend a day at the summer festival.

The Past

ADF, which critic Clive Barnes has called "the world's greatest dance festival," has a long and distinguished history. It was founded more than 55 years ago in the college town of Bennington, Vermont, as a summer collaboration for teaching, experimenting, and creating modern dance classics.

Its members were the so-called "second generation" of modern dance pioneers, who were the successors to Isadora Duncan, Ruth St. Denis, and Ted Shawn. This next generation was led by Martha Hill, and included Martha Graham, Charles Weidman, Doris Humphrey, and Hanya Holm. In 1948, a new generation of artists emerged and led ADF from Bennington to a new home at New London's Connecticut College. They were Merce Cunningham, Alvin Ailey, Paul Taylor, and others. The Festival gave these artists the chance to teach and choreograph in a stable environment, creating what are now dance classics.

In the late 1960s, the next wave of modern dance innovators were making their mark: Meredith Monk, Twyla Tharp and Yvonne Rainer. In a necessary state of perpetual evolution, the Festival responded by instituting the Emerging Generation Program, which commissioned and presented new works by these choreographers and others such as Laura Dean, Trisha Brown and members of Pilobolus.

In 1978, ADF moved to the Duke University campus in Durham, triggering an explosion of projects, professional workshops, and commissioned works.

In turn, the 1980s were a time of pioneering international efforts, including the presentation of modern dance companies from abroad, commissions to international choreographers, formal collaborative programs to develop international modern dance companies, and more informal linkages with developing dance programs in a growing number of countries.

ADF Director Reinhart admits that he and his staff struggle to balance the institution's many components. "It's a seesaw," he says. "Balance is difficult but important. I think we build it organically, which has to do with (the Festival's) history." He explains that ADF began with the school, then added the performances, then began to offer workshops in 1969. "The workshops would be totally different if they were in isolation," he says. "The fact that they are here with the school and the performances makes it all work. It makes for an absolute artistic circus, but we all survive because it's only in the six-week summer season that the volcano goes off. "

The Black Tradition

One of ADF's most significant projects in recent times has been the three-year "Black Tradition" project. Dance historian and critic Richard Long explains that while ADF has done many projects to research and preserve the history of modern dance, this program's genesis was in a pilot project that sprang from a teacher's concern with his students' lack of knowledge about the Black contribution to modern dance. Former ADF jazz dance instructor Alvin McDuffy, disturbed that his students didn't know the names of Pearl Primus and Katherine Dunham, or where the dance steps he was teaching came from historically, went in frustration to the Reinharts.

In response, ADF engaged Donald McKayle to set his classic work, the 1951 *Games*, on the Durham-based Chuck Davis African American Dance Company. Its success led to a program that combined performances of *Games* with a panel discussion by humanities scholars on the contributions of Black choreographers to modern dance.

The pilot program gained ADF a 1987 Ford Foundation grant to arrange similar reconstructions by other Black choreographers on dance companies across the country. A panel of experts chose Talley Beatty's *Congo Tango Palace*, first performed in 1960 and reset on the Joel Hall Dancers from Chicago; Eleo Pomare's *Las Desenamoradas* (1967), reset on the Dayton Contemporary Dance Company; Donald McKayle's *Rainbow 'Round My Shoulder* (1959), also reset on the Dayton company; and Pearl Primus' solos *The Negro Speaks of Rivers*, *Strange Fruit*, and *Hard Times Blues*, all first performed in 1943 and reset on two different dancers from Philadanco.

The choreographers chose the dance companies and taught the works, which were performed as part of the regular ADF weekend performance schedule in 1988. More works were recreated in 1989. Accompanying panel discussions were held by Black dance scholars, historians, and critics, with choreographers and dancers participating.

In 1990, the Dayton Contemporary Dance Company was to perform Talley Beattie's *Mourner's Bench* and Eleo Pomare's *Missa Luba*. Donald McKayle's *Songs of the Disinherited* and *Saturday's Child* were reset on Cleo Parker Robinson Dance Company in Denver.

The 1988 series of panel discussions featured all four distinguished choreographers as well as scholars in the history and criticism of the arts, including Zita Allen, William Moore, Joe Nash, Elizabeth Fenn, and Richard Long. They were a treasure trove of information on African and Caribbean roots, early dance styles, modern dance pioneers, and the recognition of Black dancers within the modern dance movement.

Joe Nash says the ADF project tried to identify the masterworks of African-American choreographers, and furnish data about the art of dance itself. "For me, the whole question is related to one's perception of what the African American is in American society, and how that culture is rooted in our history, American history," he says. "When the African began to dance, on the Southern plantations or on the levee, people saw a phenomenon that could not be explained or adequately described," so it was categorized as something apart.

"But if you think of the growth and development of American modern dance, and all the influences it had," he continues, "then your thinking becomes quite clear. When I see what Donald McKayle has accomplished, and Eleo Pomare, and Talley Beatty—they worked and functioned as artists, as choreographers with a vision, a dream, an artistic goal. Color didn't make any difference, because they took from life. When you do that, you reflect everything that is in life. They made an artistic response, so they are eclectic and diversified. They are American, and they are part of the American art of dance."

> "Our religion is modern dance. This is the American art form, along with jazz."

After one of the seminars, Long and dance critic Zita Allen sat in the well-travelled hallway of ADF administrative headquarters, dancers passing by with loaded dance bags weighing down shoulders. They chatted informally and reflected on the program.

Long traced the history of the works that had been reconstructed that summer. He indicated that some had seen occasional performances over the years, while others had not been performed in many years. "We have works that have their place in the history of modern dance," Long said, "but literally have not been seen in 40 years. It's wonderful to have these very important social and choreographic statements set on younger dancers."

Allen added, "This project has done something not just in terms of the role of the Black choreographer and Black dancer. It has had an impact beyond those simple categories. Just comparing different decades and different eras of dancer . . . You see dancers grappling with a completely different use of weight, a completely different use of movement, a completely different approach to dance where the form is not the most important thing. The content is."

The performances of the reset works were a popular triumph with sold-out crowds. There also was significant positive critical comment. Jennifer Dunning of *The New York Times* wrote, "The seven dances celebrate passions: fear and danger, life and death."

Chuck Davis says *Games* was the best thing that ever happened to his African American Dance Ensemble. He explains that his dancers were still in a developmental stage when choreographer Donald McKayle came to see them for the first time. "He saw that raw energy, and he also saw a measure of (naivete), where the dancers were open. You get many of the New York dancers and others who have an attitude of knowing everything. My dancers are like sponges in a sea of knowl-edge. They want to learn, so their eyes and their ears are open—and I insist they close their mouths.

"Donnie (McKayle) came in as a master," he says. "In my company, every-thing is based on the African tradition. You are taught to respect your elders. And when the master speaks, you be quiet, you pay attention, and you listen. And that's what they did. Donnie came in not only with the technique, but he taught them the correct way to move and dance with flair, to build and develop a character. He also brought history. It was more than choreography. It was a study in life—past, present and future. The dancers went on stage and danced as if there were no tomorrow. I think Donnie was more than pleased at that premiere performance."

The Artistic Mission

Key to ADF programs is the idea that the choreographer must be served first, and the audience will benefit as a result. The vision grows out of support for the artists, first and foremost.

Reinhart admits that his view of the presenting process may be different than most because of his background. He spent many years working with choreographers before taking over ADF in 1969. In the 1960s, he managed a number of inter-nationally renowned dance companies, including the Paul Taylor Dance Company and the Donald McKayle Dance Company. He was the national coordinator of the Dance Touring Program for the National Endowment for the Arts from its inception in 1967 until 1978.

"I am the supporter of the choreographer," he says, "so in a sense I want those audiences there as part of my support for the choreographer, not the other way around," he says. "That's what this institution was and is all all about. It's a sense of history, the serving of the artist.

"We have built an audience for modern dance. I think one of the reasons is because we are so committed to it. Our religion is modern dance. So when we go out, we pound that in, saying that this is the art form of this century, this is the American art form, along with jazz. This is where the Mozarts and the Bachs and the Shakespeares are. Their names are Taylor and Cunningham and Graham.

"We work both ends against the middle. We are saying that the creative volcano is not over in modern dance. We must help our great ones make the pieces and the young ones come up, but we must never, never forget where we have been. We must begin to look back and take care of our heritage."

Serving the choreographer means providing a structure so he or she can work, says Stephanie Reinhart, ADF associate director and "Black Tradition" co-director. "You can be simply a presenter of an art form, or you can be a nurturer of new things. ADF both presents and nurtures. To the best of our abilities, we are con-tinually commissioning new work, both from the established and the young talents. We also provide a supportive environment in which the collaborators can work together, in a way that is not possible in New York."

Mary Regan, executive director of the North Carolina Arts Council, says the commissions and the premieres benefit the North Carolina community as well as the choreographer. "It's a different mindset if people are hearing something or seeing something for the first time," she says. "That was the new thing that the American Dance Festival brought us. It has been wonderfully stimulating for all the arts in the state."

Charles Reinhart adds, "In the performing arts, without a presentation there's no performing art, period. The choreographer is the only creative artist who doesn't work by him- or herself and can't put the creation in the closet when it's finished. The playwright can do that. The painter can do that. The sculptor can do that. The choreographer needs the dancers in the studio."

Experimental tap dance choreographer Anita Feldman is one artist who has grown under ADF's wing. She explains that after 10 years in modern dance, she went back to the tap dancing of her childhood. As an instructor, "I began to wonder why tap dancing had never been explored in any modern sense. Whenever you saw tap dancing, it was unison chorus line, or it was with comedy. It never was taken very seriously. But I found it fascinating. It's complex—music and dance at the same time. I was interested in new music, and I began to think of tap dance as being new music. That was the beginning of my explorings."

Her first summer at ADF was in the 1987 Young Choreographers and Composers Program, in which she created and performed the work *Shimmer*.

"That was a major step in my development," she says. "It was the first time I had the opportunity to work with my dancers every day, six hours a day. In New York, you're lucky if you get to work three hours here and three hours there. It changed my way of working, in a positive way."

In 1987, Feldman collaborated with composer Jalalu-Kalvert Nelson. The following year, she worked with instrument maker Daniel Schmidt of Berkeley, Calif., to design and build a tap dance instrument—a floor made of different kinds of woods, metals and undersurface supports to produce a variety of timbres. In addition to being an audio innovation, the instrument is a beautiful sculptural piece which sits on the stage floor in two pieces.

"I had gotten tired of the four or five timbres I could get out of my tap shoes on the floor," Feldman explains. "Another problem is that you don't know what the floor's going to be like when you go to perform. My instrument is the floor, and I wanted to always have a good instrument, and to expand my timbral possibilities."

She was commissioned to create with composer Lois V Vierck *Hexa*, a new piece for her tap dance instrument which was performed with a full evening of her works. The program included *Shimmer*, with Jalalu-Kalvert Nelson and five other musicians performing live his specially commissioned score.

An explanation of *Hexa* in the performance program clarifies Feldman's unique approach to tap: "*Hexa* is a tap-music-dance collaboration by Anita Feldman and Lois V Vierk. It is the result of a desire by the artists to create a work in which the distinctions between the tap dance and the music are, to the greatest extent possible, eliminated. To this end, each artist participated in the creation of both the sound and the movement."

This fascinating work involved three dancers including Feldman on stage, percussionist Gary Schall in the orchestra pit, and composer Vierk at the controls of the mixing board. Microphones were placed in the undersurface of the instrument, sending the tap sounds through a synthesizer to be reprocessed by Vierk, with reprocessed percussion sounds coming from Schall. All the sounds are manipulated and modified in some way. It is a revelation, visually very beautiful, and absorbing aurally.

Feldman says ADF was the first institution to commission her to do new work, giving her the encouragement and opportunity to develop her new vision and take artistic risks.

Charles Reinhart seems driven positively by such risk, finding unknown choreographers and nurturing them, seeing them develop and create something seminal.

"We've been skirting a word, and the word is 'passion'," he says. "If you've got that going for you, you have an immediate reward. You're never going to look in the mirror and say, 'What have I done with my life?' If you put your beliefs and passions out in front of you, you will achieve everything you want to achieve on all levels. What greater satisfaction is there in the world than seeing an artist you believe in, and helping that artist go up the ladder?"

ADF in Durham

One of the greatest challenges for an arts institution like ADF—with its long and rich history, and major national and international reputation—is to maintain those assets while building local and committed support. ADF has advocate Carlton Midyette on its board of directors. He says his special mission is to try to develop pride in ADF—and support for its programs—within the Durham-Raleigh-Chapel Hill community.

"I think my role with the Festival is to be vocal and aggressive with the media—not necessarily with reporters, but with people involved in ownership of the media—and with leaders in the business community, to try to explain to them that we have something that other people would die for." Midyette acknowledges, however, that the Festival's impact on the cultural world is largely outside of North Carolina.

E.G. Schreiber, executive director of the Durham Arts Council, says ADF both fits and doesn't fit into the Durham community. "ADF, if it were located anywhere, would not fit into its community," he says. "It is certainly a nationally—if not internationally—known activity that is located in Durham. It's located here, but it's much bigger than that. It's a major element in the arts—not only in Durham, but in the Research Triangle of Raleigh, Durham, and Chapel Hill."

Midyette explains that a group of businesspeople established the Research Triangle in the 1950s to reverse what was seen as a brain drain of people leaving the area after receiving high-quality educations at one of the many universities and colleges. A large piece of land was purchased to set up and establish a research park. An astonishing number of first-class research and development organizations have moved in, and this has provided an economic engine that is enviable throughout the world. It also has done exactly what it was set up to do: ensure that many people settle in the area after completing their education. The result is an extraordinarily well-educated populace, given the size of the community. "This is one of the reasons that the Festival is here and has found as fertile a ground as it has," Midyette says. "It is also one of the reasons that there is an economy here that would support it."

Nevertheless, Durham is still in the process of shedding its image as a tobacco town. Tobacco processing once dominated the city's and county's economic activity. Now, the American Tobacco plant is closed, and Liggett Tobacco has left the state.

Liggett Tobacco and Duke University were instrumental in convincing ADF to choose Durham when it was seeking to leave its home in New London, Conn. Terry Sanford, who was then president of Duke, was particularly persuasive. Liggett has moved its headquarters to New Jersey, and Sanford is now a U.S. senator. But, ADF Director Reinhart says, there are still strong pillars of support in the community.

He singles out the city's newspaper, *The Durham Herald and Sun*, for the highest accolades. "No paper could ever be as supportive as this newspaper has been in realizing the importance of the Festival," he says. During the summer season, it runs a front-page box listing each day's activities, and has frequent articles to describe the events. The paper also has published editorials praising ADF as "the creative gemstone in the crown of the city's activities."

Another example of local support took ADF by surprise in 1988. A local supermarket printed the Festival schedule in two colors on its brown paper bags, including the telephone number of the box office. It left off its own name, and did the project on its own initiative.

The flip side of this supportive picture is the unrealized hope that ADF would have its own facilities in downtown Durham. A $2 million allocation was made in 1987 by the state to the City of Durham. Durham was to have provided an additional $4 million from its own coffers and from private sources. The now-defunct American Tobacco plant and warehouse was targeted for transformation into ADF's new headquarters. The plan has not moved forward.

Schreiber characterizes the political environment in Durham as "a bunch of different groups. As one would expect, all those groups have different agendas. It takes longer to get anything done here than I've seen almost anywhere else, except for New York City." He says the political situation is divided along racial lines and between suburban residents and in-town dwellers. "The way lines get drawn differs from issue to issue," he says, adding that there is no one clear leader.

Midyette adds that the dominant political interests in Durham respond to the fact that approximately half the city's population is Black, and that Duke University plays such a major role in the community. The 13-member city council is not controlled by a few business interests, as it would be in other cities, because the tobacco companies that once wielded much power no longer exist. "You've got a city that's run by its citizens, which is good," Midyette says, "but there is no big business impact, no strong leadership from that community. The power structure in Durham is scattershot. It's democracy at its wildest." This has meant that ADF has no strong champion within the political structure to ensure that the state's $2 million is expeditiously matched, and the building program is begun.

The Festival itself also has been said to bear some responsibility for the unrealized efforts to establish a permanent home in Durham away from the Duke University campus. The qualities that have made Charles Reinhart ADF's devoted and uncompromising soul and rallying spirit may have subverted the efforts. As good as his instincts are in modern dance, some have said, Reinhart does not have equally astute diplomatic instincts enabling him to work effectively within the business and political communities. But then, as Midyette says, "A fellow with political instincts wouldn't necessarily grow up to be a modern dance impresario."

> Key to ADF programs is the idea that the choreographer must be served first, and the audience will benefit as a result.

Through it all, Midyette's role as board member is to talk to as as many people as he can, "and explain to them the fact the Festival is here, and is still more widely recognized in New York or San Francisco or Los Angeles than it is in our area. Because I'm in the business community and in contact with people who support a variety of arts that are more generally accepted, I try to turn them on, to make them understand that there's something here that is genuinely unique and that they need to pay attention to.

"I've been trying a standard line of Charles'—that we are doing something now that will endure. The remarkable thing is that it has not come to this area to perform, it has come to this area to be created. That is an extraordinary difference that is hard to get across to people. Often, developing pride is appealing to the less-attractive instincts in people. If you tell them they may lose it, they begin to appreciate it."

Building an audience in an area that had no substantial modern dance following also has been a problem, although ADF was wooed and welcomed to Durham. Associate director Stephanie Reinhart says an audience has been built because ADF presents many of the same artists every year. "When we plan a subscription season, we put on a Laura Dean—who was not very well known when we first had her on our season—or Pilobolus or Paul Taylor or whoever, to introduce our audiences to the works of younger, less well-known talents who we strongly believe in. We put them on year after year. The next year, more people come to their performances. The first time people came to see Merce Cunningham, they walked out. Last year, he received standing ovations. So you build, and you educate."

Charles Reinhart recalls that when he worked as an artist's manager representing dance companies, he often would be told by presenters that as much as they enjoyed a company's performance, they would not bring them back to perform again for several years. He recalls thinking, "I will never, ever do that if I become a presenter.

"If you believe in somebody, you bring them back. I mean, would you say to Beethoven, 'Well, we liked the Fourth Symphony, but we're not going to bring you back even though you're going to write the Fifth, Sixth, and Seventh. We'll wait until you get to the Eighth.'? It makes no sense from a presenting point of view. The ones we bring back steadily because we believe in their talent are the ones who eventually get the biggest box office."

ADF's budget—$1.9 million for 1990—comes from 38 percent earned and 62 percent contributed income. In the 1980s, governmental and foundation support increased, with corporate support building more slowly. Stephanie Reinhart, who is responsible for fundraising, thinks the relative youth of modern dance is one reason ADF may be low on corporate giving lists.

Seventy percent of the private sector contributions are gained from outside the state. Of the total contributed income, 9 percent is from government sources, 40 percent foundation, 8 percent corporate, 5 percent donated services, and 8 percent from the ADF friends organization and from other individuals.

Stephanie Reinhart finds their most effective marketing and promotional tools are mailings and telephone work. "I think telemarketing is very important," she says. "One of our volunteers gets on the phone, and this community person can sell 40 subscriptions. It works."

Charles Reinhart comments on the difference in the critical mass and commitment of the audiences in the old Connecticut base and in North Carolina. "In New London, if we had a big house for one of the performances, it was because the dance community from New York, Boston, and New Haven wanted to come and see a specific artist. They would come on a Saturday night and the house would be full, and that would be it. Outside of that, we never counted on audiences. I never counted on box office receipts as something to keep us afloat up there. If the school didn't do well, we would have died."

But in Durham, he says, the performances are important for their livelihood. When the ADF was seriously considering Durham as its new home, Terry Sanford, then president of Duke University, told Reinhart, "We're going to help you, but you have two problems: First, I don't think there's a modern dance audience here. Second, everybody leaves in the summer."

Reinhart says people now rearrange their vacations so they can attend ADF. Midyette adds that the Festival has had a substantial effect on the community. Durham businesses show higher food and lodging revenues during the Festival schedule. "Culturally, many people build their summer around it," he says. "We have Thursday night tickets so they can be out of town on Friday and Saturday."

Reinhart still marvels that the ADF has been able to stimulate substantial interest in modern dance. "I often look at the lines at the box office and wonder, who are they? Is this real? Do people really care? I don't know who they are and where they come from, but it's wonderful."

However, he says this presents "a success problem," where the ADF needs to train its audience to come not just for the now-familiar artists, but to be receptive to the up-and-coming, less familiar artists.

Reinhart has been gratified by the ethnic mix of the audience. With "The Black Tradition in American Modern Dance" performances, their marketing targeted the Black population by working with community organizations and Black-owned businesses. A "Durham Night" event for the project also was a great success. Ticket buyers attending the performance were invited to a reception with cast members, where the special West African traditional honoring ceremony organized by Chuck Davis took place.

Kathryn Wallace is contributions administrator for the corporate giving program of the pharmaceutical firm Glaxo Inc., based in the Research Triangle. She explains that Glaxo supports ADF because "They are a major community resource, and we think it's important to encourage those types of resources. We have a commitment to keep our community strong, and support of the arts is one of the best ways to do that." Glaxo funding has helped ADF in its capital fund drive, and funded a residency by the Paul Taylor Company in 1988.

Wallace feels that the Festival is a pillar in the community because it is internationally recognized as a major innovator of modern dance, and as a teacher. "One of the things we like about the Festival is that we have dance students on campus at Duke for six weeks every summer. We can look to it as a resource not just for ourselves in our community but as a major resource to bring these students in from all over. We recognize the Festival as a major happening every summer, and it's something we feel we need to keep. The arts are important, because they're the first sign of a really thriving community."

The Future

The Reinharts say they're pleased to see that the field of modern dance has grown over the years. "It has become an international volcano," Charles Reinhart says. "We didn't know this before, but now we do. Wherever we look, we see it. Nationalities aren't so important; only the talent is." He speaks of their project at Guangdong Dance Academy to establish China's first modern dance program, and of similar programs being built in other countries. Prime funders of this international initiative are The Rockefeller Foundation and the U.S. Information Agency.

Stephanie Reinhart calls the 1980s the decade in which this international involvement began to bloom. In China, the first class of 20 students was to graduate in 1990 after finishing the three-year program. The hope is that these students will comprise that country's first modern dance company.

"Modern dance works are being created in China," she says, "based on their traditional cultural values and mores. All the international choreographers are calling on their indigenous material and using modern dance principles. They're not trying to create American work. Their work doesn't look rehashed. Nor are we trying to impose cultural imperialism."

She says ADF's yearly International Choreographer's Conference in Durham brings back three participants from the year before to set a new work on the students in the summer school.

"The Festival is being extended now, all year long," she says. "Its roots are growing world wide. In a way, we've come full circle in response to developments all over the world."

Charles Reinhart adds, "What will develop out of it will be modern dance based on Chinese tradition and culture," he says. "It will be the same thing in Indonesia, with dance that is different from all the others, and in Africa and South America, and in this country. We have all these incredible varieties of modern dance, and what we have in common is our process. But the product is different.

"I think that's dynamite. I think the artists have the vision. We just need to have the sensibility and the sense to let them recognize their talent and help them do what they need to do."

Photo by Jay Anderson

Appalshop staff

Photo by Scot Oliver

2 Cultural Reclamation in Appalachia

"America's energy colony, its third world" is one way that residents of the region surrounding Whitesburg, Kentucky describe their home. Whitesburg, a town of 1,200, is in the prime coal mining area of Letcher County. It is also the home of Appalshop.

Coal is a shadow character in the Appalshop story. Its economic and physical impact on the region runs like a vein through the people and their histories. They have burned it, fought over it, coughed it up, sold it, lived by it, and died under its weight.

But mining, once so labor intensive, has become mechanized, and advanced technology has replaced the laborers. Where once a mountain was left hollow, now it is stripped away, leaving a landscape utterly devastated.

As the land has suffered the ravages of strip mining, the indigenous culture of the mountain people also has become sanitized, assimilated or forgotten.

One need only listen to members of the Appalshop staff to hear the emotional impact that strip mining has had.

Angelyn DeBord, a founder of Appalshop's Roadside Theater and a member for the last 15 years, describes the first time she drove into Letcher County from her native North Carolina.

"I remember coming over the Pan Gap area and seeing the strip jobs for the first time. I looked down on those devastated hills and I remember thinking, 'I lift up mine eyes unto the hills from whence cometh my help. My help cometh from the Lord.' Tears just started. It is really personal when you see this land. We're an island in the middle of devastation. But the people still are here, and that's worth a lot. I want to make sure the people remain strong even if the area does become devastated."

In its 21-year history, Appalshop has restored and reclaimed a spiritual and cultural landscape. Its efforts have returned the people to their history and culture, fostering respect for the "old ways" in place of cultural amnesia.

The "Shop," as it is fondly called, has battled encroachment by the modern world in the form of satellite dishes, which have become as ubiquitous in the rural Kentucky countryside as the basketball hoop, the outward and visible sign of a statewide obsession with the sport. The dishes bring America's pop culture to the hills more unrelentingly than ever before. Young people feel the pressure to shed their regional heritage for mainstream American culture. One consequence is that bluegrass, the region's indigenous music, is preferred mostly by those 40 and older, but typically holds little interest for the young.

Coal is a player here, too. Those satellite dishes and color TVs are bought with the prosperity that demand for coal brings—a demand that accelerates the stripping. But when the industry is off, as it has been, physical destruction gives way to economic hardship.

Kelly Blair, who is in his early 20s, worked as a studio assistant at Appalshop's noncommercial community radio station, WMMT-FM. He expresses the paradox in a straightforward way.

"It's definitely love and hate at the same time. You have all this beautiful scenery getting taken by strip jobs. Youngsters look at the hills and think, 'That's a future, but I really don't want to do that, do things that God doesn't want me to. He doesn't want me to tear up His land.' Then there's the view that 'I've got to feed my family.' I couldn't really put a period to the end of it. It's just something that goes on and on, just something that happens around here."

Appalshop's Beginnings

Two developments precipitated the formation of Appalshop in 1969. First, funds for the War on Poverty, made available through the federal Office of Economic Opportunity, were earmarked to train youngsters in film and television production. This created opportunities in two industries that previously had been closed to them. Whitesburg was the only non-urban project site selected in the United States.

But no TV or film industries existed in rural Kentucky. This set the stage for the next development leading to Appalshop's founding: once trained, many young people from Whitesburg refused to leave the area to find employment.

Marty Newell helped found Appalshop when he was in high school in 1969, and served as general manager of WMMT-FM. Now, he's executive director of the Kentucky Arts Council. He recalls that the original participants didn't want to be trained for jobs that didn't exist locally. They didn't want to "follow so many others out of the region down the highway to Indiana or Michigan," he says, referring to the "hillbilly migration" of 1950–69, when four million people left Appalachia to seek jobs in the industrial North.

Appalshop's founders wanted to find a way for youngsters to stay in the area and make a living doing something other than coal mining. In 1969, and even today, those options were slim.

"It doesn't take a lot of sophistication to know that you are way ahead if you can figure out how to make a living other than to dig coal and eventually either get crushed in the mines or get black lung and die of that," Newell says.

At that time, images of a poverty-swept Appalachia were being beamed across the U.S. and the world. Several Appalshoppers recall their strong feelings about those images being viewed by outsiders who knew nothing about the region, and who saw nothing of beauty or substance in it or its people. "Somebody else was telling our story. This was an opportunity for us to tell our own story, for mountain people to have a voice," Newell says. "There are things wrong here, there are things right here. The stories on both sides are best told by the people who know them."

> Appalshop's efforts have returned the people to their history and culture by giving value to their speech, their customs, their very being.

The "Appalshop Kids," as the early trainees are still fondly called, were determined to use the new equipment to collect and show true images of their own people. In the early days, they went out to document what was familiar to them: the dirt car races, their grandparents butchering a hog, a day at the town swimming pool. According to Dudley Cocke, director of Appalshop's Roadside Theater, they captured something special about their everyday lives, showing an intimacy that the national media couldn't touch.

Word spread throughout the region, inspiring others to discover and reveal, in their own language and images, their histories and stories. When administrations changed in Washington and the War on Poverty program ended, Appalshoppers realized they would have to incorporate and look for contracts and grants on their own. They also began to work with other forms to tell the stories of the mountain people and address the area's social and cultural issues.

By 1975, Appalshop included Appalshop Films, June Appal Recordings, the Roadside Theater, the *Mountain Review* quarterly, and the Mountain Photography Workshop. The award-winning regional TV series *Headwaters* was added that year. In 1982, Appalshop moved into the Appalshop Center, a 13,000-square-foot production, distribution and exhibition facility in downtown Whitesburg. The presenting program began to operate out of the 150-seat Appalshop theater. WMMT-FM went on the air in 1985.

The ideas that led to the initial formation of Appalshop also inspired the programs that followed. Roadside Theater, for example, was founded as a people's theater built on the foundations of local culture. Director Dudley Cocke explains that the region's theatrical tradition is very rich, but its context is different from that of a "typical" theater. It has its origins in church services made dramatic with music, and in the traditions of storytelling, balladeering, and oral history.

Roadside Theater began to work with these elements, seeking both a theater and an art form rooted in history but animated by current expression. Just as the original Appalshoppers conveyed their culture through film and video, Roadside conveyed on stage the experiences of families, friends, and neighbors.

There has been a unity to Appalshop's central issues. It has spoken to the disenfranchised, been the voice of their vibrant but subtle culture, and dismantled the distorted stereotypes of the region and its people.

The Mission

Appalshop's mission is clearly understood and passionately subscribed to by those who work there. At its heart is an essential premise: Culture is not a neutral issue. It is a highly charged social and political continuum. This perception of culture—and the view of presenting and the arts that is its outgrowth—informs all of the organization's programs and activities.

Bob Henry Baber, who formerly was responsible for presenting at Appalshop, believes that every program must address what it means to live in the Appalachian Mountains. He poses a series of questions he says must always be asked, leading to an ever-evolving answer:

"What values do we want to impart? What things from the past do we want to preserve? What do we want to shed? What is really part of this culture? What part of it are the people who live in the area and dig up the minerals?" He continues, "This is a culture in flux. Appalshop's job is to preserve what is traditional and promote what is contemporary in it, and everybody has a different idea of exactly what that is."

This philosophy reflects the organization's unique sense of place and time. Appalshop values the "people's art" and tends to regard "high art" as less compelling and certainly more intimidating to those it serves. It wants to create and nurture art that people understand, theater that is human, and work that is accessible and never makes people feel ignorant or deprived. By giving value to who they are, what their customs are, the way they speak, and what makes them different, Appalshop has set out to validate the culture and people that have long been ignored, slighted, and patronized by society at large.

Debby Bays, who has worked in the presenting program, takes exception to calling it that. Bays was the programmer in charge of presenting from 1982–85, and she continues to work with Appalshop through her position with Foxfire, an association of teachers in eastern Kentucky.

"I'm not sure if 'presenting' is the word to use," she says. "You're not presenting to people. You're sharing. There is a big difference." Referring to terminology that has become *de rigeur* in the folk arts funding community, she adds, "We also don't 'collect' or 'document' our neighbors. We *share* our neighbors and ourselves with people both in our communities and outside of them . . . You are a part of what is happening, and no one is on display."

Caron Atlas describes herself as the "outsider" who moved to Whitesburg from New York City, where she was the producing director of Dance Theater

Workshop. She talks about presenting in the context of organizing. "I always thought of organizing as a creative word," she says. "To me, presenting is not only putting on a show; it's having an alliance with the community."

Bob Henry Baber explains that the presenting program has existed only since 1982, when the new facility, with its theater and gallery space, provided a home. Challenges arose immediately, the most daunting trying to serve a small population in a vast geographical area. Issues of accessibility aren't limited to physical and social barriers. How do you get the word out to let people know that an event is happening? How do you motivate them to cross a mountain pass just to see your program? How do you make attending a performance non-threatening for people who don't have a tradition of theater-going?

Appalshop has met these challenges with the work in its own theater, and through alliances with schools, churches, and other organizations in which events can be programmed. In addition, WMMT-FM is used to promote the presenting program and to broadcast events live, such as Thursday evening's "Bluegrass Express" concerts. Appalshop's outreach extends well beyond the Whitesburg area into the countryside and towns of southeastern Kentucky, southwestern Virginia, northeastern Tennessee, and West Virginia.

The organization's theater meets only part of a presenting mission that is defined in the very broadest of terms. For example, during the 1988 Open Windows festival of music, theater and dance, only three of more than 20 performances were staged at the Shop. The rest were held in schools and community centers throughout the area.

These challenges have shaped Caron Atlas' perceptions of artistic risk. "Here in eastern Kentucky, it seems silly to look at artistic risk in the traditional way, when this society is really in crisis. The biggest risk here is that this culture could die, that the local culture will not be passed on to the children, that the influence of popular culture will wipe out one of our last remaining indigenous cultures. The flip side is that this is such an insular community that it has trouble looking critically at the culture it is celebrating."

With events like Open Windows, Appalshop is attempting to deal with both sides of this issue.

Open Windows: An American Festival

Open Windows proved to be exactly the kind of program that Appalshop so uniquely conceives and presents. Described as a "distinctly American festival, a celebration of the cultural diversity of this country, an homage to the down-to-earth theatrical magic of a good story," Open Windows offered the theatrical extension of storytelling with roots in Appalachian, African American, Jewish, and Latin American cultures. Nationally recognized artists shared the stage with some of the finest local talent.

Participants included John O'Neal of Junebug Productions, one of the founders of the Free Southern Theater in New Orleans; members of Appalshop's own Road-side Theater, which hosted the events; Albert Greenberg and Helen Stoltzfus of the

San Francisco-based A Traveling Jewish Theater; Francisco Gonzalez, Santa Barbara-based musician/performer on the Vera Cruz harp, former music director of El Teatro Campesino, and a founder of the band Los Lobos; Bushfire/Urban Bush Women with New York choreographer and dancer Jawole Willa Jo Zollar and musicians Edwina Lee Tyler and Tiye Giraud; and choreographer and dancer Liz Lerman and members of the Dance Exchange of Washington, D.C. Local artists included storyteller and song-maker Florida Slone; author and storyteller Verna Mae Slone; apprentice storyteller Nikki Dixon; gourd artist Minnie Black; gospel musician Earl Gilmore; and country singer and musician Jeanette Carter.

> "You're not presenting to people. You're sharing. There is a big difference."

The idea for Open Windows came in 1981, when Dudley Cocke and John O'Neal met at a meeting of the Regional Organization of Theaters South (ROOTS). During the discussion that followed a Roadside Theater performance, O'Neal said he didn't see anything in the piece that would discourage participation in the Ku Klux Klan.

Cocke's response was quick. "What can we do about that?" he asked. O'Neal admits he was taken off guard by Cocke's ready reply and obvious desire to do something. Out of this meeting grew the idea for the festival, and a strong professional association and friendship.

Cocke and O'Neal first toured their theater companies to each other's community, one predominantly Black and the other predominantly white. In 1981, they appeared together in San Francisco at the sixth annual People's Theater Festival, along with A Traveling Jewish Theater and El Teatro Campesino. The four companies later performed together in Whitesburg; Jacksonville, Alabama; and New Orleans. All shared an interest in developing a project of larger scope and substance.

Work on a festival was well under way in 1986. The idea evolved as participating artists and companies, as well as others involved in planning at Appalshop, gave it more definition. The number and scope of performers grew, the event stretched to two weeks, and festival organizers developed workshops involving the community and the artists. Artists were to participate in programs at elementary and high schools, in community workshops, and in performances in a variety of settings. Most were to be booked for four or five days.

In 1988, Open Windows became a reality. Explaining the name and purpose of the festival in the *Louisville Courier-Journal*, Dudley Cocke said, "If you have an open window, you can see outside and you can get a cross-current of air. It's a fresh breeze that blows from these different cultures, not the harsh wind of fear and enmity."

Typically, the visiting artists were paired with local artists in some appropriate way. Each workshop or performance had at least one member of the Roadside Theater serving as a host and introducing the artists to the audience. Connections were made quickly. Many in the community had seen Roadside Theater performances in revival tents when the company travelled each summer. They had come to know and trust Roadside's members as their own kith and kin, which in fact they were. As the bridge between the familiar and the unfamiliar, Roadside was able to highlight the commonalities among cultures and to heighten the festival's impact.

Roadside Theater's Angelyn DeBord was asked at the time how the children were reacting to the strange cultures. "What I see is open mouths and shining eyes," she said. "I just see the students being overwhelmed, knocked out and loving it. Every performer is finding a way to relate to the children. They're saying, 'Look, we are like you. Look how we are the same. Now, haven't you felt this way before?'"

Debby Bays recalls, "After John O'Neal spent two days with eighth-graders, the kids said that one of the most important things for them was to talk with him, and the bonds they felt with a Black person from a rural area. This is true of almost every minority group—and hillbillies are minorities as much as anybody else. We have our own legacy of stereotypes; we have had some of the same experiences. From those experiences, you can build to experiences you haven't had. The kids made that jump just fine."

It is doubtful that many communities in the United States, much less these tiny towns in isolated Appalachia, had ever witnessed such a rich and exuberant expression of cultures.

However, other communities around the country will now have that opportunity. An American Festival and has formed partnerships with selected communities to use the programming as a tool for cultural empowerment. According to Dudley Cocke, the Festival should take place as a milestone event within each community's long-term plan to establish respect for different cultures, achieve cultural equity and advance cultural self-determination.

Fundraising

The budget for Open Windows represented half of the total presenting budget for Appalshop—clearly a significant financial commitment. The decision to build it into an American festival and make it available for national touring also required extensive fundraising.

Generally, the major public funding sources have been responsive to Appalshop's needs in regard to this program and others. The National Endowment for the Arts awarded Appalshop a $400,000 challenge grant in 1987, to be used for new productions and special initiatives in education.

Festival producer Caron Atlas points out that Appalshop also has had the support of local businesses, even when they didn't agree with certain political stands, because they recognized that they were part of the community.

Raising funds from large national corporations has been more difficult. Since corporations typically fund organizations in locations where they have employees, Appalshop finds itself without standing. Whitesburg has no corporate presence and no sizable employee base, with the exception of the coal industry. In the 1950s and '60s, companies like U.S. Steel sold their operations to multinationals that have neither a local presence nor any civic interest in the community. Even if money were available from them, there would be ambivalence about accepting it.

Individual support also is limited. The people Appalshop serves are generally poor, so it cannot organize a friends group with membership priced at $25 or more. However, a national presence is developing through Appalshop films and Roadside Theater performances in major cities. Thus, there is a chance to build a base of national supporters.

Organizational Structure

Some say that Appalshop's structure is a vestige of the 1960s. A successful worker-run cooperative for more than 20 years, Appalshop is stronger now than ever before.

After a year's service and with a vote by three-quarters of the board, any employee can become a member of the board of directors and have an equal say in how the organization functions.

The various departments that make up Appalshop include the core (administration), development, filmmaking and distribution, recordings and distribution, television, the radio station, the Roadside Theater, and the building (or presenting) program. Each department has a head, but there is no hierarchical structure within programs or at Appalshop in general. No one person is ultimately responsible for the entire organization, and there is no single spokesperson. Appalshoppers typically point to this feature with great pride.

Roadside Theater's Dudley Cocke has spoken and written on this structure. In his essay in FEDAPT's 1987 publication, *The Challenge of Change*, he writes, "An organization's structure follows from the organization's purpose, and conversely, the way we organize ourselves is a window on our purposes."

Cocke explains that in 1969, when Appalshop was being formed, participatory democracy and alternative paths to problem-solving had great currency. For the "kids" incorporating Appalshop and getting it off the ground, having a traditional board of directors with coal company executives and bank vice presidents was not an option. Appalshop was about self-reliance and independence, and out of these impulses grew a board comprised of the people who were running the organization. Who better understood their mission to act as a vehicle through which Appalachian people would have their own voice and tell their own stories? Who else had the vision to cut a path where none existed?

The fact that the board is comprised of the workers doesn't make policy- and decision-making any easier. Everybody has a stake in everything.

"We really wanted people to own a piece of this outfit," Cocke says, "for each of us to have a say. People have a sense of proprietorship about the organization. When you own something, you have much more at stake and a stronger sense of pride. It's a big strength."

But it's easy to feel a conflict between one's responsibilities as a staff member whose department has been nourishing a special project, and as a board member who must establish priorities for the entire organization. The good of the whole can mean sacrificing that project, and that's never an easy decision.

In the end, however, this structure gives Appalshop workers great flexibility and the best opportunity for collaboration. For example, different aspects of the Open Windows program touched nearly every department. The radio station was used for promotional announcements and interviews with participating artists. June Appal Records recorded harpist Francisco Gonzalez and Roadside Theater musicians Ron Short and Tommy Bledsoe. The film and video division provided extensive additional documentation for later productions. All of the events were audio-taped by Appalshop's own radio station for rebroadcast.

Throughout Appalshop, one observes an ardent commitment to the organization's mission, a devotion to its causes, a piercing intellectualism and a bias towards activism. Bob Henry Baber speaks of this dynamism and energy. "I'll bet we get more ideas in a week here at Appalshop than most agencies get in a year."

Referring to the "crazy kids" who started and sustained Appalshop in the early years, Kelly Blair observes: "They really did get something good going, and it all came from the heart. There is a lot of emotion in this place because of that. They worked hard to make this place the way it is."

Robert Sherman

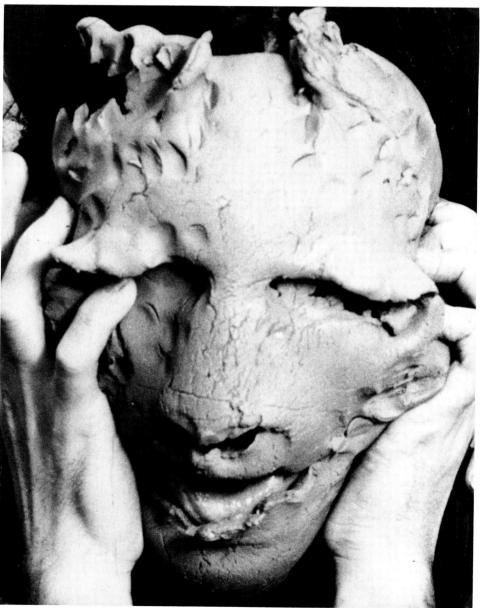

Photo by Gerry Goodstein

3 The House that Philip Built

On the edge of the Mt. Royal neighborhood, the Baltimore Theatre Project occupies a series of old and distinguished-looking buildings—the former Heptasoph Hall, and several rowhouses. Moments after ascending the steps to the second-floor theater, one encounters the manifest presence of its founder and director, Philip Arnoult. He acts like a host welcoming people into his own home, proudly showing off the accomplishments of his children or other family members near and dear to him.

Arnoult's burly and bearded presence is ubiquitous. He greets members of the audience in the lobby and encourages them to step up to the bar in the lobby for a pre-performance drink. He engages them in conversation about what they are about to see. He makes pre-curtain comments explaining where he originally saw this particular company, and why he has chosen to invite it to perform. He reappears at the end, after the applause has died down, to invite the audience to stay for a discussion with the artists, which he moderates from the stage, or to repair to the bar for informal interaction.

The Baltimore Theatre Project is a home for experimental theater artists. It also has been hospitable to more mainstream performers, but its programmatic meat and potatoes is new work, much of it identified with the avant garde. Arnoult brings in artists and companies from all over the world. In the first few months of 1988, there were groups from Argentina, The Netherlands, and Israel, and from a small theater in western Virginia whose home is in a rock quarry. Each one was provocative in its own way; each pushed the limits in its own chosen medium.

For example, the Teatro del Sur from Argentina performed *Warsaw Tango*, created by Alberto Felix Alberto. The work was nearly wordless, and minimalist in its dramatic approach. Certain scenes and actions were repeated over and over again with practically imperceptible changes. But those minute changes moved the piece toward its resolution, and revealed the four characters' inner psychic land-scape and the exterior societal landscape of their country.

Arnoult says he stumbled upon the company in 1985 during his continuing, extensive travels around the world. He was so taken by its work that he invited the company to Baltimore to make its North American debut in 1986. He then began working on a much larger North American tour for 1988. That tour, with major funding from The Rockefeller Foundation, consisted of runs at seven theaters or festivals, including the Next Wave at the Brooklyn Academy of Music, the Du Maurier World Stage in Toronto, and a month-long residency at the University of Tennessee.

Arnoult's hands-on approach to his work, and his omnipresent persona in all Theatre Project activities, convey the clear and unmistakable message that this is the house that Philip built. He and the Baltimore Theatre Project are one.

There is a real sense of personal ownership in Arnoult's approach to the Theatre Project. There also is a compelling impulse to share his discoveries with others. This impulse is evident on stage or in his office. In 1988, he urged one visitor to sit down and listen to a new CD of Tracy Chapman's debut recording, and a re-release of Joan Baez's debut album from the early 1960s. His choice of music reveals as much about him as his passions in the theater do. If he is excited about something, his enthusiasm is contagious.

Arnoult is generous in sharing the joy of personal discoveries and theatrical expressions, but less so in sharing the ownership of an organization. This has become the Project's double-edged sword: it is artistically sound but, periodically, suffers organizational difficulties.

Arnoult has pursued his own personal vision and created a unique organization serving the international, national, and local theater and dance communities. He has promoted the concept of Baltimore as the ''port of entry'' for international theater artists coming to the United States. Many of these artists appear in Baltimore long before much better-known organizations in New York or Los Angeles have invited them to their stages.

Arnoult also has provided working space for local and national artists in the process of developing new works which need honing before New York appearances or important tours. He has supported performers whose home is Baltimore, and given them the opportunity to perform at his theater. In some instances, he has assisted local artists by producing them in performances at the Edinburgh Fringe Festival during the summer.

''There would be a great sense of loss if the Baltimore Theatre Project closed its doors,'' says local newspaper writer David Bergman. ''When it closed (from 1983–85) to re-do the theater, there was a real gap, culturally and artistically, in Baltimore. It would be extremely difficult to replace this institution.''

Programming at the Fringe

The *Philadelphia Inquirer* has called the Project "... the city's leading theatrical adventurer," while Baltimore's *Jewish Times* pegs it as "... a champion for experimental and avant garde theater in Baltimore." *The New York Times* has referred to the Project's "stunning variety of theater, dance, mime and music brought in from all over the world." And the *Village Voice* has called it "a driving wedge in breaking up the cultural hegemony of New York." Although apt and complimentary, these comments don't begin to touch the breadth of the unique programming that the Baltimore Theatre Project has offered in its 20 years of existence.

> The Project has always intended to be useful in the community, and to nurture the new, the experimental, and the untried.

In his statement to potential subscribers for the 1990–91 season, Philip Arnoult wrote proudly of the "over 800 unique impulses and visions from 29 states and 19 foreign countries" that have been presented at the 157-seat theater. "Most of that work clearly met the full definition of avant garde—it was ahead of its time," he wrote. "It is my hope that much of what you will see here for the next 20 years also will fit into that category."

In the 1990–91 anniversary season, Arnoult said, the Project was to continue its deepening commitment to the presentation of international artists as well as those from the U.S. "I believe that the international bias that this theater has held onto for 20 years is more crucial than ever," Arnoult says. "The sweeping changes ... in Eastern Europe, the glimmer of hope for an end to apartheid in South Africa, and the birth of a new Europe in 1992 all mean that it is more important than ever for us to hear those other voices, see those other perspectives on the world."

The season from September to December 1990 is to feature the irreverent Theatre BUFFO from Leningrad, presenting its vaudeville/cabaret revue; two works by the Tmu-Na Theatre of Tel Aviv; Impossible Industrial Action of Baltimore in a presentation of the multi-media *The Pleasure Raiders*; and Seven Stages of Atlanta, Ga., mounting a production of South African playwright Adam Small's *The Orange Earth*.

The Project also was to house the Puppetry Project, showcasing a wide range of innovative artists whose careers have been developed with the help of grants from the Henson Foundation, founded by the late Jim Henson of *Sesame Street*.

Past seasons have been similarly unusual. In 1987–88, Arnoult presented productions he says were created by "true theatrical visionaries—artists who are pursuing their own powerful and idiosyncratic visions, rooted in, but not bound by, their different cultures ... These are theater artists who are forging new paths in theater, finding new ways to look at who we are and how we live on this fragile planet—or could live, if we try—or might live, if we stop trying."

That year, the Project featured The Adaptors; Amsterdam's Danstheater Nan

Romijn; Lime Kiln Arts' production of *Ear Rings from Oral History*; Argentina's Teatro del Sur; Israel's Tmu-Na; the Boston-based The Wright Brothers; and the Charabanc company from Belfast in a North American premiere.

The 1988–89 season included new works by new vaudeville clown Bob Berky in his *The Power Project*; mime artist Leonard Pitt in *Not for Real*; Figures of Speech Theater's *Anerca*; South African playwright/actress/director Gcina Mhlope's *Have You Seen Zandile?*; Britain's Kaboodle Theater's production of *Rasputin: The Forbidden Story*; and the world premiere of Fred Curchak's *Sexual Mythology*.

The 1989–90 season maintained the edge with a multi-media show by Robert Shields; Abel & Gordon in *The Escape*, a comic melodrama; the Ridge Theater's *The Jack Benny Program Part 1*; a piece about 19th century poet Anna Wickham; a program exploring the mythology of the serpent goddess performed by Australian actor Sarah Cathcart; *Radio Sing Sing* by the Man Act company; and *Zig Zag Zelda* from First Stage of Wilmington, Del.

Lois K. Baldwin, executive director of the Baltimore County Commission of the Arts and Sciences, says the Project's offerings are eye-opening and mind-broadening. "It's like travel; it's like reading. It's like anything where you go after something new and different. I think that's terribly important to civilization. I may not like everything I see, but being exposed to it gives me an opportunity to let some fresh air into my mind."

Fran Holden, former director of the performing arts for the Mid-Atlantic Arts Foundation, says Baltimore residents look to the Project "to bring them exciting work, and Philip delivers all the time, and consistently. It's very important here, because so little else of an experimental nature happens locally. Baltimore doesn't have a rich heritage of supporting avant garde work. Philip is the only game in town for the expression of something other than popular entertainment. This area is viewed as an old, tarnished urban center—part of the decaying Northeast—that has taken on a new identity for itself. And the arts have been extremely important. For the people who live here, it has become a very necessary part of their existence.'

Holden feels the Baltimore Theatre Project has successfully achieved one part of its mission—to become the port of entry for many international companies that go on from Baltimore to appear across the U.S. Arnoult encourages visiting companies to use their time at the Project as a linchpin for a larger U.S. tour, and he uses his contacts to help them.

Arnoult explains his fascination with international theater. "I'm a bleeding-heart, one-world . . . You fill in the blank. If the sum total of my work—when I stop it and fall over—buys the planet another minute before someone blows it up, great. I think one of the ways we'll add those minutes is to understand that we're all on this little hunk of mud, and at the base we all share things that are much more connected than artificial boundaries and differences in culture."

The work presented at the Theatre Project is rarely seen elsewhere in the region or even throughout the U.S. Arnoult says he has experienced a smugness by some of his American colleagues about international work. "But it is critical that the artists in Baltimore and around America see other visions of theater, particularly those that come out of other cultures," he says. "When you take work and transpose it into another culture, it's like adding dye to the slide. Things become more vivid, and you learn more about your own work as an artist. I'm informing an audience, preparing an audience to take new and extra steps."

Richard Swaim—professor of political science at the University of Baltimore, who has had a long association with the theater—sees the Project as a port of entry in a broader, more symbolic sense than just bringing in international work. "The term 'audience development' has referred to a broadening of the audience in terms of demographics," he says. "I'm speaking of a deepening of the audience, in terms of their appreciation and understanding of the art. The Project is the port of entry not only for international work, but for avant garde work, period. Its contribution is in terms of audience development, in the sense of educating the audience about what these works of art are, and that they are out there."

Arnoult explains how he chooses the companies and artists that perform at the Theatre Project. "I don't respond to an agent calling me up," he says. "I've never been to a booking conference. A video just gets me on the airplane." He travels to other countries and seeks out what he considers to be the best and most adventurous performance work. "I'm on the road about 26 weeks a year, and putting this old, creaky body in about 300 performances," he says. "That's the way I go looking for work." He says he is most interested in new and innovative work, and he tends to choose work "that has a humanistic cast and celebrates the human spirit."

Evolution of the Theatre Project

Even a cursory look at the Theatre Project's 20 years of existence reveals that it has gone through a number of incarnations.

It was founded in 1971 under the auspices of the Ohio-based Antioch College, which established a branch in Baltimore in response to student demands for more relevance and social awareness, says Carol Baish, the Project's former managing director and now associate artistic director. The charge from Antioch was to make the Project "useful in the community, and to nurture the new, the experimental, and the untried," Baish says. "We've always done that, although we've done it seemingly in about 19 different ways."

In 1976, the Theatre Project separated from Antioch and incorporated on its own. It did, however, retain its commitment to education and accessibility. From the beginning, it provided week-long runs for performing groups, which used the time to try out new work before receptive audiences.

This was the time when Comprehensive Employment and Training Act (CETA) monies were abundant, and municipalities were eager to make funds available to arts organizations and other deserving community groups. With the benefit of these funds, the Theatre Project did significant community projects, including the Neighborhood Arts Circus; the Rat Squad, geared toward rat-eradication education; and Baltimore Voices, an oral history project. At the height of this "CETA period," the Project's budget peaked at just less than $1 million, with a staff of 50. But Arnoult says he knew he had to be careful not to count on the CETA monies indefinitely.

Social/community theater projects coexisted with the experimental. Baish describes the 1970s as a time when a wide range of experimental work was being presented. "At times, you might see something that was still work in progress," she remembers. "The next week, you might see Pilobolus perform, or some other polished work. It was very up and down in this way." She says some thought was given to producing more "established" avant garde artists, such as Lee Breuer, but Arnoult decided instead "to present artists who maybe will never be well known, but they're trying new things."

The theater space—housed in the same building as today—was, by all descriptions, entirely different. The atmosphere of the entire operation reflected its time. Admission was free, with the customary passing-of-the-hat ceremony at the end of each performance. Revenues were split 50/50 with the visiting artists. Seating was catch-as-catch-can, mostly on the floor.

In the early 1980s, a number of concurrent realizations coalesced to create a key moment. CETA money was drying up; the audiences were getting a bit older; the theater wasn't a comfortable space to sit in for long periods of time; and the prevailing financial arrangements with the visiting companies rendered the artists the primary subsidizers of the program.

"We never found any funding agency that thought this was a noble thing to do—to not charge and to let people put whatever they could afford in the hat," Baish says. Plans were moving ahead to renovate the space, with real seats for the audiences, and there was serious talk of charging admission and giving artists a guarantee. Throughout the transition, she says, was the belief that "We're not here just to serve an audience. We're here to serve artists and audiences equally."

The Theatre Project is conceived as a meeting place—between artists and audience, between artists and other artists. Baish says that she and Arnoult began to feel that they could better fulfill this concept by charging admission and offering a more comfortable setting.

The Theatre Project existed with free performances until 1983. At that time, the theater was closed for a two-year, $2 million building renovation which provided a revamped theater facility, studios, offices, and living space for artists, plus space for an independent, privately-owned restaurant and cabaret.

Arnoult now describes the space and the concept as "packaging nontraditional work in a very traditional envelope. The seats are comfortable, the sightlines exceptional. We are warm in winter and cool in summer. The lobby is bright and pleasant."

But into this traditional envelope have gone artists and theater pieces that are quite out of the ordinary. Baish says, "It's always been clear that we are presenting unusual, demanding work that sometimes makes you feel cranky and disturbed, as well as exhilarated and happy. We don't have any intention of changing that, and we don't have any intention of apologizing for that."

Renovating the Theatre Project Space

Planning and preparations for the renovation were under way in 1976. But with the ambitious plans came a stark realization, Baish says: They had not developed the kind of constituency from whom $2 million could be raised. The cold fact that there was no base for a capital campaign spurred the Theatre Project into an innovative and creative approach to the renovation. They managed to assemble a package with a private developer that took advantage of tax breaks and public monies to realize the project.

The development is a typical story of an arts organization as urban pioneer. Today, the Mt. Royal neighborhood stands as the "artsy" part of the city, with the Baltimore Symphony's new Meyerhoff Hall across the street from the Theatre Project, and the renovated Lyric Opera House a few blocks away. Bed and breakfast places with colorful window boxes are also a common sight.

Back in 1976, this was not the environment. The Theatre Project occupied Heptasoph Hall, which even late into the 1970s was in a seedy part of Baltimore peopled by denizens of X-rated movie houses and massage parlors. "This was not the nicest of neighborhoods," Baish remembers.

> "I want people to walk in this theater and believe that it's the best theater in the world."

The Project's biggest advantage was that it owned its building, which the city had sold for $5. Four adjacent townhouses also became a part of the package, to be conveyed to the Project at a later date on similar terms. In the interim, the Project was permitted to use the townhouses at no charge.

When the renovation package was being put together, Baish says, a partnership was formed that bought the building from the Project. The partnership received tax benefits because the building was in an historic area. The capital consisted partly of federal money, a Community Development Block Grant, and an Urban Development Action Grant. The project included the renovation of the theater complex, two of the four townhouses, and the development of a restaurant/cabaret on the corner.

Baish says the Project was able to retire 85 percent of its 14-year debt, including a mortgage on the property, with the proceeds from the sale of the theater space to the partnership. A long-term lease was obtained from the partnership at a minimal amount which would graduate over an 11-year period.

When the Project reopened in 1985, it established ticket prices from $8 to $10, plus discounts for students and artists. There also was a new formulation for the business arrangements with artists. Baish says the usual contract is for a guaranteed fee against a box office percentage. In addition to the fee, the Project provides free housing in two of the four rowhouses next to the theater. There is always hospitality when the artists arrive, breakfast food in the refrigerator, and bed and bath linens. In the 1987–88 season, Baish figures, the Project provided 1,200 nights of housing for the artists—a value of approximately $70,000 that it did not have to raise in its own budget.

Ideas on programming also began to evolve at this time.

The Project launched its first international theater season to give it a renewed visibility in the community and to establish itself as a major Baltimore arts institution. The theater became a venue for new work from around the country and the world.

Programmatically, everything flourished throughout the 1980s. But by 1990, it had became apparent to Arnoult that there could be great advantages to being associated with an established and stable organization. In June 1990, a new path to take the Project through the decade was announced by Arnoult and officials at Baltimore's Towson State University. A collaborative affiliation was forged to allow the two theaters to work together on shared projects and to support each other's work while maintaining their separate identities.

"This is an incredible arrangement," says Dr. Maravene Loeschke, chair of the TSU Theater Department. "I can hardly believe it." She explains that the Project will provide internships for Towson students, offer discounts to students, faculty, and staff, and be in residence during Towson's 1991 Experimental Theater Festival and the Maryland Arts Festival. In turn, Towson will provide discount tickets to Theatre Project subscribers, and be in residence at the Project for a production in 1991, which will go on to the Edinburgh Festival as a co-production of the TSU theater program, the Maryland Arts Festival, and the Theatre Project.

In addition, Philip Arnoult will be an adjunct professor at the university, working to develop undergraduate and graduate programs, lead seminars, supervise internships, and work on special collaborative projects.

"There are enormous benefits for both of us," Loeschke says. "The Project can perform in a house more than twice as big as its own, and bring in groups that couldn't have come to its theater due to its size. The internships will expose our students to an international theater, and to professional theater people."

In subsequent years, the two theaters hope to work on more shared performances, joint production ventures, and international exchange programs for students and faculty.

Arnoult calls the affiliation "a sophisticated, perpetual repositioning for us. Now we're not alone. Baltimore is a conservative town, and it's hard to get support. I felt we needed a cover to do this kind of work."

The Man Behind the Organization

In 1987, an article in *American Theatre* magazine described Philip Arnoult as the "elder statesman" of alternative theater. It went on to call him "a large, bearded man who speaks as animatedly about his upcoming attractions as a contemporary P.T. Barnum."

Fran Holden calls Arnoult "the gracious host" of the Baltimore Theatre Project. "He's a magnet, and that has served the Theatre Project very well. He has developed a following of people who feel at home there, people who come to have a good time. He encourages informality with the discussions in the theater and at the bar. He makes the audience a partner in the process."

Writer John Straussbough, who once worked on the Project staff and later joined the board of directors, says it's hard to differentiate between the theater and Arnoult's artistic vision. "Like many small arts companies and small businesses, the Baltimore Theatre Project and Philip Arnoult are inextricably linked," he says. "His vision has been one of useful, socially relevant theater, rather than art for art's sake. Although he has broadened his reach to appeal to a wider, paying audience, he has never abandoned his original vision. Without Philip, the Project would be a different place. It would be some other theater project."

Arnoult admits that without him, there would be no Baltimore Theatre Project. But to some extent, he does share the billing with his wife, Associate Artistic Director Carol Baish. "We both have done everything in this theater at one time or another," he says. "I'm the sparkles, and she's the glue that keeps the sparkles from blowing away. Her artistic sensibilities are very refined. She's a very splendid writer. She has been very good in keeping the institutional pulse for me, but you can't get to me through her. She doesn't allow herself to play that role."

Still, Baish says, "It has always been Philip's theater. It's not theater by committee. He's always been real clear about that. It's a one-person vision, and other people buy into it." This goes for the board as well. Baish is quick to point out that "They have absolutely no input into the artistic decisions."

Arnoult talks about his background in theater. "I graduated from high school on a Friday and had a professional acting job on a Saturday." In his home town of Memphis, Tenn., he worked as an actor and director at the Front Street Theater. He also started the Market Theater, "a small theater in a bread store, with a postage-stamp stage, which lasted 3½ months and is still being written about."

After graduate work at Catholic University, he went to Europe to direct an English-speaking community theater. Back in the U.S., he produced and directed several pieces for dinner theater, and directed a community theater in Akron, Ohio. "Then I came to Baltimore," he says, "and the rest, as they say, is history."

Arnoult describes his artistic vision as "non-biased aesthetic with meetings as the central and operant image. We're not the national center of mime, puppetry, movement theater, etc. I'm not trying to focus this theater on a particular aesthetic bias. It's about meetings. This institution has been created and maintained to make the meetings happen between a number of different constituencies."

He admits that his personality dominates everything about the Project. "The historical reason is that I've done everything there is to do in this theater. This theater is my life. I built it from nothing. I want it to be the best theater in America, in the world. I want to serve artists better than anybody else serves artists. I want people to walk in this theater and have challenge and surprise, and for them to believe that it's the best theater in the world. So I work 95 hours a week.

"This has never been a collective," he continues. "I'm sure I'm very difficult to work with. I come in here and make people work at 78 rpm. And it's wonderful when I'm out travelling, because people then can do things at their own time."

He says he has been asked if he has perhaps built himself into a career cul-de-sac. "A theater looking for a new artistic director wouldn't come looking for Philip Arnoult. My answer was that in the last 18 years I have given serious thought to my career maybe for 18 minutes. I think every waking moment—and sometimes dream—about my theater."

As for the risky nature of the Theatre Project's work, Arnoult says, "I'm in the business of creating art, so it's all a risk. The next work is always a risk.

"My risk is telling Nava Zukerman (of Israel's Tmu-Na Theatre) that she can come here and do the Tel Aviv phone book if that's what she wants to do, and blocking out and contracting a work that's not created yet. And with other artists, committing to their work long before it can be seen in any form, before I have any idea what we're going to see. That kind of commitment accounts for almost half my upcoming seasons. I'm investing in the future."

Political science professor Richard Swaim says, "The value of the Project to the city and region is to provide some evidence that there are things going on other than in New York and Los Angeles. The people Philip brings together here to share his vision are exposed to a kind of aesthetic virus. Some people are immune; they've been anesthetized by mass culture. But others are not. It gets in and starts working."

Arnoult eschews the word "presenter." He sees himself as an *animateur*, "the person or institution that puts things together. In government, there's a real bias regarding those who make the art and those who are 'just presenters.' Maybe there are just presenters, people who are into a commodity. But that's the furthest thing from what gets me up in the morning. It's a long-term investment in a relationship with an artist, structuring the institution so that the rule is risk-taking, rather than the exception."

Lois K. Baldwin says Baltimore has been tolerant of presenting organizations that take artistic risk, despite its conservative nature. "But I still would never have had the courage to do what Philip did here several years ago—two one-act plays about homosexuality, with two nude males on stage throughout. Of course, it was very tasteful, but to me that was taking a big artistic risk, even as advanced as the city is. Baltimore isn't comfortable with it all yet, but we're learning. I think Philip has been largely responsible for getting Baltimore to the point where artistic risk is acceptable here."

Arnoult also has been credited with playing a unique role in fostering, promoting, and training local artists. This goes back to the organization's beginnings, when it was created to serve as a theater laboratory, and held numerous training programs for artists.

He says the availability of the theater as a developmental laboratory is important to both domestic and international work. "I'm interested in long-term, developed work," he says. "I don't think that's the only way to create good work, but it certainly is a very valid process that certain theatrical visions need. The economics and the aesthetic flavor-of-the-month mentality that we have in this country have made that very difficult to do right now. Work has to find other places to be shown. There have to be places where the work can be seen, outside the company's city or country of origin, which cannot support them by themselves. I rarely do less than two-week runs, and most are three to four weeks. Even for touring groups, that's an extraordinary luxury."

Juliet Forrest, artistic director of The Forrest Collection, a movement theater company based in Baltimore, attests to Arnoult's commitment to local artists. "I was considered very radical when I first began, and I got nothing but horrible reviews for the first three years," she says. "No one could see what I was doing. People have accepted radical departures in music and visual arts more easily than in theater and dance. But the Baltimore Theatre Project has helped to change that, to open people in Baltimore to my kind of work."

She says she also has benefited from the exposure to other artists doing experimental work. "I don't think you can create art in a vacuum," she says. "You have to be aware of what's going on, even if it's not in your own art form. It's a constant process of seeing and doing and recreating."

Arnoult feels it's possible to encourage artists in the expression of their own visions. "The first way is simply by providing a model. The longer I continue, the more people know about this idiosyncratic vision and this idiosyncratic institution. It shows that here's somebody who didn't do it for just 16 months. It's going to be 20 big ones, and that's an Ice Age in this business."

The International Orientation

Undeniably, one of the most significant ventures undertaken by the Baltimore Theatre Project in conjunction with other theatrical organizations was bringing the 1986 Theatre of Nations Festival to the city. The festival is a bi-annual program of the International Theatre Institute, which has centers in 72 countries around the world. Arnoult serves on the board of the U.S. branch of ITI, and represents the U.S. on its New Theater Committee.

In 1981, Arnoult began lobbying the city and the ITI to bring the 1986 festival to Baltimore. A city must make a proposal to ITI, whose executive committee considers the request and renders a decision. Arnoult shared the direction of the festival with Stan Wojewodsk, Jr., artistic director of Center Stage, and Hope Quackenbush of the Morris Mechanic Theatre.

The two-week festival included a wide range of companies, including the National Theatre of Bulgaria, and Martha Clarke in her *Garden of Earthly Delights*. In all, 18 companies were presented in 1986, five of which appeared at the Theatre Project. The Project also created Club 45, a gathering place for artists in the courtyard behind the townhouses

There also was a University of the Theatre of Nations—a sort of laboratory group consisting of about 25 theater professionals and higher-level students from around the world who worked with different directors and discussed various theater pieces.

Marketing and Promotion

Pamela Mansfield, former director of development, says the Project makes a point of emphasizing its national and international reputation. "We show articles from all over the world in foreign languages, with the word 'Baltimore' highlighted. We want local people to realize how extensive our international reputation is. We have to emphasize that the work we do does have a place, that it is important, and that it's work we're making accessible to people in Baltimore. We also serve as a launch point for extensive tours around the country. We're a little theater, but we're a lot bigger in terms of all these things that we do."

Annie Houston Reddick served as public relations director from 1987–88 through a special exchange program set up cooperatively with the International Theatre Institute, with assistance from the British Arts Council. Her observations as a Briton who oversaw the Project's publicity are informative.

She admits to being most surprised that so many people in Baltimore had not heard about the Project despite its long history. She also remembers being constantly frustrated by the Baltimore media's insistence on a local angle for its stories. "My point was that companies have come from all over the world, and they don't have a grandmother in Baltimore," she says.

> The Project is the port of entry not only for international work, but for avant garde work, period.

Joy Bell Tauber, marketing and development director with responsibility for promotion since June 1990, came from the New Mexico Repertory Theater in Albuquerque, where she was company manager. She describes some recent changes in the Project's marketing strategies. "We're trying to do more specific targeting of groups, which wasn't much done in past," she says. For example, the 1990 season opener of Leningrad's Theatre BUFFO called for the targeting of Baltimore's Soviet emigre population, from folk dance groups to churches to the Jewish Community Center.

"We also want to go beyond our normal advertising/brochure strategy," she says, connecting visiting artists with the the community to bring in new audiences.

An effort is being made to further target the area's extensive college and private high school population. "We want to cultivate the fairly young audience that is attracted to our kind of work. We have always had special rates for them, but now we're targeting student groups with more special deals," Tauber says.

Another innovation is their Passport, a voucher system that costs $90 and allows eight tickets in any configuration the buyer wishes. "This gives a lot more flexibility to our audience members, and to us in scheduling our season," she says.

The promotional strategies of the past have worked fairly well, Tauber says. "It hasn't been a big problem here. Even though Baltimore is culturally rich, our work is so different that it garners attention and good coverage. It's a stable area. We want to maintain it, plus reach outside the Baltimore-Washington corridor" by sending special releases to major publications in Philadelphia, New York and Boston. "I hope this will gain us more coverage and awareness, especially when a company appearing here will be going there as well."

Financing the Experimental

Because Arnoult's vision is unique to him, there has never been an organization like the Baltimore Theatre Project. But this quality also has had its drawbacks. There is such an overwhelming personal investment and ownership on

Arnoult's part that, despite its 20 years of operation, institutionalization of the operations has been elusive, at best. The artistic vision has dominated to such a degree that a desire to establish long-term financial stability has been frustrated.

There is a sense that one gets in conversation with Arnoult that he feels institutional stability and artistic risk are mutually exclusive, that evidence of the former would automatically spell compromise or even decimation of the latter. There can be no consideration of compromise of Arnoult's driving artistic vision, since it defines the organization.

The 1989–90 season was a particularly difficult time financially. Some wondered if the Theatre Project would weather the storm. It survived the season, and emerged in June 1990 with the new affiliation with Towson State University and hopes that this would bring more credibility and leverage with funders and others.

David Custy, executive director since June 1990, and business manager from 1986–89, traces the history of the Project's debt of more than $360,000 in 1988, including the mortgage on the facility.

"We've always been a hand-to-mouth organization," he says. After the Project became independent from Antioch College, it maintained itself throughout the 1970s with CETA funds. Those funds had dried up by the 1980s, and the Theatre Project was on its own. Its sources of funding had to be developed from box office revenues and contributed income, just like any other arts organization.

"The really big problem came after we reopened in 1985," Custy says. "It was the first time we had sold tickets. It was difficult to budget, because we couldn't base it on anything from the past."

The first season after the reopening was hard to budget and promote, he says, especially since the audience that had been built up from 1971 to 1983 was gone. "We had 300 performances of 18 different companies in 365 days," he recalls. "We kept our personnel down, and estimated conservatively. But this was chancey work."

Writer John Straussbough remembers this crucial transition for the theater. "In 1978, the Project had reached a peak of what it was then—part of the hippie movement, counterculture, free theater. By 1981, the money and culture had changed radically. The theater became a different animal. For 10 years, it was a place you could come to for free, which said to the public that we didn't need money. To return in a spiffed-up new package and ask for $10 admission took people by surprise. It took a few years for them to adjust, and also took Philip a while. Free theater had meant free for the audience, and total artistic freedom for the theater. You can't take the same kinds of risks any more without some regard for the audience."

Going into the corporate world looking for support also was new, Custy adds. "We got some support, but we needed some big ones to float us. They just didn't come along," he says, due in part to a board that may have been ill-equipped to effectively make the corporate pitch.

Arnoult says it's hard to sell the Project to local corporations and foundations. "The majority of those people wouldn't like the art that I do. The sell with them is that we are the third leg of a rich theatrical world in this town, and that we have national and international importance. I don't sell art to them. I sell image.''

Meanwhile, the deficit grew each subsequent year, Custy says. The theater ran into real trouble with the 1987–88 season.

''We had three groups in a row that people didn't like. We went from 500 to 350 subscribers.'' That dip in attendance, coupled with inadequate fundraising efforts, resulted in a deficit of almost $130,000.

The Project managed to stay afloat with unsecured loans that were rolled over, he says. But in 1988, the annual servicing of the debt was infringing on its artistic mission. That same year, a task force recommended that an executive director's position be created.

''Philip had been doing it all alone, both the artistic and the financial '' says Board Chairman Somerset Waters, assistant treasurer at the Black & Decker Corp. ''He's on the road a lot, and when you've got $500,000 in annual expenditures, that can be a problem.'' The executive director was to organize staff, raise money, and promote the theater's image.

Still, financial problems intensified in the 1989–90 season. ''We needed more corporate sponsorship,'' Custy says. ''It didn't happen. It looked as if we might close in January or February.'' But box office receipts went up, expenses were trimmed, and some money came in from donations, a large portion of which came from a former board member.

Since then, he says, the Project has gradually been making dents in the debt, primarily by keeping expenses down. ''We had to cut back on staff by necessity,'' Custy says, and use more interns. Salaries also were cut. In addition, he adds, some of the Project's debts were forgiven or renegotiated.

Fortunately, he says, Arnoult's extensive travels have been funded primarily through his work as a site evaluator with the National Endowment for the Arts, and as the artistic director of the Knoxville Festival.

Fundraising initiatives include renting the theater space to corporations for such programs as sales presentations, and pushing group sales to corporations, colleges and private high schools.

Public money from the county has increased, Custy says, while city money has remained stable despite city-wide budget cuts. For 1991, public support from city, county, state and federal sources amounts to $85,800. But it continues to be difficult to garner substantial corporate support, he says, and efforts to build a strong board of directors continue. He hopes the Towson affiliation will gain the Project at least one strong board member.

Board Chairman Somerset Waters III hopes the affiliation with an educational institution will open up new avenues for the Theatre Project. ''It's difficult to raise funds for a fringe theater,'' he says. ''It's hard for funders to identify with. We hope our affiliation with Towson will lend us a certain legitimacy that will help.''

It is clear, however, that the Theatre Project cannot view its affiliation with Towson State University as a financial panacea. The announcement of the collaboration stated unequivocally that each organization would remain financially independent.

Custy says the 1990–91 budget was trimmed about $150,000, from $500,000 in 1989. More reliable accounting methods also have been put into place, he says.

"Good things are starting to happen," he says. "If things continue to go well in the box office, we'll be OK despite the debt." He says he hopes to lessen the debt by $50,000 in the 1990–91 season through the trimmed expenses and fund-raising initiatives.

Arnoult is adamant that the Project resists a move toward dependence on the box office, noting that not more than 40 percent of the budget is pegged to come from ticket sales.

"I see a great danger in pandering to the box office," he says. "If you've got a 2,000-seat house, maybe you have to do that. Some people are pleased with 'three for them and two for us.'

"But, I don't want to be in the position of having to fill this theater, ever. I don't want my decisions to be based on my guess as to whether or not they're going to stand up around the corner to buy into it. The stricture of never budgeting over 40 percent earned income is a simply way to codify that.

"I want every seat in my theater filled every night, because I believe in the work. But that's not going to happen. I'm pleased when everybody wants to see something and I make a lot of money, but I'm not going to base the theater on it."

Those who know him feel that Arnoult will prevail despite serious financial setbacks. Similarly, they say, the Project also will prevail, simply because of the will and commitment of its founder.

"The thing is, I won't let this place die," he says. "It's too important . . . I'll do anything I have to do to keep this vision alive. Part of that is about money, and part is about testing the vision continually to see if it still makes sense to me and the world out there."

The Mahabharata

Photo by Marc Enguerand

4 Dreams Grounded in Cunning

It is a modern-day Quixotean drama, the saga of how *The Mahabharata* made it from a rock quarry in France to a theater in Brooklyn.

It went like this: An innovative English theater director and a French author decide to create a dramatic epic based on one of the longest and oldest books in the world. It has almost 12,000 pages, and is written in Sanskrit. It forms the core of the history, myths, and religion of Indian thought.

The dramatic adaptation is written in French, and lasts nine hours in three three-hour segments. A Brooklyn-based performing arts center, in collaboration with other international production partners, commissions an English-language version. The costs to realize this version of the piece and bring it to the U.S. are nearly $2 million. To produce it, the performing arts center has to find another theater, and convince the city to commit $4.2 million to its renovation.

Everything must be done within a year and a half, with only seven months to renovate and prepare the theater.

Unlikely? Impractical? Impossible? All three words apply. But miraculously, it happened. Harvey Lichtenstein, president of the Brooklyn Academy of Music, dreamed the impossible dream; BAM's board and staff brought that dream to life through sheer grit, determination and savvy strategic planning.

The journey of the *The Mahabharata* from the 1985 Avignon Festival in France to the stage of BAM's Majestic Theater in 1987 is just one of Harvey Lichtenstein's many dreams to have come true. Those dreams have been the driving force at BAM, and have become so consequential to the institution that an officer of its board of trustees speaks of them when defining the board's function.

"The board has two contradictory functions," says Vice Chairman Franklin

R. Weissberg. "One is to support Harvey's dreams, which are always very expensive and sometimes not totally practical. At the same time, we must keep a strong sense of fiscal responsibility."

Weissberg feels that the best managers or impresarios are "dreamers who have amazing chutzpah and a great sense of impracticality, grounded in a cunning that somehow you can get these things done. The function of the board is to support that cunning, to find the money, and to help establish an atmosphere in which things happen."

The Mahabharata

It's one in the afternoon on a Saturday in November 1987. The lights are being dimmed in the refurbished Majestic Theater. An all-day performance of the nine-hour production of The Mahabharata, which was translated by director Peter Brook from Jean-Claude Carrière's book, is about to begin. Members of the audience scurry to their seats. After so much talk about the epic, the sense of excitement and anticipation is palpable.

What follows is a gripping piece of theater. Visually, the production is a burst of bright colors, fabrics and textures. The world of natural phenomena is in full view on stage. There are two bodies of water, a river and a pond; a red clay stage floor; and elaborate pyrotechnics. The music—played by five international musicians on a variety of Asian, African, and Middle Eastern instruments—is a fascinating mélange of unusual, beautiful, and deeply moving sounds. Actors from all over the world—for many of whom English is not a first language—speak the text with clarity and drama. Many of them play multiple roles and have numerous costume changes.

As the world has come to expect from Peter Brook, the experience is unforgettable. Assuredly, those responsible for bringing the work to Brooklyn will remember not only the performance, but the process of getting it to the stage.

When Lichtenstein visited Brook in Paris in 1985, he was gripped by the idea of the monumental new project. He and Robert Fitzpatrick, then executive director of the Los Angeles Festival, discussed bringing an English-language version of The Mahabharata to the U.S. in 1987. The two had collaborated before, on the first U.S. appearances of Pina Bausch's Wuppertaler Tanztheater. At BAM, the new work would be part of its innovative Next Wave series which takes place each fall.

Brook came to New York in 1986 to find a site for the piece. He and Lichtenstein toured piers at the base of the East River, where other unusual works had been successfully staged. Finally, they went to the old Majestic Theater just two blocks away from BAM. They had to gain entrance by climbing in a window. Inside, the theater was leaking and rotting, but Brook found it promising—it reminded him of his own space in Paris, Le Théâtre Les Bouffes du Nord, where the production had played for an entire season after premiering in a rock quarry outside of Avignon.

Howard Golden, Brooklyn borough president, was enlisted to shepherd the project through the New York City budget process and to gain funds for the renovation. The design work resulted in an entirely new 900-seat house, which resembled an amphitheater. The stage was stripped to its exposed brick back wall;

all other stage space was left open and devoid of traditional stage trappings. *Time* magazine put the renovation project on its Best of 1987 list of design achievement, describing it as having "maintained the look of *désuetude*."

Lichtenstein recalls that all the work went on simultaneously: fundraising, theater renovation, work on the piece, and coordination with the Los Angeles Festival. The pyrotechnics alone took up an enormous amount of time, since clearances had to be obtained from the city's fire department.

On top of it all, the financial situation escalated in complexity with the fluctuating exchange rate between dollar and franc, in which the French production company was to be paid. After seeking advice, BAM bought currency futures to lock in the rate.

> BAM's long-term commitment to artists and their work is the key to the institution.

"We got it all done with maybe 10 minutes to spare," Lichtenstein says of the project. "It was really quite a three-ring circus. Meanwhile, we had the rest of the Next Wave to produce. At the same time, we were involved with Brook to direct a production of Chekhov's *The Cherry Orchard*. There were twice as many things as usual going on—and with the usual load, we go crazy at BAM. But it was all worth it."

Karen Brooks Hopkins, vice president of planning and development for BAM at that time, was responsible for fundraising. She knew she needed as much time as possible to come up with and implement a plan of action. First, she needed narrative and budget information: What is the project about, and what is it going to cost? How much can be expected from the box office, and how much from any other production partners? She describes the process as a critical gap between money available and time available to raise it.

She recalls that she had to write up a major proposal for the project, but Lichtenstein was the only person to have seen the work. She sent someone to the library to research it, and someone else to speak to scholars about its historical, cultural, and social context and perspective. Her staff asked Lichtenstein about how it looked and sounded. She took all the scholarly material, every piece written about the production in Europe, and Lichtenstein's eyewitness reports, "and tried to synthesize it into a cogent, brilliant, exciting, interesting, provocative, four- to six-page proposal with a one-page summary budget."

Fundraising began about one and a half years in advance. Hopkins created a two-front assault—one on foundations for production monies, and another on corporations to find a sponsor under the Philip Morris Next Wave Festival umbrella. Several fundraising events also were held, and a special "friends" group was begun to gain funds and solicit grants.

The first step was to quickly win converts and develop a roster of prestigious foundations to endorse the production with substantial grants. A trip to Paris was arranged for potential key funders—who paid their own way—to see the production in French. Some members of the BAM Board of Trustees also went. The board's Franklin Weissberg recalls seeing three hours of the production while seated on a hard bench. "It was one of the most thrilling evenings I ever spent in my life," he says. "When I came back and everyone on the board said, 'We can't do this!' I said, 'We can't *not* do this!' "

As for the theater renovation, the City of New York provided the lion's share of the money—$4.2 million. But BAM knew there would be a cost overrun, which eventually reached $500,000. Hopkins and her staff had to raise these additional dollars. In the end, they raised $500,000 for the renovation, and nearly $1 million for the production.

BAM's press/marketing department also faced a Herculean task. Vice President Douglas W. Allan acknowledges the challenge of selling three months of shows divided into three performances. He says the biggest obstacle was to convert to their advantage what might be seen as deterrents—the length of the piece and the price of the ticket, which really was one ticket for each part.

"We started with the assumption that this was a major event, like *Nicholas Nickleby* was on Broadway," Allan says. A survey helped them decide how to offer four ways of seeing *The Mahabharata*—as an all-day marathon, an all-night marathon, three nights in a row in the same week, or three weeks running on the same night. A discount was offered for cycle tickets purchased in advance, guaranteeing an audience. For the marathon performances, a light Indian dinner provided by a caterer was available on a reservation basis.

Diane Coffey, chief of staff for former Mayor Edward Koch and one-time acting commissioner of cultural affairs, says that BAM's work on projects like *The Mahabharata* has affected the entire New York City community. "It comes about because you have somebody like Harvey Lichtenstein, who is a tireless, indefatigable advocate both in terms of his own ideas for the institution and his vision for its future. He comes to the city and says, 'Here is this theater. We would like to renovate it, and we would like to do that so that we can put on this very wonderful production.' Now, you don't renovate a theater just for one production, but you do it with the thought of what lies ahead once you have your star production to initiate it. That theater was lying fallow, and there wasn't much we had planned to do with it."

Coffey says the renovation would not have happened if it wasn't for Lichtenstein's leadership. "The man never lets up for a minute," she says. "He is not dashed by fleeting disappointments or momentary letdowns, because he has a goal and he is going to get to that spot no matter how diligently he has to pursue it. He is one of the most tenacious people I have ever met. Zealots occasionally can drive people crazy, but he is easy to deal with. Because he speaks so straightforwardly, you can speak just as straightforwardly back to him."

The Path to the Next Wave

The Mahabharata saga proves how highly developed BAM's ideas and operations have become. But it wasn't always that way. The road to the Next Wave Festival and beyond was long and bumpy.

Many assume that BAM's trademark programming in the Next Wave Festival springs full-grown like Athena out of the head of Zeus. Nothing could be farther from reality. Lichtenstein's tenacious pursuit of his artistic passions is of the essence in making such projects a reality; added to this is BAM's ability to activate community interest.

Lichtenstein joined the Brooklyn Academy of Music as president in 1967. He describes the institution at that time as "quiescent." A membership program included many kinds of activities—lectures, chamber music concerts, weekly folk dancing sessions, travelogs—all for $25 per year. Its constituency was primarily older, retired people who also attended a celebrity series promoted by an outside producer affiliated with the Sol Hurok organization. Lastly, there was a series of five concerts per season by the Boston Symphony Orchestra, which had performed there since the 1880s.

Lichtenstein says he came to the BAM position with little experience, after a Ford Foundation fellowship program to develop arts administrators from former practitioners. He had studied dance at the Martha Graham studio and at Connecticut College, and danced professionally until he was in his late 20s. After the fellowship, he spent a year as an administrative intern with the New York City Ballet, and subsequently was hired to start a subscription series for the ballet and the New York City Opera. Two years later, he got the BAM job.

He also had spent a summer at Black Mountain College in North Carolina, which at that time was an artist's colony for contemporary generative artists from across the disciplines. There he met Merce Cunningham, Robert Rauschenberg, Charles Olsen, John Cage, Franz Klein, and Jack Twerkow, all of whom had a tremendous impact on him.

He recalls arriving at BAM a novice, but with basic expertise in programming. He learned about running the institution as he went along. He was sustained by his broad experience in the arts, "and an instinct for what would make sense to do, what would be interesting and important," he says.

Lichtenstein saw much interesting work going on in dance—outside the mainstream and in the studios—which was not being seen by a wider public. He decided BAM could do something unique in this area that would not duplicate efforts by Carnegie Hall, Lincoln Center, the 92nd Street Y, or Hunter College.

He was interested in other off-beat things "that could really create a stir," like Jerzy Grotowski's Polish Theater Lab, and the Living Theater, a politically engaged expatriate American company. BAM was the host to both theater companies in the late 1960s.

After these early ventures, there was the first appearance of Robert Wilson's work, *The Life and Times of Sigmund Freud*, in 1969; Twyla Tharp's performance in 1969 with the audience seated on stage in the Opera House; Merce Cunningham in 1969 and 1970; and minimalist composer Steve Reich and his ensemble in 1971. Now, Lichtenstein says, BAM is "better, more professionally organized, more experienced, and presenting a lot of experimental work that has developed an audience—but a lot of what we do has taken 20 years of maturation to continue and develop."

Dr. Mary Schmidt Campbell, commissioner of cultural affairs of New York City, credits BAM with overturning the myth that the outer boroughs of New York are more provincial than Manhattan in artistic taste.

"BAM has created one of the leading avant-garde spaces, along with an aura that makes people very willing to cross the Brooklyn Bridge for its performances," she says.

Lichtenstein says that program development takes energy, patience, and "a real belief in what you're doing. When we first presented Robert Wilson, we would have 300–400 people in a 2,000-seat house; Merce Cunningham often drew very small crowds that left during intermission. We went through lots of depressing times." He was carried by his belief in the work.

Lichtenstein first met Peter Brook in 1969. Brook's connection with the Royal Shakespeare Company as its co-director led to an important relationship with BAM during a period of years. This long association with Brook explains why *The Mahabharata* was such a compelling project for Lichtenstein.

Many of the artists on BAM's program today are those with whom Lichtenstein has developed long-term relationships, artists to whom he has a long-term commitment. He has figured significantly in their development and they have figured significantly in his.

This long-term commitment to artists and their work is really the key to BAM; what it presents today is an organic outgrowth of the work it has been doing for more than 20 years.

"I think the work we're presenting as part of the Next Wave originated with work that we presented when I first got here," Lichtenstein says. "That came about through my predilection, and also my feeling that these were major artists who had no place else to go. Presenting them gave our institution an identity and a visibility."

Lichtenstein has been challenged by two other areas during the past 20 years. One is building the organization through staff development. The other is the growth of his own vision as he has expanded his interest into theater and opera.

The development of the BAM organization took a long time. Lichtenstein admits, "I was a slow learner at first. It took a while because I didn't know how to manage when I began, how to communicate with and develop people." He now feels he has a vital group of people who feed him with their energies and ideas, and who do not hesitate to challenge him. He has fostered the concept that they all are administrators who serve and support BAM's artistic mission. Key staff members meet weekly to learn what's going on in all departments.

Dr. Alberta Arthurs, The Rockefeller Foundation's director for arts and humanities, credits the management team's talent and perspicacity for BAM's significant accomplishments. "BAM is brilliantly managed," she says. "It has got to emerge as one of the most creative teams in the country."

The Work Onstage

BAM's programming is still evolving. So far, it has consisted of several major components: the Next Wave Festival; spring events including opera and theater; the chamber music series directed and hosted by violist Scott Nickrenz;

the performing arts program for young people; the DanceAfrica program events; and other programs held at the renovated Majestic Theater, most notably the offerings of 651, an organization established to celebrate Brooklyn's cultural diversity.

Of BAM's programs, the Next Wave Festival has received the most attention, renown, and notoriety; it has come to serve as the signature for the organization. In reality, it is simply BAM's fall season. The Next Wave is set apart from BAM's other programming—even if many of the artists' names are the same—by its breadth and depth.

The development of the Next Wave Festival has been a process of natural growth. What began as isolated events—a short season for a single dance company, or the presentation of a new music-theater piece—gathered momentum. As isolated events, the impact had been ad hoc and transitory. When gathered together—first in a year-long series, then as the three-month fall season—the aggregate impact added to the individual impact of each event.

> "Program development takes energy, patience, and a real belief in what you're doing."

Ironically, the Next Wave began after an unsuccessful attempt to establish and house at BAM a professional classical repertory theater modeled after the Royal Shakespeare Company. The BAM Rep, which began in 1979 and ran for two seasons, was not well received either by critics or audience. In the end, the project left a deficit of more than $2 million.

Lichtenstein says it took almost three years to regroup from that monumental financial setback. But with all of the disappointment and stress it placed on the institution, the BAM Rep moved it from being a presenting organization to an organization that also produced. That production experience fed into converging paths that soon led to the Next Wave.

After the financial losses, Lichtenstein retrenched. He decided to focus on the avant-garde work he had championed for many years. In 1981, he assembled a modest effort that included four events. There were three dance companies: Trisha Brown Company, Laura Dean Dancers and Musicians, and Lucinda Childs Dance Company. There also was Philip Glass' new opera, *Satyagraha*, with a libretto in Sanskrit about Gandhi's South African days.

The press/marketing department decided to try something new: offering all four events in a subscription package which would be called the Next Wave series. To everyone's amazement, the five performances of the Glass opera sold out more than a week in advance of the first performance; the dance companies sold at least 25 percent more than anticipated.

A series was born.

It moved along for two seasons and in the fall of 1983, in expanded form, it became the Next Wave Festival.

Steve Reich offers his perspective on how Lichtenstein's original programming led to the Next Wave aesthetic. "As an outsider observing it," he says, "the Next

Wave is basically Harvey scratching his head and thinking about all these people
that he's been committed to over the years in various ways. He probably thought,
'I've been doing this right along. Why don't we put it together under one name
at one time of the year, and put a focus on it?' And at that point, the cannon
went off.''

The Next Wave

Peter Sellars, Bill T. Jones and Arnie Zane, Pina Bausch, Meredith Monk,
John Cage, Maguy Marin, the Kronos Quartet, John Adams, Cecil Taylor, the World
Saxophone Quartet, the Art Ensemble of Chicago, Ping Chong, Mark Morris, Lee
Breuer, George Coates . . . Each of these outstanding generative and/or interpretive
artists, and many others, has been regularly produced or presented on the Next
Wave Festival schedule.

It is important to note that the institution is not ''discovering'' totally unknown
artists breaking through at the earliest stages of their careers. That kind of work
is nurtured in the smaller environments of Dance Theater Workshop, P.S. 122, and
The Kitchen. Lichtenstein enters the picture when he feels an artist is ready for
the next step to a more fully-realized production.

The festival has several distinctive touchstones: It is a national and international showcase for large-scale, contemporary performing arts work; much of the
work is commissioned and produced by BAM, either alone or in concert with other
national or international festivals, opera companies, or presenters; there is an
emphasis on forming artistic partnerships for creative collaborations, which combine, for example, a choreographer, sculptor, lighting designer, and composer all
working together on a new piece; and artists are challenged to enlarge the concept
of their own work—what might have been created for a loft space is slated for the
46- by 50-foot stage of the Opera House.

Many say BAM has affected their career, and influenced their creative process.

Nina Wiener—choreographer, dancer, and director of her company—says two
important things happened after Harvey Lichtenstein saw her perform at Dance
Theater Workshop. First was his vote of confidence that her work was ready to be
presented at the Next Wave. The other was the challenge he offered through the
BAM engagement to work with artists with whom she might not otherwise have
worked.

''Sometimes, presenters see a possibility in your work that you haven't been
aware of yet,'' she says. ''They get there before you, and they offer that as a possibility
for you to look at, to see if you also feel maybe that's a direction you want to
go in.''

David Gordon—choreographer, dancer, and founder and director of the Pick
Up Company—says Lichtenstein gave him the opportunity to work collaboratively
on *The Photographer* with composer Philip Glass and director JoAnne Akalaitis. He
then was offered the opportunity to perform at BAM in 1986, and again in 1988,
when his full-evening work *United States* was presented.

Gordon says it was a challenge for him to leave his own studio and other performance/loft spaces and work on the Opera House stage. "If you up the ante on the scale of things, it's an interesting thing to do," he says. "When you're working in an opera house, it's an astonishingly exciting thing to run around and look at what you've done from there, from there, from there—because you're seeing something else entirely."

Author, designer, and director Robert Wilson says BAM confirmed that he was on a viable track in his ground-breaking work. "I began to develop a technique and a style and my vocabulary. I began to see my work in reality." After his work at BAM, Wilson was invited to France, where his career was established. He says BAM's effect on contemporary generative artists is substantial. "It's been a window, a place where we can come together," he says. "Theater is a forum where you meet and exchange ideas. People go to BAM, they see things, they discuss them. It's unique."

Performance artist Laurie Anderson says her work involves music and pictures, "and sometimes it comes out as concerts, sometimes videos, sometimes film, sometimes records." She first became aware of BAM after seeing some of Robert Wilson's works. She went to the organization when she realized that they were the only people in New York who were interested in doing several nights of a long performance.

Lichtenstein supported the length of her work, and the technical and rehearsal requirements. Appearing at BAM was a capstone to her work on *The United States, Parts I-IV*, she says. "It meant finishing something that I had been working on for a while, and putting it in a definitive form so I wouldn't have to do it anymore. There are just so many times you can keep working on a work in progress." It was satisfying for her to say, "That's it. This is the last time."

In 1983, Lichtenstein hired Joseph Melillo to direct and produce the new, expanded series that was the Next Wave. Melillo served until 1990, when he moved on to direct the New York International Festival for the Arts.

Melillo previously had been the general manager of the New World Festival of the Arts in Miami Beach; while there, he produced several performances of 22 world premieres at 13 different venues over a three-and-a-half week period. He calls that experience his trial by fire, "and my complete immersion into this strange animal called a performing arts festival." It was perfect preparation for the Next Wave Festival.

A festival of this complexity, density, and scope previously had not been undertaken at BAM, and the stakes were high. "I only knew a few things," Melillo says. "No one else had produced a festival like this within this institution. I knew what a festival was all about, having come out of Miami. And I knew it all had to scream, 'Contemporary!' That's all I knew."

Melillo immersed himself in art—from attending performances of all kinds to reading voraciously—so that new ideas for the season could surface. He and Lichtenstein both agree that the process of putting together the Next Wave Festival each season was one of collaboration. "Much of the decision-making for the Next Wave came out of what Joe and I did together," Lichtenstein says. "Still, a lot of people on the staff contribute ideas and responses to artists' work. They are not just good administrators; they also have artistic judgment, and that is respected and used. We see things together, and we put it together jointly."

Both also keep in touch with artists with whom they have an established working relationship, who are creating new ideas for potential productions. "Through the process of distilling all that data, a form emerges," Melillo says, "and we begin to plan the festival." This process of program development is ongoing; often, it is very slow. Some ideas take years to conceive, mature, fund, create, and produce. Others have a shorter gestation period—seen in February, programmed in March, and on stage in October.

For the works created specifically for BAM, it is a challenge to translate the artist's dream onto the stage. Melillo says that what goes on in between is "a toboggan ride through hell," which is different with each artist and depends on his or her idiosyncrasies, personality, temperament, and ego.

Although Melillo's ultimate responsibility was to deliver the opening nights, "Let there be no mistake: I was intimately involved in raising the money and selling the tickets. But it wasn't my responsibility." He says he was blessed with partners in the planning and marketing departments."We spoke the same language," he says. "We participated in what is a strategic management process of achieving objectives, and we were consistent in the positioning of the Next Wave Festival in the contemporary culture—what's right for us and what's wrong for us."

He targeted marketplaces in the performing arts and in the visual arts—fashion showrooms, night clubs, and restaurants—that are a part of contemporary culture. He also helped create the subscription brochure, working with graphic artists in conceiving state-of-the-art design. He reviewed telemarketing scripts, brochure and press release copy; scheduled and oriented the press; and helped to target group sales efforts.

Melillo takes exception to the notion that the Next Wave Festival created an interest in and a market for contemporary work. "There were people who were ready for this work," he says. "We identified them. We galvanized that audience, brought them to Mecca. Now, they're spending the time to stretch that base and develop the audience further."

The Festival has been stretching the base on the production side as well. To successfully bring to its stages mammoth projects like *The Mahabharata* or *Nixon in China*, it must enter into partnerships with other commissioners and producers. Each project offers unique challenges. Some are initiated by BAM, while others germinate from other institutions. The opera *Nixon in China*, with a score by John Adams and a libretto by Alice Goodman, was co-commissioned by the Houston Grand Opera, BAM, and the Kennedy Center in Washington, D.C. The English-language version of *The Mahabharata* was co-commissioned by BAM and the Los Angeles Festival. After its three-month run at BAM, and its five weeks in L.A., the production continued its world tour to other production partners: the Australian Bicentennial Authority, and the City of Zurich.

Melillo says co-commissions and co-productions are necessary to make these works possible. On its own, BAM could not singly bear the financial liability. Equally important, the Festival renders a service to the artists by putting their work in front of more people, and allowing that work to grow and evolve through the experience.

"Large-scale work cannot tour according to traditional touring notions," Melillo says. "It has to sit down in a community and be presented, and presented consistently. It is by creating these co-commissioning, co-producing relationships that we are altering and redefining the verb 'to tour' for Next Wave's large-scale work."

A touring program has been an important outgrowth of the Next Wave. The program has been a hit-or-miss effort, according to Chris Tschida, former director of touring and spring programs at BAM.

BAM has a special fund for commissioning and touring. These monies were used to co-commission *Nixon in China* and *The Gospel at Colonus*. More conventionally-financed tours have included Nina Wiener and Dancers, Steve Reich and Musicians, Meredith Monk and Ping Chong's *The Games*, and others. The Peter Brook production of *The Cherry Orchard* toured to Russia and Japan.

Tschida says the touring program is trying to make the special work that BAM produces and presents more widely available to audiences. "BAM has access to things that other presenters just don't have access to," she says.

But there are many serious problems in achieving that. Most have to do with the size and scale of the productions, their technical demands, and whether they must involve union stagehands.

Alberta Arthurs says that when The Rockefeller Foundation agreed to help fund and promote the Next Wave, it was with the understanding that it would be a presenting and touring fund. "I think the presenting part of that has been brilliantly realized," she says. "The touring part of it has been much less well received, and that's been a disappointment to all of us. Many presenters are still somewhat traditional in what they want to see, but also—and perhaps more importantly—they hesitate because the work that BAM has done has been on such a tremendously large scale, and therefore is very difficult to move."

The Next Wave's ongoing challenge is to not let the vision become stale. Laurie Mallet, president and chief executive officer of the fashion company WilliWear, has been a member of the BAM Board of Trustees since 1982. Mallet was involved with Lichtenstein and Melillo in their quest for significant work. She says continual redefinition is the only way to keep the Next Wave concept fresh. It is important, she says, to reformulate the next Next Wave, "because otherwise everybody will be doing the same thing. We must redefine, and develop a new identity."

A new era began at the Next Wave with Melillo's departure. Liz Thompson, formerly executive/artistic director for Jacob's Pillow, has brought her own unique artistic vision and human sensibilities to the position. She is beginning to broaden the definition of international contemporary arts that has been celebrated at the Next Wave. That conception by and large has been a Eurocentric view excluding non-European cultures and the rising tide of pluralism within the U.S.

Thompson chooses her words carefully. "I think we must be careful not to jump on the bandwagon of multiculturalism, as if it were something new," she says. "America had an indigenous population that was completely multicultural. The American Indians did not have one culture."

She observes that the Next Wave has not presented a lot of work grounded in the Asian, Latino, African, African American, and Native American cultures. Artists from these cultures frequently create "contemporary work which doesn't fit in the definition of what was the Next Wave, which was to break new ground and find new forms. People whose roots are not in European cultures often rework traditional forms rather than create new forms. We must recognize that the reworking of these forms *is* groundbreaking" and make a commitment to present that work to audiences side by side with the Euro-centric work. "That makes BAM potentially a wonderful common ground to create a place where people can come together, as I wish they would in the outside, everyday world," she says.

> What BAM presents today is an organic outgrowth of the work it has been doing for more than 20 years.

She says this effort is not audience development; rather, it is a social commitment that won't happen just because of a well-developed marketing plan. It will happen only if BAM is sincere in its efforts to acknowledge cultural equity for work and audiences from diverse backgrounds.

Thompson also wants to integrate some of the Next Wave programming with BAM's children's programs, and encourage participatory work that involves the local community. Jawole Willa Jo Zollar's Urban Bush Women and Garth Fagan's Dance Company are on her list for presentation.

During her tenure at Jacob's Pillow, Thompson was known for her preserving and pioneering work. She maintained the spirit of the original mission founded by Ruth St. Denis and Ted Shawn more than 50 years before, and pioneered a broader-based approach that included gospel, jazz, and African dance and music programming. She proudly characterizes her accomplishments at Jacob's Pillow as "a well-balanced Calder mobile of all kinds of work, side-by-side."

Much of what she wants to initiate at the Next Wave began at Jacob's Pillow. And in Brooklyn, she has a more culturally diverse community to work with than she did in western Massachusetts.

Fundraising

For more than a decade, Karen Brooks Hopkins has been a major player in BAM fundraising. She arrived as a development officer in 1979, and moved on to become vice president of planning and development. She became executive vice president and managing director of BAM in 1988.

Her accomplishments are formidable, including forging a funding plan with a philosophical base and an activist strategy. Her approach offers significant symbiotic and complementary roles for government, foundation, corporate, and individual support.

There is nothing haphazard in her approach. Although her most recent title has brought an expanded set of responsibilities, she still oversees fundraising. She says a good fundraiser has the ability to organize and strategize a coherent campaign beginning with the identification of various constituencies and choosing an appropriate approach on each front. Certain personal skills are necessary: dogged determination; the ability to take rejection well, coupled with a good sense of humor; instincts regarding how much to ask for from each prospect; a talent for meticulous detail work; a good memory for names and faces; and a "killer instinct."

"To be successful," she adds, "you have to believe in what you're raising money for. If you don't, you shouldn't do it. I believe in the institution, and I believe in a lot of the work, and mainly I believe in what we're trying to do on stage. I may not like everything in the Next Wave Festival, but I believe in the rightness of presenting a body of work that is contemporary."

A good fundraiser doesn't "just take the money and run," she says, but properly thanks people and builds relationships with funding sources. She says this approach is particularly important for presenting organizations. Generally, the people who support a single-discipline producing organization usually have a commitment to that particular field. "When you are a presenting organization like BAM, you do something different every year, so your constituency is changing all the time. This is difficult for a fundraiser.

"That's why we've become so program-oriented at BAM," she says. "Part of my job is to size up the right donor for the right project, to keep people involved and find projects that make sense for them year after year, and to find new donors."

It is impossible to read anything about the Next Wave and not notice that it is sponsored by the Philip Morris Companies. This relationship did not happen overnight. Hopkins traces its development in light of her fundraising philosophy.

She says Philip Morris became a major sponsor not only because BAM already had a working relationship with Board Chairman Hamish Maxwell, but because its presentation made sense in terms of the corporation's philanthropic/cultural program. BAM chose to ask the corporation to fund the Next Wave because the festival seemed consistent with Philip Morris' goals. "For BAM, it has never been enough to know somebody," Hopkins says. "You must know them, and then ask for something that makes sense."

Stephanie French, director of Philip Morris' cultural affairs and corporate contributions programs, says the corporation identified the arts as an area that enhanced its relations in the community because the arts make a community a more stimulating place to live. "It also fits with the company image, which is one of being very forward-thinking, on the cutting edge, very creative," she says. "We want to communicate that we are a creative company." She says the corporation decided to support the Next Wave because "We saw the fit, and took the chance."

Hopkins also courted and won a group of Next Wave backers from the foundation world and from government funders. The Rockefeller Foundation has allocated $250,000 a year.

Visual artists and people who collect contemporary art also entered the fund-raising picture. Hopkins worked with Anne Livet and the late Steve Reichard, consultants with extensive contacts in the visual arts world, to help sell subscription tickets in that market.

On Reichard's recommendation, BAM formed a support group for the festival, a kind of "private patron arm." She says this Producers Council was the first time BAM reached out to a constituency in the city that had some wealth but was not organized. Some members were the sons and daughters of patrons of the Metropolitan Opera or Lincoln Center; some were downtown visual artists and art collectors; some were people in the fashion or entertainment industries. These people were more off-beat, not threatened by BAM's programming—and with enough money to give $1,000 or $1,500 a year. The Council has drawn on such celebrities as Bianca Jagger, Richard Gere, Bette Midler, Claes Oldenburg and Jann Wenner. As much as $175,000 per year has been contributed. However, Hopkins says the dollar figure is only part of the story. The Producers Council also has provided a way to develop a new network of supporters.

Marketing and Promotion

The positioning strategy for target donors and supporters was as important to the planning and development department as audience development efforts were to the marketing, press, and promotion department. The efforts of both departments have dovetailed.

The marketing efforts have set the tone for BAM's artistic and programmatic direction throughout the 1980s. Douglas Allan, vice president of marketing and promotion, says they were looking for a younger-than-usual audience interested in the contemporary visual and performing arts. They got involved with Soho art galleries, "because on a Saturday, that's where these people are." They also knew that these same audiences were going to The Kitchen, Dance Theater Workshop, and small spaces and clubs to see work on the cutting edge.

"We knew that our visuals had to be special," Allan says. They established a fresh visual image by commissioning Next Wave posters from the likes of artists Roy Lichtenstein, Francisco Clemente, Frank Stella, Susan Rothenberg, and Willem de Kooning.

The rest of the marketing approach, Allan says, "is adaptations of standard marketing techniques: direct mail, newspaper advertising, telemarketing. What we did differently is how we designed and approached the direct mail, and how we advertised, picking the publications that would reach our target audience."

In creating "the Next Wave handle," the marketing department is credited for having set the tone for BAM's significant artistic and programmatic direction throughout the 1980s.

New Initiatives

Alberta Arthurs of The Rockefeller Foundation says the Next Wave aesthetic has permeated BAM's other programming, including the more traditional. "I think that a lot of work that once would have been part of the Next Wave has traveled, has meandered into the spring season, has affected the programming at BAM in every conceivable way," she says. "I don't think it's easy for BAM to present conventionally any longer. It has become an organization devoted to the energies of new artists in virtually everything it presents."

This influence often takes the form of a contemporary interpretation or re-interpretation of classic works, plus the creation of new works by contemporary artists. In theater, for example, BAM followed up the opening of the Majestic Theater with a production of *The Cherry Orchard*, directed by Peter Brook. *Hamlet* was then performed in Swedish in the Opera House by the Royal Dramatic Theatre of Sweden, directed by Ingmar Bergman.

In the 1988–89 season, BAM initiated its first opera season and presented Verdi's *Falstaff*, performed by the Welsh National Opera in its American debut with stage director Peter Stein, who is regarded as a commanding presence in inter-national contemporary theater. On opening night, BAM demonstrated to the world that it had truly arrived on the international social circuit, when the Welsh com-pany's patron—Princess Diana—attended the production and post-performance din-ner.

There also was a BAM production of Kurt Weill and Bertolt Brecht's *Mahagonny Songspiel (Das Kleine Mahagonny)*; and *Conversations with Fear and Hope After Death*, selections from Bach cantatas and other works. The opera season ended with the American debut of the baroque opera by Jean-Baptiste Lully, *Atys*, performed by the Théâtre National de L'Opéra de Paris.

In the 1989–90 season, BAM presented the American debut of Brussels Thé-âtre Royal de la Monnaie in a production of Mozart's *La Finta Giardiniera* and Purcell's *Dido and Aeneas*.

BAM did face a setback for the 1991 season, for which it had planned a major opera initiative—a collaboration with the Metropolitan Opera. Peter Sellars was to have directed Gluck's *Orfeo ed Euridice* and *The Death of Klinghoffer* by the composer John Adams and librettist Alice Goodman. However, the Met withdrew from the project, reportedly due to fundraising problems.

Lichtenstein says BAM still will produce *The Death of Klinghoffer*. It also will follow through on its own explorations of new and unusual opera, perhaps through its association with Dennis Russell Davies, music director of BAM and the Brooklyn Philharmonic, and director of the Bonn opera.

Community

For any arts organization, the issue of community is serious, provocative, and challenging. For the Brooklyn Academy of Music, it takes on very significant proportions because the property is owned by the City of New York. In response, the organization serves a series of concentric circles of ever-enlarging communities.

BAM is located in downtown Brooklyn, a primarily African American and Caribbean neighborhood. Karen Brooks Hopkins, who is responsible for BAM's community relations program, sees BAM as the premier arts institution in the Borough of Brooklyn, whose population of several million people would qualify it as the fifth-largest city in the U.S. were it not a part of the City of New York.

"BAM is an international institution, a national institution, a city institution, and a Brooklyn institution," she says. "You have to maintain that balance very delicately. You cannot let one be abandoned in light of the other. They are all important."

BAM's response to Brooklyn communities has been less focused than have the inspired, well-conceived and executed Next Wave Festival and related programming. Undeniably, some outstanding programs have been created and established; the 30-year-old Performing Arts Programs for Young People, and the 13-year-old DanceAfrica are two examples.

In response to a combination of factors—community pressure, the need to keep the new Majestic Theater more actively utilized, and BAM's own realization that its community efforts were less developed than its Next Wave ventures—BAM inaugurated the nonprofit arts organization 651 in the spring of 1989.

It derives its name from the address of the Majestic Theater, 651 Fulton St., and spearheads a multicultural arts program at BAM. The organization is an outgrowth of the Fund for the Borough of Brooklyn, an arm of the Borough President's Office. Both BAM and the fund provide financial and administrative support. Programming has been created and produced by Mikki Shepard, an expert in multicultural music, dance and theater; and ethnomusicologist Leonard Goines. The eight events in 651's 1989 season were intended to evoke a particular kind of sound characteristic of New York's various clubs and neighborhoods. The 1990 season brought performances of calypso, salsa, jazz and ballroom music by some of the most prominent of today's musicians.

Cultural affairs commissioner Dr. Mary Schmidt Campbell welcomes the addition of 651 to BAM's programming. She acknowledges Shepard's "superlative history of programming DanceAfrica," and credits her with bringing that same kind of leadership to 651.

BAM's DanceAfrica program has been under the artistic director of Chuck Davis of the African American Dance Ensemble, based in Durham, North Carolina. Since it began in 1977, DanceAfrica has explored African dance traditions and their influence on today's dances and dancers.

DanceAfrica events are authentic and organic to a significant part of the Brooklyn community. An outdoor bazaar draws thousands to buy African, South American, Caribbean, and African American foods, crafts and books. The sold-out performances—which have showcased both African and American performers—bring together people of all ages for what has become a joyous community event in the formal surroundings of the Opera House.

A Commitment to the Artist

Dr. Arthurs of The Rockefeller Foundation says Harvey Lichtenstein has put BAM on the national and international map. So significant is his leadership that in 1986, Lichtenstein received a presidential appointment to the National Council on the Arts to advise the National Endowment for the Arts on policy, programs, and procedures, and to make recommendations on grants.

Lichtenstein considers himself "one of the really lucky people in this world, to be doing work which I not only enjoy doing, but which is stimulating and allows me to continue to develop and grow—and having the opportunity to work with these artists and this staff, and seeing them develop and grow. At first, I was a one-man band, because that was all I knew. As I began to understand what was needed, I began to understand who I needed to help me, and I began to allow my staff to do what they could do."

Composer Steve Reich makes an analogy in trying to capture BAM's essence through Lichtenstein. "You support the climate, the soil. You water the garden. You hope the sunshine will come in. And you pull out some weeds. Harvey's a real good gardener. His general attitude seems to be to encourage the work, and I think ultimately that is correct. All a gardener can do is create a really good climate, and that's the best way to get the best work to survive."

Roots of Brasil

Photo by Tony Bennia

5 A Mirror of Its Communities

The Caribbean Cultural Center's annual tribute to Oya and Yemanja, the Yoruba goddesses of the whirlwind and the sea, is more than just a concert or performance. It is a total experience, engaging all of the senses and penetrating the soul.

The tribute to the West African deities celebrates cultural history, cultural memory, cultural continuity, and cultural pride. The typically sold-out event attracts a diverse audience that includes a remarkable number of families. Children sit in the laps of parents and grandparents to watch and listen as Yoruba drummers and dancers, Cuban Santeria singers, Brazilian musicians, and African American dancers offer their individual expressions in honor of these goddesses, who are an integral part of numerous African-based cultures. The event becomes a sweeping experience, a celebration of the kinship of these cultures—which, though sometimes separated by geography, are linked by a world view in which art, religion and daily life are inextricably intertwined.

The tribute—which also features lectures, speeches and an African/Caribbean market—is characteristic of the work of the Caribbean Cultural Center. The presentation of the arts in the context of the culture that gave rise to them is one of the cornerstones of executive director Marta Moreno Vega's concept for the Center, which she founded in 1976. Culture is a continuum, she says. The arts cannot be extracted, examined, and practiced in isolation from everything else in society.

"The notion of culture is holistic, by definition," Vega says. "It expresses your philosophy, how you identify as a group, then it begins to develop the aspects that create a society. Your educational system reflects that philosophy, as do your legal system and your creative expressions. In looking at cultures of color, you see that they're all interrelated. Most cultures of color do not see art apart from the total scheme of living. That's how we developed the notion of the Center."

In his book, *Before the Mayflower: A History of Black America*, author Lerone Bennett Jr. describes the extent to which this world view is operative in African-based cultures. "Art, like religion, was a life expression," he writes. "There were no art museums or opera houses in pre-white man Africa. Art and aesthetic expression were collective experiences in which all the people participated. Art, in short, was not for art's sake, but for life's sake."

Another philosophical underpinning for the Center is the kinship of African-based cultures in the Americas, whatever their geographical home. As the Center's 10th-year report puts it, "The slave ships from West Africa made many stops— and wherever they stopped they left a legacy of tradition, customs and creative expressions with their human cargo. The variety and spectrum of the Center's programming unites these traditions, encouraging cultural exchanges and understanding not available through other avenues."

This notion of a shared background is commonly acknowledged by people of African descent, says C. Daniel Dawson, director of special projects for the Center. It's a controversial notion, he says, only among "Europeans who have a stake in that not being the truth, because of the political power of people seeing themselves as one, or at least unified." Dawson, who has worked as a filmmaker in Martinique, Guyana, and Brazil, recites a saying common in those countries: "Same boat, different stop." This unity among peoples in the New World defies international borders and language barriers, and has survived the imposition of European languages, customs, and religions.

The depth of the Center's work reflects the essence of the cultures it presents. Its activities have more meaning than just "creating a program," "putting on a concert" or "putting up an exhibit" since the Center also provides the context for the work, so it will be authentically presented and appropriately apprehended by the public.

The annual tribute to Oya and Yemanja is an example. In addition to the dancing, singing and music-making, the tribute offers participants a wealth of other experiences. Every year since 1985, the lobby of Aaron Davis Hall on the campus of City College in New York's Harlem has been transformed into an African/ Caribbean marketplace. Vendors sell colorful fabrics and clothing, fine imported and domestic crafts, jewelry, books, and posters. Enticing smells waft from food booths representing a variety of Caribbean cuisines.

The din heightens as the crowd gathers in the lobby. What follows is part performance, part political rally, part a conjuring up of a shared cultural memory and a transmitting of that memory onto the next generation.

At the 1988 tribute, TV producer Angela Fontanez hosted the program, which opened with a slide lecture depicting visual manifestations of the goddesses. Babalorisha John Mason, a Yoruba priest who writes and lectures on religion, spoke about feminine power as the foundation of civilization. He provided a context for the work that was to be performed, and showed slides of the unique expressions of Oya and Yemanja in Africa, the Caribbean, and across the Americas. He traced the thread that ties all of these expressions together at the source—Africa.

Nigeria's Babatunde Olatunji and Drums of Passion then performed four pieces honoring Yemanja. Milton Cardona and the Eya Aranla Ensemble drummed and chanted Cuban music in honor of a number of Yoruba gods: Obatala, the god of creativity; Chango, the god of fire, thunder and lightning; and to the honored female divinities Oya and Yemanja.

After intermission, Adelaide Sanford—a member of the New York State Regents, an elementary school principal, and former president of the New York Association of Black School Supervisors—spoke with passion and eloquence about how the city's educational system must be changed to derive strength from and support for communities of color.

Dance of the Wind, a tribute to Oya, was then performed by the Marie Brooks Caribbean Dance Theater company of dancers and drummers, ages 8 to 18. Roots of Brasil presented the dancing and drumming of Brazil's African-based cultures.

All of the groups were brought back on stage together and then down into the audience for an overpowering conclusion of drumming and dancing. At once, everyone became participants as the entire audience stood and moved to the rhythms. They had

> The Center is based on the idea that culture is a continuum, that the arts are intimately intertwined with everything else in society.

been involved, enlightened, and challenged by the experience, and they left the theater totally energized.

The same sense of unity and celebration permeates the Center's annual "Chango Celebrations," a music and dance tribute to the Yoruba god of fire, thunder and lightning. To welcome people to the 1988 celebration, Adeyemi Bandele, director of the Advanced Education Programs of the New York State Martin Luther King Jr. Institute for Non-Violence, requested from the podium that each person in the room introduce him- or herself and shake hands with the people immediately nearby. The handshakes, smiles and greetings warmed the theater with a sense of community; no one could feel like an outsider. This approach, although carried out in a spirit of spontaneity, was a very carefully thought-out part of the celebration. It was no chance inspiration.

In his book, *Flash of the Spirit, African & Afro-American Art & Philosophy*, Dr. Robert Farris Thompson, professor of art at Yale University, describes the Yoruba people of West Africa as the largest and most urban of traditional civilizations in Black Africa. He writes that the Yoruba "show their special concern for the proprieties of right living through their worship of major goddesses and gods, each essentially a unique manifestation of àshe—the power-to-make-things-happen, a key to futurity and self-realization in Yoruba terms."

He says the Yoruba remain the Yoruba, despite the diaspora, "precisely because their culture provides them with ample philosophic means for comprehending, and ultimately transcending, the powers that periodically threaten to dissolve them. That their religion and their art withstood the horrors of the Middle Passage and firmly established themselves in the Americas (New York City, Miami, Havana, Hatanzas, Recife, Bahia, Rio de Janeiro) as the slave trade effected a Yoruba diaspora reflects the triumph of an inexorable communal will."

The Yoruba tradition is only one of the many on which the Center has focused. The Caribbean Cultural Center's goal is to "chronicle the cultural roots and living traditions of people of African descent in the New World." For example, an October 1990 conference was to examine the Kongo-Angola culture and its global impact, yet another example of an African tradition with international manifestations.

While it points to a shared cultural background, the Center's programming also celebrates diversity, according to Dr. J. Michael Turner, associate professor at Hunter College, who specializes in African and Latin American history and has been a consultant for the World Bank and the U.S. Agency for International Development. There is strength in diversity, he says; it can bring about social transformation and change when it is accepted and celebrated. He points to a 1989 concert by "the queen of salsa," Celia Cruz, held at the Abyssinian Baptist Church in Harlem as part of the Center's "Expressions '89" series.

"To have salsa and a Latino tradition in a Baptist church in the middle of central Harlem was a celebration of diversity," Turner says. Latinos had the chance to see what they have in common with African-Americans, and vice versa, and people could get beyond the fact that one group speaks Spanish, and the other English. With events like this one, the Center demonstrates how important it is to look at the things that bring people together, Turner adds. "I think that's fundamental. It's Marta's vision of the world and the cosmos, the vision that she brings to New York City."

In this context, the Caribbean Cultural Center is joyously and respectfully acknowledging the belief systems and the cultural expressions of its communities' ancestors. The Center's significant impact is due to this continuing expression of the communal will.

The Roots of the Center

How did this unique institution come into being, and how does it continue to flourish in New York's competitive arts and cultural world? Marta Moreno Vega, who has been the inspiration from the beginning, sustains the ideas that keep the Center at the cutting edge of community building and involvement, and of aesthetic and cultural growth. She is a skillful and visionary institution-builder.

Vega also was one of the founders of two other important New York cultural institutions—El Museo del Barrio, a community museum devoted to Puerto Rican history and culture; and the Association of Hispanic Arts, an information and service organization. She served as director of the museum from 1968–1973. During that time, she began to research and document collections of Puerto Rican visual arts in an effort to determine where they were, why they were not accessible to the public, and how El Museo del Barrio might utilize them.

In describing this research, Vega acknowledges the strong influences of Pre-Columbian and African cultures. She says she could not have looked at Puerto Rican art in isolation from the other islands, other cultures, and other experiences in the Caribbean. She realized that an entire area was not being examined, and determined that she had to create a comprehensive research project to do so. The focus: how the visual arts in Puerto Rico are a part of the cultural continuum of the entire Caribbean region.

A fellowship from The Rockefeller Foundation through the Metropolitan Museum enabled her to begin documenting Caribbean collections. She was determined to find out where they were, how they were being used, why they were not accessible, and whether they had been properly documented. Working in a basement office at the Phelps-Stokes Fund, Vega thoroughly surveyed Caribbean collections in the U.S., and moved on to survey collections in Europe and elsewhere.

She found that a great deal of material had been acquired by museums but typically was not on view. She also found that most of the collections were poorly documented, or documented from a Eurocentric point of view. That is, items were being viewed as art objects or artifacts—shown solely as art, stripped completely of their importance to the total culture, and not seen as a form of ritual or as expressions with deeper meaning.

At the conclusion of the research project, Vega began to search for an institution in which to house the information. It became apparent that there was no such institution. Those that might be interested in it were oriented to viewing the objects solely as art for art's sake. Vega wanted to create an institution that would bring together the variety of cultures under one roof.

She asked the Phelps-Stokes Fund to house her nascent organization while she tried to build an institution. She knew a solid foundation would have to be built, and how difficult it would be to take an organization from idea to reality.

The late Franklin H. Williams, then president of the Fund and a former ambassador to Ghana, pledged support by providing in-kind services, advice, and resources. The fund already was doing work relating to West and South Africa, and was sponsoring educational projects in the U.S. and the Caribbean.

"The marriage was excellent," Vega says of her association with the fund. "Their support allowed us to get off the ground. It also gave us the opportunity to do work that began to express the concept in programmatic terms. This was very important. The concept on paper is one thing, but people were able to see the various cultures coming together in exhibitions, in concerts, and in conferences."

Two and a half years later, in 1976, the organization was incorporated as the Visual Arts Research and Resource Center Relating to the Caribbean. By the early 1980s, it became known more directly as the Caribbean Cultural Center. In 1990, it was officially renamed the Franklin H. Williams Caribbean Cultural Center/African Diaspora Institute.

The Programming

The Center's fact sheet notes that it is the only organization of its kind in the U.S. researching the common heritage of all people of African descent. "Through its many programs, the Center explores the ways in which African tra-

ditions in music, dance, art, and belief systems have survived, evolved, and found
new expressions in the cultures of North, South, and Central America, and in the
countries of the Caribbean," it says.

When Vega puts together the programs, she depends on advice from a network
of traditional, community, and artistic leaders. Afro-Cuban jazz musician Mario
Bauza, for example, says he and his group have had the opportunity to perform
and musically advise the Center.

> "I've never looked at us as a presenting organization. I've looked at us as an extension of our culture, of our people."

"I hope that it's a mirror of what our community
is," Vega says of the Center's programming. "The activities that you see are activities that happen within
our communities throughout the world. We're not imposing anything that's not there already. When we put
our programs together, that network advises us, and
traditional leaders are very much part of what is done."

Many of the Center's celebrations honor Yoruba
deities (orishas) like Oya and Yemanja. Orishas and
their powers have formed a central core of the belief
systems for people of African descent. In honoring
them, the Center is respectfully acknowledging a living
cultural tradition.

On a deeper level, the fact that knowledge of the
orishas still exists is a tribute to the Africans who were
forcibly brought to the New World as slaves, and to their descendants. Keeping
alive the religion and the resulting belief system in the face of prohibitions and
punishment took courage, commitment, and ingenuity.

Hunter College's J. Michael Turner adds insight to the significance of these
celebrations. He points out that the Center has understood that, as the composition
of the population in large U.S. cities has changed during the 1960s through 1990s,
there are more newcomers who practice Yoruba traditions. Frequently, these traditions have been maintained in private. "The number of people practicing this
religion is increasing all the time," he says. "This is a very important religious
tradition and should not be seen by the community as marginal. It should be
celebrated." He is quick to point out that the Center's programs are celebrations,
rather than religious ceremonies. "They are aesthetic presentations of performances
that are inspired in the religious tradition," he says.

In honoring the orishas, Turner says, individuals are led through celebration
to personal reflection.

"The reflection is of the part that is linked to social change and social transformation. In turn, this can lead to positive social change and transformation.

"Recognizing one's religion, history, and tradition keeps a person or community from becoming complacent or static . . . It means you take the religion out
of the closet, take it with you inside of yourself when you go to your classes at
Hunter College, or Amherst, or Smith," Turner says. "That becomes part of your
identity, part of your strength. You know that you can be faithful to your religious

tradition and also be a nuclear physicist. One does not exclude the other. That is the reflection that comes with celebration."

The Center's unique programming has been central to meeting its goal to "chronicle the cultural roots and living traditions of people of African descent in the New World."

Each October, the ambitious Expressions Festival includes films, art exhibits, concerts built around certain themes and a major conference.

In addition, its annual Caribbean Carnival in New York takes place outdoors in August, and includes a parade, a concert that is part of Lincoln Center's Out of Doors Festival, and a street festival. The carnival draws about 20,000 people each year.

The Center also sponsors exhibitions of art, crafts, artifacts, and photographs reflecting the survival of African cultural traditions. It presents concerts of traditional and contemporary music and dance from Africa, the Caribbean, and the Americas. Conferences bring together scholars, artists, traditional and spiritual leaders, and community activists to examine aesthetics, cultural history, and belief and value systems. The Center holds classes in Afro-Caribbean dance, drumming, and chanting, and in Yoruba language.

Finally, it researches and documents African traditional cultures in the Americas. The Center has a developing research center of audio and video tapes, photographs and publications. It also publishes *Caribe*, a seasonal journal of African-Caribbean-American cultural history and trends.

The Expressions Festival, which began in 1979, is the major focus of the organization's autumn programming. The 1989 festival featured four concerts, two mini-concerts, an evening of films, an exhibition celebrating salsa musician Celia Cruz' birthday, and a four-day international conference examining cultural diversity. Concerts included "We Came Before Columbus," a celebration of the indigenous peoples who preceded the colonial era; and the "Trumpet Traditions" concert featuring Wynton Marsalis, which traced the evolution of the trumpet from Mali to Haiti to New Orleans. The other concerts focused on the island nations, and on Harlem. The serious and coherent mix of musicians from around the world at all the concerts resulted in a depth that celebrated the cultural continuum.

Journalist Kalamu Ya Salaam, writing in the New Orleans music publication *Wavelength*, points out how the Center's events translate its philosophy into practice. "The first half (of the 'Trumpet Traditions' concert) established both the existence and the musical importance of a unique 'trumpet' tradition that existed outside of the Eurocentric frame of reference. (Artistic Director Dr. Maurice) Martinez had the vision to aurally walk the audience through the tradition, so that when the 'traditional jazz trumpet styles' were presented, the links were not abstract nor conjectural. One had heard the roots and could thus much more greatly appreciate the fruit."

The Center's presentations are remarkable in that even an outsider to those cultures can be swept away by the power of the event. How does the Center elicit such a visceral reaction from its audiences? Vega cites the intrinsic aspects of the cultures themselves. "Native cultures, Asian cultures, and cultures of color throughout the world are a total experience," she explains. The Center tries to make its events as participatory as possible to counteract the fact that, too often, people have been placed in the role of observing the arts, rather than participating in them.

Vega is on a quest to create the right "mix" to maximize audience participation. "We do education as well as creative expressions," she says. "Our children and our communities have been taught that art is a certain thing. We must constantly show that what you do in your home is valid." She reflects this in programming that encompasses the family and community as extensions of the home, and presents events in the most appropriate context. The Center's vision is always changing, always being pushed further, she adds. "That's what culture is," she says. "Once it becomes static, it dies."

She explains that the Expressions Festival was created because she felt uncomfortable with doing discrete visual art exhibitions, or conferences, or concerts. "I was looking for the mix that brought it all together. That's what should happen. We should be looking at all aspects of our lives in the same way, because they are all part of a continuum. We go to school, we go to arts activities, we come home, we think, we do ritual, and so on. It doesn't happen in little compartments. That's why our programming is as it is. One piece is not apart from the other piece. We try to maintain the linkages among activities. Each should spur you to think further and to think of the past and the future."

She expresses surprise that the Center is regarded as a presenting organization by funders like the National Endowment for the Arts. "I've never looked at us as a presenting organization," she says. "I've looked at us as an extension of our culture, of our people, and tried to mirror back what it is that happens within our communities. If that's being a presenter, then I guess that's what we are. The Center is just a mirror. At a given point in time, it highlights an aspect of who we are."

J. Michael Turner of Hunter College, who is a member of the Center's board, says he initially was attracted to the Center because he saw it as a community development effort, "using culture as its social force. This was fascinating to me. I've worked with community development problems that were more traditional— lack of city services, day care needs, community education needs, sexism, violence against women. But here was a community development agency whose main advocacy was culture, using culture for social mobilization, development, and social change. This was a grass-roots community organization based around culture, which I feel is extremely powerful."

Peter Pennekamp, vice president for cultural programming at National Public Radio, first met Vega when he was director of the NEA's Inter-Arts Program. He says she has refused to compromise her programming to gain funding. "She hasn't fallen into the trap of saying, 'OK, here's my culture, and here are the things I do to get my money so I can pursue my culture. Instead of doing a festival to the goddess of the sea, I'm going to do a subscription series because everyone wants me to show I've done one so I can get funding.'

"Her programming is very much based on the values and concepts of her own culture and her own commitments," Pennekamp adds. He says she has asked funders who are skeptical about her organization either to make the case that what she is doing is not valid, or to accept that there are different ways of doing things—and to give her the resources to do them.

Indeed, Dr. Mary Schmidt Campbell, commissioner of cultural affairs for New York City, credits Vega with unfaltering tenacity in her insistence that these cultural traditions be presented in their most authentic form. Another admirer is Dr. Alberta Arthurs of The Rockefeller Foundation, who characterizes the Center as "a very remarkable organization whose existence is due to the persistent stubbornness of its management and to this sense of total commitment to an idea."

Pennekamp says Vega's uncompromising position has helped the Center gain credibility. "We tend to assume that if there is a debate, and there are two different points of view, that compromise rests in the middle. Forces push us toward compromise. The forces of compromise that face community-based centers like the Caribbean Cultural Center all lead toward an acceptance essentially shaped by our racist past. Even though we've thrown off the concepts of cultural superiority, in fact every system in this country continues to keep them alive."

Vega has a vision of what's right "that 20 years ago most people thought was off the wall," Pennekamp adds. "There are still people who do. But she has held to a vision of a quality and vitality of cultural expression. Many people are beginning to realize that she has been right all along, that the underlying truths that she has pursued are correct."

The Pursuit of Cultural Equity

Vega is concerned about the low level of support for organizations whose constituencies are people of color, even though the Center itself has been successful in obtaining funding from both the public and private sectors. "It's clear that the funding to organizations of color hasn't been equal to that of major Eurocentric institutions," says Vega, who has served as the co-chair of the cultural arts task force established by the state's Black and Puerto Rican Legislative Caucus. "That would indicate to me that there is a cultural bias in funding patterns, both public and private, that is to the detriment of our institutions." The task force has published a report which examines the structures that perpetuate this pattern of underfunding.

Vega is particularly concerned about the way in which public funding organizations are beginning to recognize and respond to issues of cultural diversity. In the Center's spring 1990 newsletter, she cautions people to "beware the recolonization of people of color. Increasingly, the jargon prevalent in national education, social, and economic circles has embraced as 'common' the terminology of inclusion. Words and phrases of inclusion—such as cultural diversity, multiculturalism, cultural pluralism, and the like—are used by institutions and agencies that previously refused to address the concepts embodied by such inclusive terms."

In her analysis, Eurocentric organizations are now being funded to include more diverse programming, and to market their already-existing and new programs to more diverse populations. These populations, now referred to as "new," or "non-traditional," are the very people of color long ignored by the same institutions, she says. She sees the established institutions "putting on 'Black masks' or 'Asian masks' or 'Latino masks' or 'Native American masks' in an effort to maintain control. In essence, these Eurocentric institutions and curators are being encouraged by funding agencies to duplicate the work of culturally grounded institutions of color, which historically have been underfunded and considered less than professional based on Eurocentric criteria."

Typically, she says, these organizations are receiving this money in addition to their regular allocations. She says this rewards them for suddenly doing what they should have been doing all along, to the detriment of cultural organizations of color that have established track records for creating substantive programs that address cultural diversity and draw on a diverse population.

As a result of funding organizations' new emphasis on multiculturalism, established institutions are increasingly interested in artists of color, Peter Pennekamp says. "However, we don't trust the communities of the artists of color. We've put all the focus and generally all the money into the established institutions, some of which are more than glad to exploit the funding," he says. "Few of them actually believe in it. They'll go that way, even though they don't have any deep commitment."

J. Michael Turner sees the current funding trend in the context of leaders and followers. He finds it ironic that the Center "is now becoming victimized by its success, to a certain extent." He says major funding is now going to mainstream cultural institutions for the same kinds of programs that the Center created years ago at much less cost.

"In the 1990s," he says, "it's a very odd situation. Those ground-breaking institutions—because of their good work and because they were on target—are now finding themselves once again being marginalized for trying to continue the kind of work that they have pioneered."

The Center on West 58th Street

In 1983, the Center moved into its current location and first permanent facility in a brownstone on West 58th Street in Manhattan. The building was completely renovated, and a major capital campaign drive was launched for the $800,000 needed to purchase it. With much hard work and determination, Vega says, and by "being consistent and being a pest," the Center secured a $150,000 challenge grant in 1986 from the NEA toward the building fund and to establish a cash reserve.

The Center acquired the building in February 1990, and the organization and building were renamed in honor of the Center's long-time chairman, Franklin H. Williams, who died in May 1990.

The four-story building is narrow but deep. The ground floor houses the reception area, which includes the box office and the International Shop containing books, records, textiles, clothing, carvings, instruments and other items. There also is the Resource Center, which is the repository of documentation for most of the Center's activities and events. It contains a full range of audio and video tapes, equipment to hear and view them, photographs and slides of conferences, exhibitions and concerts, and books and periodicals on African, Caribbean, and African American cultures.

The second and third floors contain a gallery and activity spaces where exhibitions, lectures, and other programming take place. The fourth floor houses the administrative office. Since there is no theater or auditorium space, the Center must rent a variety of theaters and other spaces to present its large-scale performing arts events.

Fundraising

Vega began the process of fundraising early in the organization's existence. At first, she did everything herself. By the mid-1980s, it was clear that the Center needed someone devoted to fundraising, with Vega continuing to broaden the base of the institution's support, and to do programming.

In 1985, the Center received a two-year, $150,000 Ford Foundation grant to establish a development office. Fundraising consultant Barbara Bratone conducted a search, and Melody Capote was hired as development director. She had worked as a student volunteer at El Museo del Barrio, and as a staff member at the Association of Hispanic Arts. She became responsible for all of the Center's fundraising.

In addition to the fundraising problems and challenges the Center shares with other nonprofit arts organizations, some are unique to organizations of color. This difficult situation is compounded by the Center's strong philosophical concept. While it makes for a clearly-defined set of goals and objectives, some funders find it difficult to understand the level of support needed for the Center's seriousness of purpose and broad-based constituency. Some also still view such organizations and their constituencies of color as marginal to their funding imperatives.

Capote says that when she goes to city banks, she is told the Center is eligible for local and neighborhood grants of from $500 to $5,000. It's good to receive a contribution, she says, but it is disappointing to have the funding come in at such a low level. Capote says many cultural and arts organizations share this same experience: No matter what the level of excellence they have achieved, no matter what artistic arena they operate in, they will always be relegated to "neighborhood" status by some funding organizations.

On the other hand, the Center has cultivated support and received substantial ongoing funding from Consolidated Edison, the New York City gas and electric utility company. The funding has been earmarked for the Expressions festivals, for which Con Edison has always been the major sponsor. Annual funding from Con Edison initially was $10,000, but has grown to $60,000. Capote calls this one of the few ongoing commitments that the Center can count on each year.

As with other nonprofit organizations that are successful in the fundraising arena, the Center must prove a rock-solid program, and have advocates with power and influence. The Center's Board of Directors and advisory board includes many people important within the New York community. Board members helped open the doors at such corporations as Con Edison and the Chemical Bank.

One important advocate has been New York Mayor David Dinkins, who was borough president of Manhattan when the Center launched its capital campaign. He worked with the Center as a member of its building fund committee, and concentrated his efforts on investment bankers. In early 1986, he co-hosted a fundraising event with former congressman Herman Badillo, a member of the Center's board, who at that time was deputy mayor.

> # The Center's activities reflect the activities of African-based communities throughout the world.

Other substantial support has come from the Avon Products Foundation. President Glenn Clarke hosted a luncheon to interest corporate giving officers in the Center's building fund. Today, the Center's brochure lists contributions from an impressive list of corporate and foundation donors, as well as public agency support.

Of the Center's 1990 budget of $850,000, roughly 55 percent comes from government sources, 30 percent from the private sector, and 15 percent from ticket sales, conference registration fees, and gift shop revenues.

Vega has been savvy in her approach, and has cultivated numerous political contacts. She enjoys a significant involvement with the state's Black and Puerto Rican Legislative Caucus, which has successfully lobbied for sizable annual grants from the New York State Natural Heritage Trust.

The city's Department of Cultural Affairs also grants about $150,000 to the Center each year. Dr. Mary Schmidt Campbell, commissioner of the department, says the Center represents a cultural tradition which until recently was "virtually invisible on the American cultural landscape. It seems hard to believe now, when you look around and see the many African and Caribbean groups. But, in fact, there were no institutions that represented these traditions 20 or 25 years ago. The Caribbean Cultural Center has made an extraordinary contribution."

At the February 1990 rededication ceremony, Campbell said, "So much of our history has been submerged, hidden and denied. Places like the Center have disclosed our history in all its beauty."

By doing so, Vega and the Center's development staff are building a strong and stable fundraising base.

Public Relations

Kristen Simone was public relations consultant to the Center from 1983–1989, responsible for audience development, the promotion of each event, and support for fundraising and advocacy work. She produced all promotional materials, and also wrote and prepared them for distribution.

Some of the issues which drive the Center naturally have an impact on the objectives of its public relations approaches. The first is the core audience. To whom should the Center's public relations efforts first be targeted? Since its programs are constantly changing, and represent a wide variety of African and Caribbean cultures, its target audience also changes.

Simone says the staff must focus on the unity of cultures as opposed to separating them from one another. "Society has emphasized the differences rather than the common thread among these groups," Simone says. "The thrust of the Center is to trace the common roots and to bring people together to celebrate that common heritage."

These issues affected Simone when she approached the community newspapers which cater to particular cultural groups. For example, some serve Spanish-speaking people from the Caribbean, while others are for the English speakers. Some are geared to New York's African-American communities. Thus, if the Center is publicizing a Jamaican group, it may not expect as great a response from the readers of newspapers for Spanish speakers. Or, if the group is of Cuban nationals as opposed to Cuban immigrants, one community newspaper with an anti-Castro editorial policy would not be receptive. Still, these publications are instrumental in communicating with the core audience for a particular event, and Simone says they have consistently provided publicity.

After the core audience is solicited through its specific media, including print and broadcasting, Simone then approaches the other New York City media. She was successful in gaining extensive coverage from *The New York Times*. Music writer and critic Jon Pareles, and Robert Palmer before him, have taken a keen interest in the Center's unusual programs. Its concerts are often reviewed by *The Times*, and are frequently the subject of a feature article or a special mention in a critic's choice column.

The Center also maintains a mailing list of 10,000 people who have attended events, made a contribution, become a member, or purchased something in the gift shop. They receive the seasonal newsletter and regular mailings about events. Other lists are rented or borrowed as needed for special audience promotions.

Simone says she was challenged by the need to bring in new audiences and to make the Center's work more known. However, she saw her responsibility in even larger terms: to educate the public about the cultures, not simply publicize the work. She found it rewarding to send out information that people have not had access to in the past, and to create a new awareness of the cultures.

The Global Vision

Marta Moreno Vega brings to her work a global vision which never allows for circumscribed thinking. She is pleased that the Center has grown rapidly, and now runs year-round programs on the local, national, and international level.

"The institution is still in its adolescence, almost pre-teen," she says. "I would hope the ability to maintain that newness is always integral to its growth—the ability to change, to shift, to do what culture does and reflect the conditions and the time of the people, and project the future and the past."

The analysis she brought to the founding of the Center is being extended as her sphere of influence widens. Her ability to think globally has thrust the Caribbean Cultural Center into the position of acting as a service organization to the extended family of people of color all over the world.

"The history of the Center of what was originally perceived as being an Hispanic institution is now seen as having a world vision where people of all traditions and cultures can go and feel validated," says J. Michael Turner. "Having this kind of open door to different cultures makes it a stronger institution."

Global vision by definition is antithetical to thinking small. Consequently, the Center's activities always embrace the widest possible sphere of inquiry and influence. It is not difficult to view the Center and Vega as cultural and community leaders. However, Vega says she doesn't believe in taking on a leadership role. "I don't think that's real. I think it's bestowed on you by the community you're serving. And if you're serving that community well, that expression will be there in support and attendance."

She hopes that she and anyone who follows her as executive director will never appoint themselves as leaders, prescribing what should be done for the community. "That's absolutely what we are not designed to do. That's contrary to the reason I developed the Center."

Institutional Growth

Vega frequently is called upon to represent the Center at conferences, task forces, and initiatives on cultural diversity in the arts. She brings with her a passionate and well-articulated perspective on cultural equity, and comes away with a growing network of colleagues.

In 1989, the Center hosted a meeting of national leaders from other cultural centers of color; these leaders organized the meeting to determine the feasibility of establishing a touring network. Applications forms are pending with a number of foundations, and the NEA has earmarked money through its Expansion Arts program to support the venture in the 1990–91 fiscal year.

"Cultural Diversity Based On Cultural Grounding," a four-day conference that was part of the 1989 "Expressions Festival," is another example of the Center's leadership. More than 70 artists, scholars, panelists, and other guests brought their cumulative historical knowledge and experience to document the systematic exclusion of groups based on race and ethnicity. Participants reflected the opinion that the contributions of these groups too often have been misrepresented, erased, destroyed, submerged, distorted, and marginalized.

Experts in philosophy, sociology, law, politics, public policy, education, management, and the arts participated in a series of rigorous panel discussions. These discussions already have begun to form the agenda for future activism in the movement to achieve cultural equity for all racial and cultural groups.

Beyond Vega's personal influence, the Caribbean Cultural Center itself appears to be providing leadership. For its modest size, it has taken on the most pressing and compelling agenda of the day for all communities of color.

Its "Stay in School" program of concerts and rallies for young people entered its third season in the summer of 1990. The program was initiated by the Center and other community organizations in conjunction with the New York City Board of Education in response to the high dropout rate among communities of color. Vega says it sets out to reinforce the message of Nelson Mandela that "Education is the most powerful weapon."

"The public school system is not educationally responding to the needs of our young people to live effectively in today's society," says Vega. "The concerts and rallies provide a vehicle for our young people to experience their cultural and artistic expressions as valuable" and to offer role models.

The summer-long series of events introduce young people to artistic expressions of diverse cultures, and to educational support services Vega says are often missing from their formal learning experience. In the last of five free events held in 1990, hip-hop song and dance acts Stetsatonic and Tashan were to perform, plus rappers Get Set and Latin Empire, the Revelations singing ensemble, and the Marie Brooks Caribbean Dance Theater. Motivational speeches were to be given by youth leaders, along with informational presentations by organizations that offer services to city adolescents.

In his book, *Flash of the Spirit*, Robert Farris Thompson describes the Yoruba concept of àshe as "spiritual command, the power-to-make-things-happen, God's own enabling light rendered accessible to men and women."

Events at the Center sometimes end with a communal chanting of the word. The force of àshe seems to inform all of the Center's activities. It is on a constant quest to make things happen, to realize potential by holding up a mirror to reflect the cultural expressions and belief systems of African cultures and their manifestations in the Americas.

Says Vega: "I think the Center is doing what every institution should do: strive to provide and service its community with the highest level and highest quality of what reflects itself."

6 Excellence Has an Audience

It was St. Patrick's Day 1988, and shark repellent had turned the normally-murky waters of the Chicago River to a bright Kelly green. Everything and everyone on North Wacker Drive was ready for Chicago's famous parade: the floats, the high school marching bands, the piping brigades, the politicians.

But perhaps the main event for a Chicago sojourner was an extraordinary concert, lovingly presented the night before by Chamber Music Chicago. It featured Gidon Kremer and Friends of Lockenhaus at Pick-Staiger Hall in nearby Evanston. It was a concert to remember.

A marathon of sorts, beginning at 7:30 p.m. and lasting more than three hours, the concert provided Chamber Music Chicago's audience a rare exposure to a characteristically European—and uniquely Kremerian—sense of programming. Offering four major chamber music works with two intermissions, Kremer and his Lockenhaus colleagues treated the capacity audience to performances of Mozart's Quintet in G Minor, K. 516; two of Shostakovich's string quartets, numbers 13 and 14; and the Schubert Trout Quintet. This was serious music-making at its finest.

It was but one of 12 events in Chamber Music Chicago's 28th season, one that saw significant artistic and managerial growth. The offerings included a nine-concert subscription series and the Kronos Quartet's new three-concert Festival of New Music. Works by Keith Jarrett and Dick Hyman, commissioned by the organization, had their world premiere performances. There also were Chicago premieres by Peter Schickele, Ellen Taaffe Zwilich, and Leos Janacek on the subscription series, and nine premieres on the Kronos Quartet series. For the first time, jazz compositions were included on the main series rather than in a ghettoized setting, integrated into programs that also included Bach, Stravinsky, Debussy,

Bartok, Beethoven, and Janacek. That season, the organization received the ASCAP award for innovative programming in chamber music.

On the management side, there was a 100 percent paid attendance average, with subscribers turning back for resale the tickets they were unable to use. The number of single-ticket buyers attending their first Chamber Music Chicago performance increased by 187 percent. There was a 30 percent rise in earned income, and a 273 percent increase in corporate and foundation giving. The organization had seen a growth rate of 56.6 percent of its total operating budget during the previous five years.

In the midst of this phenomenal growth and financial health is an organization driven by its devotion and commitment to art and artists. At its core is an artistic vision, surrounded by a mission and philosophy that organically follow the vision. Chamber Music Chicago realizes its mission in a sophisticated manner, marketing and communicating it to the public with dignity, enthusiasm, and purpose. It has won a loyal following, and a confidence that its audiences will go where the organization takes them. Everything flows from the artistic vision.

At the helm of Chamber Music Chicago is Susan Lipman, who as executive director for the past seven years has restored vitality to an organization that was in a severe midlife crisis when she took over. Through her love of music—indeed, her obsession with it—she has rebuilt a once-important Chicago cultural institution. Her programming ideas are generated by her desire for the audience to hear certain repertoire or be exposed to composers or performers she admires. She is unequivocal about the priorities: "This is an organization whose first commitment is to music."

From this simple and direct statement flows the managerial savvy to market the season's offerings and to raise funds from public and private sources. The motivation to be fiscally sound and operationally stable comes from a desire to keep the artistic purpose on track, to reach the public and carve out a place in the city's significant music scene.

From the Beginning, to Midlife Crisis

The caption for the 1959 *Time* magazine cover story read, "Not All Chicagoans Carry Machine Guns in their Violin Cases!" It featured the Fine Arts Quartet, which had just returned from a successful European tour. The article lamented that the quartet, although lauded internationally, had no home in the United States, not even in its native city.

From this story, an idea was born. Chamber Music Chicago board member Jean Evans relates the straightforward beginning of a new organization: "Four suburban women, nonprofessionals all of us, just loved the music and thought it was an outrage that these fine artists were being ignored by their own city. We decided to put on a series of chamber music concerts featuring the Fine Arts Quartet in their home city."

The Fine Arts Music Foundation was founded in 1959. It presented concerts by its first resident ensemble, the Fine Arts Quartet. During the course of many seasons, the foundation and the quartet grew and prospered together. In 1976, Evans says, "The quartet began to disintegrate, three of the four musicians resigning one at a time. They tried to work with substitutes, but it was not what it had been, and the audience began to feel it right away. Ticket sales began to decline. We were very saddened, but we felt that we could no longer base what we were doing solely on the Fine Arts Quartet." The foundation began to present chamber ensembles from all over the world, with programming decisions made by the board's music committee in conjunction with the executive director.

Susan Lipman, who was selling real estate in Chicago at the time, had been a young subscriber to the Fine Arts Music Foundation concerts. She believes she was invited in 1976 to join the foundation board because she did not fit the subscriber profile—she was younger than most—and because the board recognized the need to bring in new blood.

By 1981, the Fine Arts Quartet was restructured. It no longer was the same group with which the foundation had developed a long-standing professional and personal relationship. It was time for the quartet and the foundation to go their separate ways.

Lipman describes the foundation as experiencing serious decline, losing subscribers, losing money, "and, frankly, losing its position in the community as a valuable cultural resource." The organization met and spoke about ending the foundation, perhaps even closing its doors before the end of its season. "Some of us didn't want that to happen," she says. "Jean Evans was one of the board members who put her heart into keeping this organization alive."

They decided that if it had to end, it would end honorably, completing the season. "We did that, but no one really knew what to do next," she recalls. "Then, one day out of the blue, the president called and asked me if I would take over the organization." During the brief discussion of her proposed responsibilities, Lipman was not pleased to hear that she would have to keep the books and oversee financial planning and management. By her own admission, she could not even balance her own checkbook. But the board, recognizing a latent talent and proclivity for management, was convinced she was the right person at the right time.

Lipman called a close college friend and accountant, Gladys Nunley. Nunley assured Lipman that if the opportunity was as challenging as it appeared and she wanted to take it, Nunley would help her go through the books for as long as it would take to make sense of them. With this offer of assistance, Lipman accepted the "part-time" job—which turned out to be 80 hours a week—and proceeded to save the organization from extinction.

She reminisces that the two would come into the office every night for four months to unravel the finances. Lipman began to enjoy the process; she came to see how this aspect of the job could be as creative as the others, and that tight financial controls would enable the organization to realize its artistic purpose.

The foundation changed its name to Chamber Music Chicago in 1982. Since then, Lipman's leadership has propelled the organization to become "the standard-bearer for imaginative chamber concerts" (John von Rhein of the *Chicago Tribune*), and "the nation's hottest chamber music series" (Robert Marsh of the *Chicago Sun Times*).

A Sharply Focused Mission

What happened between the organization's decline and its phoenix-like rise from the ashes? The first giant step had been to bring on an executive director who could plot a new future. The board deserves credit for spotting in its midst an extraordinarily capable person who could keep the organization alive, lead it into its next phase, and bring it to greater artistic and managerial heights. Susan Lipman was all that, even though she had never run a nonprofit arts organization.

> At the core of Chamber Music Chicago is the artistic vision; the mission and philosophy follow organically.

The first thing she did was bring the organization's purpose into focus. That mission, clearly understood by all involved in Chamber Music Chicago, is to bring the best of chamber music to the community; to support Illinois artists; to support educational activities through the education of tomorrow's audiences; and to support young and emerging artists.

Having clarified the why of the organization, Lipman began to work on the how. She drew up a marketing plan, the number-one priority because Chamber Music Chicago had been losing its audience. Instead of hiring an expensive market research company or conducting a formal survey to find out what the audience wanted, Lipman rolled up her sleeves and began her own research.

Even though she was a Chicago native, Lipman didn't assume she had all the information she needed. She visited record stores in metropolitan Chicago to determine where the most classical music was being sold. Once she was convinced that she had identified those areas, she bought mailing lists with the appropriate zip codes.

Soon, everything began to change. Lipman understood that the public perceived chamber music as dull and boring, and she observed that the message and graphics of the brochures weren't helping. She set about printing new brochures that were colorful and lively. She also began to bring managerial stability to Chamber Music Chicago by establishing office procedures and putting tight budget controls in place. Most important, these controls were in the service of a new artistic vision that was to be the bedrock of the organization.

Lipman takes her own enthusiasms and makes them public. This inner strength, flowing from her profound love of the music, propelled the recrafting of Chamber Music Chicago. Lipman knew that if she could communicate her own excitement to potential audiences, they would buy tickets to hear exciting music and experience new ideas.

Stanley S. Madeja, chairman of the board, says Lipman catalyzed several bold moves at the crucial point when the organization's future was most in doubt. The first was to move the concerts to the Chicago Civic Theater, a 900-seat hall in downtown Chicago. It was twice as large as any the organization had used, and represented a doubling of the number of tickets available for sale.

Simultaneously, the programming began to get more adventurous. Most organizations faced with the loss of more than half their subscribers would stick with the tried and true, but Lipman's attitude was just the opposite. One of the first ventures into a less-than-traditional format was the a presentations that paired clarinetist Richard Stoltzman and Bill Douglas, composer, bassoonist, and pianist. It was the first time that jazz had appeared in a Chamber Music Chicago concert, and the audience responded enthusiastically. The organization also began to commission new works from American composers, while at the same time maintaining and continuing to develop interest in the standard repertoire.

The risks panned out. Chamber Music Chicago began to grow phenomenally. When Lipman became executive director in 1982, she inherited a $4,000 deficit and a $63,000 annual budget. For the 1989 fiscal year, the budget was $575,000. This growth has been achieved without deficit. Rebecca Riley, director of special grants for the John D. and Catherine T. MacArthur Foundation, draws the obvious conclusion: "Chamber Music Chicago reaffirms that excellence has an audience, and that institutional leadership can make a difference."

The Vermeer Quartet and the Early Talent Recognition Program

After the alliance with the Fine Arts Quartet was discontinued, the organization wanted to reestablish itself as a strong support structure for a similar chamber ensemble. In 1984, Chamber Music Chicago entered into a relationship with the Vermeer Quartet, the ensemble that for many years has been in residence at Northern Illinois University in nearby De Kalb. Each season, Chamber Music Chicago presents the quartet in three concerts as an integral part of its season subscription. In fact, the Vermeer is the organization's resident quartet.

The organization has commissioned new works for the Vermeer, and has made it the focal point of the Early Talent Recognition Program, its educational component. Inaugurated in 1986 with a performance by the quartet at a Chicago high school, the program enables students from schools in economically depressed inner-city neighborhoods to develop as artists by working directly with the Vermeer.

The program includes performances by the quartet at high schools; lecture-demonstrations; student attendance at Chamber Music Chicago concerts; two workshops at each of the nine participating high schools; informal meetings with the students; and, ultimately, performances by student ensembles with the Vermeer as their audience. There is a strong commitment to the program by all those involved, and there are plans to expand it to accommodate more participants each year.

In the 1987–88 season, the program added interaction between the Kronos Quartet and the students. While in Chicago for its three concerts, the Kronos performed in the schools for program participants. In a short time, these concerts have begun to influence the music programs of several of Chicago's public high schools; in two of them, the Kronos concerts have been directly responsible for saving the string instrument programs.

Commitment to Young Artists and Ensembles

Chamber Music Chicago has demonstrated a commitment to young artists and ensembles. When it began to present emerging ensembles in the early 1980s, there was concern that subscribers would turn back those tickets for resale, that audiences would be smaller, and that critics would not attend.

Disturbed by this concern, Lipman sought to increase attendance and attention for what she and the board considered a vital part of the organization's mission. Her figuring led to the birth of the Discovery Competition, Chicago's only international music competition.

Its purpose is to identify an "important" young ensemble through a rigorous screening, audition, and live competition process, which is broadcast nationally on WFMT, Chicago's classical radio station. The winner receives a cash prize and a place in the next season's Chamber Music Chicago subscription series. In 1987, the winner of the first prize was the Shanghai Quartet, which initially came to the U.S. to study with the Vermeer and then went on to study with the Juilliard Quartet in New York.

Lipman says the organization is not thrilled about adding significantly to its work load and budget to administer the international competition. Still, she and the board view the Discovery Competition as the only way to gain public attention for the support of young and emerging artists.

The competition proved so successful that Chamber Music Chicago initiated a competition for composers at the crossroads of their careers. In 1990, after reviewing more than 100 scores, a distinguished group of American composers chose Steven Mackay as the competition's first winner. His string quartet was performed by the Vermeer in the spring. The winner also received a cash prize, plus a commission for a world premiere to be performed the following season. A three-year pledge of support from a board member will bring stability to the program and guarantee continuity for the immediate future.

With its international competitions, Chamber Music Chicago continues to foster a creative atmosphere and engender excitement for new works. Chicago's critics, at first less than enthusiastic, now come to hear the Discovery contestants and review the performances.

The Presenter-Audience Partnership

When it comes to relating to audiences, Lipman says, presenters have a responsibility to make things happen. "You have to go out on a limb. I view myself as a catalyst. Of course, when you take a programmatic risk, you must do everything in your power to make it work, to maximize the success because of your responsibility to the musicians. If you have the process of education and nurturing going on, it is amazing what you can program. You should not underestimate your audience.''

Lipman has an unusual notion of the presenter-audience relationship. The common wisdom is, that if an audience does not like the programming, the presenter is obliged to make adjustments. But Lipman feels differently. ''An organization has to have a strong notion of its identity,'' she says. ''Sometimes, that idea is at cross-purposes with an audience. But that often happens because the audience doesn't understand what you are trying to do. It is your responsibility to educate the audience to see the light, to come to understand, support, and agree with your purpose.''

Chamber Music Chicago mails preview program notes to subscribers 10 days before each concert. Audiences arrive at the concerts informed about what to expect. The notes are written by Andrea D'Alessio, the program administrator at WFMT. The notes give the historical context for the works being performed, followed by a biography of the composer that Lipman says is ''extremely well-written, with life and excitement. This is not a dry bio pulled out of the Grove Dictionary.''

> ''When we take risks, I think we are responding to what an audience is willing to allow to happen.''

The biography is followed by a description of the works to be performed, and the notes conclude with profiles of the performers. Included is a comprehensive discography of available recordings, which give the record company, the artists, and the catalog number of all works on the program. A complete list of other works recorded by the guest artists also is provided. Under an arrangement with Rose records, subscribers receive a discount on any recording included on the discography.

Chamber Music Chicago also has made arrangements with restaurants near the Civic Theater for dinner discounts the night of the concerts, and with nearby garages for discount parking.

Long-time subscriber Gilbert D. Totten has some observations as a member of the audience. ''We feel we are as important to the artists as they are to us. We come with a heightened expectation that, through active listening, we will make the music part of ourselves . . . You see students, older people; you see people who are obviously without too much money, and others who can fly in on the mink jet set. We all enjoy one another's company, and nobody coughs and nobody talks, and if somebody did they would be booted out, which is nice.''

The Presenting Process

Lipman's approach to presenting is grounded in music and artists: what repertoire she feels is important for her audience to hear, what repertoire has not received the attention it deserves, and which artists she wants to support in their development.

''You're always talking to people, and you're always thinking,'' she says. She has been listening to a lot of music by the English composer Michael Tippett. "Tippett's music, so far as I'm concerned, hasn't received the attention it merits here in the United States. Lately, I've been listening to his four quartets. I know that eventually he will write a fifth quartet. I know that this city will hear all five of those quartets real soon, because this city has not had an opportunity to hear that music. I also know the group that performs his music the best—the Lindsay Quartet—and so we will go to that group because they are the best interpreters of Sir Michael's music."

Chicago may become one of only three sites in the U.S. to participate in a commemoration of Tippett's 85th birthday in the 1990–91 season. If sufficient money can be raised for this very costly program, Tippett will compose his fifth quartet, and Chamber Music Chicago will present it, with Sir Michael present.

Lipman also is thinking about developing a series that would focus on contemporary and historic chamber music composed by women. For the past several years, she has done research to determine the best way to program this idea.

"The process starts with what we think we can do that is worthwhile to be doing," she says. "Then, sometimes there is a performer who you hear and you think is quite wonderful." She finds the work of young English violinist Nigel Kennedy captivating. "Very few people in Chicago know who he is. But we are going to bring Kennedy over and introduce him to this city. His philosophy is that there is something joyful to be communicated through music. Well, that is exactly what we think. We go to great lengths, we spend a lot of money to communicate that message to our audience. When we premiere a work here, even just for a Chicago premiere, we always try to have the composer present. It enriches the experience for everyone."

Lipman says much of her negotiation is done directly with the artists. "I work with management—it's a very supportive and cooperative arrangement, of course— but the programming and arranging can be done directly with the artists. This works out to everyone's advantage."

She describes her approach to the presenting process as "a running dialog with several artists: 'What are you doing?' And even, 'What do you want to do?' 'How can we help; how can we fit in; where can we be supportive?' That's it. That is our presenting process: ongoing conversations with people."

Programmatic Risk and Marketing

Chamber Music Chicago gets high praise for its record of risk-taking from Rebecca Riley of the MacArthur Foundation. "What is important is being comfortable enough with the artistic vision to do things that you think are important to the artists, or a canon of existing work that might not necessarily be popular with audiences," she says. "Risk is focusing on artistic opportunities, and less on marketability. Audiences that support an organization for its artistic excellence, I think, are generally educated and in a way following what is important to them, a contribution to their own knowledge and interests. Chamber Music Chicago takes risks much more than, say, the Chicago Symphony Orchestra, and they are investing intelligent time educating their audience."

Lipman also balances risk and responsiveness by programming the repertoire with the groups that she engages. Earlier in the same week in which Gidon Kremer and Friends of Lockenhaus performed its concert of Mozart, Shostakovich, and Schubert at Pick-Staiger Hall in Evanston, Chamber Music Chicago presented on its subscription series in the familiar downtown location the Borodin Quartet from the Soviet Union in a program of Borodin, Shostakovich, and Schubert.

"We asked a great deal of our subscribers that week," Lipman says. "We asked them to come Monday night to the Civic Theater to hear Schubert and Shostakovich, and then we asked them to hear Schubert and Shostakovich again Wednesday night, in a community outside Chicago, at a starting time (7:30 p.m.) that is earlier than they normally anticipate. We fully expected that there would be problems, and we went out of our way to try to compensate for them." In fact, she says, fewer tickets were turned back than usual at the Monday night downtown series.

One critic did mention in his review that he was "not prepared to hear two Shostakovich/Schubert programs from one management in three days." He missed the whole point, Lipman says. "That was deliberate. We wanted to do that because we learn from it. You get to hear different interpretations. Gidon Kremer and Lockenhaus play very differently from the Borodin Quartet, and you got to hear it. You got to hear the same composer interpreted differently. That was the strength of what we were doing."

Lipman does not think Chicago is as conservative as people say it is. "I frequently feel that we underestimate our audience. I don't think we give them enough credit for what they are willing to do and listen to. We have a tendency to see ourselves as noble, and as doing great things because we are taking risks. I think we are responding to what an audience is willing to allow to happen. It just doesn't happen on its own. If it's working, it is because there is an audience there. You work with your partners in this. That's one of the reasons I like our audience so much."

Lipman takes her programmatic risks with her eyes open. She is fully aware of the artistic and financial exposures, and has a specific plan for managing that risk.

Jazz presenting offers another insight into Chamber Music Chicago's approach to risk. Its original impetus to move in this direction came from a desire to present more of the music of America. They asked what they could do that would be different and to which the audience would respond.

Acknowledging that jazz is the music of America, Lipman began to think about what it had in common with chamber music. She saw them both as an endangered species, and asked, "Why not help both by fostering a collaboration between the two forms of ensemble playing—one that is improvised, and one that is not?" She commissioned Keith Jarrett to write two new works for the program. Jarrett was a purposeful choice, since he already had functioned effectively in both serious classical music environments and classic jazz settings.

A group of artists was gathered especially for the 1988 performance, which was held in Orchestra Hall, the 2,600-seat home of the Chicago Symphony. Artists included the composer at the piano, Richard Stoltzman on clarinet, Paula Robison on flute, Fred Sherry on cello, and Lucy Stoltzman on violin.

This concert was a command performance for the city of Chicago. It took place nowhere else in the U.S., and it happened only because Susan Lipman and Chamber Music Chicago pursued the financial backing to commission two new works (another world premiere and a Chicago premiere were added later), and to bring together five artists of significant stature.

The concert was not easily sold. Although there were the beginnings of an audience in Chamber Music Chicago's subscription base of 1,000, another 1,600 seats had to be filled. Jarrett was not unfamiliar to a classical music audience due to his international appearances in solo recitals of classical music, apart from his solo concerts of jazz improvisation. In addition, his compositions for classical ensembles have been commissioned by and performed at the Chamber Music Society of Lincoln Center.

Still, he had never appeared in Chicago in this guise. Chamber Music Chicago was careful to make it clear just exactly what this concert was to be, since it did not want to sell tickets to people expecting Jarrett to perform one of his free-form solo improvisations or appear with his "Standards" trio.

Ticket sales were slow but steady. With days to go, two things conspired to fill the event with suspense right to the end. The Chicago Bears were in a playoff bid, and the first major snowstorm of the season was predicted (forecasts called for 21 inches). Lipman was convinced that there would be a sparse crowd, expecting that those with tickets would not attend due to the weather, and certainly anticipating no single-ticket sales. Much to everyone's surprise, almost 2,000 people turned out. Box office sales were so strong that a late start was made to accommodate the last-minute rush for tickets.

The experience confirmed something for Lipman and Chamber Music Chicago: Audiences respond to substance and challenge, and it is possible to program to the highest level and still sell tickets and have a successful event.

Lipman feels it's risky to depend on subscription sales. This leaves no opportunity for developing the audiences of tomorrow if there are no tickets available outside of subscriptions. She has initiated a new marketing approach by creating several miniseries that enable people to make a commitment to a smaller number of concerts in the season. Lipman says this will bring in younger listeners who want more flexibility and aren't subscription-oriented. This approach also will encourage more people to buy fewer concerts on a modest-sized subscription, increasing the organization's penetration into the Chicago community. Instead of selling 700 subscription tickets, for example, Chamber Music Chicago can reach nearly twice as many people by splitting the subscription season in two. This has great import for long-term audience development.

Board Structure

Chamber Music Chicago's achievements are the result of an engaged and committed board that understands and supports the organization's mission. The board has a two-tier leadership structure: The president looks after the internal functioning of the board's committees, and makes certain they are accomplishing the work that keeps the organization moving forward; the chairman has an external focus, and looks after the organization's long-term future.

This system was adopted after the greatly increased growth in budget and activity made it clear that Chamber Music Chicago needed a stepped-up organizational structure. This would ensure strong and active board involvement, and develop a way to disseminate information about monetary needs for stronger and more substantive programs.

Fundraising is an essential part of the support that board members provide. Approximately 45 percent of Chamber Music Chicago's budget comes from income earned from ticket sales. The monies received from the Illinois Arts Council and the National Endowment for the Arts are, respectively, 3 percent and 1 percent of the annual budget. The rest must be raised from individuals, corporations, and foundations. This task requires the board's full commitment, particularly in raising the individual contributions which come primarily from subscribers. Telemarketing is used to contact subscribers for valuable feedback, and to request contributions.

> "This is an organization whose first commitment is to music."

Lipman handles most approaches to foundations and corporations, and the organization has seen a marked increase in the amount of contributed income it has received from these sources. In 1988, the organization brought on nine new board members. In addition to being devoted to chamber music and supportive of the organization's mission, they have significant contacts in the Chicago business and corporate community.

This has been an important move for the organization, since its board had been composed almost solely of chamber music devotees who helped develop the organizational mission, but who had little experience in fundraising. Because they were of modest means, they were unable to make major monetary donations. Now, with bylaw changes, the board can be increased to 40 members from its current 30.

Corporate, foundation, and public funders seem to respond to the same things that the audience responds to in Chamber Music Chicago: the substance of its innovative programming and high-quality concerts; the seriousness of purpose and the stability of the organization; the leadership that it is asserting in the city of Chicago and nationally; its commitment to developing young audiences through the Early Talent Recognition Program; and its commitment to emerging ensembles through the Discovery Competition.

The Borg-Warner Foundation is one of the most substantial supporters of the Discovery Competition. Ellen J. Benjamin, Borg-Warner's director of corporate contributions, describes one of the most important elements in making a contribution: "The magic for me when I am considering a grant is when I know that the resources we give an organization will become something very special to the community. I knew that would be the case with Chamber Music Chicago."

Mary Lee O'Brien, presenter development coordinator for the Illinois Arts

Council, says Lipman's approach to managing Chamber Music Chicago has been the reason for the organization's success on stage, with its audiences, and with funders. "The strength of the organization is that the director has such faith in her staff and an eagerness to see her staff develop, to fulfill their ambitions, to realize their potential. Susan Lipman does not see Chamber Music Chicago in a proprietary way. It belongs to the board, the staff, and the audience. She sees the growth of her staff as an asset to the organization, not a threat."

The Continuing Challenges

Chamber Music Chicago has a proven record of artistic and managerial achievement. Many challenges still remain, and Lipman acknowledges that there is a long way to go.

Its stability was threatened most when the organization was about to go to press with its season brochure for an ambitious 1988–89 season. Lipman received word from the Civic Theater, its home for the previous six seasons, that scheduling difficulties would make it impossible for them to return there.

Alternative arrangements were hastily made, but the series is now in four different halls in Chicago and environs, not a convenient or consistent posture for any organization. Lipman reports that subscribers are balking, and major efforts are again under way to maintain community support. It is a serious problem when a presenter does not own, or have assured access to, a specific facility.

Lipman faces another challenge, this time in the presenting area. She is developing programming in response to current movements toward cultural equity in the arts world, and wants to engage Chicago's communities of color. In her 1990–91 season, she will focus on music of the Americas, and co-sponsor performances of the Puerto Rican Ensemble with the city's Old Town School of Folk Music. In her inimitable style, Lipman—who majored in philosophy at the University of Chicago—is now completing a two-year program on the music, history, thought and literature of non-Eurocentric cultures.

Whatever the arena, the organization's impact on the Chicago music scene has been great, and that may sustain it in difficult times. John von Rhein, chief music critic for the *Chicago Tribune*, says: "Susan Lipman very definitely has asserted cultural leadership in the Chicago arts community. I would say that Chicago's music history, by and large, has been the history of what one person can do with a given group or genre. She is that one person when it comes to chamber music in Chicago. Think of Theodore Thomas as the one person who started the Chicago Symphony, or what Carol Fox did for Lyric Opera and what Ardis Krainik is doing now. She's right up there in terms of single-handed initiative. The residual benefits of that kind of vision, programming, and innovation will be felt for many years to come."

Keith Jarrett

Silly Wizard

Photo by Stephen Matyi

7 Of the Neighborhood, and Beyond

The Victory Theatre in downtown Dayton, Ohio has seen a lot of performances in its time, but seldom has it ever housed anything like "Masters of the Folk Violin." The concert, organized by the National Council on Traditional Arts and sponsored by Dayton's CITYFOLK, brought together six prodigiously talented fiddlers performing in six distinct styles: Irish, Texas long bow, Cajun, Cape Breton, bluegrass and jazz improvisation. The artists—Seamus Connolly, Allison Kraus, Michael Doucet, Joe Cormier, Kenny Baker, and Claude Williams—each made it seem that the fiddle was created for the sole purpose of making his or her particular kind of music. That night, the capacity crowd laughed and clapped along as the artists shared both personal and musical styles with them, and they applauded each flourish of virtuosity.

In the grand finale, the musicians all gathered to perform a reel, each fiddler taking a solo turn between the choruses. It was a rousing end to almost four hours of superlative music-making—so superlative that, despite the length of the concert, there was not a hint of restlessness on the part of the audience. Everyone seemed to hope that this entrancing marathon would never end.

"Masters of the Folk Violin" was an ideal introduction to CITYFOLK, Dayton's ethnic and traditional arts presenting organization. The concert, part of a national tour, was a microcosm of what the organization is all about: an eclectic, professional presence in the city, devoted to preserving and celebrating traditional folk expressions from a variety of cultures.

From its modest beginnings in 1980 as a neighborhood arts project started by five volunteers, CITYFOLK has grown into a vibrant presenting organization with a full season of events and programs. Maureen Moloney, a Dayton attorney and trust officer at a local financial institution, serves as the organization's immediate past president. She says its mission is to promote cultural diversity and understanding among ethnic groups by enabling them to experience the arts of other cultures. Each season is designed to encourage pride and understanding among members of those groups, and to celebrate the differences among people while promoting the bonds that join them.

Dayton is a city with active, recognized, and well-supported symphony, ballet, and opera companies that have dominated the urban landscape for many years. Like similar mainstream institutions in many cities, these companies constitute the performing arts pillars of Dayton. It is frequently difficult, if not impossible, for smaller, fledgling organizations to win credibility in such an environment, much less receive significant funding. This is further complicated when the new organization presents not the standard recital, chamber music performance, or family fare, but an ever-changing array of ethnic expressions.

This was the case with CITYFOLK, a completely independent organization unaffiliated with any larger parent institution. Throughout the years, it has fought hard for, and won, the respect of the city's many cultural groups and the largess of the city and state public and private funders. In the course of that struggle, CITYFOLK has created a place for a traditional folk arts organization in Dayton, and become a model for others in other cities.

Much of the credit for its record of achievement must go to Phyllis Brzozowska, one of the organization's five founders, and the organization's guiding force since its early days. It is through her vision and energy that CITYFOLK grew from a fledgling project in response to a neighborhood need into the organization it has become.

The Founders' Vision

"Many people who are involved with traditional arts see themselves as different from the rest of the arts world," Brzozowska observes. "But I always felt differently, partly because the funding was there, partly because I was seeking legitimacy for the traditional arts. I always wanted CITYFOLK to be accepted, just like the ballet, the philharmonic, and the opera. We had every right to be, and that became a goal to work toward. That's why we set up a sound structure and a business-like approach to all we did."

In 1980, Brzozowska and four other residents of Dayton's Five Oaks neighborhood responded to an initiative from the Ohio Arts Council/Ohio Humanities Council's Joint Program in Folk Art and Culture. They submitted a proposal for a series of five events that they dubbed the CITYFOLK Folk Arts Series. They received an $8,000 grant to fund the series for one year.

The series included an Irish music concert, a Greek dance workshop, an Appalachian square dance, an African drumming and dance workshop, and the creation of a mural in a neighborhood park. Each event spoke to a particular ethnic group in the city and was designed to stimulate citywide interest in the community's cultural variety and wealth.

The enthusiastic response convinced Brzozowska to embark on her crusade to build an organization that could carry on this effort.

CITYFOLK's beginnings were modest. Concerts often were held in bars or churches because these settings provided a ready audience and required no rental fee. In addition, sound equipment sometimes was available without charge. This approach, combined with ticket sales and small grants from the Ohio Arts Council, enabled CITYFOLK to meet its expenses for each event while it gradually assembled the structure and foundation for a more ambitious operation.

During the early years, Brzozowska worked as a volunteer, seizing borrowed moments during the days and evenings while maintaining a full-time job in a hospital audio-visual department. Slowly, as the concerts began to attract larger audiences, and promotion and fundraising efforts paid off, the organization was able to provide her with a paying part-time job. Since 1986, she has worked full-time for the organization. CITYFOLK has undergone remarkable growth since then, and now has four full-time employees and another who works part-time.

> CITYFOLK is an eclectic, professional presence in the city, devoted to preserving and celebrating traditional folk expressions.

Brzozowska describes herself as a self-taught, intuitive administrator. She takes full advantage of technical assistance opportunities offered by the Ohio Arts Council, and avails herself of workshops and publications to hone her skills and ideas. She calls Thomas Wolf's book on managing the nonprofit organization her bible, and she gives a copy to every new board member. Also important have been Joan Flanagan's *Grass Roots Fund Raising* and *The Successful Volunteer Organization*.

CITYFOLK is an arts organization that grew from an idea shared by a few people who wanted to bring something new to their community. "I just wanted to hear more Irish music," Brzozowska explains. "Then I wanted an organization so I could continue to hear Irish music. In creating that organization, I recognized a need in the community that was bigger than my own, and that need became my passion. To see the public respond has been an incredible reward."

Dayton's Ethnic Communities

Dayton is a cauldron of cultures and CITYFOLK grew organically from the character of the city.

Brzozowska explains the CITYFOLK phenomenon by outlining the classic progression of migrating populations. "When the immigrants arrived, they still had their own structures. Each immigrant group stuck together for survival. In Dayton, however, those immigrant groups were relatively small, so there were pressures to assimilate. It was typical of the first and second generations to move away from their heritage because they felt that holding on would hold them back. CITYFOLK's role is really to help the second and third generations reclaim that heritage."

Fred Bartenstein, executive director of the Dayton Foundation and former director of Dayton's Victory Theater, says the city was a hotbed of music in the 1940s and '50s. That was the result of the migrations of southern blacks and rural Appalachians who came to the city for its job opportunities in manufacturing. They brought their music with them and, depending on the neighborhood, one could hear jazz and blues as well as bluegrass. There also were pockets of Eastern European and Irish immigrants who had their own cultural traditions.

But today, these cultural ties have loosened, as they have in many cities of the United States. In addition, the loss of most heavy industry in Dayton has changed the area to a white-collar, service-based economy, further separating people from their roots.

Bartenstein says this is where the organization finds its niche. "CITYFOLK is not an indigenous folk organization," he says. "Its audiences are not primarily folk people. In an area like Dayton, in which people have become alienated from their origins and in which there is no dominant folk activity, you need a CITYFOLK. The audience responds to it."

Private Traditions and Public Performances

The issue of artistic and cultural authenticity concerns serious organizations like CITYFOLK. Brzozowska delineates the elements of authenticity: "Traditional art is taught informally, orally, with the tradition being passed on from generation to generation," she explains. "It is passed on within a community, from a master to an apprentice. And the art itself reflects the shared values and standards of that community."

Brzozowska says that the difficulty begins when staging an event. The folk arts are not meant to be staged. By and large, people perform their folk dances, rituals, and concerts for their own enjoyment within their own community. When these artistic expressions move on to a public venue outside of that community, the orientation and perhaps the form of the art are irrevocably changed.

Compromises often must be made in order for a folk event to be interesting and exciting as a public performance, Brzozowska says. Her first priority is quality, and her second is authenticity. By presenting the folk arts, she says, one is by definition altering its historic function. In so doing, one must find the groups and the events that communicate to an audience in the most immediate, compelling, and vivid ways.

CITYFOLK sometimes finds itself in the sensitive position of reintroducing people to their own culture and acting as an agent of cultural renewal. Brzozowska stresses the importance of approaching each ethnic group with caution and respect, always honoring the customs and internal structure of that community. It takes time to earn the trust of each group, she says, and to communicate that CITYFOLK is committed to presenting the culture with integrity.

As contacts have become solidified with the various cultural populations of Dayton, Brzozowska reports that collaborative efforts between CITYFOLK and indigenous organizations have been developing. She points to particularly successful relationships that have been fostered with the Puerto Rico Society and the area Hispanic association. She worked with these groups to present and promote the sold-out performance of Tito Puente and His Latin Jazz All-Stars at the January, 1990 grand reopening of the newly-renovated Victory Theatre, which has been renamed the Victoria Theatre.

Risks and Rewards

In its 10 years of operation, CITYFOLK has developed an annual season format that consists of its "Jazz Tradition" series, a Celtic series, and the "American Heritage" series focusing on significant regional music, dance, and oral traditions. Each season also offers an international dance performance. On occasion, there is a special event, like the performance of the South African Zulu men's choir, Lady-smith Black Mambazo, on its first tour of the United States in 1987.

The range of traditional expressions has included concerts of zydeco, blue-grass, Cajun, traditional Yiddish, traditional African American, Irish, and Scottish music. There also have been storytelling workshops, clogging classes, African dancing, and many other programs.

One of the challenges of presenting the traditional arts is that there is no one audience for everything. In Dayton, as in most cities, the enthusiasms of a small number of folk music aficionados embrace all cultural traditions; but, typically, each event draws a specific audience.

One of CITYFOLK's ongoing efforts is to develop an audience for each new concert. For events that reappear each season, such as the jazz and Celtic music series, this has been a rewarding process of evolution. But for single events that focus on a particular genre, the challenge is much greater and requires ongoing promotion and outreach. When these efforts are successful, the result is a diversified audience expanding its own cultural and artistic boundaries.

Joe Wilson, executive director of the National Council on Traditional Arts (NCTA), a Washington, D.C.-based nonprofit organization that promotes and protects folk arts, has collaborated with CITYFOLK on three occasions. NCTA-produced tours of "Saturday Night and Sunday Morning," "Masters of the Folk Violin" and "Races Musicales (Musical Roots: A National Tour of Regional Music of Mexico and the Hispanic Southwest)" were presented in Dayton.

"An outstanding presenter of traditional events deals with its audiences and performers in a way that makes them comfortable and enables a good interchange between them," Wilson says. "That can be very complex. CITYFOLK is highly responsible, and it manages to assemble people who truly love the event being presented. It can target a specific audience and still fill the house."

This kind of audience development requires an organization that knows its city much better than most presenters, and that brings a certain combination of sophistication and sensitivity to the promotion of each event. In addition, folk expressions are often perceived as being less socially acceptable than the fine arts; so, according to Wilson, there is a social risk in choosing to present them.

"Masters of the Folk Violin" was the second national tour produced by NCTA.

The first tour of "Saturday Night and Sunday Morning" consisted of blues, gospel, storytelling, and buckdancing. For each tour, NCTA assembled and curated groups of musicians and performers who showcased a variety of styles and genres around a central theme. It was the first time such a variety of performers had toured together, but the result was an identity as a group that was greater than the sum of its parts.

Finding presenters who were willing to take a chance on "Masters of the Folk Violin" was difficult, since it was the first tour of its kind. Nor was it accompanied by critical acclaim from the likes of *The New York Times*. Each presenter had to recognize the intrinsic value and viability of the program within its own community. The fact that Brzozowska took this risk with both tours, Wilson says, is another indication of what sets CITYFOLK apart.

> "Our purpose is not to serve an audience that is already being served."

Brzozowska describes herself as a born risk-taker. She insists on presenting the unknown to the Dayton audience, and her board of directors anticipates the risks by budgeting for losses on certain programs.

Brzozowska recalls how the organization took a major risk several years ago by presenting the Chieftains, a popular Celtic music group. The group's fee was very high for a small organization, and CITYFOLK also had to rent a theater and sound system, hire technicians, and aggressively promote the concert. The group was largely unfamiliar to the Dayton audience at that time, so the event was a gamble. But the positive response and strong attendance figures encouraged CITY-FOLK to book a return engagement. The second time around, the concert was a money-maker.

Brzozowska considered a third engagement by the Chieftains, but decided it was again time to challenge the audience and broaden its horizons. In the 1986–87 season, the organization presented "Cherish the Ladies," a tour of Irish music that underscored a fascinating development in that field: the increasing number of young women of Irish ancestry studying and performing traditional Irish music and step dancing.

Ironically, the Dayton Philharmonic that same season elected to present the Chieftains with James Galway, and had a tremendous success. Certainly, the Philharmonic's good fortune owed a great deal to audience development efforts already undertaken by CITYFOLK. Although CITYFOLK lost money on the "Cherish the Ladies" performance, those who did attend told Brzozowska that, musically, it was the best concert on the Celtic series. Brzozowska states unequivocally, "Our purpose is not to serve an audience that is already being served."

Another example of Brzozowska's approach to presenting was the appearance of Ladysmith Black Mambazo. The *a cappella* group gained recognition in the U.S. as a result of its association with singer Paul Simon on his *Graceland* record and tours. The opportunity to present the group on its own came on very short notice and with a fee that was considerably higher than what CITYFOLK is used to paying.

But Brzozowska and the board felt that it was a unique opportunity. Their plan included approaching a major corporation for assistance in underwriting the concert, as well as an appearance at one of Dayton's elementary schools in the Black community.

James Young, a board member who works for AT&T, initiated what turned out to be a successful relationship with the AT&T public relations office in Columbus, Ohio while raising funds for that concert. In announcing its contribution, AT&T spokesperson Jackie Williams commented on the corporation's interest in supporting a "deserving, up-and-coming institution like CITYFOLK." Black Mambazo performed for 1,200 people in Dayton's Memorial Hall on the evening before Thanksgiving Day. The performance at Wogaman School was an equally important and special experience for the students and teachers.

The Jazz Series

In 1986, CITYFOLK instituted "Jazz Tradition," a series that reflects CITYFOLK's interest in presenting America's indigenous art form as a way to collaborate with Dayton's Black community. Since she was less knowledgeable about jazz than about the other art forms that she presents, Brzozowska organized a committee of jazz aficionados whose members, both Black and white, represented a broad commitment to the music.

The committee's charge was to oversee the development of the new series, to serve as its curator, and to provide the expertise to allow the organization to establish the program quickly with the same high standards that characterized its other activities. Early funding from the Dayton Performing Arts Fund and the Ohio Arts Council was crucial in this effort.

About that time, a young man named David Barber arrived on the scene. He was a jazz programmer for the local public radio station, WYSO-FM, where he worked in public relations. Barber joined CITYFOLK as a volunteer and began assembling the elements for the Jazz Tradition series. He then became a part-time employee doing public relations and overseeing the series.

The jazz committee was formed through the Dayton jazz grapevine. One of the people who responded was James Young, who heard through friends at his record store about an organization that was trying to launch a significant jazz program. Young and Barber met each other and, along with other members of the jazz committee, began the process of planning and implementing the series. Characteristically, the CITYFOLK approach was to eschew pop-jazz in favor of the more substantive expressions, and to build the audience slowly while engendering a commitment to the music and musicians. A regional focus without compromise also was slated for each year.

The first series of three concerts included the Dirty Dozen Brass Band, Booty Wood, and Craig Harris in a program called "Two Generations of Jazz Trombone." It ended with a solo concert by pianist Randy Weston.

Barber notes that the most commercial of the performers was the Dirty Dozen, far from a household name. The Booty Wood concert had special significance because Wood was Dayton's native son. His 50-year career had included stints with Duke Ellington, Count Basie, and Lionel Hampton. Wood died soon after the concert, and it became the only tribute to him in his home town.

The series was presented in the Dayton Art Institute, whose auditorium seats 500 people. In the first season, the series drew few more than 200 people at each performance. But in the second season, also at the Art Institute, attendance more than doubled.

The second season also consisted of three concerts. In addition, a pre-series celebration included a screening of *The Last of the Blue Devils*, a documentary film on Kansas City jazz, featuring performances by Count Basie, Big Joe Turner, and Jay McShann. A symposium on "Tradition in Transition," with critic and writer Albert Murray as keynote speaker, also was held. A panel discussion included Oscar Treadwell, jazz announcer and programmer from Cincinnati; Chuck Nessa from Nessa Records; Willard Jenkins, then jazz coordinator for Arts Midwest; and Ted McDaniel, director of jazz studies at Ohio State University.

The series' third year included a symposium, this time on jazz education, with participation by New Orleans musicians and educators Ellis Marsalis and Alvin Batiste. Performances were given by Marsalis and Batiste, the Art Farmer Quintet with Clifford Jordan; and pianist and singer Shirley Horn. In the fourth season, CITYFOLK continues consistently to provide Dayton with quality, content and depth in its jazz programming, bringing significant names from the jazz communities in other cities and building on strong jazz traditions from within Dayton itself. The 1989–90 series included the Detroit Jazz Summit, featuring Charles McPherson and Marcus Belgrave; pianist Tommy Flanagan with bassist George Mraz; and a homecoming for trumpeter Eugene "Snooky" Young, Dayton's native son and a trumpeter in *The Tonight Show* band.

As a result of his work on the jazz committee, Jim Young was invited to join the CITYFOLK board in 1987; he remains a leader in the activities of the board's jazz committee. Young says the experience has been a rewarding one. He feels he has benefited most from the "educational" sessions Brzozowska provides at board meetings: She plays the music scheduled next on the calendar so that board members can speak knowledgeably about it to their friends and colleagues.

Leadership and Funding

Central to the impact that CITYFOLK has had on the Dayton community is the role Brzozowska fulfills as artistic director. "So much of presenting *is* artistic direction," she says, "and I feel very comfortable with that role. I don't know how I developed the taste and aesthetics that I have, but I know that they work, and I trust them implicitly. I think they're a gift from God. I remember that when I was five, I used to organize the kids in the neighborhood and we would put on variety shows using someone's back porch as the stage. How does a child of five decide she wants to put on shows? Where does that come from?"

She says she trusts what she thinks will work, and protects that role very carefully. "The only time I let go of the artistic direction is when I trust the aesthetic of the person or group I'm giving it to, as I do with the jazz committee and Dave Barber. I know that the people on the committee will choose excellence, and I encourage them to resist people who differ with their standards or who are trying to move them toward more pop-oriented events."

The respect and support for CITYFOLK within the community also are based on the tight budget control Brzozowska asserts over the modest but growing budget, which was $290,000 in 1990. From the beginning, CITYFOLK received grants from the Ohio Arts Council/Ohio Humanities Council Joint Program in Folk Art and Culture. It also has received funds from the city's Dayton Foundation that Executive Director Fred Bartenstein describes as risk investment. "We never really knew if CITYFOLK would survive, but they were doing good work, bringing in new art forms, engaging people in learning about and being proud of their own heritage. It was well worth the risk. Now, CITYFOLK has a real shot at being an ongoing part of the cultural landscape of Dayton."

The organization's chances in this respect were greatly enhanced with its inclusion in 1987 as an associate member of the Dayton Performing Arts Fund, which conducts an annual federated campaign for the arts in the community. CITYFOLK previously had received only ad hoc project funds. The Arts Fund finally decided that the organization had reached an appropriate level of professionalism and was eligible for ongoing operating support. By 1989, CITYFOLK had become a "full member" of the renamed organization, Arts Dayton, and was assured annual funding. In the 1991 fiscal year, that funding will amount to $59,500.

Jim Van Vleck, a senior vice president with the Mead Corporation, whose world headquarters are in Dayton, served on the fund's board. He says he was impressed with the organization's soundness and with its accomplishments.

"It seemed to me that CITYFOLK was performing a unique function in this community," he says. "Dayton is ethnically and economically diverse, and I believed that the Performing Arts Fund needed to be more broadly based. I had previously served on the Dayton Philharmonic, the Dayton Opera, and the Dayton Ballet. When we attended the events of those institutions, we saw many of the same people over and over again, usually the more affluent population. Yet, we knew that there was a large community interested in the arts that was simply not present. My experience in going to CITYFOLK performances was that I saw an entirely different audience."

He says it helped that Brzozowska came to the Performing Arts Fund with an open mind. "Some groups are afraid they will lose their control or identity," he says, "but Phyllis had figured out both how the fund could be helpful to CITYFOLK and how CITYFOLK could help the fund broaden its base. It is the only organization in town that has an urban flavor, and because of that, it plays a unique role. The performances are more informal, more fun in a certain way. It has an earthy, down-close-to-the-people feeling about it, and a very strong sense of roots."

Internally, Brzozowska reports that one of the most significant steps for the organization is the process of institutionalization. The staff is growing, and the board is taking more ownership of the organization. "Board members are taking the organization out into the community, talking it up with the people they have contact with, and garnering growing support that way," she says. She admits that it's a relief not to have her finger on everything related to CITYFOLK.

Marketing Traditional Folk Arts

CITYFOLK wins high praise from many quarters because of its ability to draw audiences for the widely varied events that it presents. Ira Weiss, director of the performing arts program for the Ohio Arts Council, praises the organization for working closely with educational institutions and with folk and ethnic groups to develop audiences both through grass roots methods and through more sophisticated means like telemarketing.

In the early 1980s, each event was promoted separately and had to find its own niche in the community. Since each was designed in conjunction with a different ethnic group, the promotional efforts began by including each group in the planning process.

This encouraged a sense of ownership in the event and a feeling of partnership with the organization. Slowly, these ethnic groups and their organizations were convinced of CITYFOLK's sincerity and respect for their cultures. Ultimately, they permitted the use of their mailing lists, and they inserted a listing or article from time to time in their newsletters. This process generated audiences and won credibility for the organization.

In 1986, CITYFOLK issued its first season brochure listing all the events for the year. It offered subscriptions to its Celtic and jazz series, and single tickets to the other presentations. This brochure displayed a handsome illustrated image of Dayton's skyline superimposed over a collage of the various groups and individuals representing the season's offerings. It was a graphic image that established the tone of ethnic diversity in the context of the urban landscape.

Brzozowska reports that since the first season brochure was issued, ticket sales have grown steadily. In a single year's time, from 1989 to 1990, season sales jumped from $76,000 to $100,000. This represents about 30% of CITYFOLK's total income for the 1990 fiscal year.

People can now subscribe to three different three-part series: "Jazz Tradition," "The Celtic Series" or the new bluegrass series. They also can buy single tickets to any other event. Up to now, CITYFOLK has not felt that there would be a significant number of people who would want to subscribe to the entire season, since each event is targeted to an entirely different population. But they are now seeing a growing crossover in their audiences, no matter what cultural group is presented. This being the case, a subscription to the full range of events might actually be popular.

Brzozowska's long-term plans include hiring a folklorist and expanding CITYFOLK's functions to include exhibitions, documentaries, educational projects, and other community-based undertakings. "We would like to be an organization that offers a focus for the study and dissemination of information on traditional and ethnic arts," she says.

Brzozowska is very excited about a special project to take place in April, 1991. CITYFOLK will host a month-long residency with actor and writer John O'Neal, whose character Junebug Jabbo Jones presents material drawn from the rich and varied African American oral tradition. While in Dayton, O'Neal will interact with the local community and with artists, and will make a series of informal appearances before his final performance at Wright State University's Festival Playhouse. Brzozowska made efforts to fundraise specifically for this program. She was successful in reaching the special Allegro fund at the Dayton Foundation, which is designed to help support an annual month-long residency in Dayton; the O'Neal project seems tailor-made for it. In addition, a substantial grant for the project came in from the Ohio Arts Council.

Brzozowska sees CITYFOLK as a resource for individual artists and other arts organizations; it often assists these organizations with presenting, technical assistance, publicity, and fundraising. This backstage role became more public in 1988, when the board of the Dayton Black Cultural Festival asked CITYFOLK to help reorganize that event to ensure its stability and future operations.

The organization accepted the project on a consulting basis, and ultimately served as the fiscal agent for the festival. The five-day event in the summer of 1988 was a great success. It also emerged without a deficit for the first time in its history. Since then, Brzozowska has been invited to join the organization's board, where she serves on the personnel committee.

Still, CITYFOLK's primary work lies in giving the people of Dayton the chance to experience the talent of performers onstage. With presentations like "Masters of the Folk Violin," it has touched a responsive chord within the community.

What evoked the overwhelming emotional response that the audience gave the artists who performed in the "Masters of the Folk Violin" program? Joe Wilson, producer of the tour, believes he knows.

"Why did those people stand up and scream? Why did they stay in their seats for almost four hours? If I create and I want you to like it, I have to put some of myself into it. It has to be a part of myself that you can look across this table and see some of yourself in. Then we can say that you and I understand each other; we found this piece of music in which we could share an intimacy. That feels good because all of us pass through this vale of tears alone, and we all have to reach out to each other as we go.

"This concert did that," he continues. "We took a little instrument and showed how different people have put their feelings and heart and intellect into a piece of wood. What they've done is beautiful, and it makes a statement about ethnicity and race, a statement that says there is quality in *all* people."

CITYFOLK reaffirms that spirit of humanity with every program it presents. This is the treasure that it offers to its audiences and, ultimately, this is its power as a presence in Dayton.

LA LA LA Human Steps

Photo by Edouard Lock

8 7,500 Square Feet Above a Tire Store

David R. White's description of Dance Theater Workshop as "7,500 square feet above a tire store"—which until recently literally was true—is unpretentious and unprepossessing. But the executive director and producer's characterization of this New York-based organization, which was founded in 1965 by three choreographers, belies the overwhelming impact DTW has had on artists and the performing arts for many years.

DTW has not simply changed the face of the performing arts in the United States. It also has changed the way administrators in the field and funders outside it think about the work of contemporary, experimental, generative artists, about the presenting of performances, about the value and credibility of small alternative/ artist spaces, and about their impact in the larger context of the arts and society.

Of necessity, presenting organizations reflect the thinking and experiences of their founders or long-time directors. The acute, astute, and almost prescient vision behind DTW comes straight from White. In fact, director and organization seem all but fused.

White brings to his work his own accumulated experiences from within and outside the arts, and the philosophical lessons he learned from them. These experiences, and the people with whom he interacted, all powerfully influenced his approach to DTW and to the broad, inclusive agenda he developed to render it a service to artists.

His great talent is his ability to process and assimilate experience, information, and ideas from far afield, and to apply them in a practical way to realize his vision. He refers to the underpinning of many of his innovative programs as combining "ideas and means" to achieve a particular goal. One of his colleagues, Jeremy

Alliger from the Dance Umbrella in Boston, calls him an "incredible manic visionary."

He can spot clear but unmet needs, analyze them carefully, search the storehouse of his intellect, and find uniquely fitting and deceptively simple solutions. He likes straightforward ideas, celebrates the small over the large, and invents alternative structures to realize goals. He champions the strength of working cooperatively to solve problems, and knows how to build coalitions of like-minded people.

The concept of "community" is a driving force, a clear legacy of his political activism in the 1960s. "We always see what we do at DTW in the context of the larger community," he says. Community has many different meanings for him: the community of artists, the community of work, DTW's Chelsea community on New York's west side. Each has its own important presence, and together they assume an even larger significance.

Despite DTW's national and international impact, White still views it as a local organization. "Everything we do is to support local artists or artists from the outside working here," he says. "All the outside services and activities have been designed to accomplish our own in-house purposes, which must be approached from a cooperative point of view."

What is Dance Theater Workshop?

DTW almost defies description, because it is so many things. The simplest characterization appears in the organization's membership brochure. It "is in the forefront of revolutionary artistic support. Originally a pioneering cooperative of modern dance artists, DTW has developed into an alternative performing arts institution . . . DTW's goal remains distinct and uncompromising: to identify, encourage, and sponsor independent artists and companies whose work is both visionary and provocative in the field of dance, theater, performance, music, literature, visual, and allied arts."

Statistics support DTW's claim that it is the single most active dance theater in the U.S. Since 1975, when the organization moved into its current production facility, it has presented some 500 different choreographers and companies. As it has broadened from dance into other forms such as theater, contemporary music, literature, and visual arts, DTW has presented scores of theater artists, composers and musicians, writers, and visual artists.

The sponsorship program—as its presenting arm is called—is only one in a range of services enabling artists to create and survive. DTW also functions as a partial alternative to conventional arts management organizations by providing resources for out-of-town artists or companies producing a New York season. The DTW Presenters List is a honed selection of national presenters who have a demonstrated interest in the types of artists that DTW sponsors.

Membership services include a computerized audience direct-mail operation; a discount advertising agency; a quarterly newsletter; press lists that are fully researched, updated, and cross-referenced; a national performing arts presenter mailing service; an international sponsor and producer reference list; a video documentation and archival project; and consulting on an array of issues including promotion, management, and budgeting.

DTW also administers three major programs that enhance and recognize the work of individual artists and companies: the National Performance Network (NPN), a loosely federated group of member organizations that facilitate the touring of experimental dance, music, theater, mime, and performance artists; the Suitcase Fund, which enables U.S. artists to tour abroad, and helps international artists tour in the U.S.; and the New York Dance and Performance Awards, known as the Bessies (after Bessie Schönberg, DTW's chairman).

In the grand scheme of things, the presenting organization aspect of DTW is just one part, although an important one, of the way the organization has come to support artists and their work.

The Philosophical Underpinning

David White was first exposed to dance at age 19 in Paris, at the time of the student upheaval in 1968. He was studying film, and he observed Jean-Luc Goddard filming the protests. He says he experienced the "absolutely integral relationship of art and society, and the ability to look at one through the other." After returning to the U.S. in 1970 and briefly pursuing film production, he became interested in dance as "an arena for ideas and live social interaction."

He began to study dance at Connecticut College and attended the American Dance Festival, then based in New London at the college. That summer was revelatory, he says. "It was an isolated world where everything just seemed to revolve around this art form, and all of it seemed to make sense, including the social connections." That summer, he met two people involved with DTW, and he decided to move to New York. He describes DTW in the early 1970s not as a counterpart of the Judson movement toward minimalism, but something else entirely. "Dance Theater Workshop was a group of people who dealt with dance theater," he says, rather than with postmodern expressions. The DTW loft on 20th Street became a place to share resources, ideas, and information, and to create new works.

After study at DTW and a brief stint with the Kathryn Posin Dance Company, White recognized that he was not destined to be a dancer, but that he was challenged by management and the production of performances. He began to think about how to make Posin's company work better administratively.

At that time, he met Ted Striggles, a lawyer who became a dancer in Jamie Cunningham's company. White says Striggles revolutionized the small company by pooling resources to pay for expenses and salaries. He also made sure that the proper records were kept and filed to enable the dancers to receive unemployment insurance. Striggles' seminal contribution to the field, White says, was "the idea of using the available systems and seeing those systems as part and parcel of how you promulgated the art form." This philosophy strongly influenced White's own thinking.

Still, White says, no existing system "would create a living situation for the artist." New and inventive solutions to that problem were needed. If everybody pitched in, operated imaginatively, and created alternative structures to survive, companies could do important work with limited resources. To provide some of those solutions, in 1974 Striggles organized the Economic Survival Workshops for DTW's dancers.

White came to believe that "companies are in fact the presenters." But to realize this concept, he had to put into place a concomitant idea. One small dance company doing highly theatrical work could not afford to do a New York season because the rental, rehearsal, and publicity costs were astronomical. By formulating ideas with the 1960s in mind, White began to think about cooperative activity. If several companies could pool resources from public and private funding organizations, they could amortize the costs over a longer period, share advertising expenses, and publicize the combined seasons as an event. This would create a critical mass that could capture significant press attention.

> ## DTW identifies, encourages, and sponsors independent artists and companies whose work is both visionary and provocative.

Thus, the Dance Umbrella was born: 12 companies sharing a publicly-supported facility with funds coming from the National Endowment for the Arts (NEA) and the New York State Council on the Arts (NYSCA). The companies remained aesthetically autonomous, but shared resources. The first Dance Umbrella, consisting of two four-week series, was held in 1975. Its $300,000 budget was raised in advance from the NEA, NYSCA, and the Andrew W. Mellon and Ford foundations. The Dance Umbrella lasted for five years, and was undone partially because the groups did not control an appropriate facility.

White says the most important aspect of its first season was that "We were producing a community of work, not just a company. The Dance Umbrella's function was not to serve the public, but to serve the artists. If it works for the artists, it works for the public."

At that point, White says, "I began to conceive of my work as being a systems artist. I was molding an environment within which an artist can create. The situation clearly identifies the 'producer' as a creative individual, not as a passive person just occupying a job. There had never been a full-time dance theater in the United States, and that is what I set out to do—to create a year-round identity for this work." White wanted to establish a constancy, volume, and flow of activity that would become part of the organization's identity, and he wanted to assemble the production resources to make that possible.

When White took over DTW, the rather insular 10-year-old organization had not yet perceived and reacted to changes in the artistic community. He wanted to dovetail the activities of various organizations to constitute a community, and to build a bridge for emerging artists between the avant-garde and the mainstream. He believed that the first thing artists needed was a way to perform that included both a space and an audience. "Too many presenters do not seem to care about the work," White says, "but rather about getting the audience in to pay the bills. There is no clear idea that there should be an integral relationship between the work and the community from which it emerges."

The care and husbanding of the community at large was essential, White says. "We could create a situation in which all possibilities of good work were going to have a chance to come through. If work fell on its face on its merits, at least it would have had its moment to say what it had to say and to have someone see or listen to it. We wanted to animate a real and binding relationship between the public and the work that emerged from its midst."

White also wanted to keep ticket prices low. "Box office had to be irrelevant to our programming," he said. "The issue was that artists had to be presented, and people had to catch up with the artists." During the past 15 years, this approach has gained DTW a dedicated audience. "They've become an audience not for isolated events, not for this performer or that artist, but an audience for the field," he says. "Every event now fits into a context."

There is no one DTW audience, but myriad audiences that respond to the diverse programming. The great strength of DTW's approach to audience development is its capacity to draw a responsive audience to almost any kind of programming. The programming comes first, White says, and the audience follows.

On Presenters and Presenting

White's well-developed view of presenters and presenting is philosophical and pragmatic. "I believe that the best presenting has been based on personal commitment to the artwork, just as artists make a commitment to their work," he says. "Presenters have to work by intuition, not on the basis of established reputations or what will draw. Most presenters have lost their imagination. They have to see exactly what they'll be getting before they book it. But no matter how much you try to know beforehand, you'll never know enough to take the chance. You have to assume that you're taking a chance, and jump."

White says the producer/presenter—he dislikes the term presenter—has three roles. The first is that of *animateur*, a French term that implies investing life and liveliness into a situation. "You create a situation in which other people can create," he says. "This goes beyond simply putting people on stage and people in the seats. We have a more profound responsibility to anchor the culture of the country."

The second role is that of gatekeeper, the intermediary between the artist and the public. "You give artists what some of them have never had—the final laboratory," White says. "There is only so much artists can do in the studio and with others who share their assumptions. Once you put it up on the runway in front of a group of people who do not share those assumptions, that's when they begin to understand what they need to do in the work."

The third role is that of an archaeologist who draws conclusions from incomplete information. "You are going to surface various things from an archaeological dig," he says. "As you begin to find these shards, you piece them together, and you have very small, partial pictures of what this thing was. But you extrapolate. You draw conclusions. And something clicks. An intuitive light bulb goes on, and that is the point at which you produce."

White says there are two fundamental ways to produce. "You either produce artists or you produce work. At DTW, we produce artists. Artists produce works."

Investing in a commissioning or co-commissioning project is simply the enabling of an artist's next work. "Art is about things that you don't know yet," he says. "It's about defining and redefining. It means that the producer believes in the artist as a distinct sensibility, not that the producer knows what will be created."

He also is concerned with the presenter's motivation. "We should think of ourselves as amateurs in the best sense—people who love something. You aren't totally learned and indoctrinated. You come out of curiosity. To me, that is the motivation that's most important to encourage. And if it is going to be made manifest in your public, it has to be made manifest among these *animateurs*-gatekeepers-archaeologists-producers-presenters."

To drive home the point, White characterizes his work in the most basic human and emotional terms. "This is one of the best jobs in the world—and it's not a job. In fact, it often feels much more like a love affair that is about as rocky as anything you could get into. It offers a lifetime of anticipation, temptation—all sorts of extraordinary despair with misery thrown in just to keep whetting your appetite."

From Philosophy to Pragmatism

To the outsider, David White has brought DTW his eloquence and his unique vision, in addition to his ability to translate those into concrete programs that are developed and refined as new circumstances emerge. To him, though, the process is completely the reverse: "Out of the practical proceeds the philosophical," he says.

But however it proceeds, both thinking and pragmatism are abundantly evident in DTW's programs. Its components show a significant progression from building a local constituency—the artist—to broadening service to those artists, to a national and international presence and agenda.

Practically, that has meant developing and securing the base of support through Membership Services, the sponsorship program, the National Performance Network, the Suitcase Fund, and the New York Dance and Performance Awards.

MEMBERSHIP SERVICES

When White signed on as executive director, a pressing concern was to devise services that would meet concrete needs. In 1975, there were approximately 100 member companies and individuals. Today, there are more than 500. Annual membership is $60 for the independent choreographer, dance company, or theater company. For presenting organizations, the dues are scaled from $75 to $200, depending on the organization's budget. Of all DTW programs, Membership Services generates the most earned income, a hefty 75 percent of its specific annual budget allocation. This high level of user support speaks to the program's health, and to its relevance in providing badly needed assistance in the field.

DTW PRESENTS

DTW's presenting programs are a flexible set of stylishly monikered series, some of whose names reflect DTW's former proximity to the tire store—Fresh Tracks, Border Crossings, Economy Tires Music Hall, and others. There also are exhibits in the DTW Gallery and Out Loud/New Readings in American Fiction.

Although the costs for each of the companies far exceed the income guaranteed by DTW to the company, the opportunity to be well presented in an "important" New York downtown space, and to have access to press from the New York and national media, is a significant draw.

> "This is one of the best jobs in the world—and it's not a job. In fact, it often feels much more like a love affair that is about as rocky as anything you could get into."

DTW also has become a place where presenters from other organizations come to see the development of new talent, and the refinement of more familiar artists.

Nina Wiener, who first appeared at DTW in the mid-1970s, mentions White's support of young artists. "He tries to make things possible for you. Of all the presenters I've ever worked with, he gave me the most support. He nurtured me when I needed nurturing. When I went on to a different type of work, there was no bad feeling. He continued to nurture me."

Another voice is that of choreographer David Gordon. "David White presented me in New York at a time when no one else would touch me with a 10-foot pole," Gordon says. "He presented me for several years running, and kept upping the ante each time from one week to two to three. We had a party during the three-week run, and the dancers who worked with me at that time toasted me for the longest run of dancing that they had had in their entire career. David was and is responsible for that kind of thing."

As a result of his three-week run at DTW, Gordon—who earlier had characterized himself as a nonprolific artist—"began to know that I could be oiled, and I did have the possibility of being productive in a more continuous way and even on a schedule. That's a process you don't know about until somebody says, 'Here's an opportunity. Go do it.' "

Choreographer Susan Marshall says her appearances at DTW precipitated major developments in her career. "With me, it's hard to disassociate David White from DTW. But I guess if you take the two of them as a whole, they've essentially launched and secured my company's career."

White spread the word about Marshall, and interested many presenters in her work. "He's a sort of hub," Marshall says, "and people do call him for recommendations." Since then, Marshall has been a regular with NPN sponsors, and received an important commission from the Boston Ballet because Artistic Director Bruce Marks had seen her perform at DTW.

Performance artist Ann Carlson describes the DTW audience as quite a bit more "uptown" than those at many other downtown spaces. "The press coverage I got there was amazing," she says. "You perform at DTW, and *Elle* magazine calls you up."

NATIONAL PERFORMANCE NETWORK

Established in 1985, the NPN serves two important roles. It is a national program that facilitates the touring of experimental artists. It is sustained by a decentralized network of alternative presenting spaces—the primary sponsors—in selected cities and communities throughout the U.S. NPN is a regranting program; presenter members apply to DTW for support for the touring artists' residencies. DTW receives funding for NPN from a combination of public and private sources, including the NEA, the Ford Foundation, the Pew Charitable Trusts, and the Lila Wallace-Reader's Digest Fund.

The network does not create an "approved list" of eligible artists. Rather, the presenters must be accepted into NPN. They must meet certain standards to deliver the proper producing and presenting services to the artists. The network grew to 19 primary sponsors in the 1989-90 season. It subsidizes 35 percent of the fee for a one-week residency, and 50 percent for two weeks. Fees are set to cover transportation, salary, and per diem for each company member, and a fixed administration fee for the group. There is no negotiation. Every company is entitled to the same fee for performing, and all have the same access.

Renata Petroni, touring projects coordinator, administers NPN. "The idea was to create an incentive for the network members to be adventurous in their presenting," she says, "and to really take risks with young companies that otherwise would not have been booked." With the subsidy, the NPN member will at least break even.

Part of the idea behind NPN is to shift the artistic focus away from New York. In its pilot phase, NPN stipulated that each primary sponsor engage no more than two artists from New York, or half of the four residencies available to each site. Petroni says this rule is now unnecessary. Because of NPN's effectiveness, more generative work from outside New York is being toured, both to New York and elsewhere.

NPN's annual meeting, each year in a different city and region, brings network members and guests together for three to four days to foster communication, share successes and problems, discuss artists and their work, look at videotapes of performances, and refine the program's guidelines and administration.

Jeremy Alliger, executive director of Dance Umbrella in Boston, a charter NPN primary sponsor, says presentations by artists from each region are a major attraction of this meeting. "Having this kind of exposure was an education for me," he says.

Each year, as more people speak of the fascinating programs performed by artists they've presented, other network members also present them. Seattle's On the Boards has been a major support of choreographer Pat Graney. In fact, Graney's work was performed at On the Boards during an annual meeting of the NPN in Seattle. As a result, other NPN members decided to present her in cities to which she would not have had access without the network's exposure.

This self-selecting component of the program, as opposed to an approved roster of artists, leads Alliger to say, "This is the only system I know of that is funded on a national level as part of a network where the selection process takes place entirely at the local level. This makes us all rugged individuals, as well as a community of presenters with a shared mission."

Each new year brings administrative refinements and innovations in response to members' ideas and experiences. Petroni lists two improvements: a co-commissioning component, and a travel fund enabling network members to see work around the country.

SUITCASE FUND

White says the Suitcase Fund was inspired by something from the Watergate era. He describes Maurice Stans, President Nixon's secretary of commerce and later the chair of the Committee to Reelect the President, carrying a suitcase containing $200,000 in cash to meet pressing problems. The idea intrigued White. Stans' notion could be applied to moving people around, to fund what experimental artists have always had difficulty finding money for: travel expenses.

White translated the Watergate-era image into the Suitcase Fund, subtitled "A Project of Ideas and Means in Cross-Cultural Artist Relations." This simple idea is based on a complex but refined philosophical foundation. The fund is not a simple "throw money at a problem" program, but the result of a keen analysis of how and why international artist exchanges have been lacking.

White describes the goals of the Suitcase Fund: "To redress the imbalance of international and cross-cultural artistic exchange, to encourage practical relations among the world's diverse artist communities, and to foster a broader context for the global communication of cultural ideas. These goals are addressed by ensuring and regularizing the traffic of artists, producers, and writers."

The Suitcase Fund sends American artists abroad, enabling international audiences, presenters, producers, and artists to see their work. This work and these artists are largely unfamiliar to the public abroad. The companion part of the program subsidizes U.S. tours by international artists, producers, and writers, and provides important interchange. Part of the fund's beauty is that it feeds into NPN's already established structure. International artists who come to the U.S. can tour the country under the network's auspices.

The Rockefeller Foundation provided pilot project funding of $25,000. DTW also applied money from its NEA challenge grant. The project's budget grew to $225,000 for the 1988–89 season.

Petroni says the Suitcase Fund has won the credibility of international producers, companies, and artist representatives because she and White bring with them the ability to back their ideas for collaboration with money. European companies often receive travel funds from their governments, which enables the Suitcase

Fund to allocate an equivalent amount for per diems, for example. Each of the U.S. presenters provides a fee to tour the company through the country. It is a partnership in the same way that many of DTW's programs are partnerships, bringing together people and organizations with shared interests.

THE BESSIES

The New York Dance and Performance Awards were established in 1984 with a grant from the Morgan Guaranty Trust Company. The creation of the Bessies illustrates DTW's ability to serve as a conduit between funders and one segment of the New York creative community.

Morgan Vice President Jeanne Erwin Linness, who directs the bank's philanthropic program for the arts, says the firm wants to encourage new work and develop emerging artists. "This has been deliberate, not accidental," she says. "Some people have likened it to research and development. We don't use that analogy, but that is really what I think it's about—making sure that the arts are vital. Not just preserving the past, but developing in as dynamic a way as contemporary society makes it possible to do."

Linness says the company tries to be proactive as well as responsive to specific proposals. It wants to identify needs it perceives in the arts in New York.

"In 1982, we were looking for an initiative in dance that we hoped would address some of the needs of individual artists, and enable us to support them through a major organization in a way that we couldn't do directly. I give David White credit for bringing the Bessies to us, but it fit our objectives extremely well."

White says the bank's support speaks to DTW's ability to create partnerships in the field. "People have to see you as a partner in their process," he says. "Once they begin to look at you in that way, not simply as an applicant, things change."

Morgan came to DTW with a proposal for the organization to regrant money to individual artists. DTW responded with the awards idea. White says that Morgan first was talking about a commissioning program. "I felt that sometimes money focusing on commissions does the wrong thing. People begin to look at the end product: 'This is the work we paid for? Whoops, it's not so good.' So I suggested we find a way to recognize what people have done already. Giving money as awards would allow artists to use it in any way they saw fit."

The award selections are made by a committee of 23 artists, curators, and administrators who are active in the field. They attend performances throughout the year at all the alternative downtown spaces, as well as at uptown spaces that present larger-scale works from the contemporary dance and performance community.

White says Morgan is a very conservative bank with a progressive arts policy. "Even though they provide major funding for the Bessies, they don't know where that money's going until they attend the ceremony, like everybody else."

Linness says people have told her the awards are very important for the dance community. "They've brought the dance community together in a way that it has never been brought together before. But they've also provided very practical funding for some very talented artists," she says.

DTW has been able to attract additional funding for the Bessies from several other sources, including grants from Dom Ruinart Champagne and Best Products Foundation, and gifts from the JCT Foundation and Philip Morris Companies, Inc.

The event itself has become a focal community evening for the New York, national and, to a certain extent, international arts scene. Each year, the Bessies are hosted by a pair of performers in a downtown version of an awards show reminiscent of the Tonys or Oscars. Instead of Hollywood-style production numbers, there are performances of short selections from some of the year's most fascinating and outrageous works. Such hosts as new vaudeville clown Bill Irwin; dancers Valda Setterfield and Carolyn Adams; and performance artist Ethyl Eichelberger appear in an array of costumes and carry on the expected banter. Even with its tongue-in-cheek manner, the event still rallies a significant presence and has fostered the sense of a community of artists.

Marketing the Unknown

DTW's approach to the media utilizes the standard techniques of releases and followups, cultivation of press contacts, and targeting stories to reporters who have shown a particular interest in certain kinds of work or artists.

What is singularly DTW is what could tamely be described as its newsletter, sent to people on its extensive mailing and press lists. *DTW New(s) in Revue* is an irreverent quarterly tabloid that is a take-off on the *National Enquirer*. Each issue is crammed with photographs of the performers, hip descriptions of their work, and what others have said or written about it. Regular features and columns include "Financial New(s)," a listing of public and private support; "Long-Range Forecast," a three-month calendar of events; "Arts New(s)," a gallery listing; and "Literary New(s)," a readings listing. Then, there is "Consumer Alert," DTW's pitch for advance ticket sales and subscriptions.

This regular communiqué keeps DTW on people's minds. Its satirical tone takes the edge off the fact that, more likely than not, most of the artists listed in the *New(s) in Revue* are not familiar to the readers. The reader is engaged, instead of feeling threatened by a lack of familiarity with the artists and their work. It invites and cajoles readers to take a chance and go see an artist or company.

DTW has garnered a big share of press coverage because of the quality of the artists, the credibility of the work, and its service to the field. A steady stream of reviews appear in *The New York Times* and *Village Voice,* among many newspapers and magazines. DTW also has been successful in gaining the more difficult-to-get feature stories. This is accomplished by gentle prodding, but most of all by the trust that critics and reporters have for DTW.

New York Times dance critic Jennifer Dunning says, "At DTW, I think most readily of the performances I have seen from around the country in its Out-of-Towners and Border Crossings series. It's a wonderful feeling to think that you have a chance to see people's work that you would not see any other way. It's very lovely to feel the world shrinking that way, on the level of alternative arts." Significantly, these two series have been greatly enhanced in recent years by the stepped-up number of appearances by non-New Yorkers and international artists, as a result of the National Performance Network and the Suitcase Fund.

A sense of partnership pervades DTW's attitude and philosophy toward the media. The organization sees them as partners in the process of promulgating new work and new artists. In turn, Dunning says she frequently calls White as a resource for information about the field.

DTW Day to Day

Keeping the organizational home fires burning is the task of Laurie Uprichard, DTW's managing director. She is responsible for day-to-day operations, long-range planning, overall budgeting, and fundraising. Uprichard says White has an idea of how he wants things to run and what he wants to happen, and she makes those tangible. "The analogy I use is a translator," she says. "I translate from one set of words into another set of words, depending on if it's a grant proposal or working with staff or whatever."

DTW's annual $2 million budget is substantial by any standard, but simultaneously ironic. Like White's modest characterization of DTW as "7,500 square feet above a tire store," a budget of this magnitude is not what one would expect for an alternative arts organization.

Uprichard says about 25 percent of the budget is earned income. This picture is somewhat skewed, because the NPN and the Suitcase Fund are based entirely on grants from private foundations and the NEA. Nonetheless, the accumulated deficit has reached $200,000. She says DTW won't be able to "nickel and dime" itself out of the deficit. Her proposed solution is to fund the deficit as part of DTW's planned capital campaign, including a sum like $500,000 in a $5 million goal to cover deficit retirement and the building of a cash reserve.

Real Estate and the Arts in New York

DTW must begin to consider a capital campaign, because the future in its current space is in question. In New York City, real estate plays a major role in the life of any arts organization, large or small, establishment or alternative. It hits harder for the smaller ones, whose financial stability is usually more precarious, and whose rented property is frequently located in the urban frontiers. Arts organizations often set the stage for a marginal neighborhood to become of interest to developers. Just as the organization starts to build toward stability, the developers are ready to raise the rent 300 percent, or decide that the piece of property is prime space for a luxury apartment building.

This is what DTW is now facing. The Chelsea section of New York's west side has seen a slow but steady rise in popularity. DTW's two-story building is on the demolition list, to be replaced by a high-rise, high-density apartment building. In response, DTW is exploring a few options. In coalition with Creative Time, another alternative New York arts organization, DTW made a proposal to take over and renovate the now-defunct Maritime Ferries Building at the tip of downtown Manhattan. Their proposal was accepted, and they have been named the provisional designees for the space. This only means, however, that they have the right to raise the several million dollars it will take to gut and renovate the building. This project is at least five years down the road. In the meantime, DTW must secure a home.

The organization has bought some time, because the landlord has been persuaded to extend their lease at a whopping percent increase for the next five years. This involves an annual commitment of $112,000. Undoubtedly, the real estate saga will continue until DTW is safely ensconced in a new facility.

Fundraising

Uprichard spends half her time on fundraising activities, working with White to develop grant proposals, cultivating corporate and foundation donors for White to visit and talk with in his persuasive way, and working with staff and board to schedule and implement in-house benefits.

Grant proposals to city, state, and federal arts agencies have been met with a consistent pattern of funding. DTW also has garnered major multi-year grants from among the most important private foundations, and has received some expressions of corporate largesse.

Board members like President Patricia Tarr, a young New York philanthropist, cultivate individuals capable of making substantial donations. Tarr says DTW does very well pursuing and receiving government and foundation grants, but she and other board members feel the individual and corporate sides of giving need development.

This cultivation begins with an invitation from Tarr or another board member to attend a DTW benefit, which always is combined with attendance at one of the performances. Benefits are held at least twice a year. With tickets selling at $100 each, DTW nets around $10,000 per benefit.

Supporting the Vision

With someone as charismatic as David White at the helm, is there room for anyone else's vision at DTW? Staff members seem comfortable with their roles in support of White. Uprichard, who has worked with him since 1984, says it's important to have one person with an artistic vision in charge.

"It is the same way in a dance company," she says. "You've got a Paul Taylor or a Merce Cunningham. The dancers aren't trying to become the choreographers. On the other hand, perhaps in the same way as one of the dancers might do something that has an impact on the choreography, we might have an impact as well. It's a two-way street."

White is sometimes seen as a prophet by his colleagues at other alternative spaces, and sometimes as a somewhat overbearing, almost dictatorial presence in the field who is trying to garner attention for himself when other people and spaces are doing work that is just as good. A number of directors of alternative spaces point out that informal networks were set up in various regions of the country long before the NPN existed. They resent the attention that is focused on one space and one person.

Still, it is difficult to deny White's effectiveness at making the case nationally for contemporary, challenging, experimental work and for all the organizations and spaces that present it. White's presence and point of view often are sought and recognized.

Stephanie French, director of cultural and contributions programs for the Philip Morris Companies, Inc., and the first corporate representative on the DTW board, says DTW is important because it is discovering tomorrow's talent. "They take even more risks than the Brooklyn Academy of Music. They are getting the artists that are just emerging and developing. They give them one of their first big showcases and launch their careers. What would we do if Dance Theater Workshop didn't exist? That's where the new talent first comes forward."

Dr. Alberta Arthurs, director of arts and humanities at The Rockefeller Foundation, points out what is unique about DTW. "There just isn't anybody like David White and the Dance Theater Workshop anywhere else in the world, right? David is an example of a set of qualities that we seem to be talking about. One is absolutely dedicated management—of ideas as well as of people and place. David in some ways has been a manager of ideas more than of anything else, and he has this total commitment to artists, to artistry, and to experimentation in the arts."

No Anointments

Whatever major influence DTW has had on the world of contemporary, experimental arts, it also has influenced popular culture. This may sound paradoxical for an organization that supports untried artistic territory. But DTW has played host to new expressions from the nether reaches of the artistic community when no one else was willing to take a chance.

Whoopi Goldberg was known to a very few people for her biting one-person monologs in which she created an array of distinctive characters. As a result of her run on the Out-of-Towners series, director Mike Nichols brought her one-person show to Broadway.

DTW also gave a platform to the new vaudevillians like Bill Irwin, the Flying Karamazov Brothers, and Bob Berky and Michael Moschen. This is not to say that they were discovered by DTW; much of this activity was simmering on the streets and in underground and alternative spaces around the country. But DTW gave new vaudeville its platform in New York, and raised the public consciousness of the work so it could be acknowledged as art.

Wouldn't it be easier to continue to present once-unknown artists who now are well known, in part because DTW presented them? "There are continuities in our program of certain kinds of material," White says, "but they don't have to be the same people. There's not a question of anointing people."

And so, no anointments of White, either. Still, it is hard to imagine how the field of presenting would be without the seminal work being done on the second story of a building on Manhattan's west side.

David Parsons

Photo by Lois Greenfield

9 Educating the Whole Human Being

The little boy was crying because he had to go home after lunch hour at his rural New Hampshire school. With winter's first snowstorm on its way, his father needed his help hauling wood to keep the family warm. But leaving school early meant that he would miss the art project with his sixth-grade class, working with the weaver who had been in residence that semester.

Mary Sue Glosser, former curator of arts education services for the Hopkins Center and the Hood Museum of Art at Dartmouth College, tells this story to illustrate the impact the arts have had in the rural area served by Dartmouth's Hopkins Center. "If you or I want to know about something, we will find a way," she says. "We will open the door and go in. But for children in an area like this, just the idea of opening the door to the arts accomplishes as much as the art project they might do or the play they might see."

Indeed, for this little boy and many others like him, access to art has become a welcome and essential part of life.

Arts education is only one of the many facets of the Hopkins Center, which celebrated its 25th anniversary in the 1987–88 season. But it exemplifies the broad approach and serious agenda that the Center embraces. "The Hop," as it is affectionately known, belies preconceived notions that the arts at an Ivy League college are the province of a privileged few. The reality here is just the opposite. The Center is at the fulcrum of a delicate balance between academic and extracurricular interests, between Dartmouth College and the community, which includes the town of Hanover and the extensive rural area that surrounds it in New Hampshire's Upper Valley.

Early Dreams, Later Reality

A unique vision underlies the bustle of daily activity at the Hopkins Center. Shelton g Stanfill, executive director of the Center from 1981 to 1988, recounts its history as the singular vision of the founder and first director, Warner Bentley, and Dartmouth's former president John Sloan Dickey. This vision—to make the arts an integral part of the student's college experience—was incorporated into the design of the arts center like a retaining wall. Add to the vision a strong dose of tenacity, and you have the elements that went into the foundation of the Hopkins Center, elements that are still apparent.

The Hopkins Center was conceived as a theater and drama building in the late 1920s, when Ernest Martin Hopkins was president of the college. He hired the young theater activist Warner Bentley, fresh out of the Yale School of Drama. First the Depression and then World War II forced the postponement of the new building. Then, postwar prosperity and optimism began to sweep the nation. During John Sloan Dickey's administration, the concept of an arts center at Dartmouth expanded and took shape. The controversial modernist structure, which housed much more than the theater that was envisioned 35 years earlier, opened in 1962.

Some view the Hopkins Center as a bellwether in the trend that swept the country from the 1960s through the 1980s, when palaces for the performing arts were built in the guise of performing arts centers in cities and on college campuses.

But the Hopkins Center is hardly a palace. It is more a symbol of a fascinating and rare approach to educating the whole human being. Its contiguous spaces deliberately blur the boundaries between academic functions and extracurricular "campus life" events. The Center was conceived with a variety of anchors—student mailboxes and the food service, for example—that serve as magnets to bring students into the building and make it attractive for them to stay. Intermingled are the music, drama, and visual studies departments and the dance program, along with design workshops used both for instruction and extracurricular activity.

The community's access to the Hop also is important. "Access" has been worked into the fabric of the Center's operating assumptions and is based on enlightened political reality. When the Hop was proposed, part of the plan was to close off a town street to accommodate the structure's expansive design. Stanfill says the citizens of Hanover were concerned about this plan. The ensuing discussion led to the implicit understanding that the Hop would be a community facility in which Hanover would hold town meetings and other important functions.

Then, there is the fact that the Center houses four theaters and concert halls, each used for a different purpose.

Spaulding Auditorium with its 899 seats serves as a concert hall (it has a shell, but no fly or wing space); it is also used as a film theater and as the site for large academic classes, visiting lecturers, and occasions of moment on campus. Many of the events of the Hopkins Center's "imported performance season" take place in Spaulding.

Next in size is the 470-seat Center Theater, with all the accoutrements of a well-equipped stage house. Dance, drama, and musical performances are produced or presented here.

The Warner Bentley Theater is a flexible, black-box theater that can be set up as a proscenium, thrust, or in-the-round configuration. Depending on the stage setting, the capacity ranges from 100 to 250. This is an intimate space that allows for maximum experimentation, and enables performers and audience to communicate.

Completing the array is the Faulkner Recital Hall, part of the Music Department, which regularly provides recitals by students, faculty, and guest artists.

The Hopkins Center controls the scheduling of three of the four theaters, excluding Faulkner Recital Hall, which is scheduled by the Music Department. With this choice of spaces, the Center has a great deal of flexibility in selecting the appropriate theater for each of the 70 or more performances it presents annually.

In many academic institutions, the presenter has to plead for space or enter into complex negotiations for a date in halls that are considered academic spaces and are controlled by departments of music or theater. But the executive director of the Hopkins Center also

> The Hopkins Center belies the notions that the arts at an Ivy League college are the province of a privileged few.

functions as the fine arts dean—a unique feature of Dartmouth's administrative structure.

This structure is in place because Warner Bentley set the precedent. At the opening of the Hopkins Center, Bentley unequivocally expressed its underlying mission:

"In the past at Dartmouth, one hand of art has never known what the other hand was doing," he said. "In the Hopkins Center, we cannot escape each other, even if we should want to. We will have here for the first time the opportunity to show our students how the arts complement each other and have affected our culture since the beginning of history." That vision prevails today.

The other person whose presence is felt even years after his retirement is John Sloan Dickey, president of the college from 1945 until 1970. Stanfill says Dickey was passionate about the issue of access. "I can imagine him in all those early meetings about the Hopkins Center, wanting that ease of access by eliminating physical barriers," he says. "I can imagine his enthusiastic response to the technical director of the building, who suggested that the student mailboxes be placed in the building. But for him, issues of access also were symbolic, access in the sense of openness. He wanted everything that went on at the Hop to mean more availability."

Stanfill built a staff of senior program directors that takes the mission of the Center as seriously today as Warner Bentley and the first staff did in 1962. Stanfill now is president of the Wolf Trap Foundation in Vienna, Virginia, and several staff members have moved on since his departure. But at the Hopkins Center, nothing is stagnant.

The Presenting Program

The Hopkins Center's so-called "imported" events speak to the Dartmouth tradition of education beyond the classroom. Since 1986, the director of programs and operations—the official title for the presenter—is Colleen Jennings-Roggensack, who has been in the field of presenting for more than 10 years.

She has a firm hold on her own vision as a presenter, and is committed to cultural diversity and contemporary art. Jennings-Roggensack has extraordinary energy and enthusiasm. In a sense, she is a cheerleader for the arts. The image does not affront her, since she recognizes that element in her own personality. "I think that part of cheerleading for the arts is saying to the public, 'There is wonderful stuff out there that you may not understand right away, but it deserves to be experienced—and I am going to offer it to you.' "

When she organizes the annual series of imported events for the Center's performing arts season, her style is to develop programming around themes—sometimes encompassing an entire season, sometimes ad hoc. In 1988-89, for example, she created a season around the theme "Westward Oh!," bringing to New England a representative sample of the full range of artistic expression from the western United States. The programs included performances of classical music and ballet, contemporary music and dance, and traditional expressions of Hispanic Americans, native Americans, and cowboys.

Jennings-Roggensack did not simply put the work before the public and expect it all to be crystal clear. Instead, she made a point of presenting it in a context that enabled the public to understand and appreciate it. On the day before one performance, for example, the poets and musicians of the group Cowboy Poets and Horse Sense participated in panel discussions that explored the impetus for the songs and poems of ranch people, and traced the development of the work. Several of the "Westward Oh!" events featured pre-performance "bull sessions" that introduced the audience to significant aspects of the evening's program.

Jennings-Roggensack also schedules some smaller series programs within the Hopkins Center season. In 1988–89, they included a jazz program of four events with Billy Taylor and Ramsey Lewis, George Russell and the Living Time Orchestra, Dartmouth's own Barbary Coast Jazz Ensemble with special guest Max Roach, and a trio consisting of Anthony Davis, James Newton, and Abdul Wadud. There also was a Canadian miniseries with two French-Canadian artists—I Musici de Montreal, and pianist Louis Lortie.

Above and beyond her responsibilities for the imported events, Jennings-Roggensack schedules and coordinates the performances of Dartmouth's 10 student and student/community ensembles. As if to illustrate the Center's central role at Dartmouth, these ensembles are referred to as the Hopkins Center Instrumental and Vocal Ensembles.

Quartet-in-Residence

Jennings-Roggensack believes in developing an audience for ensembles that are presented every year in concerts and residency programs, so that a relationship between the community and the artists evolves. A good illustration is Dartmouth's commitment to a quartet-in-residence.

In 1974, at the invitation of then-director Peter Smith, the Concord String Quartet became the Hopkins Center's first quartet-in-residence. The Concord was formed in 1971, won the coveted Naumburg Foundation Chamber Music Award that same year, and was committed to the performance and commissioning of contemporary works. Despite the quartet's impressive beginnings, it was not well known in 1974. But as Smith observed in a fall 1987 article in *Chamber Music* magazine, the Concord was chosen primarily for its "refreshing adventurousness." The choice also speaks volumes about the adventurousness of the Hopkins Center, to take a chance on a young group whose reputation was still very much in formation.

The Concord's residency was a tremendous success. When it disbanded at the end of the 1986–87 season, the quartet had developed a respected place for itself not only at the college and in the hearts of people in the community, but also in North America and around the world.

A natural impulse for Dartmouth would have been to replace the Concord with another quartet at the same level—a world-class ensemble with a full touring season of performances. Instead, Stanfill decided to reassert the original philosophy of the residency by encouraging new and young quartets to apply for the position.

"I believe very strongly that an organization like the Hopkins Center has to give back to the arts," he says. "To go to the young quartet again was to give those individuals that kind of opportunity. There is also an excitement about a young quartet, an energy and a kind of edge to their playing that you will not find in a long-established ensemble."

The search committee sifted through 27 applications for the position. It decided on the Franciscan String Quartet, which had won the Banff International String Quartet Competition in 1986, and the 1987 Press Prize at Evian, France. The all-female quartet members are graduates of the San Francisco Conservatory of Music, where the group was formed. The group was the conservatory's Fellowship Quartet until it won the Wardwell Fellowship at Yale University to study with the Tokyo Quartet.

The group has been at Dartmouth since the 1987–88 season, occupying the same studio and teaching some of the same students as did the Concord. Members Wendy Sharp and Julie Kim, violinists; Marcia Cassidy, violist; and Margery Hwang, cellist, say their selection as quartet-in-residence was a dream come true. They say that almost every string quartet is looking for a college at which to base itself so as to combine touring with teaching.

Each season, the Franciscans play four formal concerts at Dartmouth. For their first performance at the Hopkins Center in 1987, they played for an audience of 700 in Spaulding Auditorium. They undoubtedly will build a large and loyal following as the community becomes better acquainted with them.

The Hopkins Center remains committed to commissioning works for this quartet, as it did for the Concord. In their first season, the Franciscans performed the world premiere of a quartet by Charles Wuorinan, which Dartmouth had commissioned for the Concord before it disbanded. Other young composers with whom the quartet has worked are Ned Rorem, Gerald Cohen, Paul Moravec, David Evan Jones, and George Tsontokis.

Cultural Diversity

Cultural diversity is a pressing issue at Dartmouth. An old and established Ivy League college, it sometimes is assumed to be a conservative institution, one that is not at the vanguard of progressive race relations. Recent, highly-publicized campus incidents might seem to support this assumption.

As a Black woman, Colleen Jennings-Roggensack often is confronted with questions from friends and from colleagues in the field about why she is at Dartmouth. Her quick reply is, "The college is going through a tough time now. It is trying to say, not only to itself but also to the greater academic community, 'We are not a conservative, racist institution.' You see that in our student body makeup, in our curriculum, in our programs, and in the administrative personnel. Why have I chosen to come to Republican heaven? Because I am needed here, even more so than I would be needed anyplace else. Dartmouth needs people who represent other ideas and viewpoints."

Toward this end, she has aggressively programmed events from a wide cultural universe. She acknowledges that there was some diverse programming in the past, but Black artists usually were presented only during Black History Month, and Hispanic artists only during Hispanic Heritage Week. There was no integrated approach that asserted that "Art comes in all shapes, sizes, and colors. Art by Black artists does not just happen in February."

In the 1987–88 and 1988–89 seasons, the community saw and experienced Native American, African-American, Hispanic, African, and Asian artists and companies. These were integrated into the season, not ghettoized from the rest of the programming, so that their value to the total presenting program was clear.

Jennings-Roggensack also is passionate about presenting challenging contemporary work and international work. Through her efforts and insistence, the Hopkins Center was one of just two organizations in the United States to present French choreographer Daniel Larrieu's *Waterproof*, otherwise known as "the swimming pool piece." The setting required a swimming pool, underwater lights, film and slide projection, and a complex sound setup with underwater speakers. Few presenters had the facilities or money to undertake such an unusual venture—or the willingness to take the chance.

Artistic direction is important to her. She sees her role at the Hopkins Center as that of the artistic director of her season, and she accepted Shelton Stanfill's offer of the position only when he assured her that he would support her desire to function this way.

"Over the last 10 years, I have developed my own personal resources and my own taste," she says. "My vision has broadened in the way I look for work to be presented. I used to think of the booking conference as my major avenue for looking at, knowing about, and booking work. I now turn to many other avenues—including little festivals, international work, and American traditional work—to reach artists who are out of the artist management mainstream. The core of my vision has always been to broaden my own horizons personally, and to broaden the horizons of my audiences."

Jennings-Roggensack says she sees a fair number of people who regard the role of a presenter as "a janitor or custodian. Presenters have to have a passion for the work they see that makes them want to present it to their public. It is philosophically and practically important to acknowledge that presenting the arts goes beyond the mechanics of how to put on a show. You cannot teach passion. That comes from inside. But you can plant a seed and hope that passion will spring from that seed.

"There are times when I sit in the theater, when the lights are dark and the house is full, and something wonderful happens on stage," she says. "Sometimes I start crying. I don't know if I am crying because the art is so beautiful, or because all these people are seeing it, or if it's a combination of those things. But it's a very passionate thing to sit in your theater and think that people are seeing or hearing something wonderful together. I have to think that there are many presenters out there who share the same kinds of feelings."

The Film Program

Bill Pence, director of the Hopkins Center Film Program, is another senior staff member with a passion for his work; his life revolves around film, filmmakers, and film programming. As the founder and director of the annual Telluride Film Festival in Colorado, Pence brings to his position at Dartmouth a lifetime of experience and commitment.

Stanfill, who hired Pence, calls him "one of the best film people in the country, first class. Bill will stay at Dartmouth only if he can do the things that he wants to do, the things that he feels are important to the film program here." In order to get Pence to accept the job, Stanfill had to expand the program both in quantity and quality, and to provide a budget that would enable this expansion.

Pence describes himself as "a bit of a maverick. What excites me is going against the grain, because that's what creates the sparks that make life interesting and worth living." He has found at the Hopkins Center a unique opportunity to create programs that combine the screening of films with a series of special guests—actors, actresses, and directors—who talk with students, faculty, and people in the community about their films and their careers. He sees film as an intellectual medium that provides a way to explore issues.

The film program consists of at least four films a week, not including specials, sneak previews, and marathons. The Dartmouth Film Society, the organization behind the campus film program, has been in existence since 1949. The Film

Society shows films in the Spaulding Auditorium, which has high-quality projection equipment, a large screen, and a Dolby stereo system. The viewing experience there is far different from what the public has grown to expect from the multi-screen, shopping mall type of movie theater.

Each semester, an outstanding person in film receives the Dartmouth Film Award. Recipients have included Lillian Gish, Michael Powell, Chuck Jones, Les Blank, Robert Wise, Teri Garr, Dusan Makavejev, Ray Harryhausen, Louis Malle, Werner Herzog, Athol Fugard, Marcel Ophuls, Andrei Tarkovsky, Robert Redford, Nagisa Oshima, Cab Calloway and Liv Ullman.

> "It's a very passionate thing to sit in your theater and think that people are seeing or hearing something wonderful together."

As in other areas at the Hopkins Center, there is a blending of purpose between the academic and the extracurricular. The Dartmouth Film Society and the Film Studies Program complement each other for the college and the community beyond. The Film Studies Program, while not a film production school, places film in the context of liberal arts studies, exploring its historic and aesthetic character as well as its technical side.

Pence brings his years of experience, serious purpose, and commitment to the film exhibition program. Like Colleen Jennings-Roggensack, he finds his motivating factors to be his engagement with his field and his artistic vision. "I have to say this with humility, but I think that we become artists ourselves. Programming is not primarily an economic decision. Rather, it is what works, what is the most beautiful, most exciting, most thrilling, most serendipitous . . . what is the combination that seems to fly. I feel that I have to take that responsibility. Otherwise, my work could be done with a computer."

Part of his job is to achieve a balance between the films the public wants and the tougher, more subtle and more challenging films. The balance is very important, Pence says. "You can't just be going public with your own enthusiasms, or you may be playing to empty theaters."

The more popular films also may provide a bridge to other Hopkins Center programming, he believes.

"Film gets them into the building and then they get a feeling for the vitality of what is going on inside. They might take a chance on a Dartmouth Players production, or a Franciscan Quartet concert, or something else. Film is one of the great entryways into the Hopkins Center."

Arts Education Services

Passion and fervor also are in ample supply in the person of Mary Sue Glosser, former curator of arts education services. While she was in the job, her intense commitment to arts education was matched by her dedication to the area's children and teachers. (She left the post in 1988 to become director of arts education at the Art Institute of Chicago.)

Glosser says she was always touched when she saw a child become fully involved in or changed by an experience at the Hopkins Center. She is keenly aware that the child might never have had such an experience were it not for the Center's programs, and she has a rich repertoire of stories showing how the arts education program has opened doors for children and their teachers.

The Hopkins Center describes the programs of the Department of Arts Education Services, now in its 16th year, as central to its mission as a regional arts center and a resource for the region. The idea is to involve educators, regional artists, and students in a year-long performance program that examines the arts through experience. To that end, the Center offers a number of educational programs to the teachers and school children in the area. More than 30,000 students in 120 schools throughout Vermont and New Hampshire are served by performances and workshops.

Glosser says the program was based on the celebrated model of the Lincoln Center Institute, an artist-based, teacher-student program of aesthetic education. The concepts and ideas were modified to suit the needs of New Hampshire's rural Upper Valley.

"The idea was to set up a program here that would be so tight that it would live forever at the Hopkins Center," Glosser says. "Sometimes, arts education programs are personality-based, and I don't think they should be. They should be learner-based—based on where you are and who you're working with.

"In this area, the learner varies from the sophisticated child in Hanover who has traveled to China and may have three computers at home, to the rural kid who has never been to any city, even to Hanover."

She says the Hopkins Center decided also to focus on teacher education, because "If the teachers were involved, then the kids would obviously get more out of the experience."

And how the teachers have responded! The stories come one after another about the extraordinary teachers in some of the rural communities. "Did you know that here in these mountains, there are still some one- or two-room schoolhouses? Some of these people are islands out there," Glosser says. "It's touching when we are able to bring these islands together for a magical encounter in the Hopkins Center. The institute gives them that energy to take back and try to make the arts happen on a more modest scale in their own schools. This holds them over until they can get back here for the next round."

Glosser says that aesthetic education empowers the learner. "When they begin to understand the difference between a slide and a real painting, or a tape and an orchestra, they want the painting and the orchestra. They will do what they must to see the painting or hear the orchestra again. We can help teach these children how to get themselves to the arts over a lifetime. The arts are not always going to come to them. That's what it's all about."

Marketing the Arts in Rural New England

John Hall was director of communications at the Hopkins Center from 1986 to 1988, when he left to publish a newspaper in his native upper Midwest. While he was at Dartmouth, Hall managed a sizable department consisting of media relations, marketing, graphic design and the box office. He and his staff worked as a team on the creative aspects of promoting and publicizing the season and individual events.

One of his biggest challenges was to draw attendance from a sparsely populated rural area to the Hopkins Center's array of performances. "We have to be sensitive to the many different lifestyles in this area of New Hampshire, and over the state line in Vermont," he says. "This is a small community, and the public expects a great deal of care, attention, and service. Trust also is extraordinarily important. We're introducing people to artists and ensembles they've never heard of before. They have to trust us, and what we say they're going to see has to match or exceed their expectations. Building trust starts with copywriting, goes to working with newspapers and developing the general graphic image, and extends to how we treat people at the box office."

Beyond the Upper Valley, there has been interest and attendance from as far afield as Burlington, Vermont (150 miles away), Boston (100 miles), and Montreal (180 miles). People typically travel to Hanover when the Hopkins Center becomes the only presenter beyond New York offering an event of exceptional merit. Hall says the local media also show interest when such an event takes place.

Hall worked equally hard to develop the student audience, which represents approximately 35 percent of the total. Students are drawn most to events that have student performers—the chorus, orchestra, players, dance performances, and jazz bands. These events are all part of the Center's regular season.

Fundraising

An important part of Shelton g Stanfill's responsibilities when he arrived at Dartmouth was managing a major fundraising campaign, which had been underway since 1978, to expand the Center's facilities and to build the Hood Museum of Art. He raised $16 million toward that campaign.

Stanfill describes Dartmouth's well-oiled fundraising process: "Dartmouth has incredibly loyal alumni who expect to be asked for money. In any kind of fundraising we do—whether business, corporate, foundation or family—there is almost always some connection to Dartmouth."

The gala program celebrating the Hopkins Center's 25th anniversary lists 36 endowment funds. Stanfill says that the campaign on which he worked raised a total of $21 million in 10 years. He calls the effort, although time-consuming and requiring focused attention, surprisingly enjoyable. "No one was ever shocked that I asked them for money," he says. "They all understand that this is the way Dartmouth operates, and the college needs the money. For most of them, their regard for the college is high enough from their memory of it—even if they have differences with the current administration—that they want to be asked to contribute. I don't think that I could go anywhere again and have such an easy time of it in terms of development."

Pride and Priesthood in Academia

Presenting organizations within institutions of higher learning have unique challenges. The most prevalent is the tension between presenters and the related academic departments. Those tensions frequently manifest themselves as conflicts over access to academic facilities, and over who influences and controls the programming. Often, there is friction about competing curricular and noncurricular issues.

Tensions may arise as a result of the Hopkins Center's physical setup, where the curricular and noncurricular spaces intersect and intermingle. What's more, the fact that the directors of student groups like the jazz band and the film society all report to the Hopkins Center executive director, rather than to the head of the corresponding academic departments, has surely created some raw feelings among academic staff.

Stanfill is frank in expressing his view of the difficulties that result from this type of arrangement. "It is a matter of pride and self-respect," he says of the tension. "For some of the faculty, it is inconceivable that somebody who does not have a Ph.D. might be better at selecting what will be included on a music presenting program than they would be. An exaggerated analogy would be the English Department saying that no book in English can be in the library unless that department has passed on it. It is a matter of pride and of priesthood, in a way.

"For example, I had a faculty member who would not go to hear an artist-in-residence whom he had to review for a faculty appointment because the pianist was performing nothing but Bach, and the faculty member believed that Bach should not be played on the piano. When you encounter something like that, you cannot argue about their expertise or knowledge, but the end that you're after is so different that it's impossible to mesh the points of view.

"The real issue," Stanfill says, "is not so much the particular decision as who is making the decision, or where the prerogative should lie. The question for the institution then is, 'Does music belong to everybody?' Of course it does, because it is a part of all of our lives and culture. Is there an institutional role to serve broader interests as opposed to the particular and parochial interests of a department and its students? I think there is."

Despite any discontent that academic faculty may feel about the way that artistic decisions are made, members of Dartmouth's senior administration say the Hopkins Center is one of the best tools they have to recruit new and high-quality faculty in all academic disciplines. Others in the community feel that Hopkins Center programming provides arts offerings unparalleled for a rural area. Others remark on the important role the Center plays in educating local children in the arts.

Peter Robbie, the director of the Center's design workshops, cites part of what makes the Center unique and extraordinary. "The basic premise of a small liberal arts college is the education of complete individuals, individuals who see

learning as a continuum rather than a collection of facts or little bits of things,"
he says. "In the Hopkins Center, we have a living example of what can happen if
you are patient enough and smart enough to put together teams of people.

"I think the students learn a great deal more about the arts in general from
having access to all of them here in one building than they ever would if each of
the departments and programs was separated."

Robbie's statement perhaps should be enlarged. The Hopkins Center experience is unique because of the breadth of its vision within the college and the
community. Members of the staff operate each day with a sense of responsibility
for the most basic integration of the arts into the lives of people throughout the
region. They care about the rural community, and they try to open the doors to
the arts.

They maintain a welcoming atmosphere for those arriving to attend an event,
but they aren't afraid to challenge audiences with unusual or provocative work.

Most important, the staff thinks about the arts, and they are passionate,
engaged, and enthusiastic. They go public with their enthusiasms, giving the community a rich environment in which the arts strengthen the quality of life. This is
a stunning achievement.

The Myrna Loy Theater, circa 1920

10 "Meet You at the Myrna Loy!"

Traveling around Helena, Montana, with Arnie Malina is an experience that has many starts and stops, many interruptions. Practically everyone in this town of 25,000 people knows him—and they all have something to say to him.

On the other hand, Arnie—as he is called by everyone he encounters—does a lot of talking himself, about the Helena Film Society/Series for the Performing Arts. He is eager to hear what people think, learn from their reactions, solicit their ideas, and try out his own. He is a walking public relations agent for the organization that he and two others founded 13 years ago, and that he has lovingly directed ever since.

The history of the organization is his personal history. In 1974, Malina arrived in Helena from the University of Colorado-Boulder to write his dissertation in English literature. He and his wife, Alexandra Swaney, lived rent-free in a small cabin outside of town.

After receiving his Ph.D., he went to work for the state Commission on Local Government as a public information officer. Eventually, he became frustrated with the state bureaucracy, but he liked living in Helena. The only problem, he says, was there was nothing to do there. Having grown up in New York City, one of the things he missed most was being able to see a wide range of films. The four commercial theaters in town showed mostly commercially-popular fare such as Walt Disney classics and teen-age exploitation films.

Scott Hibbard, immediate past president of the Film Society/Series for the Performing Arts, says that anyone who looks at a map can see how long it takes to get to Helena and how far it is from other places. The sense of isolation is an accepted part of the life of Montana, both because of the location of the state and because the local industry consists of agriculture, logging and mining.

Hibbard, who comes from a pioneer ranching family of German immigrants who settled in the Helena area in the late 1860s, says that his great-grandfather and one of his great-uncles walked beside a wagon train from St. Joseph, Missouri to Montana. These early pioneers brought with them a set of expectations about what a community should offer its citizens, and more recent settlers like Malina have continued the tradition.

In late 1975, Malina, Swaney, and a friend began to brainstorm about starting a society that would show high-quality films. "We had a great time fantasizing about how we would program the series," Malina says, "what double bills we would put together, and so forth. At that point, we just decided to do it. Everything began within the next six months."

They found a place on the second story of 9 Placer, off Last Chance Gulch in downtown Helena. With a $6,000 investment, they located 88 theater seats, constructed a tiered structure on which to install them and acquired 16 mm projection equipment and a screen. They called the facility the Second Story Cinema.

The programming philosophy was eclectic from the beginning. They presented diverse genres, including foreign films, American independents, cult classics, documentaries, and silent films, sometimes with live piano accompaniment. They also presented a series of informal, illustrated talks before each film.

Malina's partners soon moved on to other projects, and he was on his own. He began to present local artists—poetry readings first, then plays and a playwrights' competition. His first touring event was *Orlando, Orlando*, a theater piece with music and words based on the Virginia Woolf novel, created and performed by the 10-member Illusion Theater from Minneapolis.

"In those days," Malina says, "we did a lot of going up and down the street. To anyone we sort of knew, we would say, 'Hey, are you coming to this, are you coming to that?' We called people on the telephone and tried to get them to help spread the word. We put up posters all over town." He was able to get about 250 people to attend *Orlando, Orlando*, held in the high school auditorium. "I was disappointed," Malina remembers, "but the performers were amazed. And so I learned about the poverty of audiences elsewhere."

Two years after the Helena Film Society was up and running, the performing arts director of the Montana Arts Council encouraged Malina to present the Portland Dance Theater. A modern dance company had never performed in Helena, Malina says, so he took a chance. He managed to round up a huge audience.

"I loved the performance," he says, "and I assumed that everybody did. I was a bit naive, because everybody did *not* love it. My relationship with my audience was self-righteous. To me, doing this stuff was the most important thing in the world, and I didn't understand that people had other interests, other priorities, or just didn't care."

Over the next several years two things happened. Malina came to understand that not everyone in the community was as compelled as he by the work that the

Helena Film Society was presenting. On the other hand, because the organization was consistently offering exciting events, it began to gather more and more interest and support.

The Montana Arts Council then invited the film society to participate in the Western States Arts Foundation's Pilot Subscription Series project, which made funds available to a few presenters to put together subscription series. Helena and Billings were the only two communities in Montana to be included. The 1979–80 season marked the beginning of the first "official" Helena Series for the Performing Arts, featuring four companies from the West. In addition to presenting film programs at the movie house, the Society rented the 800-seat auditorium at the city's middle school, and at the 2,000-seat Civic Center for season programming.

The series had about 500 subscribers in its first season. There was no marketing plan. "We just corralled people at films and got them to subscribe," Malina says. The first subscription of four events sold for $20 or less. A decade later, there are 13 events annually, selling for $108.

Building the Montana Performing Arts Consortium

As the Helena Film Society/Series for the Performing Arts embarked on planning its second series, Malina became aware of exactly how isolated Helena really was. He wanted to bring in events from beyond the West, but no tour was just "passing through" Helena on the way to someplace else.

It didn't take him long to recognize, as had presenters in other western states, that an alliance of Montana presenters would provide a block of dates that would be far more enticing for a tour than a single performance. It also would be economical for both presenters and touring artists. When Malina began trying to build an alliance with his colleagues, he discovered that they saw each other as competitors and did not want to present the same events. But he persevered, and the result was the Montana Performing Arts Consortium.

As a result, Montana presenters have been able to include dance companies and some headline-name performers—both mainstream and avant-garde—that they never could have considered without the cooperative efforts of the consortium. They have saved money and upgraded the quality of the events they provide for their audiences. Five or six presenters actively take part in the major consortium tours; some 80 other presenters in various communities throughout the state occasionally take advantage of the block-booking opportunities.

As president of the consortium, Malina tends to generate many of the programming ideas and puts the tours together. Bill Pratt, director of organizational services for the Montana Arts Council, says Malina's strong personal style and propensity to work long and hard hours is sometimes a problem with the other consortium participants, many of whom are volunteers.

"He has mellowed in the past few years," Pratt says, "and seems to have found a more collaborative working style. Occasionally, there is a clash of ideas, but the controversies and conflicts have been healthy. The consortium has become an important resource for other states in the region."

The Challenge of Producing Events in Helena

In 1988, the organization sponsored a three-day residency with the California E.A.R. Unit, a nine-member group from the Los Angeles area that performs contemporary music. The Helena Film Society/Series for the Performing Arts was the only presenter in Montana willing to take the significant financial, logistical and artistic risk to expose its community to the experience.

The E.A.R. Unit is a young group, not well known, that performs music that is difficult to embrace on first hearing. Most of it was composed after 1950, with a few exceptions; therefore, it is unfamiliar except to a few contemporary music cognoscenti. The group tries hard to acquaint its audiences with this music. Their presence in Helena attests to Malina's commitment to education, and his eagerness to make the arts accessible.

The challenge to the organization was considerable from the technical standpoint alone. It had to acquire two marimbas, one cello, two nine-foot grand pianos and an enormous sound system. In addition, it had to obtain housing for the nine musicians. Malina tries to have services and equipment donated, but the organization picks up the tab when volunteers are not available or equipment must be rented. (He now is paying more for technical support than he did for the entire year's artists' fees when he began the series in 1979.)

One of the most impressive events of the E.A.R. Unit's residency was an interactive concert for 2,000 fourth- and fifth-graders at the Helena Civic Center. The Helena Capital High School Orchestra opened the program with Schubert's *Rosemunde* overture, giving a remarkably good performance that showed careful preparation by the conductor and his students.

Still, they did exhibit the tentativeness typical of young musicians. And as they played, it was obvious that the bows for almost all the string instruments had barely any hair on them. What hair there was hung loose, so that the students were practically playing on the wood of their bows. It must be inconvenient and expensive to have the bows rehaired during the school year; indeed, there might be no instrument dealer in Helena who does that kind of work. It was striking how dedicated these students were, to perform so ably under the circumstances.

After the overture, the California E.A.R. Unit made its entrance with Steve Reich's *Clapping Music*, a rhythmic contrapuntal dialog between two clapping musicians. With this, the Unit began its explanation of the elements that are the building blocks of music: rhythm, melody and harmony. This served as a fitting introduction to the children's concert. The musicians invited four student volunteers to join them; together, using symbols painted on posters, they improvised a piece for full orchestra. It had shape, rhythm, dynamics, drama and excitement. All of a sudden, the orchestra had lost its tentativeness. It sounded like a professional group, not a student ensemble.

Other residency events included a fairly technical lecture-demonstration. Composers Arthur Jarvinen and Rand Steiger spoke about the music—their own and other composers'—that the group would perform the next evening. They answered questions and played pieces or parts of pieces with members of the Unit.

Later, the group reassembled in the bar of the Park Plaza Hotel, and the Unit performed Terry Riley's *In C*, one of the seminal works of the minimalist school. The fact that Malina held this event in a bar added another off-beat element to the experience. People were encouraged to order drinks and enjoy the evening. One of them said, "This bar will never be the same!"

> The organization has chosen to develop an audience and to trust their intelligence, taste, and receptiveness to the unfamiliar.

The next morning, Unit members gave instrumental classes to Helena public school students; that evening, the full-length concert was held at the middle school with more than 400 people attending. The program consisted of seven works—compositions of Arthur Jarvinen, Michael Torke, Elliott Carter, Sylvano Bussotti, Rand Steiger, John Bergamo and Morton Subotnick. (The Bussotti piece was composed in 1959, but the rest are post-1981.) In one work for prepared piano, three of the musicians climbed into and underneath the instrument to produce all the required effects. Jarvinen, who did most of the performing underneath the piano, wore satin boxing shorts with high-top sneakers.

In the audience, wild enthusiasm was mixed with stunned puzzlement. Some people told Malina it was the only kind of event he should ever program. Others felt just the opposite.

Meanwhile, Rand Steiger says the Helena experience was wonderful for the California E.A.R. Unit. "You might think that a repertoire such as ours doesn't reach people in a town like Helena, but you can see that it does. There are kids and people here who have never heard this kind of music, but because of that they approach it with an open mind. Whenever we do a residency like this, we always wind up talking to a handful of people who then pump us for all the information we have as to where they can hear this music, get the recordings of it or the printed music itself. For me, personally, that's the best part about doing a residency—spreading the word on this other way of thinking about music."

Programming Philosophy

From his early forays into presenting the performing arts, Malina realized that presenting live events on a regular basis would require careful thought. Everything had consequences for the community's image of the organization.

But this awareness did not force him into a cautious, no-risk programming stance. Instead, he chose to go another route: to develop his audience and to trust their intelligence, taste, and receptiveness to the unfamiliar. "I decided that I would present a wide range of events," Malina says. "Some would make people uncomfortable. There would also be events they would love that would coax them into seeing new expressions with which they might be unfamiliar. Throughout, I would call people to get their thoughts and reactions." As a result, people came to trust Malina and the organization.

"Being a presenter is presenting the unexpected," he continues. "To me, the importance of presenting is that you reach people, you entertain them, you get them together, you educate them, you give them something to think about, you enrich their lives, you get them to be tolerant. To me, getting an audience to accept things they're not familiar with is an aesthetic that expands their lives. Ultimately, it should expand their lives to everything, open them up not just to art, but to other people and ideas that are unusual or unfamiliar as well."

Malina concedes the importance of balance, and he carefully plans each season with a combination of the familiar and the unfamiliar, the classic and the contemporary, pieces representative of the full spectrum of American culture and international events representing other cultures. He has been willing to take a chance on a number of dance and music ensembles—including the Kronos Quartet, the Philip Glass Ensemble, and the Merce Cunningham Dance Company—offering work totally unfamiliar to audiences long before some larger presenters in major cities have done so.

Malina also says an important part of his organization's mission is to "enrich people's lives with a variety of cultural events in media, performing, and literary arts that have great cultural diversity—because we're in a community that does not have cultural diversity."

The series also has sought to build an international perspective. This impressive diversity of events is even more significant because Malina, his staff and board have built the kind of community interest that supports both quality and quantity of programming in a small, isolated city. He has found a felicitous balance between headliners, challenging contemporary events and performances of mainstream interest, while offering a wide and culturally-diverse spectrum of artists.

Steve Browning, President of the Helena Film Society/Series for the Performing Arts, says, "Part of the success of this organization is the trust that the community has in the programming." There seems to be an understanding that not everyone will like everything that is presented, but that cultural life in the state's capital city would stagnate unless the community is asked to stretch a little.

From Jail to Art Center

A measure of the organization's recent growth and development is the evolution of what has become its single most challenging, expensive and expansive project: converting the 1891 Lewis and Clark County Jail into a performing arts center.

The idea of finding or building a new, more inviting facility had been on Malina's mind for some time, but he had been unable to locate a space. Then, about a year before the county jail was to be phased out in favor of a newer facility, Malina and board members Al Lundborg and Martin Holt—who later became chairman of the building committee—went to look at the space.

In an article in the organization's newsletter, *Front Row Center*, Holt wrote of his excitement at sensing that "It would be possible to turn this massive stone building, associated for nearly a century with darkness and pain, into an arts center that would strive to free the spirit."

Malina shared Holt's enthusiasm for the jail's potential. He also realized that the building could be more than just a new home for the Second Story Cinema. It could be the well-equipped, comfortable, and intimate performance space that Helena seriously needed. He felt that many diverse events could be scheduled in the converted two-story, 28-foot-high cell block. He also wanted to build the right kind of performance space to make them eligible to become a part of the National Performance Network. Finally, Malina felt that preserving the jail would generate community excitement and broaden the project beyond the interests of his own organization.

The first step was a feasibility study, from which developed a list of "gate-keepers" in the community—those with money, power, and influence whose support or lack of it could make or break the project. Some people responded to the call for help; others did not. It was a long, slow, and painful process, but Malina used it to develop the board of directors into a committed working body that knew its way around the community well enough to garner support.

The next step was to deal with Lewis and Clark County, which owned the building. Public hearings were held, and the organization eventually signed a lease for one dollar a year.

When the architectural master plan and construction budget were completed, the price tag on the project was $1.1 million (it since has become $1.6 million). When the building has its grand opening in January of 1991, the renovated space will house a 230-seat main auditorium with a 38-foot-wide proscenium opening and a 44-foot depth; Cinema II, an 80-seat movie theater that will replace the Second Story Cinema; a conference room; staff offices; lighting control and projection rooms; a video editing suite; classroom space; and an atrium courtyard with concession areas.

As appealing as the plans for the jail sound, $1.6 million is a substantial sum to raise in Helena. Montana itself is in an economic depression. The bedrock industries of the state's economy—mining, ranching, and farming—have all come on hard times. Montana is the only state that is losing population. Helena, the capital, is a government town, and government workers have not had a salary increase in more than three years. There are no major foundations or corporations in the state.

The state's three major industries by their nature require that workers spend most of their time away from the main population centers, Scott Hibbard says. "Work takes place outdoors, in very harsh elements, during winters that are nasty and long. It requires some real backbone on the part of people who are able to tough it out and stay here. The feeling of community is very important to promote a sense of togetherness, of associating with your kinfolk." Residents have an investment in trying to make Helena a better place to live.

Because this desire is so strong, the board decided to proceed despite negative fundraising forecasts, confident that the project was compelling enough to succeed. Monies from two government sources primed the pump. The organization received a $75,000 advancement grant, requiring a three-to-one match, from the National Endowment for the Arts; and a $50,000 cultural and aesthetic project grant from the Montana Coal Tax Trust Fund.

When the consultant who did the feasibility study suggested that board members donate an aggregate of $75,000, Malina thought

> ## "Being a presenter is presenting the unexpected."

the consultant was crazy. The most that he had ever raised from the entire board was $4,000 a year. But in the end, the 21-member board contributed $118,000.

In 1987, with more than $200,000 raised, it was time to approach foundations and corporations. Even though there are no foundations or corporations particularly associated with Montana, the fundraising committee, with the help of the staff, developed a small but targeted regional and national list of potential donors.

The board also enlisted the support of an ally whose interest in the project as an important community venture could substantially aid the fundraising effort—U.S. Sen. Max Baucus. He had grown up in Helena, was interested in the arts, had attended Helena Film Society events, and his mother served on the board.

Baucus accompanied Browning to New York to visit Philip Morris Companies Inc., renowned for its support of the arts. The company sent its regional manager for governmental affairs to look at the jail and explore the plan with Malina. The Philip Morris Company decided to make its first major grant in the state of Montana to the Helena Film Society/Series for the Performing Arts for $100,000.

Another early grant came from the Steele-Reese Foundation, based in New York with an office in Carmen, Idaho. The foundation is interested in projects and organizations in rural areas, but it seemed at first that Helena was not rural enough to be considered. The foundation sent a representative to meet with Malina, visit the jail, attend a sold-out showing of an Australian film and have dinner with the board. Before she left the next day, the representative told Malina that the foundation would allocate $100,000 to the project.

For any organization, under any circumstances, either of these grants would be a thrill to receive. Given the peculiar circumstances at work in Montana, each one was a veritable triumph. Every grant or contribution thereafter raised the project's credibility with the community and with each fundraising prospect that was approached. Soon after the first $400,000 was raised, Shell Oil, U.S. West (Mountain Bell), the Ruth and Vernon Taylor Foundation, and the John D. and Catherine T. MacArthur Foundation all made donations.

In June 1988, the organization received the best news yet. The Michigan-based Kresge Foundation had awarded a $150,000 challenge grant that required the balance of the budget to be raised by June, 1990. The Murdoch Foundation of Vancouver, Washington awarded another $150,000 as a challenge grant. The Burlington Northern Foundation of Seattle followed with a donation of $100,000.

One startling statistic is that $600,000 in capital funds was raised in Helena from individuals, including the $118,000 in contributions from the board. Helena's citizens also contributed another $300,000 for an endowment fund. After touring the jail, two donors contributed substantial sums that no one knew they were capable of giving. Steve Browning says the organization's exemplary record contributed to the success of the fundraising efforts. "We're not proposing a whole new idea," he says of the project. "Rather, it is a continuation and expansion of an organization with a strong history."

Former Montana Gov. Ted Schwinden is another enthusiast for the jail conversion. He likes to talk about the pioneering spirit of Montanans who have built up the arts in the state. He calls Malina an "adventurer" in the arts, but credits citizens for responding to innovation and exciting new ideas.

The organization has chosen a name for the performing arts center: the Myrna Loy Center for the Media, Performing, and Visual Arts. Malina says that no building in Helena is named after a colorful personality. "The fact that she is a woman, I feel, is also important. It's an affirmation that the town is named after a woman."

The actress grew up in Helena, a few blocks from the jail. In her memoir, she credits her Montana heritage and the live performances she attended at the town's Marlow Theater as significant influences in her early life. Loy was a great social activist in her day. She was the U.S. representative to UNESCO, avidly supported the United Nations and fought mightily against McCarthyism. Malina loves to quote from a speech that she made at the U.N.: "The cause of peace is the world's greatest drama." After explaining all the good reasons that Myrna Loy had been chosen to be honored, Malina adds, "Besides, I like the sound of 'Meet you at the Myrna Loy!' It has a nice ring to it."

Steve Browning and Sen. Baucus visited Loy at her home in New York and received her permission to name the building in her honor. Loy's agent, Robert Lantz, has agreed to help the organization set up a National Friends of Myrna Loy fund. Several actors who have had a close friendship or association with Loy have permitted the organization to use their names in national solicitations. Further fundraising efforts are being undertaken to develop a local Friends of Myrna Loy in Helena.

In 1990, The Helena Film Society/Series for the Performing Arts changed its name to Helena Presents, a name that Malina believes better represents all of the work the organization does. The name change was announced at a "sneak preview" party at the jail on August 2, Myrna Loy's birthday. Malina also used the occasion to acknowledge the $350,000 program endowment fund, which was the gift of Helena resident Pauline Knight Allen.

Festivals

Even with the current limitation on space in Helena, there has been no limitation on the creative programming ideas developed by Arnie Malina. Of particular note have been the festivals, both large and small, that he has brought to fruition in the past few years.

The festivals reflect Malina's broad scope of thinking and the development of the organization's mission as a center that programs films, performing arts, and visual arts. The festivals also speak to the development of a humanities component to the organization's programs.

Malina also wants to be responsive to both community and global concerns. This kindled the idea for the 1987 event, "Let a Hundred Flowers Bloom: A Festival of Chinese Culture." The pivotal live event and festival grand finale was a performance by the Peking Acrobats but there also was a film festival; a free program of lunchtime documentaries; a children's weekend with films and educational activities; and a series of lectures and workshops on Chinese decorative and visual arts. Chinese American writer Shawn Wong read from and discussed his work, and introduced a 1919 D.W. Griffith film, *Broken Blossoms*. Symposia were held on "China and the U.S.: Economic development, trade, politics and cultural exchange," with 14 presentations by 25 different participants.

> "Getting an audience to accept things they're not familiar with is an aesthetic that expands their lives."

The culinary aspect wasn't neglected. The festival included a gala banquet with opening remarks by then-Gov. Schwinden and Tang Shu-bei, minister of the Embassy of the People's Republic of China in Washington, who came to Helena especially for the event. The banquet also featured a lecture on the diversity of the Chinese population, a tai chi presentation, and a concert of Chinese music.

To present the festival, Malina had formed a working partnership with two other Helena institutions that became co-sponsors: the Mansfield Center for Pacific Affairs, and Carroll College. Funding came from the Montana Committee for the Humanities. The grant was matched with cash and in-kind services raised in the community.

The breadth and depth of the program spurred the Montana Committee for the Humanities to nominate it for the 1988 Helen and Martin Schwartz Prize for Public Humanities Programs.

A similar in-depth festival was scheduled the following year to highlight Japanese culture.

Malina's favorite festival was "Re-enchanting Island Earth: *The Tempest* Weekend." He came up with the idea while sunning himself on a Greek island and reading John Fowles' *The Magus*, a novel that tells and retells the story and symbols of *The Tempest*.

"I thought that this would really make an interesting festival," Malina says, "to talk about the influence of *The Tempest* on the modern world, to have a group of scholars, theater people, and also films, and mix it all up. You would think that something like this would not be a popular thing. It's not like taking Howdy Doody and turning it into a festival. It wasn't everybody's cup of tea, but it was a real adventure."

For the time being, there is a hiatus on festivals so the organization can concentrate on a final fundraising effort for the renovation of Myrna Loy Center. But, once this effort is complete, it's a safe bet that festival programs will return at an increased level.

Nurturing Local Artists

A crucial part of the organization's planning process involves local performing artists, writers, and scholars. This is a tradition that goes back to the organization's early days. In a real and meaningful sense, the needs and initiative of local artists transformed the Helena Film Society from a movie theater into a community cultural center. Malina provided an open door for the creative spirits of Helena, who were encouraged to come to him with ideas for poetry readings, theatrical drama and satire. Local bands came to jam at the Second Story Cinema. Local artists provided some of the early moral support for importing touring events; in turn, they developed their own expression as a result of interaction with artists from outside the community.

"When I came to Helena (from California), I was very worried that there would be no input anymore," says Lorna Mills, a teacher of tap dance. "I was afraid that I would have to go out of state to get those valuable experiences. But the Helena Film Society has provided incredible experiences in dance and music and art. Without them, I'd be dying on the vine here."

Each year, the organization allocates $5,000 in support of artists' projects through its Grants to Artists Program. Funds for this program have been raised in an annual art auction and exhibition sponsored by the Friends of the Helena Film Society/Series for the Performing Arts.

Budget and Staff

One of the most impressive things about the organization is how much it gets done with so little. Malina says the staff has been kept very lean because money hasn't always been there in abundance. What is abundant are the ideas, energy and commitment of the six people Malina has brought together during the years.

Malina reports a 1988–89 budget of $300,000, of which 55 to 60 percent is earned from ticket sales, advertising revenue and concessions. The balance comes from the annual campaign, event underwriting, and grants. He and his staff have become expert at stretching every dollar.

Marilyn Bailey, who serves as administrator, has been on staff since 1984. As in many small nonprofits, her responsibilities vary widely depending on what is needed at a given time. One of her most important roles is assisting Malina in grant preparation. She also keeps a watchful eye on the budget, referring to herself as "Attila the Hun." The organization has been reluctant to resume the annual fund drive, she says, until they finish raising money for the Myrna Loy Center. "We have been running on cash reserves and very tight management," she says. "We could not tap this small community twice in a year for different kinds of giving to the same organization."

The staff must deal with the pressure inherent in a small organization that does so much. "There are days when we have to dig deep to be highly productive during the day and then show up and work a performance that same evening," Bailey says. "But two days later, when we're recovered, we feel, 'Boy, that was great! Now, what can we do better for the next event?'"

Les Benedict, who is responsible for media arts, has relieved Malina of the administrative details of running the film and video program. Benedict chooses the films in conjunction with Malina and Dee Dawse, who oversees marketing and audience development. Benedict also develops the video programs, deals with the film distributors, and schedules the projectionists.

Dawse's arena is publicity for the live events and films. She also sells advertising in the program booklet and the monthly newsletter, which brings in a substantial amount of revenue. Originally a board member, Dawse participated in the interviewing process that brought several of the present staff members to the organization. Volunteer coordination is also within her purview. More than 200 volunteers now give their time to the Helena Film Society, helping to make each event function smoothly. Dawse also coordinates the sale of desserts at live events. Bailey says "Desserts just show up at all of our events, as if by miracle." The volunteers get free tickets in exchange for their desserts.

One Individual Makes a Difference

Originally Malina was an outsider, coming into a town that was completely new to him. But Scott Hibbard says that the nature of the west is that almost everybody who lives there moved there in the recent history of the U.S. There are not the deep social enclaves that might exist in the East, and those that do exist are easy to break into.

"As far as Arnie goes, in bringing something that alters the dimension of the community he has been embraced, because it has been such a positive factor," Hibbard says. "Through his sheer determination he has added a cultural dimension to this community that just wasn't here before."

Malina often talks about how "ennobling" and "humbling" it is for him to see how the board and staff have made the organization's mission their own. He says the staff has worked long and hard to achieve the organization's vision, and that board members have put huge amounts of volunteer time into the jail conversion project.

Clearly, this is ennobling for Malina because the Helena Film Society/Series for the Performing Arts was originally his own personal dream. But the fact that others in the community have embraced it makes the effort all the more meaningful.

Arnie Malina has had an immense impact on Helena. He and his partners had an idea and a vision in 1975. A few years later, their venture became Malina's sole obsession. Through it all, Malina maintained an open door, receptive to ideas from others in the community who were embracing the new organization. The community began to feel that the organization was worthy of their time, money and commitment.

Once complete, the Myrna Loy Center for the Media, Performing, and Visual Arts will become a tribute to this commitment. In the course of the fundraising campaign, Malina and his board have attracted national attention. *Newsweek* magazine selected Malina as one of 50 national "unsung heroes," recognizing his work in Helena. The photo in the July 4, 1988, issue shows him jumping for joy in front of the county jail.

Malina has demonstrated that a person whose realm of activity and interest in the arts can become a leader in his community, someone who can challenge the minds and spirits of people and enable them to keep growing.

But this, too, is reciprocal. "If you ask what is the most amazing thing about this organization," he says, "the answer is that it exists in a town of 25,000 and that it has existed for 15 years. It has grown and the community has nurtured it, and because of that it still continues to grow."

Former Gov. Ted Schwinden expresses it differently: "In Butte, Montana—or Butte, America, as the folks there like to call it—the finest accolade they can give is, 'You done good.' Arnie Malina's done good in Montana."

Photo by Allan B. Lairson

11 Culture Refusing to Die

Nothing prepares visitors for the mural *Song of Unity* at La Peña Cultural Center in Berkeley, California—not word of mouth about its impact, not even photographs.

In the great Latin American tradition, the mural—which covers the entire facade of La Peña's building on Shattuck Avenue—has a cultural, social, and political message. Its presence declares to the outside world the essence of what is going on inside the building. It sings out a sense of spiritual and human unity among the peoples of the Americas.

The story of La Peña is a story of commitment, social activism, and community. The story opens in 1972, when a group of Latin Americans and North Americans agreed to try and educate the public about the political situation in Chile and the U.S. government's attempts to destabilize the democratically elected socialist government of Salvador Allende. After organizing the 1973 Bay Area New Chile Festival, some of them decided to continue focusing attention on these issues.

Eric Leenson, one of La Peña's founders, studied in Chile on a Fulbright fellowship during the Allende era, and was taken by the strong cafe tradition that exists in that country and in all of Latin America. During Allende's time, the peñas—which are cafes or coffeehouses—functioned as community cultural centers. "I attended peñas in Santiago," he says, "and was impressed by the combination of cultural and political education."

Leenson says that much of the peña tradition is rooted in class structure. Many people cannot afford to attend cultural events, "so they replace them with their own sociability, and their willingness to share what they know, who they are, and what they have. In the peñas, food, drink and conversation come together with

with music and poetry. Gathering in the peñas makes people more relaxed, more willing to reflect on some of the issues."

Leenson wanted to bring the feeling of the peña to the U.S. "When I came back," he says, "I began doing a lot of speaking and writing, trying to educate people about what was happening in Chile. But in the back of my mind was the notion that we should recreate a physical setting where people could gather socially and exchange ideas through the medium of culture. This could be an extraordinarily effective means of political education."

After the 1973 military coup in Chile, Leenson found some kindred spirits in Hugo and Patricia Brenni and a group of other exiles from Chile and Argentina. This group began to develop the collective vision for a peña, which they finally incorporated on Sept. 11, 1974, the first anniversary of the coup. The founders saw La Peña as a constructive response to the horrifying events of the year before.

The original plans for a coffeehouse became of necessity more grandiose, because a small, modest space could not be found in Berkeley. When a French restaurant went bankrupt and abandoned its commodious quarters, La Peña rented, repaired and renovated the space, with the restaurant as its focus. La Peña opened in June 1975 with several paid staff members, the restaurant staff, the Brennis as chefs and organizers, and a host of volunteer waiters and waitresses.

In the beginning, the restaurant and the cultural center were one program. The members of the original collective were involved in every aspect of management, from planning the menus to developing the programming, to providing leadership for the new venture.

The music heard at La Peña was Nueva Canción—New Song—a cultural movement that flourished throughout Latin America and promoted social change and solidarity through music and song. Typically, New Song is performed on traditional instruments with contemporary lyrics. This meshing of indigenous roots and current politics makes New Song haunting and unusual, says Marie Acosta-Colón, formerly the special assistant to the director of the California Arts Council and now director of the Mexican Museum in San Francisco.

The work of New Song's most inspired and popular exponents—Victor Jara and Violeta Parra—influenced La Peña's history and development. In 1985, La Peña's restaurant was renamed Cafe Violeta in honor of Parra, a Chilean poet, folk singer, and cook.

Jara became one of the dominant images in La Peña's mural. Long a hero to the Chilean people, he was mutilated and murdered in 1973 by members of the Pinochet military junta. Jara's hands were either cut off or crushed (depending on who tells the story) in front of some 15,000 political prisoners in the Santiago soccer stadium. Popular legend has it that the soldiers told him, "Now, sing; now, play your guitar!" Jara is said to have gone on singing, with the prisoners joining him as if with a single voice. According to Osha Neumann, one of the three artists who designed and painted La Peña's mural, "Jara has become a symbol of culture refusing to die."

Song of Unity

In 1978, Commonarts—a Berkeley community arts organization funded by the Comprehensive Employment and Training Act—was seeking sites for murals to be created by several painters. Fortuitously, La Peña had just bought the building it had leased since 1975, and wanted to make some improvements.

The original mural lasted for more than six years, but then some of the three-dimensional elements, which were made of *papier mâché* over chicken wire, began to deteriorate. The original muralists—Neumann, Ray Patlan, O'Brien Thiele, and Anna de Leon—re-did it, keeping the same themes and design elements, but reflecting more recent history.

Song of Unity can be appreciated on different levels. As a work of public art, it is arresting because of its vibrant colors, larger-than-life figures, and enormous size. The work gives off energy and movement. Three-dimensional elements emphasize an already striking work of art.

But the mural's symbolism makes it even more arresting. The piece mixes images of real and historic individuals with generic images that symbolize people and ideas. North America is represented by the eagle, South America by the condor, and Central America by the Quetzal bird, which rises from the center of the mural. The birds' spread wings serve as an elliptical frame that embraces masses of people—some nameless faces, others recognizable: Oscar Romero, the slain Archbishop of El Salvador; Violeta Parra; and Augusto Cesar Sandino, inspiration of the Nicaraguan revolution.

Several figures playing Latin American musical instruments lead this procession into the bottom center of the mural. There, three laborers with saws and hammers symbolize the building and rebuilding of the movement for freedom. To the right, on the North American side, are several jazz musicians; Woody Guthrie; beloved Berkeley folk and political songwriter Malvina Reynolds; and Paul Robeson—all embraced by the eagle's wing.

Dominating the mural is an unforgettable sculptural image of a guitar being played by the disembodied hands of Victor Jara, whose face fills one corner. His mouth is open, singing out—loudly, one thinks—and gathering all the voices and music of the others in the mural into a universal chorus to freedom, unity, and liberation. In its symbolism, *Song of Unity* graphically represents all that a peña embodies.

Neumann describes the conception, design, and creation of the mural as a collective process. "This mural is not just one artist's vision," he says. "It is an artistic interpretation of a collective vision. The process seemed quite appropriate in view of what La Peña is all about."

Molding the Cultural, Social, and Political

The peña's melding of the cultural, social, and political, which so impressed Eric Leenson and other Berkeley-based North Americans, continues to attract like-minded people. Marie Acosta-Colón, who returned to the Bay area in 1975 after living in Mexico for three years, was drawn to La Peña because "It was common political ground that supported and nurtured discussion and cultural activity that I couldn't find anywhere else."

The mural expresses it, but La Peña reinforces it: There is no exclusivity here, certainly not in the economic sense, and particularly not in the cultural or social sense. No one involved with La Peña suggests that it is only a place for Chileans, or Latin Americans, or Spanish-speaking people. In fact, the feeling is very much to the contrary: La Peña welcomes and embraces various cultures, just as the wings of the birds in the mural embrace individuals and their causes.

> The people at La Peña have a passion for, and commitment to, justice for people who don't have justice.

This singular spirit and energy is quite apparent to visitors.

At the entrance, a bulletin board is covered with notices of an array of political meetings. Flyers announce concerts and performances of every kind to be held at La Peña and elsewhere.

One Friday night, Cafe Violeta was buzzing with activity and discussion; in the Cultural Room, the technical set-up and run-through was under way for that evening's event—Sambazul, a Bay-area Brazilian band. When packed, the performance space can fit in about 180 people. It is a flexible arrangement, sometimes with chairs and tables set up, other times completely open for dancing. In another wing of the building is La Tienda, the gift shop that sells all things Latin American and serves as box office for La Peña and for other community events.

Loni Hancock, Berkeley's mayor, confirms that La Peña has brought a special mix of culture, fellowship, and politics to the city. "For a very small place, La Peña has touched an enormous number of lives. It's a great resource for a wide cross-section of people and political and cultural organizations. This is hard to find in mainstream arts centers. La Peña calls itself a cultural center, and culture cuts a very broad swath."

Because it was founded by both Latin Americans and North Americans, La Peña has had this spirit of unity from the start. That is the point of La Peña: to find a way, through cultural expression, to spread the word about the reality in South and Central America, and to form alliances in North America to help fight for the cause. (Although Pinochet's ouster in 1989 is seen as a great victory for the people, Chile still faces many problems, as do many other countries in the region.)

Chilean musician Lichi Fuentes has been in the U.S. for nine years, and on the staff of La Peña for seven. At La Peña, she found a home away from home, a job and a forum for her musical expression. Fuentes speaks of the cultural center as "a place where people are willing to share different cultures, where people are interested in 'the reality' in different countries. It is one of the few organizations that strongly supports the continuing struggle in Chile. La Peña is a place where many expressions have the opportunity to be heard. It's also a place to find good friends."

La Peña has a reciprocal relationship with the community. The center seems to be in a perpetual cycle of giving and receiving. By embracing a broad ethnic, cultural and political spectrum, La Peña offers itself to the community as a friendly, receptive place; in turn, it receives the community's loyalty.

When it was founded, it focused on educating people to the Chilean political reality and agitated on behalf of Chileans seeking their democratic freedoms. But La Peña quickly became more than that. It became a place where others in the community with different concerns could find a meeting place or have a benefit to raise money for their own causes.

These strong community ties also brought volunteers to La Peña to help build and run the facility. At every juncture, volunteers have contributed materials and labor. When the restaurant needed remodeling in 1985, an army of volunteers came forward to do the work in just one month. Literally dozens of community tradespeople contributed an estimated $20,000 in donations and low-interest loans, and some $75,000 worth of labor. According to La Peña's 10th anniversary calendar, "Their handiwork is a testament to the value of collective community efforts."

David Pontecorvo oversees La Peña's volunteers, approximately 90 people who work regular jobs with defined responsibilities. "Volunteers have been the key to the survival of the organization," says Pontecorvo, who began as a volunteer himself in 1979. "If we had to pay for all the work that volunteers do here, the annual budget would have to be increased by $60,000. That's how much time these dedicated people contribute each year." That volunteer work is crucial for an organization that operates on a small budget—$325,000 for the 1989–90 season.

In the Cultural Room, volunteers arrange the chairs and tables, set up the sound system, and run the equipment during performances. They also staff the box office and serve as ushers. Volunteers work in the restaurant and in La Tienda, as well as in a variety of other programs throughout the week.

"The term 'community' gets thrown around a great deal," Pontecorvo says. "In the Bay area, there are many different communities—neighborhoods, ethnic communities, political organizations. La Peña doesn't represent any one of those. It is a gathering place. La Peña's community is by definition anyone who feels attached to the place, comes to programs, eats dinner here . . . The crowd is different every night. Our constant goal is to reach out to other communities."

Organizational Structure

La Peña's essence is the seamless whole that embraces many social, cultural, educational, and political aspects. A collective of seven people directs the flow of activity. They relate to each other as peers rather than in a hierarchical way. Each oversees separate and distinct aspects of La Peña, but there is some overlap in responsibilities. Although everyone has a title—partly because grant applications require them—the organization is administered with a large measure of flexibility. A La Peña "*pot au feu*" symbolically bubbles on the back burner at all times; each person who joins the collective brings ingredients to the stew, inevitably changing the flavor slightly. The result is an evolving creative effort that responds to La Peña's needs as they develop.

Members of the collective are paid according to seniority, from $16,200 for newer employees, to $18,600 for those who have worked there longer. Other workers earn about $7 an hour. Staff members have gone without their paychecks during cash flow crises, but the organization has been working to financially stabilize itself so that this kind of drastic action will no longer be necessary.

Mayor Hancock comments on this kind of commitment: "We see many people today with so much short-term economic self-interest, and so much cynicism. In contrast, what makes La Peña extremely important is its rooted commitment to democracy, egalitarian values, and high artistic standards."

Executive Director Paul Chin has been with the organization since 1979, the longest of all the current staff. Chin lived in Chile, Argentina and Brazil from 1971 to 1974, and married an Argentine woman. He discovered La Peña quite by accident one day as he and his wife were walking down the street. Their curiosity was piqued by a poster announcing a performance. When they went into the center, they immediately felt at home. After attending the event, they decided to volunteer.

Chin volunteered for three years, and then was recruited to join the staff. "At first, I made a one-year commitment because I did not think I could live on such a low salary. But after a year, you develop a habit of working in a collective situation. There's a lot of leeway to grow, and many opportunities to show initiative. Many of us are motivated to take on tasks that in another structure we might not, because there is no boss here."

Chin's major responsibility is producing the monthly calendar of events. This means booking the events, negotiating and signing contracts, collecting publicity materials and making sure all technical specifications are clearly understood. A five-member programming committee meets weekly. Chin works closely with personnel responsible for booking/technical direction, and publicity/tours and special events. The programming committee deals with problems, publicity, contracts, current business, ads, technical demands for current shows and future bookings.

Each calendar usually has a theme or an overriding message, and the artists engaged for that month try to reflect those concerns. The programming committee strives to balance the presenting program. La Peña doesn't just offer Latin American arts—although that is an important feature—but also presents a wide and culturally diverse set of performers. Of the 68 concerts in 1986–87 by Bay-area, national and international musical groups, some of the music was New Song; the balance included traditional music from Latin America, Asia, Africa, Europe and North America. There also were 54 fiestas, which featured Bay-area bands performing salsa, reggae, and Afro-beat dance music. The programmers are committed to presenting emerging performers along with more familiar names.

There is balance in La Peña's staff as well. Cathy Mahoney, who does fund-raising, says that the strength of the staff comes from the fact that people are from different countries and backgrounds, men and women both. Not everyone is Latino, but everyone is bilingual, a necessity for answering phone inquiries that come in

Spanish. Still, Mahoney says, "It is not a Latinos-only perspective." Mahoney also started as a volunteer and was tapped for a paid position seven years ago. She had been active in Latin American solidarity work and enjoyed coming to La Peña to see the cultural programs.

Mahoney describes the process of developing an appropriate definition for the organization so it can take full advantage of funding possibilities. Through membership in the California Consortium for Expansion Arts—a statewide alliance of multicultural organizations—La Peña participated in the Professional Management Assistance Program, in-depth workshops at which consultants help arts organizations develop a more sophisticated sense of representing themselves.

> "The arts are a vision of hope, freedom, and liberation that are not come by through other means."

The program pointed up a huge gap between the long-established mainstream arts organizations and the smaller, younger ones representing the varied interests of California's vast multicultural population. "We weren't speaking the same language as the mainstream organizations," Mahoney says.

The workshops helped La Peña's staff see their organization in a new light. "In grant applications," Mahoney says, "we had always called ourselves a neighborhood arts center. Jeff Jones, our consultant, helped us see that we were a presenting organization, and had been applying for funding in the wrong category." When La Peña made the adjustment, which did not change its mission or programming, funds were available from other California Arts Council programs as well as from the National Endowment for the Arts. "We knew we were serving both artists and the community," Mahoney says, "but we really had not understood the value of being called a presenter."

Mahoney says participation in the consortium opened doors with other, similar organizations. "We used to have contact only with artists and the community," she says. "Now, we've discovered ways to identify common issues with other organizations." La Peña is one of the 12 founding members of the new Cultural Centers of Color network.

Roberto Johansson, formerly the collective's public relations and marketing voice, sums up La Peña's new-found consciousness as a presenter. "We came to presenting through the back door, from being many things—a community cultural center, a contemporary artists' space, an ethnic restaurant. We never considered ourselves presenters. As we began presenting more artists in facilities outside of La Peña, we began to think about how to reach more and new audiences, and we saw exactly what we are. We are presenting artists to the community. Now we have that consciousness and vision to go forward."

Mahoney says the staff is getting better at communicating what La Peña is all about. "Our cultural mission is to present socially conscious art and art from a wide variety of international cultures based in the U.S. and from other countries. In the beginning, people thought we should only do political art, but we soon realized everything La Peña presented didn't have to be a political 'pamphlet.' We look for alternative arts that have many different kinds of messages."

Whatever the art, the community is clearly behind La Peña. Mahoney says about 2,000 individuals make donations every year. This solid individual support is a strong vote of community confidence. The response to the two direct-mail fundraising appeals each year is impressive, although the contributions generally are in the $5 to $25 range.

Paul Chin says that La Peña's top individual donor has contributed about $5,000 a year; two or three others each contribute about $1,000 a year. "The bulk of our donations are from people who come to a program and put themselves on the mailing list to receive the monthly calendar for $2 each year," he says. There are about 3,000 people on the mailing list. Once they have received the calendar for a year or so, they typically donate about $25, he says.

This base of support helped La Peña become one of nine state multicultural arts presenters to receive a two-year, $80,000 advancement grant from the California Arts Council. The grant helped cover the basic budget, allowing La Peña for the first time to think about the future, and to plan for growth rather than just survival. Part of the funds went to salaries for full-time staff in grant writing and fundraising, and publicity and marketing. By concentrating on those two areas, Chin says, they have begun to make significant progress toward increasing contributed and earned income.

The advancement grant has enabled them to develop a long-range plan. The resulting vision for the future is to focus on the strengths of the current programs, to enhance their quality, and to uncover new and talented groups. La Peña wants to increase its ability to reach out to the community, especially through its artists-in-residence and schools program, and to build audiences.

The Cultural Program

La Peña has grown during its 16 years of existence in modest and incremental ways. The cultural presentations that once were an auxiliary part of the restaurant/cafe operation are now a main focus. In the 1986–87 season, La Peña presented more than 300 music, dance, theater, and film programs; children's programs; and community events.

This growth hasn't been undertaken at the expense of the founders' original aims. La Peña has not watered down its mission or its political convictions to obtain grant support. Cathy Mahoney says they were afraid at first that the NEA and the California Arts Council wouldn't support La Peña because of its political messages. "But we haven't found that to be the case," she says.

Marie Acosta-Colón assesses the quality of growth she has witnessed at La Peña. "While La Peña is a part of the presenting world, its artistic vision goes beyond a nurturing of the art to a deep commitment to social change," she says. "I do not think they've faltered in that in spite of what might be perceived as a professionalization of the organization."

La Peña's presenting program is seen as part of an integrated whole, one way for the organization to carry out its mission to present New Song musicians, or performers whose work reflects an empathy for that musical movement.

"We're looking for people who make us think, maybe shock us, cause us to have a vision of a future we all need to construct," says Roberto Johansson in describing those artists that La Peña invites to perform in the Cultural Room. "We're also searching for artistic quality. The two need to go together. We find many artists who are involved in political struggles and have high artistic quality. They may not be well known because their forms are unusual, but we are aware of them."

Over the years, La Peña has presented Chilean groups Quilapayun, Illapu, Inti-Illimani, and Osvaldo Torres; Bolivian charango player Ernesto Cavour; Mexican guitarist Flaco Jimenez and norteño singer Lydia Mendoza; and the Andean music ensemble, Sukay. American performers Pete Seeger, Holly Near and Sweet Honey in the Rock also have appeared. Literary events have included readings by Chileans Ariel Dorf-

> The creation of La Peña is a story of commitment, social activism, and community.

man and Antonio Cadima, and other Latin American and Bay-area Latino writers. Bay-area artists working in compatible traditions are frequent performers in music, dance, and theater.

Children's programming is featured every Saturday morning. Appearing twice monthly are the Plum City Players, a trio with guest artists that performs songs, stories and games from around the world. The other weekends are filled with performances by the group Amigitos de La Peña, which grew out of a troupe composed of the children of La Peña workers. The children, ages 2 to 12, dance and sing songs in Spanish.

Other children's programs feature folk singers Nancy Raven, Jose Luiz Orozco and Gerry Tenney. In 1988, a double bill featured singer and songwriter Al Einhorn and Joel Ben Izzy, a storyteller who has collected stories from many cultures. As expected, the audience of children and their parents was culturally varied, with representation from a cross-section of the population. Lichi Fuentes, one of the coordinators, says the audiences change from week to week, depending on who is performing.

The La Peña Community Chorus has been an integral part of the cultural program since its founding in 1979. It concentrates on the repertoire of New Song writers, including Victor Jara, Violeta Parra and Osvaldo Torres, as well as North American folk and protest songs. The chorus has had two unusual opportunities to participate in the creative process. In 1981, Berkeley composer and conductor Peter Adler composed *Ode to Paul Robeson*, a 45-minute work based on a poem by Nobel Prize-winning Chilean poet Pablo Neruda and adapted by Aurora Morales Levins. Another milestone was the 1987 performance of the cantata, *The Heights of Machu Picchu*, also based on a Neruda poem and composed by Peter Maas, the former director of the chorus.

The chorus also has a political mission. Typically, its performances benefit community groups; some have raised money for the Sanctuary movement, and others have supported a music and theater workshop for young people in Chilo, an island in southern Chile.

Joel Ben Izzy offers his observations on La Peña: "I tend to think of Berkeley as an enclave of new ideas, and La Peña is a part of that. California and the Bay area are filled with immigrants from Central and South America and the entire world. They generally get blended into the mainstream, but here they find a voice, a voice with integrity. Many things that get imported to this country get watered down; look at Taco Bell! Here, there's a sense of authenticity, in the people who come to perform as well as those in the audience."

A Commitment to Touring Unique Work

Some presenting organizations are committed to extending the reach of the special programming they have commissioned, produced, or nurtured. This extended reach has frequently taken the form of touring unique work or groups not available through regular channels.

La Peña has acted on this impulse by doing five tours in the last few years. Two of them featured the Chilean folk groups Quilapayun and Illapu. Both ensembles have long been associated with the New Song movement, and Victor Jara performed frequently with them in the 1960s and early '70s. For artistic and practical reasons, La Peña took on the challenge of arranging two U.S. tours for Quilapayun. The artistic goal was to enable this group to be heard throughout the country. In addition, the visa arrangements required to bring a group like Quilapayun to the U.S. are so complex that it made practical sense to extend the tour.

To find presenters for the tours, La Peña goes to its network of similar organizations throughout the U.S. Generally, these are Chilean or Latin American solidarity groups; sometimes, they are small clubs or small groups of people who have taken an interest in Chilean culture and politics. Some of the cities touched by La Peña's tours are Minneapolis, Austin, Denver, Portland, New York, and St. Albans, Vermont.

Roberto Johansson formerly oversaw the tour arrangements, and served as road manager. He came to La Peña from a California legal aid society where he was an advocate/social worker for farm workers, the poor and the disadvantaged. He has traveled throughout Latin America. The son of missionaries, he grew up in Chile and attended Chilean schools; consequently, he is fluent in Spanish, although English was spoken at home. Johansson's bicultural background served him well at La Peña and in the Bay area in general.

Johansson feels that La Peña's new awareness of itself as a presenter provides substantial challenges for the future. In fact, the Quilapayun and Illapu tours were an important learning experience. "We found out a great deal about presenting from the tours and from operating outside our community with other presenters all over the U.S.," he says.

La Peña's main marketing tool is the monthly calendar that details the programs scheduled in the Cultural Room. On the flip side are highlights of the month's offerings, with photographs and more detailed descriptions. Approximately 10,000 copies are printed each month; 3,000 are mailed to subscribers, and 7,000 are distributed to bookstores, restaurants, libraries and other public places in the Bay area.

Large-scale events like the Quilapayun and Illapu concerts are presented in a rented facility, the Calvin Simmons Theater in downtown Oakland. The staff believes the large potential audience justifies the financial risk of renting a theater. Marketing and promotional efforts for these events go beyond the usual calendar distribution. La Peña buys time on Latino radio stations, works closely with public radio stations to build support through public service announcements, seeks lists from appropriate organizations for target mailings and places ads in area newspapers.

The *Oakland Tribune* also is courted for its coverage. Music critic Larry Kelp has taken a keen interest in the events at La Peña. He has been receptive to listening to records or tapes of groups about to perform, and has given credence to La Peña's program by writing seriously and critically about their efforts and the artists' performances. He has written that "La Peña is critical to exposing noncommercial music that reflects real life, for the benefit of the local public that couldn't see and hear such things elsewhere."

Johansson says the organization is on the verge of making major structural changes in the cultural program so as to establish itself more firmly as a presenting organization. This includes trying to create a seasonal format and selling subscription tickets to a certain number of performances. This kind of thinking will help the organization plan for the long term.

Whatever the lead time, it seems unlikely that the volume of what La Peña presents will diminish substantially. There is at least one event every weeknight, a Saturday morning family program, and frequently two performances on weekend evenings. In one typical month, there were 28 events. In addition, Cafe Violeta and La Tienda are open and operating daily, and various classes go on in addition to the activity in the Cultural Room.

One problem that must be dealt with quickly concerns facilities. In reaction to 1989's earthquake in the region, a local law requires the organization to do seismic structural reinforcement within the next five years. La Peña is planning a feasibility study to determine if they should reinforce, or move to larger quarters.

Whatever happens, Johansson feels that the volume of activity in the presenting program will help build support and attendance from the community. Staff members know that many of their programs will not attract a large crowd, but they take the risk when they feel a program is important. The volume of activity makes these risks possible, because no one event can make or break a season the way it might on an eight- or ten-concert series.

La Peña has been a supportive partner to many artists who have come into its orbit. The center has provided a showcase for the work of artists who could not find a place or organization to take an interest in them, much less present them. In addition, La Peña refers artists to people who ask for suggestions or who want to contact a specific performer. Johansson says the La Peña family now includes many artists with whom the center has developed a long-term relationship. La Peña also has a small recording company that has issued six or seven titles on record and cassette. This helps promote artists performing in the Cultural Room, or on tour.

People speak about La Peña with a high level of emotion. This comes from those who are on staff and at the core of the organization, those who founded La Peña and those who are associated with it as artists.

"On the deepest level," says Osha Neumann, "the arts are a vision of hope, freedom, and liberation that are not come by through other means. They're a place where the imagination can show what could be, rather than simply what is. Without the arts, there is not a whole lot of relief from life. Entertainment is just a quick fix. On a deeper level, the arts provide an avenue to a realm of beauty and truth, hope, imagination, love—all the things that people long for."

Marie Acosta-Colón echoes this sense of emotion. "The people at La Peña are exemplary to me because they are constantly inspired. They have a passion and commitment that goes beyond art and into an international perspective. It's a passion about justice for people who don't have justice—that's the motivation and the inspiration. Too often, we don't have such passion in our lives. But at La Peña, this passion—the cultural, social, political, and economic relationships—really matters."

Photo by Laura Ruiz

Sankai Juku

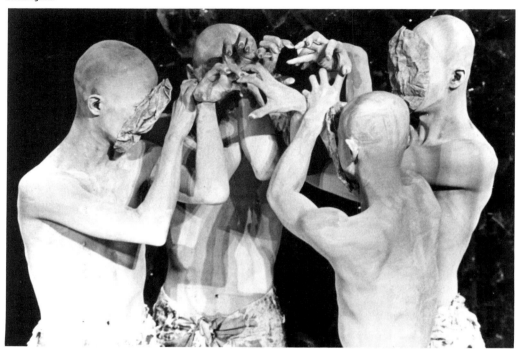

Photo by Jack Vartoogian

12 Navigating Through Controversy

It was an evening to remember—March 9, 1990, the 10th anniversary of the Madison Civic Center in Wisconsin. That night, seven world-class musicians—members of the Juilliard String Quartet and the Billy Taylor Trio—strode onto the stage of the Civic Center's Oscar Mayer Theater and plunged into the world premiere of Billy Taylor's *Homage*, written for string quartet and jazz trio.

The work, commissioned by the Civic Center to celebrate its anniversary, was a triumph. It was one of the first and most successful pairings of a jazz ensemble and a chamber music ensemble in performance of a composition written in a straight jazz idiom—not third-stream music, but out-and-out modern jazz.

It is a rare and treasured occasion when people can hear the premiere of a new work. It is rarer still when that new work gets such an enthusiastic response as this one. The audience received an encore, the short and snappy *One for Fun*, also written by Taylor. Then, when the standing ovation would not be quashed, the musicians played the final movement of *Homage* a second time. The premiere was a triumph beyond any anticipation.

The next day, all the doors of the Madison Civic Center were thrown open, not only the entrance doors but also the interior doors to stage, technical and mechanical areas, which normally are off limits to the public. Families were encouraged to come in and see what goes on behind the scenes. Children could explore the center with the help of volunteer guides and a beautiful cross-section map. Volunteers protected the public from anything dangerous, and stagehands explained the technical side of the operation.

That day a host of live events engaged spectators in the public lobby spaces, including the Crossroads, an amphitheater-like space that was packed with people all day. There were exhibits in the Madison Art Center, slide shows, an organ recital in the Oscar Mayer Theater, and a rehearsal of the Madison Symphony Orchestra. Birthday cake and lunch were served. It was a very busy and very special day, one that illustrated fully the level of interest the Civic Center has always engendered among Madison-area residents—although the feeling in the Center that day was more uniformly positive than has always been the case.

Since the Center opened its doors in February of 1980, it has been a focal point for the passions and prejudices of the citizenry.

The building, which is comprised of renovated spaces carved out of the old Capitol Theater and a former Montgomery Ward store, occupies a place in the figurative and literal heart of the community; its Moorish-deco facade is a landmark on downtown State Street, the six-block thoroughfare that links the state capitol and the University of Wisconsin campus.

Because Madison is the home of three major centers of influence—the Wisconsin state capital, the county seat and the flagship campus of the state university system—the city is exemplified by an intelligent, vocal citizenry that crosses the political spectrum. From left-leaning liberals who came of age during the political turmoil of the 60s to independent-minded farmers proud of the progressive traditions of their Scandinavian and German forebears, to conservative businesspeople concerned for the economic and social stability of the community, Madison's lively and sometimes contentious populace of approximately 175,000 firmly adheres to the belief that every citizen should have a say in the life of the community.

In 1988, then-Mayor F. Joseph Sensenbrenner said that not everyone in city government was as enthusiastic as he about "the sense of a special quality of life" that the Civic Center gives Madisonians. These mixed feelings hold true for the general population as well. In fact, tax support of the center is an issue in every election.

But Sensenbrenner says the Madison Civic Center has won a place of importance in the thinking of a significant number of citizens; that spot in the collective heart of the community has made the Center's existence and its municipal subsidy unlikely to be shaken in the foreseeable future, although this position was not won easily, and continues to be debated.

Indeed, the site for a civic center was an immediate source of contention when such a facility was proposed for the city more than 124 years ago. The fact that it took more than 110 years to bring that proposal to reality attests to the bitter community and political divisions that have surrounded the building. Even after the center was built, some Madisonians continued to question its financing, programming and—in a never-say-die exercise in futility—the site itself.

But even the most vociferous critics of the Center will generally acknowledge its commitment to providing a mix of significant, high-quality programming and events that speak to the diverse tastes of the community.

The broad range of offerings that celebrated the Center's anniversary is typical of its activities year-round. They are especially noteworthy because the center is a city-owned and partially tax-supported public facility. And while municipalities increasingly want to own or sponsor civic centers as a showpiece for downtown revitalization, similar organizations in other cities often provide only the most popular of attractions.

When Ralph Sandler became managing director in 1981, he made a loud-and-clear statement that the Madison Civic Center would offer a variety of events to appeal to the broadest range of tastes in the city, that these events would be of the highest quality available on tour, and that while some would meet an expressed need or interest, others would challenge audiences. Some events would be fun, some would be very serious, some would be family entertainment, and some would require advance preparation for maximum enjoyment.

The Madison Civic Center has been host to Broadway shows, classical and popular concerts, ballet, modern and ethnic dance, experimental performance work, significant exhibits in the Madison Art Center, musical odysseys with the Madison Symphony and Wisconsin Chamber Orchestra, and theatrical events from the Madison Repertory Theater, Classic Theater of Madison and other local arts groups. There also have been important community-oriented events,

> Since the Center opened its doors in 1980, it has been a focal point for the passions and prejudices of its community.

including the annual International Holiday Festival, the Crossroads Concerts, Kids in the Crossroads events, artists-in-residence, outreach programs, accessibility for the disabled and many other community and social events. All contribute to the personality of the Civic Center as an exciting community cultural center that hosts more than 350,000 people annually, some 167,000 of them actual ticket buyers.

In addition to its role as a programmer, the center also has served as landlord, renting out the space either to resident constituents like the Madison Symphony Orchestra, Wisconsin Chamber Orchestra, Madison Repertory Theater, and Classic Theater of Madison or to independent promoters who typically book rock or pop concerts.

When he was in office, Mayor Sensenbrenner viewed the balance Sandler brought to the programming as critical. "I would point to the breadth of things, which run from the avant-garde to the traditional, to stretching local artists by exposing them to the work of a touring performance or composer," he says. "The range is a great measure of what he has accomplished."

Sandler had been a Madison resident for many years before he took over the reins of programming. After graduate school in English at the University of Wisconsin, Sandler worked on the staff of the university's Wisconsin Union Theater with then-Director Bill Dawson. When Dawson left the theater in 1976, he recommended Sandler as his successor.

The appointment marked the beginning of Sandler's full-fledged career as a presenter. He remained at the Union Theater for five years, building the residency programs, expanding the subscription series, and developing and refining the concept of presenting that he later brought to the Madison Civic Center.

Sandler had a broad vision and was sensitive to serving the needs of the full community, says Ben Sidran. Sidran, a nationally known jazz pianist and radio personality, is also a member of the Wisconsin Arts Board and a resident of Madison of more than 25 years. "Madison needs people who think of it seriously," Sidran says, "and Ralph is one of those people. He thinks it has a world-class audience and is deserving of world-class events."

In 1987, the center began a coming-of-age process typical of arts organizations as they gain a foothold in the community and begin to broaden their base for financial stability and long-term support. The process began with two separate sold-out fundraising galas, each featuring a legend of the ballet world—Rudolph Nureyev and Mikhail Baryshnikov.

That same year, the center received a $200,000 challenge grant from the National Endowment for the Arts. These grants require a three-to-one match over a three-year period. Raising the match has been one of the more important challenges the center has faced. The Madison community has neither enormous wealth nor an abundant corporate or foundation presence from which to draw. Seeking the matching funds has required pursuing many smaller contributions and gifts, rather than a smaller number of major ones.

The Presenter as Community Leader

"It's like giving birth," Sandler says of the presenting process. "It's agonizing and exhilarating at the same time. I love it."

He sees the process as creative and curatorial, an artistic and financial balancing act that requires a great sensitivity to the community and to the changing expectations of audiences. "The balance artistically is important," he says, "and I spend much time thinking and working on that. The diversity is important because of what the Civic Center is and who it has to program for—the entire community."

Sandler says a presenter can and should be a community leader. Madison's weekly newspaper, *Isthmus*, acknowledged his leadership role by characterizing him as the "culture czar (who) sets Madison's arts agenda." Still, his personal style favors working quietly behind the scenes, getting the performances on stage and letting the artists take the applause.

He thinks part of a presenter's job is to provide the community with what it wants, but believes the job does not end there.

"If you decide to have Sankai Juku or Meredith Monk come, it's not that difficult to book them," he says. "The real challenge is to let the audience know what this is, and to entice them to come to the theater. We spent a lot of time working on that—the marketing approach, getting the people to decide to take a chance.

" 'We know you like the Flying Karamazov Brothers, the Chieftains, Mummenschanz, and the Vienna Choir Boys'," he says to a hypothetical member of his audience. " 'But why don't you take a look at this? You might get a kick out of this. You haven't seen it before.' "

Simply stated, the Madison Civic Center's mission is to provide a broad spectrum of the highest quality arts events for, and accessible to, the entire community. This speaks to two essential issues: quality and diversity.

For Sandler, quality is the core of everything that he presents. "I learned from Fan Taylor and Bill Dawson (his two predecessors as director of the Wisconsin Union Theater) that quality is the most important thing. You have to establish a tradition of quality and an expectation of quality so that people will say, 'I don't know if this is something that I am really interested in, but if it's going to be happening at the Civic Center, it's going to be good, so let's try it.' That's of the utmost importance. The other important issue is the diversity of programming necessary because we are a tax-supported institution."

In his nine years at the Civic Center—before his recent move to the directorship of the Colden Center for the Performing Arts at Queens College in New York—Sandler expanded the center's mission to include the presentation and support of the new. He felt this was imperative because no other institution offers this kind of work to the people of Wisconsin and towns on the northern Illinois border.

"It is vitally important for us to introduce new artistic concepts, images, and forms to the community," he says. "I think it's a boring community that can only have the best of the traditional world. This is not to say that Mozart, Beethoven, Shakespeare and Petipa are not wonderful. They are wonderful. But if you fill out a season only with the works of those artists, there is a screaming gap."

He says he is excited when he finds his audience in heated discussion about a work they have just seen. "Stimulating people to think, to talk, to stretch themselves is one of the things that is very important, and one of the things that I enjoy most about presenting."

New and challenging works are also risky works. Sandler encountered impassioned reactions of all kinds to Sankai Juku, the first Japanese Butoh dance company to tour the U.S., and to *The Photographer*, a collaborative piece by Philip Glass, JoAnne Akalaitis and David Gordon, which came to Madison as part of the Brooklyn Academy of Music Next Wave On Tour program. Some people loved the works; some hated them. But even for those who did not find either performance a transcendent experience, attending a performing event of historical significance seemed to be exciting. "It's always interesting to think that at some point you will bring that seminal piece of art to a community," Sandler says. "The community has been exposed to it and can say, 'We were there! We saw it happen.' "

The NEA challenge grant has set a minimum of $800,000 for the center's new endowment fund. Sandler thinks the fund will enable the institution to become involved in creative commissioning programs with contemporary performing artists.

Sandler's eagerness for this kind of collaboration is spurred by memories of a five-week intensive residency at the Union Theater with the Alwin Nikolais company in which Nikolais created a new piece, *Aviary*. Sandler planned and implemented this project, and involved the university's Dance Department in working with Nikolais. Scores of students and faculty participated in that residency, making it an unusually rich experience for the community.

The motivation for commissioning new work is multifaceted. Artists need financial assistance to enable them to maintain creative productivity. For the institution, sponsoring the creation of new works contributes to a sense of community pride, Sandler says.

"It helps to establish, reinforce, and cement the reputation of the presenting organization that is doing the commissioning. It is another piece in that continuing puzzle of trying to counter the American notion that the arts are a frill, that they aren't important. Presenters, artists and managers must fight to make the arts a more accepted part of the daily fabric of society, the way they are in Europe. In a leadership capacity, that's what I tried very hard to do in this community, and I feel that commissioning premieres of work, having artists of that stature in the community for longer periods of time, contributes to that feeling."

> "Presenters, artists, and managers must fight to make the arts a more accepted part of the daily fabric of society, the way they are in Europe."

New works also are newsworthy. "As a country and as a people," Sandler says, "we are so used to having our perceptions spoon-fed to us. We feel that if something is on the six o'clock news or on the front page of the newspaper, it must be important. But how many times do we see or read stories about the arts on the front pages of our newspapers or on the evening news? The more we can make that happen, the more people might say, 'Maybe there's something to this.'

"Those are the *events*, as opposed to just performances," he continues. "Commissioning, long-term residencies, major benefit performances by super-star artists—those are the kinds of things that make the evening news and the front page of the papers. You hear and read about the Hollywood producers, who like to put deals together. Well, this is the kind of deal that I like to put together: getting the composer or choreographer, getting the dancers or the musicians, getting them together, finding the money to do it, bringing them to the community. That's a challenge. That's fun."

In 1987, Sandler approached the Juilliard String Quartet to commission a new work by a composer of their choice which would have its world premiere in Madison at the center's 10th anniversary celebration. The quartet, long known for championing 20th century composers, jumped at the chance to premiere another contemporary quartet work. They chose jazz composer and pianist Billy Taylor. Taylor, a fan of the quartet, proposed a work for the quartet that they could perform together with his trio.

Sandler loved the idea. "Joining together artists who come from a classical background and artists who are performing in a jazz milieu could create something that would be of extraordinary interest," he says. "It gave us the opportunity to put together a piece of music unlike virtually anything that has been created before."

Taylor was equally enthusiastic. "I was intrigued that the quartet wanted to play jazz. That put another type of pressure on me. There are certain things about jazz that I hold to be rather special— the rhythmic aspects, the manner in which the individual presents himself, the fact that it comes out of an African American tradition, the certain specific qualities that make the music unique. How do you approach people who play Bartok, Beethoven and Haydn with the same ease and familiarity that I play the blues? It was a formidable challenge.

"I wanted them to come away with a clearer understanding of what I think jazz is," he continues. "I saw in their work the same kind of interplay that one sees in a fine jazz group. Between the four of them, there were all these sparks flying, all these things happening that indicated to me that the music was not only coming off the page, but was coming alive in a very special way. I tried to write something that would get them to do this, within the structure of mainstream jazz."

Juilliard String Quartet cellist Joel Krosnick and Taylor had met soon after Taylor's premiere of *Peaceful Warrior*, his piece in memory of Martin Luther King, Jr. for jazz trio and symphony orchestra with Taylor's own trio and the Atlanta Symphony. Krosnick knew that Taylor composed works for groups beyond or in addition to his own. "When I brought that up to the quartet, there was an immediate sense of adventure," Krosnick says. "If we do this, we're going to go somewhere that we haven't been—and in very special circumstances. We set out to have an adventure, and we are having a very special one."

In conjunction with the world premiere, Sandler had the trio and quartet in residence for three days to take part in a panel discussion, master classes, rehearsals and press interviews. Both groups had the chance to interact with students on the high school and university levels.

As if to graphically illustrate Sandler's point that new works are newsworthy, a camera crew and producer from *CBS Sunday Morning with Charles Kurault* taped the residency. (Taylor is a commentator on the program, but he says it is usually harder for him to convince CBS to pay attention to his work than to do another story where there is no personal association.)

Sandler won assistance for the program from the Norman Bassett Foundation, with additional funding from the NEA and the state arts board. Commissioning funds were made possible in part with a grant from the Meet the Composer/ Rockefeller Foundation/AT&T Jazz Program. The evening benefited the Madison Civic Center's endowment campaign.

Sandler's conception of uses for the endowment fund combines elements of two past experiences he says are seminal to his development as a presenter.

The first was the artists residency program he coordinated at the university's Union Theater. The program developed alternative performance settings to the concert hall, including schools, hospitals, nursing homes, factories and senior citizen centers. Through his work with the program, Sandler gained an appreciation for what artists could mean to a community, beyond their performances. He also discovered that the longer term and more informal settings of the residency process offered the artists unique pleasures and benefits, and that meaningful human interaction is possible between artist and audience.

Another experience resulted in a new appreciation of the critical importance of presenting contemporary and experimental works as part of a well-rounded program. This "conversion experience" came about when David White, executive director of Dance Theater Workshop in New York, invited Sandler to travel to France for the Avignon Festival under the auspices of the DTW's Suitcase Fund. Sandler was "bombarded with words and works" for two and a half weeks. In his own responses—not all of them positive—he recognized the necessity of exposing his audiences to work they had never experienced, regardless of how they might respond.

Outreach and Audience Development

The Outreach Program is one of the most important ways the Madison Civic Center fulfills its mandate as a tax-supported institution. There are two components: programs geared to human services and accessibility, and programs of interpretation designed to edify audiences regarding the artistic content of works presented at the center, particularly those of a contemporary or experimental nature.

Human services outreach is directed at five target audiences: the elderly, the disabled, the community of color, low-income citizens and children. Norma Sober, the center's former outreach specialist, says these five groups are not commonly regarded as traditional ticket buyers. She explains that the existence of the Outreach Program in part speaks to the issue of the Madison Civic Center as a tax-supported city facility.

The Outreach program is not, however, treated as a marketing function, and these groups are not viewed as eventual ticket buyers. Instead, the program helps to fulfill the center's dual mandate to establish itself as an indispensable part of community life and to make everyone in Madison feel at home within its walls. "We want the people in these five groups to feel that the Civic Center is a part of their city," Sober says, "that there are things going on here that are relevant to them and have meaning for them, and that they can feel comfortable here."

The outreach specialist's salary is the only portion of city funds spent on the Outreach Program, which is otherwise self-supporting through grants. Fundraising is an ongoing challenge, and there is never any certainty what kind and level of support will be available. Consequently, long-term planning is difficult. Programs are discussed and planned with the assistance of an outreach advisory council. Each target group has its own committee made up of members of the target group and/or professionals in the field. The outreach specialist consults with the council and seeks its ideas on program development.

Among the program offerings are the Grand Barton Organ Singalongs, which are targeted to senior citizens. The organ, installed in the Capitol Theater in 1928, is the oldest Barton organ still housed in its original site. With its free admission and refreshments, the program has become very popular.

Another popular component of the program is the Kids in the Crossroads series on Saturdays. Then, each February, the center turns over its Crossroads space to Madison's Black History Month, Inc., which plans a month of presentations from the Black community, such as gospel choirs from area churches. These programs always draw a large, multi-ethnic, family crowd.

Edith Hilliard, executive director of Black History Month, Inc., says the Civic Center has been instrumental in these celebrations. "They have been so wonderful as far as giving us the space, donating the time, doing the publicity. It seems there just isn't enough that they can do for us. They've been so receptive, not just to Black Americans but to all Americans. It doesn't matter where you come from; you're always welcome to come through these doors. With the Civic Center in the heart of Madison, it makes it accessible to a lot of people, including the handicapped. The Civic Center has been a vital part of rejuvenating the downtown."

> "It doesn't matter where you come from; you're always welcome to come through these doors."

The Arts on the Edge series of performances and lectures is devoted to contemporary experimental works; programming has included Sankai Juku, the Mark Morris Dance Company, trombonist Miles Anderson and violinist Erica Sharp and others. Because many of the artists and works are unfamiliar to large segments of the audience, Sandler and Sober wanted to demystify the art forms and begin the slow process of building a broader, better-informed ticket-buying public.

To that end, the series includes adult education lectures presented in conjunction with the University of Wisconsin department of continuing education. Each Arts on the Edge event—four are presented each year—includes two course lectures, one given by a university faculty member in advance of the performance and the other by the artist on the night of the performance. At season's end, there is a final lecture giving an overview and review of the course.

About half the registrants in the Arts on the Edge lecture series have been arts teachers in the Madison school system, who receive continuing education credit for this course.

Arts on the Edge exemplifies the center's commitment to developing audiences for quality programs. Another example is Sandler's support and promotion of Keyboard Conversations, a series of concerts with commentaries written and performed by pianist Jeffrey Siegel. Siegel generally develops the programs around themes, such as concert waltzes, rhapsodies, Russian music, or virtuoso works by Schubert. He then delivers his comments on each of the works, their similarities and differences, and how they relate to and in some cases develop from one another. After intermission, he performs the works, then concludes the performance with questions and answers. The program provides audiences with intimate evenings of music making and ideas.

Keyboard Conversations has proven itself to have "legs"— over time, to have developed the capacity to stand firmly on its own. Sandler stayed with the program even though the center was unable to sell more than half the tickets for the first season. He says that he was persuaded by Siegel himself, who had managed to find

funding for the series, and who insisted that the audience would grow incrementally
from year to year.

He was proved right. In the second year, the audience climbed to 250 (from
160 the year before) for the three-concert series held in the small Isthmus Theater;
in the third year, the programs were completely sold out months in advance. It
became the hottest ticket in town, Sandler says. In its fourth season, it was expanded
to four concerts, and a complete sell-out was again achieved. Sandler says this kind
of programming, which requires time to build its audience, will benefit most from
an endowment fund.

"I think the Civic Center has become an integral part of the community and
of the new Madison," says Fan Taylor, director of the university's Wisconsin Union
Theater from 1939 to 1966, and a central force in the arts in Madison for more
than 50 years. "It's a different audience and a different community from what one
would remember even 25 years ago," she says, when the center of cultural life was
at the university's Union Theater.

A History of Controversy

In 1939, architect Frank Lloyd Wright, who lived in the nearby town
of Spring Green, challenged Madison's citizens to "Wake up, go places, do something with the beautiful site Nature gave you."

In the ensuing years, the voters passed referendum after referendum authorizing substantial funds to begin construction of a civic center on the picturesque
lakeshore site to which Wright referred. Every time, progress was brought to a
screeching halt by political maneuvering. The last false start began in 1954, when,
despite vigorous opposition, voters passed a referendum authorizing a $5.5 million
appropriation for construction of the facility. It was never built.

It is difficult to isolate one predominant issue that prevented Wright's vision
from being realized in bricks and mortar. It seems that much of the controversy
swirled around Wright himself. Madison's Mayor Paul Soglin says, "Wright was a
very opinionated person, with a bohemian lifestyle. Despite Wisconsin's Progressive
tradition, you must remember that Progressives are Republicans; they're not fellow
travelers. Some people had this image of Wright sitting out there in Spring Green
with a bunch of communists and other bohemians practicing all kinds of satanic
rituals."

Jazz pianist Ben Sidran says he had high hopes for a Wright facility, "which
was shot down by a government official who personally did not like Frank Lloyd
Wright—at a terrible loss to the city and to all of us who could have had a living
tribute to one of the geniuses of our time. Madison is a small town that is very
conscious of itself as a small town. They're not going to let anybody get too big.
They didn't build that civic center by Frank Lloyd Wright because they were going
to cut him down to size, boy. 'If he's going to live here, he better not think of
himself as too special.' So they showed him, didn't they!"

When Mayor Soglin first came into office in 1973, he was committed to
resolving an issue that had torn the city apart for nearly five decades. He wanted

to keep his campaign promise that the citizens of Madison would have their civic center. He preferred Wright's plan, by that time redesigned by Wesley Peters of the Wright Foundation. But when that plan proved hopeless because of escalating costs, Soglin boldly confronted strong opposition from the Common Council and—as Sidran puts it—"bulldozed" through a plan to renovate the old Capitol Theater.

The dissension surrounding the Civic Center was tenacious. Even when the city was preparing to begin staffing, people in the city government tried to derail the process. Edgar Neiss, hired in 1977 as the first managing director to oversee the construction and opening phase, recalls that when he had only the confirmation hearing with the city's Common Council left to go through, he received a disturbing telephone call at his home in Los Angeles from a Madison alderman.

The caller insisted that the council would never approve the center's budget, and that Neiss should not waste his own time and that of the council. Neiss went to Madison to undergo the hearing anyway, the Common Council approved him and appropriated the money, and the new managing director reported to work.

Because the process used to garner support for the project from local arts organizations seemed to promise them more than they eventually got, Neiss immediately had to deal with the fallout. One of his biggest problems was negotiating fair-use fees with the local constituent arts groups that were to perform and exhibit in the Civic Center. He also had to deal with demands from certain local groups regarding the technical design of facilities—demands that he believed were disproportionate to the limited use those groups would make of the Center.

At first, Neiss thrived on the excitement of seeing the project to completion and then planning the opening events and festival celebration. But after a season and a half, he tired of "living in a fish bowl, with the news media camped out" for his comments on anything relating to the Center. In October 1981, he left Madison to become managing director of the Fox Theater in Atlanta. Ralph Sandler was his successor.

Sandler recognized the substantial challenges confronting him. He knew that what ailed the Center could not be turned around overnight. Deliberate, incremental steps would be required to engender confidence and community pride in the Center, get the resident arts groups to work cooperatively among themselves and with the staff, and schedule the use of the facilities fairly and effectively.

Ten years later, though, controversy still rages. One might think that after 10 years of stability, after effectively serving a cross-section of civic needs for so long, the Madison Civic Center would have proven its worth.

This has not happened, due to the city's unique ethos. Bill Kraus, a native Wisconsinite and learned hand at state politics, puts the controversy in context: It is not so much that the Civic Center is controversial, he says, it is that *everything* is controversial in Madison. "The blessing and curse of Madison is that there are too many outgoing, articulate, smart people in that city," he says. "Madison is bedeviled by expertise. They freeze because the sides are usually evenly divided, and equally persuasive."

The Madison Civic Center must be viewed in this community context. Just like the inevitable Wisconsin winter snow and below-zero temperatures, controversy and contention are a fact of life for the Civic Center's staff and supporters. A substantial part of the city's population seems proud of it and thrilled to have it—and another portion persistently opposed to spending city funds on it.

As the community changes and grows, the Madison Civic Center will share in that process by remaining sensitive to the needs and aspirations of the audiences and artists it welcomes through its doors. It also will need a seaworthy ship with a steady hand on the rudder to steer its way around and through the tempestuous political waters of its community.

Mikhail Baryshnikov

Gerard Schwarz and the New York Chamber Symphony

Photo by Jonathan Atkin

13 The Care and Feeding of the Arts

What one feels on entering Kaufmann Concert Hall at the 92nd Street YM-YWHA in New York City must be similar to what Tamino felt on entering the Temple of Wisdom in Mozart's *The Magic Flute.*

Here is a temple of ideas. It is finished in finely polished mahogany and overseen by those whose gilded names adorn the friezes around the ceiling's perimeter: Virgil, Spinoza, Brahms, Bach, Beethoven, Lincoln, Washington, David, Moses, Isaiah, Jefferson, Shakespeare, Dante, Goethe, Maimonides, Emerson, Homer, Einstein. Their collective presence hovers over the hall, serving as notice that the 92nd Street Y is a serious place. People come here not for superficial amusement, but to be immersed in the arts. And if one's entertainment lies in exploring knowledge and ideas, the performing arts program at the 92nd Street Y offers the best.

The long tradition of the performing arts at the 92nd Street Y dates back to 1935, when William Kolodney was hired to head the educational department and serve as director of Kaufmann Concert Hall.

Kaufmann Concert Hall provided a home for the creative expression of the era—art forms that were hard pressed to find a hospitable place elsewhere in New York City. The Y's aesthetic was Kolodney's, and it embraced chamber music, modern dance, poetry and literature, and foreign films. Into the hall came the newly arrived emigrés of the Budapest String Quartet; the American modern dance companies of Martha Graham, Hanya Holm, Charles Weidman, Agnes deMille, Alvin Ailey, and José Limón; the writers W.H. Auden, T.S. Eliot, Langston Hughes, Marianne Moore—and Dylan Thomas, whose *Under Milkwood* received its first American reading there.

In 1973, Omus Hirshbein took over. He has steered the performing arts program of the 92nd Street Y ever since. The son of a Yiddish playwright, poet, journalist and world traveler, Hirshbein was born in New York and grew up in Hollywood, Calif. He began studying piano at age 3, and decided to become a concert pianist. His professional studies were at The Juilliard School with renowned piano pedagogue Rosina Lhevinne. He abandoned his ambition 27 years later, and began his career as a concert manager. He worked at the Aspen Festival in Colorado, then at the Hunter College Concert Bureau during its halcyon days in the 1960s, and ultimately at the 92nd Street Y, where he has presided over a renaissance of activity in the performing arts.

A wiry, energetic, and gregarious man in his 50s, Hirshbein is driven by ideas. From him and from his artistic directors come the programs and concepts that have become the essence of the 92nd Street Y's performing arts program.

When Hirshbein took over the program, four years after Kolodney's retirement, things were "a little quiet," he says. The performing arts program had always been subsumed under the educational department, which also offered classes in crafts, dance, and arts, as well as lectures about general and Jewish topics, and in recent times Kaufmann Concert Hall had become primarily a rental facility with few events presented by the Y. The once-important modern dance performances had moved to other theaters in New York City whose stages were larger and more suitable to the art form.

Hirshbein says he first set out only to revive the presenting program. But by 1974, he had decided that presenting alone was no longer enough. Since then, he has shepherded the performing arts program through a period of intense growth. In addition to the celebrated Poetry Center, still flourishing when he arrived, the 92nd Street Y under his aegis has created a series of programs which fulfills its purpose of offering serious content-based presentations.

These programs include the New York Chamber Symphony series, under the direction of Gerard Schwarz; Chamber Music at the Y with Jaime Laredo as artistic director; the Distinguished Artists series of major international recitalists; a variety of "bonus" concert series attached to each of the other series, presenting less well-known artists in concert, and emerging artists and ensembles in debut recitals; and the monumental Schubertiade, under the artistic direction of baritone Hermann Prey. The latter, a 10-year festival begun in 1987, was designed to culminate in the celebration of the bicentennial of Franz Schubert's birth.

Some of the arts programming also is generated by the Y's School of Music, with Hadassah Markson as director. These include a summer jazz series and winter piano-jazz concerts directed by pianist and jazz historian Dick Hyman and a winter jazz series directed by Max Roach, world-renowned composer, arranger and percussionist. The 1990 season marked the 20th anniversary of the Lyrics and Lyricists series directed by Maurice Levine. This ever-popular series of five programs on weekday afternoons explores the songs of selected American musical theater writers. Because of outstanding response from the audience, musical theater programming was augmented with the Dialogues in Musical Theater series moderated by

Martin Gottfried. Gottfried leads discussions with actors, directors, producers, com- posers and critics about life on the musical theater stage.

Hirshbein brings his own perspective to the programming he has created, and the way in which he conceives of it and in turn talks about it. He has made the performing arts programming—largely music programming—work in a kind of platonic harmony. His drive to discover programming that is totally organic to the Y, his perception of risk, and his notion of concept-based programming have all helped to create the Y's singular voice.

Hirshbein is a principled man who expresses despair about the state of the concert business, worries that the transmission of cultural memory and history will end unless corrective steps are taken, and mourns the loss of public education in the arts. His is not a casual involvement with the world of the arts and ideas, or the field of presenting. He is completely engaged, combining intuition with a keen mind, a savvy sense of politics, an entrepreneurial spirit and a special ability to create an environment in which the performing arts can flourish.

Hirshbein's passionate involvement in his work comes from his deep feelings about the arts in general, and music in particular. Gerard Schwarz, music director of the New York Chamber Symphony, tersely describes Hirshbein's unique qualities and abilities. "He cares about the future of music. He cares about the artists, and he cares about the repertoire itself. He takes chances and has a tremendous imag- ination."

Dr. Mary Schmidt Campbell, Commissioner of Cultural Affairs for the City of New York, lauds the 92nd Street Y for maintaining a level of excellence in several different disciplines at the same time—and for doing so well within its role as a community-based organization.

"They are an example of the fact that the terms 'community-based' and 'excellence' are not mutually exclusive," she says.

The Force of Nature

A persuasive example of Hirshbein's style is the planning for the gala that was organized in 1987 to celebrate the 10th year of the New York Chamber Symphony. Without question, it was appropriate for Gerard Schwarz, the orchestra's founding and current music director, to conduct. But what, Hirshbein wondered, would make the event distinctive for the occasion, and unique to the institution that founded it?

Why not commission a piece of music especially for the occasion? And in so doing, why not enlarge the scope of the event to celebrate two additional anni- versaries: the 20th season of Nobel laureate Elie Wiesel's four-part lecture series, and the 50th season of performing arts presentations at the Y?

The result was the cantata *A Song for Hope* by the American composer David Diamond, set to a text by Wiesel, and performed in Kaufmann Concert Hall by the New York Chamber Symphony and eight solo voices under the baton of Gerard Schwarz. The program also included Bruch's *Kol Nidrei* with cello soloist Yo-Yo Ma; and the Andante from the Brahms Piano Concerto #2 with piano soloist Joseph

Kalichstein. Ma and Kalichstein both have been closely associated with the Y for many years.

In planning the event, Hirshbein says he and others looked to the Y itself to determine what would be most meaningful. Asking Wiesel to write the text for a cantata was "a force of nature, an idea that bubbled to the surface and was naturally accepted by everyone." Likewise, inviting David Diamond—a well-established Jewish composer who had written a number of opuses dealing with Hebraic substance—to compose the music also was natural. This idea was thoroughly organic for the Y; it might not have had the same kind of fit for another organization.

As for the artistic and emotional substance of the gala, Hirshbein says, "That's what we are about. This is what we do." Other institutions might have produced an "all-star occasion" with little serious content, or without relevance to what was being commemorated. By contrast, the Y capitalized on and celebrated its abundant artistic riches and traditions.

Hirshbein says that finding what is natural and organic is the prerequisite for artistic growth—but it is a sometimes painful exploratory approach that takes time and commitment. It is not surprising that he also sees the presenting process as more than simply engaging talent and selling it to the public. "Presenters provide that part that makes it possible for artists to have a place to ply their art," he says. They also supply the opportunity for artists and audiences to interact. But unless the presenter moves into producing, he adds, the job is essentially only a business function.

"Some of us have become anomalies," he says. "We have taken positions in the world of the arts and have started to produce one or another kinds of art forms. Let's face it—there is not much you can do with load-in and load-out of your theater or concert hall. That's picking and choosing, rather than taking an artistic position and pursuing an artistic direction. The ability to shape the artistic mission is much less for a presenter who brings in talent than it is for a producer who has a particular vision and point of view."

Chamber Music at the Y, Hirshbein's first venture into production, represented an expansion of the presenter's traditional role as buyer and seller. The concept fit squarely in the tradition of the 92nd Street Y's performing arts program. Back in 1938, when the program was still new, William Kolodney had augmented the Budapest String Quartet's annual series with appearances by Rudolf Serkin and Adolf Busch, who had performed several concerts, bringing together a loosely-knit group of musicians to explore the classics of chamber music. Later, members of the New York Philharmonic under Dimitri Mitropoulos came to the Y to perform groundbreaking concerts of modern music.

In 1974, with this history in mind, Hirshbein invited noted solo violinist and chamber musician Jaime Laredo to help create a chamber music program at the Y. Rather than establish a standing ensemble, Hirshbein hoped to take advantage of the abundance of outstanding musicians in New York City who he believed would jump at the opportunity to perform a variety of chamber music works and forms on a high level.

With Laredo as artistic director, Chamber Music at the Y was born. Three concerts comprised the first season. At its height, it grew to seven pairs of concerts and four bonus performances of emerging ensembles, many of them making their New York debuts. In the 1989–90 season, Laredo planned four pairs of concerts, including an all-Brahms program, and an all-Czech program with pianist Rudolf Firkusny. Four bonus concerts with debuts for two ensembles also were included.

Hirshbein says that recruiting Laredo was a completely natural development, given the history of chamber music at the Y.

"Jaime is a direct descendant of the German and middle-European tradition of chamber music performance, which was brought to the United States in the 1930s. Symbolically, he is the son of Serkin, of Alexander and Mischa Schneider [members of the celebrated Budapest String Quartet], and of the whole Marlboro Festival tradition."

Laredo recalls that when Hirshbein first approached him, it was to plan a single season of three concerts. "I thought that was all that was meant to be," he says. "I looked forward to it and loved the whole idea. Somehow, it felt like I was going back to

> The 92nd Street Y is an example that the terms 'community-based' and 'excellence' are not mutually exclusive.

my Marlboro days. At the beginning, we were very conservative. Then, we became much more adventurous and even commissioned new music. Chamber Music at the Y has given me an opportunity to play with the people I love to play with, and to play music that I truly love and believe in." Another direct offshoot of Laredo's involvement is that it provided the circumstances for the formation in 1976 of the Kalichstein, Laredo, Robinson Trio.

Risky Business

Someone looking at a brochure of the Y's program might not regard it as particularly risky, since much of what it presents is old, tradition-based classical music. But Hirshbein says that there are risks in the programming and kinds of artists the Y presents.

Recitalists on the Distinguished Artists series and guest artists with the New York Chamber Symphony, for example, mix recognizable names in the international world of music with less well-known artists of the highest standards. Almost everyone who appears on the Chamber Music at the Y series is likely to be known at least within the New York music world, but may not be known beyond that.

According to members of the Y's board and staff, risk is one issue about which everyone is clear. The risk that the Y faces may be qualitatively different from that encountered by institutions presenting large-scale, multi- and interdisciplinary contemporary arts events. But, Hirshbein maintains, "if you look carefully at our programming, you'll see that we take a lot of risks. They're subtle, and harder to finance."

The founding of the New York Chamber Symphony provides one of the clearest pictures of risk-taking at the Y. Creating an orchestra was never a part of his vision for the performing arts program, Hirshbein says. It began because he wanted to present Bach's complete Brandenburg Concerti, but didn't want an existing ensemble to perform them. He wanted to contract for an outstanding group of freelance musicians to perform the repertoire, in keeping with his proclivity to create unique programs.

He knew about Gerard Schwarz, the gifted young trumpet virtuoso who was then with the New York Philharmonic and who reportedly performed the Brandenburg Second Concerto better than anyone else in New York. Schwarz was beginning to develop his conducting career, and there was word that he would leave the Philharmonic the next season. Hirshbein met with Schwarz and engaged him for the concerts, which were held in December 1976.

The Brandenburg Concerti concerts were an overwhelming success. Audiences loved them, and the press was full of praise. Critics Joseph Horowitz of *The New York Times* and Speight Jenkins of *The New York Post* enthusiastically wrote that the chamber orchestra was fine enough for the Y to continue to present it.

Immediately following the concerts, Hirshbein met with Schwarz and the two began a series of discussion about creating a classical, chamber-size orchestra to be housed at the Y. They assembled a plan for the 1977–78 season that included five concerts by a classical-sized, 45-member ensemble. Guest artists included violinist Itzhak Perlman, pianist Alicia de Larrocha, soprano Judith Blegen, and a new piano trio—the Kalichstein, Laredo, Robinson Trio—that had grown out of Chamber Music at the Y the previous season.

This sparkling program also carried a $40,000 deficit in the first year. But even with the deficit, Hirshbein was elated. "We saw eye-to-eye on the aims of the New York Chamber Symphony," he says of his interaction with Schwarz. "In all our meetings and talks, we were on the same track with respect to what we wanted to create here—the kind of music, the composers, the commissions for new work."

Was there risk? "You bet," he answers. "All kinds of risk. I was taking the Y on a path it had never been down before. Founding an orchestra is very different from founding a chamber music society. In the second year, I convinced the board that it was more economical to do five pairs of concerts than five singles. Then, in order to get the name of the orchestra around and respected, we had to embark on recordings. The board had to subsidize that as well."

Schwarz points out that the Y had a tremendous amount of foresight in supporting the notion of a symphony orchestra. "The Y felt that in order to have an important cultural center, one had to have institutions exist only for that center. (We asked ourselves), 'What can our hall do besides being a rental house or a house where we present artists that other halls around the world present?' One way was to have an orchestra and a chamber music society."

It is not unusual for presenting organizations to present touring orchestras, or even to rent their facilities to their city's orchestra. But few presenters specifically create a professional orchestra as an integral part of their program, and as a significant part of their programming, budget and support structure. Few presenters administer not only their own programs, but also become full-fledged orchestra managers. This is what the Y took on in creating the New York Chamber Symphony.

Another gamble involved the symphony's leadership. Although Schwarz was well known in New York music circles, he was not a celebrated conductor, much less a music director. But Hirshbein says he would not have considered founding the orchestra with anyone else at the head, even someone better known.

"Gerard Schwarz was a part of the organism, the key," he says, sounding a familiar theme. "That's what this act of creation is all about. It was nature." Today, in addition to his post with the New York Chamber Symphony, Schwarz is the music director of the Seattle Symphony, Lincoln Center's Mostly Mozart Festival, and the New Jersey Waterloo Festival. Hirshbein's confidence in Schwarz was not misplaced.

Risk has programmatic as well as financial dimensions. After the first few seasons, a programmatic philosophy emerged that included a strong commitment to the performance of new music. Contemporary works, many of them by American composers, were integrated into the programs of every New York Chamber Symphony concert. In recognition of this commitment to American composers, Schwarz received the 1989 Ditson Conductor's Award for his "passionate and eloquent advocacy of American music." In addition, much of the more standard repertoire has focused on lesser-known works by well-known composers. The approach has not been to separate out new music concerts from the regular season, but rather to expose the audience to new and unfamiliar works and composers, and to catalyze a discovery process.

When the symphony began to aggressively promote new music in its fifth season, it lost 400 subscribers. "We had looked at our programming," Hirshbein notes, "and finally took the step you cannot take: You cannot ask a mass audience, night after night, to hear programs where they don't recognize one piece. All was unfamiliar. We finally pushed them too hard, and they rebelled. That's artistic risk. You want to educate, and you push too far. They voted with their feet and pocketbooks." The performing arts department has since built the audience back up, without having to abandon its commitment to new and unusual work, and the New York Chamber Symphony regularly plays to 75–95 percent capacity of the 916-seat Kaufmann Concert Hall.

The financial dimensions of risk are always present. The board was not pleased at losing 400 subscribers. The budget for the symphony alone—which is only one part of the performing arts program, which in turn is only part of the Y's total budget—stands at $1 million annually. Touring, commissioning, and performing more new music, and doing more recordings, require a total commitment by the institution. There are plans for the New York Chamber Symphony to tour to Germany in 1992. This will impose an additional fundraising challenge. But it is a challenge that the Y feels is worth the effort; the international acclaim such a tour can bring greatly enhances its national profile as a unique cultural institution.

Another significant example of Hirshbein's risk-taking artistic vision is the unprecedented Schubertiade project, an odyssey through every single work of Franz

Schubert. Established on the initiative of baritone Hermann Prey, the project will present the complete works of Schubert in chronological order for ten seasons.

In its first season in 1987, the series of eight Schubertiade concerts utilized the talents of more than 125 musicians and singers. Those numbers will vary from year to year depending on the repertoire, but will only increase as the later, larger works are performed. Each season, the deficit for the annual installment of Schubert's music is $225,000, an investment above and beyond any other performing arts programs at the Y. It is an expensive project but, although Hirshbein has not been successful in snaring a major national sponsor to subsidize the entire canon, there have been donations from foundations, government and individuals to sustain the first three years.

Concept-Based Programming

The performing arts programming of the 92nd Street Y always seems to evolve in response to the next artistic imperative or opportunity. Hirshbein cites a particularly fortuitous development that occurred during the 1986–87 season which forever changed his thinking on how he wants to program.

The Y was approached by the Museum of Modern Art to create a set of musical programs as a companion to its exhibition, "Vienna 1900," which featured the works of Gustav Klimt and Egon Schiele, among others. The companion concerts were performed in the museum's own 500-seat hall, and consisted of eight programs organized around the second Viennese School of Schoenberg, Berg and Webern. Also presented were works by Debussy, Ravel, and Zemlinsky, all of whose works had been presented at Schoenberg's Society for the Private Performance of Music in turn-of-the-century Vienna.

Having had the chance to experiment without any financial risk to the Y, Hirshbein had found a new way to present. Concept-based programs with a particular theme could be accompanied by an intellectual overlay that gave broader meaning to a body of work. It also struck him that the concerts drew a completely different audience from the one he observed at most chamber music concerts. He now believes that programs of this kind offer a great opportunity to challenge existing audiences, while building new ones.

The Schubertiade is currently the best example of Hirshbein's idea of concept-based programming, in which a particular focus is put on a body of work which is explored in musical and human/historical terms. Each year of the Schubertiade brings with it a very significant humanities component. This includes a program booklet with extensive program notes, texts and translations, essays about the focus of the year, and a complete listing of all performers, with biographies. The booklet is mailed to subscribers in advance, so that that they can be properly prepared when the first note sounds.

A one-day symposium is a regular part of the program. The symposia have been planned and directed by Joseph Horowitz, program annotator at the Y, and author of many books on music. Year I brought "Schubert and the Romantic Lied;" Year II, "Schubert Lieder in Performance" and a master class of Schubert Lieder

coached by Hermann Prey; and Year III, *The Erlkonig* and another master class
with Prey.

Hirshbein speaks of the concept-based programming presented in the Schubertiade as "an examination of the art, life and milieu of a composer. We are finding
some startling things about him that we did not know. The next Schubertiade will
address some of the data that shows much of the reclusive life of Schubert was a
result of his being part of a homosexual subculture. There will be people at that
symposium who will conceivably assert that the young
and impressionable Schubert's art was shaped by this.
Others will argue against this point of view. It will go
deeper into the individual than we have ever gone."

Hirshbein is also in the process of developing a
similarly concept-based program for a future season
on Schumann's complete piano music. He intends to
work with pianist Martha Argerich to perform the
works. Again, symposia will be planned and led by
Joseph Horowitz.

In 1989, a new structural development may have
provided Hirshbein the means to realize an eloquent
expression of his concept-based programming ideas. Hirshbein was promoted to
the position of director of the arts and humanities, supervising the development
of collaborative and complementary programs between the two departments to
enhance interpretation and education. In choosing Hirshbein, the Y chose a person
who is sympathetic to the interrelation of these two areas, and who also has the
entrepreneurial and fundraising skills to approach funding agencies.

> "You have to be willing to tough it out and find your own voice. That's what artistic direction is about."

Artistic Direction

Taking a position on artistic matters is something that comes naturally
to Omus Hirshbein. He cares passionately about the presenter's role in artistic
matters.

"You have to be willing to tough it out and find your own voice. That's what
artistic direction is about," he says. "It is simply not possible to abdicate your
responsibility as a presenter. You can't let the Philistines take over the world."

The Y is distinguished from many other New York City presenting organizations because it eschews trendy programming. This is not where the music of
minimalist composers is showcased. Rather, the Y often commissions composers
who may not be currently in vogue. It seeks to develop a commitment to certain
artists and composers whose work is considered particularly notable. This commitment may manifest itself with a significant composer or musician whose work
is widely known, or with a well-known performer who is eager to do a project that
differs from what audiences expect from him or her.

For many years, Gerard Schwarz has been interested in the music of Andrzej
Panufnik, a Polish expatriate composer and conductor who lives in England. Although his work was championed in America by Leopold Stokowski in the 1960s,

Panufnik had not developed a significant career in the U.S., although he is better known in Europe.

Out of his love of the music and commitment to the composer, Schwarz has made Panufnik's music a regular part of the repertoire of the New York Chamber Symphony. At first, Schwarz conducted the performances himself. Then, in 1988, he brought Panufnik over from England to conduct his own works, one a New York premiere of his 1985 bassoon concerto. This was followed in 1989 with a premiere of a new work, *Harmony*, for the New York Chamber Symphony, which the composer also conducted. In the spring of 1990, a compact disc of Panufnik's *Arbor Cosmica* was released on the Nonesuch label with the composer conducting the New York Chamber Symphony.

The Y's Distinguished Artists series annually presents some of the concert world's finest performers. For his recital in May 1989, cellist Yo-Yo Ma performed a program of 20th century works by Bloch, Hindemith, Stravinsky, Leon Kirchner, William Bolcom, and Roger Kellaway. Ma's recital dates are some of the most highly prized of any performer today, but the Y is the only venue that not only enabled but requested he perform a recital consisting of solely 20th century works, none of which is in the standard cello repertoire.

Likewise, pianist Peter Serkin—always considered a maverick and long known for his commitment to 20th century music—was engaged for two performances of a recital of world premieres for the Distinguished Artists Series. The Y's performing arts department provided funds to commission 10 new works for Serkin by composers of his choice specifically for this recital. Hirshbein raised more than $60,000 for the composers' fees from the Mary Flagler Cary Charitable Trust, the National Endowment for the Arts and the New York State Council on the Arts. This was a serious dedication to new music and to an artist who both derives and projects immense joy in performing such works. Interestingly, in that same season, the Y also engaged Serkin to perform the complete violin and piano sonatas with Young Uck Kim.

The Commitment to Education

As passionately devoted as Hirshbein is to music, musicians, new works and audiences, he is equally concerned about the lack of arts education for school children. He cites a statistic that, by law, 10 percent of every New York State school district budget must be allocated to arts education—with one exception. That exception is New York City. Acting on the paucity of arts education in the city's public schools, the performing arts department of the Y, in concert with the New York Chamber Symphony, initiated an arts education program in 1983.

It is different from many other arts education programs in that it is not geared to giving a large number of children a one-time exposure to some event. Rather, it is meant to be more in-depth, with students in grades 4–6 having three encounters with the orchestra for each of three years. Teacher preparation is required, with attendance at five seminars per year helping them to prepare complementary curricular lessons. The program serves the same group of children over a three-year period. Because the choice was made to structure the program in this way, it is able to serve only 1,800 students each year.

Gerard Schwarz originally developed and led the programs. Since 1988, Amy Kaiser—conductor of the Dessoff Choirs and the Y Chorale, and director of choral music at the Mannes College of Music—has been engaged for the program. Funding has been provided by the New York City Department of Cultural Affairs and the Sidney A. Wolff Fund.

Community Center and Jewish Institution

The 92nd Street Y is a multi-purpose, multi-use community center. The performing arts is but one department among many—including the humanities, education, School of Music, group services, residence and physical education. In this context, the performing arts department must compete for its share of institutional resources.

Even though the innovative programming approach of the performing arts department frequently produced a deficit, the leadership of the Y for many years looked on it with favor and recognized its national and international renown.

In fact, Judith O. Rubin—former president and current chairman of the board, who recently became Mayor David Dinkins' commissioner of protocol—acknowledges that the Y's national reputation is due largely to the performing arts program. It's unusual enough to find the performing arts fully integrated into a community center, she says, but the center becomes even more special when that program is of the Y's scope and substance and includes its own professional orchestra. In return for the abundant attention and acclaim that the program brings the Y, Rubin says, the institution must accept the fact that the program should receive special support.

The performing arts program also must be considered as a part of a larger Jewish institution. Discussions of this issue at the Y are in cultural, not religious terms. Rubin says that the Y is a thoroughly secular agency. "The Jewish legacy has been an intellectual tradition, one of history and cultural memory," she explains. "The Y is a reflection of that."

Fundraising and Institutional Priorities

Hirshbein reluctantly acknowledges the institutional conflict over the "most favored nation status" that the performing arts program has enjoyed for so many years. "The Y is a multi-purpose urban center in which you can take care of your mind or your body," he says. "The growth of the arts at the Y in the past 10 years has been due to a political situation in which the leadership made the arts a priority, understanding that it was not only an image, but a practical necessity. Without the arts being strongly represented, the institution would lose its national and international visibility." That visibility also enabled the Y to raise money for all its programs.

He thinks this awareness has diminished, and that the current leadership perceives the Y primarily as a community center. This has serious ramifications on the way in which a very limited number of facilities will be utilized. As the institution has grown and other departments increased their activities, there has been greater demand for access to Kaufmann Concert Hall for lectures. This has limited the performing arts program's expansion possibilities. As a result, Hirshbein has been forced to look elsewhere for facilities for off-site programming. At one time, this would have been anathema to the Y's board because of the attendant loss of identity, but they now realize that, because of limited financial resources, it makes sense to use existing facilities. Currently, Hirshbein is exploring a relationship with another city institution to gain access to other facilities that will enable expansion of the scope and depth of programming.

A related issue is the state of fundraising for the 92nd Street Y. The performing arts program receives its share of funding from the NEA, the New York State Council on the Arts, and the city's Department of Cultural Affairs, as well as from an array of private foundations and individuals.

Private philanthropy is well developed at the Y. Hirshbein says the Y originally was built with major contributions from the private philanthropic families of the Warburgs, Buttenwiesers, Kaufmanns and others, in whose honor various facilities have been named.

Unfortunately, the great wealth of many of today's *nouveau riche* has not found substantial expression in the same kind of major philanthropy. Hirshbein says today's wealthy people operate by a different ethic and ethos. This is a problem not only for a Jewish institution, he says, but also for other cultural, educational, community, and health care institutions. Hospitals and universities have been particularly affected. "People are interested in living a high life," he says. "They are not community minded, as the others were."

This is a serious situation for an institution that depends on the generosity of private donations. Undoubtedly, the annual contributions of private individuals committed to the performing arts will continue to support the ongoing programming. But the truly major donations are more difficult to cultivate and actualize.

One notable exception is the $5 million pledge from Joan and Robert Preston Tisch for the Tisch Center for the Arts and Humanities. This is a significant part of the Y's five-year, $40 million fundraising campaign.

Belt-Tightening for the 1990s

In response to a projected $1.5 million institution-wide deficit on a $17 million total budget for 1991, the administration of the 92nd Street Y is cutting back on programming and expenses throughout the organization.

Despite the critical acclaim and audience response for the Schubertiade, the performing arts share of that cutback will postpone the 1991 installment for one year. The Y is hoping to realize a $250,000 savings by the postponement. Sol Adler, executive director, was quoted in *The New York Times* as reaffirming the institution's "highest priority" commitment to cultural programs. However, this is a serious blow to one of the most important classical endeavors on the New York musical scene in a long time. It also is a blow to the impressive decade of growth enjoyed by the performing arts program at the Y.

Hirshbein reluctantly accepts the cutback, saying he recognizes that the Schubertiade presents itself as the logical place to trim, from a financial standpoint. Since the program is structured to present the works in chronological order, the early years inevitably have and will deal with Schubert's lesser-known and less-formed works. This has a serious ramification for the size of the audiences and the box office income. In its first three years, the Schubertiade averaged only 60 percent capacity in sales, which was partially responsible for creating the $225,000 annual deficit. However, Hirshbein maintains that the audience has been very devoted, well prepared, and considerably younger than regular audiences.

Chairman of the Board Judith O. Rubin is quoted in the same *New York Times* article: "The 92nd Street Y does many things well, but I believe that it is the arts and humanities programs that have put this place on the map, and turned it into a major institution rather than just a neighborhood community center. These kinds of programs don't grow overnight. And the moment they are lost, the institution becomes more ordinary, and less a place that a large segment of the public is likely to seek out."

This is a critical time for the 92nd Street Y in general, and particularly for the arts and humanities programs. The Schubertiade postponement may be a har-binger of further cutbacks, and a denuding of the high level of programming for which the performing arts department has built a significant reputation. Still, the situation may rally supporters to provide the financial wherewithal to enable con-tinued in-depth growth of the unique programming path. The fear is that there will be a loss of substance, and seriousness of purpose and of soul. The commitment to the serious pursuit of learning and the arts can all too easily be lost. But as long as Hirshbein is at the Y, he will bring to bear his determination to maintain a serious approach to performing arts programming.

What is compelling about Hirshbein's leadership is his ongoing commitment to the highest artistic standards, and his ability to realize unique programs that pique the intellectual curiosity of the audiences.

Jaime Laredo speaks of the breadth and depth of Hirshbein's accomplish-ments. "Omus has put lots of enthusiasm and love into that place. When you think of the amount of music, art, poetry, and everything else that goes on at the Y, it's enough for a whole city, period, without any other arts organizations. This is all very much his doing."

Debbie Poulson and Wade Madsen

Photo by John Klicker

14 "Best Stuff in Town"

The neatly penned phrase on the wall of the women's restroom in Seattle's Washington Hall Performance Gallery reads: "On the Boards: best stuff in town." The anonymous lines are an unsolicited testimonial from a sort of contempo Everywoman to the quality of work that On the Boards has been producing and presenting in Seattle for more than 10 years. Others may speak at length about the organization's accomplishments but somehow these words, in their minimalism and spontaneity, are the most eloquent.

The story of On the Boards is the story of a grass-roots initiative. The organization grew out of the work of a community of contemporary artists and it continues to support the local contemporary arts scene. It has won almost universal respect in Seattle from both the established and the emerging arts communities, as well as from funders and journalists. And it has developed a national reputation because it nurtures artists from the community who have gone on to tour nationally.

Contemporary artist Robert McGinley, one of the co-founders, describes the genesis of the organization in 1978, when six artists came together out of a need for community and for a space in which to work and perform. Things were happening for artists in Seattle at that time, he recalls. An influx of people from a summer institute run by choreographer Bill Evans had brought together "all these folks with nowhere to go, no venue to show their work."

"We all knew about Dance Theater Workshop in New York, and we wondered why there wasn't anything comparable in Seattle. We wanted a place where we and other artists could show work and bring in people from time to time to see if we could develop an audience."

One day, McGinley saw a for-rent sign in an old Masonic building belonging to The Most Wishful Sons of Haiti. He was shown upstairs to a "trashed ballroom." Co-founder Pam Schick, whom many consider Seattle's equivalent to New York choreographer and teacher Bessie Schönberg, was ecstatic when she saw it. "This is it!" McGinley recalls her saying. The rest of their informal group shared her sentiment, and negotiations for the space began. They spent late summer scraping, painting, and cleaning. The first event was scheduled for fall.

The group decided to focus on performance, dance and experimental theater. The space, which the founders named the Washington Hall Performance Gallery, gave them the ability to launch a spectrum of activities, including dance classes and workshops. It was also a popular rental hall, often used for commercial rock concerts which helped support the organization's projects.

The income from the rentals also supported a small part-time staff. For a while, day-to-day administration was handled by one of the co-founders. Eventually Andrea Wagner, a student of Schick's, became the first work-study intern, a job that proved to be more enduring that the title would suggest. Wagner is still with the organization today—as its managing director.

The nonprofit organization On the Boards was born in the fall of 1979, when McGinley and Wagner realized they would qualify for funding if they were properly designated. Programming developed around workshops, the two-event Interface Performance Series, and a monthly showcase for local performing artists called Choreography, Etc. The showcase offered a combination of informal performances and provided an opportunity for audience feedback. (This has evolved into "12 Minutes Max," now offered four times a year. The Interface series also has changed names, and is now known as the New Performance Series.)

By the 1981–82 season, On the Boards had found its operational and programmatic footing. A National Endowment for the Arts grant enabled it to hire a managing director, and to present its most ambitious season on the "New Performance Series." The organization was secure in its dual mission: to introduce Northwest audiences to the work of world-class, contemporary performers, and to encourage the development of performing artists in the region.

The 1981–82 season consisted of Bill T. Jones & Arnie Zane; the Off the Wall Players, a Seattle-based comedy and satire group; Mabou Mines' production of *Dead End Kids: A History of Nuclear Power*; Laurie Anderson's *The United States: I-IV*; and Eiko & Koma.

The subscription count rose from 35 to 200. "Suddenly," McGinley says, "our phone calls to the newspapers were being returned. People began to acknowledge that our programming recognized a cross-disciplinary body of work that included dance, theater, music and performance art. We had some important goals to meet. We wanted regional representation, and we wanted a culturally diverse base. The programming suddenly took on a very solidified and sophisticated point of view."

On the Boards has presented a wide range of performing styles on its "New Performance Series." The artists may come from as near as California or from as far away as Asia and the Middle East. Most, however, are North Americans. From the U.S. have come the Trisha Brown Dance Company, Fred Curchack, the Harmonic Choir, Paul Zaloom/Paul Krassner and Bebe Miller and Company; from Canada, Carbone 14, LA LA LA Human Steps, and the Inuit Throat Singers. In addition, the international groups Compagnie Maguy Marin from France, the Needcompany from Belgium and Sankai Juku from Japan have also appeared.

The parallel development to the highly polished "New Performance Series" was "Choreography, Etc.," which was intended to support local artists and their work. The program began in 1979 and was run by Pam Schick; many of the artists who showcased work were her composition students.

Although the program was successful and met certain artistic needs in the community, it proved to be not enough. "We had achieved a certain level of media and audience awareness," McGinley says, "but we wanted to do something more."

In 1982, an evening called "Three New Works" began. The following year, it was increased to "Four New Works." By 1984, it had evolved into the "Northwest New Works Festival," a program that supports local artists whose work was ready for a more elaborate level of production.

"We realized that between 'Choreography, Etc.,' 'Northwest New Works' and the 'New Performance Series,' we had developed a three-tiered system that gave local artists a structure for evolution," McGinley says. "We weren't just presenters; we were also producing." He mentions Pat Graney, Llory Wilson, and Robert Davidson as three "Choreography, Etc.," alumni who have developed a national reputation in the contemporary arts world.

Managing Director Andrea Wagner also speaks of the "stepping-stone" approach to supporting the development of local artists. After more than a decade of operation, On the Boards' programs in support of local artists consist of "12 Minutes Max," the performance exhibition in which artists selected by audition perform new works or works in progress; "Intermission Impossible," an annual performance marathon to celebrate the organization's anniversary; and "Northwest New Works," a juried festival of new productions of more "finished" works by Northwest artists.

Pat Graney affirms the organization's significant impact on her artistic life. Graney, a choreographer with her own national touring company, says she was drawn to Seattle because of its thriving choreographic community and her desire to study with Pam Schick. She participated in "Choreography, Etc.," which enabled her to develop and refine her choreographic and compositional ideas. Eventually, she served as the program's artistic director, and then as artistic director of "Three New Works."

Graney was among several artists selected for the first "Northwest New Works" festival in 1984. She used the opportunity to expand the conception of her work, collaborating with two other Seattle-based generative artists—visual artist and lighting designer Beliz Brother, who designed an environmental piece around which Graney created the work, *Childrenz Muzeum*; and composer Michael Micheletti, who wrote an original score.

"Choreographically, I took a huge jump," Graney says of that experience. "I felt that On the Boards helped me take that risk and was supportive, whether the work was a big smash commercial success or not."

A videotape of the work was circulated to members of the National Performance Network, resulting in engagements and residencies in New York, San Francisco, and Minneapolis. On the Boards enabled Graney to rework the elaborate production for a proscenium space and give a single performance at Washington Hall Performance Gallery before the national tour.

After a few years away from On the Boards, Graney made her triumphant return in the 1987–88 season, when she appeared for four performances on the "New Performance" series. *High Performance*, the magazine of the artistic avant-garde, wrote of her work: "Graney has emerged as one of Seattle's strongest performance artists, and one reason (that) name acts from out of town have an increasingly difficult time looking good in comparison to Seattle work." This praise is as much a tribute to On the Boards as it is to Graney. In the summer of 1988, she was invited to perform in Lincoln Center's "Serious Fun!" festival, one of the country's most important engagements for contemporary performers.

Developing the Season's Programming

Andrea Wagner says assembling On the Boards' annual programming boils down to achieving balance—between work that represents diverse geographic, cultural, and disciplinary approaches; between intimate solo work and production-oriented work; between meditative or somber work and raucous work; between various works dealing with contemporary issues. In addition, On the Boards each year tries to sponsor a return engagement by at least one artist to show the public how his or her work is developing.

Wagner locates the artists and companies in a variety of ways. Visiting artists, many of whom tour the U.S. and Europe, happily recommend people whose work they admire. Wagner keeps up to date by reading as much as possible and by networking with other presenting organizations. The National Performance Network (NPN), of which On the Boards is a founding member, is particularly helpful. The NPN annual meeting is a way to learn from colleagues about what's happening around the country in cities other than New York.

On the Boards also has benefited from the Suitcase Fund, a project of New York's Dance Theater Workshop. McGinley and Wagner have traveled abroad under Suitcase Fund auspices to see European and Middle Eastern work and, with assistance from the fund, have brought to Seattle artists and works they have seen.

King County Arts Commission Director Kjris Lund describes the significance of On the Boards' membership in the NPN: "That migration of ideas from one region to another helps provide the work we see here in Seattle as well as the cultural exchange we experience with other parts of the country and the world."

Closer to home, projects initiated and produced with local artists are organic to On the Boards' mission. Diane Shope, business manager for the Seattle Arts Commission, says the organization has earned a unique niche in the arts community as the only presenter and producer of cutting-edge, new, and experimental work.

"It's difficult for individual artists both to do their art and to produce or present themselves," she says. "Having people in an organization who can advise and assist them is very important."

On the Boards' role in the "Performa '87 Festival," conceived and sponsored by the King County Arts Commission, is further evidence of its support of locally-generated contemporary art, and its willing participation in community arts events. The festival was designed to provide the same kind of support for new performance work that the visual arts community had been receiving from the arts commission. The festival also addressed what the commissioners saw as a vacuum in its funding of generative artists.

On the Boards was enthusiastic about "Performa '87." It received a $20,000 grant for the production of a collaborative project by nationally known performance artist Ping Chong and Seattle-based composer Norman Durkee. Vickie Lee, performing arts coordinator for the county arts commission, says the work—*Without Law, Without Heaven*, a history of the Chinese Cultural Revolution—was one of the festival's major events.

> On the Boards has won almost universal respect in Seattle from both the established and the emerging arts communities.

As one outgrowth of "Performa '87," the arts commission instituted an individual artists program that supports new works by generative artists. Each work must receive at least one public exposure—not necessarily a polished, fully produced performance, but some exchange with the public. Lee says On the Boards has provided valuable support for the program. A number of individual artists are fulfilling the public exposure requirement of their grants through On the Boards' different programs. "A lot of emerging artists feel that their work is validated if they can perform at On the Boards," Lee says. "On the Boards has also been very influential in getting regional artists national attention."

Special Projects

Two very different special projects—the 75th anniversary production of a Danish play with Seattle roots, and a contemporary rap musical—exemplify On the Boards' involvement with the community, the way it helps artists realize works of unusual interest. Projects like these are central to the organization's mission.

Seattle-based theater artist and actress Lori Larsen is known for creating "crazy, experimental stuff," Wagner says. She proposed to On the Boards that she adapt the Danish vaudeville *En Sondag Paa Amager (A Sunday on Amager)*, for the 1985–86 New Performance Series. Larsen said that being in the Washington Hall Performance Gallery brought back childhood memories.

She explained that the hall was built by a Danish fellowship association shortly after the turn of the century, and the Danish community had communal meals in the cafeteria-meeting hall, often followed by dances and light entertainment upstairs in the ballroom.

A production of *En Sondag Paa Amager* had opened the hall in 1911, and had been presented every 25 years to celebrate the birth of Harmonien, an important Danish theater society on the West Coast Scandinavian touring circuit. Larsen—by playing the leading role of Lisbet for the local production's 75th anniversary at Washington Hall Performance Gallery—was following her grandmother and her mother in a family tradition.

Larsen traveled to Denmark, where she researched the playwright and the play, and located a copy of the original handwritten musical score in the Royal Danish Library. She had the production translated into English, and gathered a company of Seattle and West Coast artists, many of whom had performed their own work at On the Boards. Among the participants were composer Wade Del, who adapted the musical score for the six-piece orchestra, and San Francisco-based performance artist Rinde Eckert, who also served as the music director.

The more Larsen became involved in the play, "the less she was able to do anything crazy with it," Wagner says. It ended up not as one of Larsen's unorthodox performances, but as a "very sweet version of a very sweet play about a love triangle." Attending the performance were many older members of Seattle's sizable Danish community, and representatives of the old fellowship organization. "They were just in seventh heaven," Wagner recalls. "Artistically, it was not the kind of thing that we normally do, but it was really special for those eight performances."

A co-production of a rap musical, *Boys Will B-Boys*, with the Madrona Youth Theater allowed On the Boards to engage in a cooperative and collaborative project in its own neighborhood. The organization is situated in Seattle's Central District, home to much of the city's lower-income African American community.

The musical included rap, rock, gospel, and hip-hop music. It was a collaboration between the Emerald Street Boys, Seattle playwright A.M. Collins, and Seattle composer Reco Bembry. In a synopsis of the book for the show, Collins wrote, "Beat boxes and gospel choirs come together in this musical fantasy, which uses a large cast of actors, rappers, singers, dancers and musicians to tell the story of a somewhat jaded angel sent by the powers above to save a trio of young rap musicians from an evil path leading to bad news." The musical was given an eight-performance run in July 1988.

Sankai Juku

The event that really tested the organization's strength, stability, and community support came in its sixth year, with the Seattle engagement of the Japanese Butoh dance company, Sankai Juku.

The company was scheduled to stage its ritualistic "hanging" performance, presenting its dancers, white makeup covering their bodies, in a "dance of birth and death" as they are slowly lowered head first from the roof of the building by rope.

On the Boards' fall newsletter predicted, "When Sankai Juku's boat arrives in Seattle from Paris, where the company is now based, they will bring Northwest audiences an opportunity to share in a performance experience that is startling, new, and unforgettable."

No one knew how startling and unforgettable the event actually would be. As a large lunchtime crowd gathered to see the company being lowered from the Mutual Life Building in Pioneer Square, something happened to dancer Yoshiyuki Takada's ropes. He fell to the ground and was killed instantly. It was a tragic accident for a dancer in the prime of his life, a great loss for his family and for Sankai Juku, and horrific for those who had gathered for the event.

Wagner recalls how deeply affected the entire city was. For days after the event, there were piles of flowers, poems, and photographs at the site where the dancer had fallen. "The artists in the community were deeply touched by it," Wagner says. "Many artists who were at the performance wanted to express their sorrow somehow."

On the Boards organized a vigil to give the community an opportunity to grieve. Takada's father, who came to Seattle for the ceremony, became "a sort of quintessential father for many people at the vigil," Wagner says. "He was very moved by the expressions of sympathy, respect and honor from the local artists."

On the Boards brought Sankai Juku back less than a year later to open its U.S. tour, which had been rescheduled as a result of the tragedy.

A Solid Administrative Approach

On the Boards' solid, conservative fiscal policies provide the stability to support experimental work and a risk-driven approach to programming. "Artistic risk-taking does not preclude sound fiscal management," Wagner says. "Our sound fiscal base allows for 'wild and crazy' work."

In the early days, 80 percent of the budget came from earned income. As the organization has matured and become better known, the proportion of contributed income has risen. Wagner says approximately 60 percent of the $350,000 annual budget is earned from box office, rentals, and advertising sales; the other 40 percent is raised through grants and contributions from individuals, corporations and foundations.

Volunteers are critical to On the Boards' operation. Like the organization's programming, its volunteers tend toward the nontraditional. They are younger and of a different economic status than volunteers at establishment arts organizations. Many of them can't afford financial contributions. Instead, they often assist with technical, office, and promotional work. Wagner says one volunteer did structural repair on the balcony and then repainted it and all the offices.

Wagner proudly says that the board of directors is one of the best arts boards in Seattle. In the beginning, it consisted mostly of artists and their friends, but it has broadened to become an active working board charged with fundraising and community development.

Board President David Holt, owner of two stylish restaurants in downtown Seattle, is enthusiastic about On the Boards. "The work we do is exciting, and our role in the community is very important," he says. "The way we go about doing it—staff and board interaction—is also appealing. We do things with a tremendous amount of responsibility and success, and yet often unconventionally."

Holt has a sound grasp of the functioning of a nonprofit arts group, and of On the Boards' unique vision. He says the organization has an unusually active board. The amount of time board members are willing to commit—and not their financial resources—is a major consideration in their selection. "We're more after people who have a lot of energy, a lot of ideas, and are leaders," Holt says.

He irreverently points to On the Boards' financial health. "We are one of the few organizations in Seattle that is chronically in the black," he says, which may be due to the fact that On the Boards was artist-initiated and remains artist-operated. "This artist involvement contributes to our sense of responsibility," he says.

> "We're not trying to do something just to please an audience. We're trying to contribute to the field."

Holt also is proud that individual giving has quadrupled in the last four years. Under his guidance, the board has been especially active. It developed the Ambassador Club, a "frequent flyer" program for donors of at least $500. As a benefit of membership, On the Boards arranges for the donor to attend performances in other cities on the National Performance Network. He or she reports back to compare the out-of-town performance with what goes on at On the Boards. The club has more than doubled its membership in the last few years and has enthusiastic supporters.

An annual phone-a-thon is the source of the organization's large base of small contributors. It also provides an opportunity to gain feedback. "It's actually kind of fun," Wagner says of the effort, "but very labor-intensive." She says it is nurturing a future giving base.

An advancement grant from the NEA helped to build a base for the future. It was awarded to establish an endowment, and provided the impetus to begin developing links with the Seattle corporate community. "We're encouraged by the reaction we've gotten from Seattle corporations," Holt says. He cites Safeco Insurance company as one of the important corporations that has been particularly responsive to the organization's funding applications.

Jill Ryan, Safeco's community relations manager, administers the Seattle-based corporation's national program of contributions and community relations. She first became aware of On the Boards through its fliers, "which always show outrageous-looking people with descriptions of performances that sometimes sound other-worldly." When she attended the performances, she found herself challenged intellectually and emotionally, "and I liked what I saw."

She did not seek out On the Boards to offer funding. "They came to us on their own," she says, "originally because they needed a fire alarm system at Washington Hall Performance Gallery, and thought an insurance company was a logical place to go." The company funded the $2,000 request.

Two years later, the organization received a contribution of $5,000 from Safeco to develop an endowment fund. "We generally don't give to endowments, but this was an exception," Ryan says. "It was an opportunity for Safeco to lend its good name to On the Boards' endowment campaign, and help the organization appeal to other corporations. For a small organization, On the Boards has always had a high-quality and concise way of presenting its case. To any funder, that is a godsend."

She underscores the unique capabilities of On the Boards: "Their budgets are lean, and they've done a lot with very little. When they get national attention or national grants, you look at them in a different way. It's an endorsement of their professional capabilities."

Marketing the Unusual

Co-founder Robert McGinley vividly recalls the moment when a marketing rationale for On the Boards "clicked" for him. As he looked around the hall during a performance by a local artist, he noticed that maybe 80 percent of the audience members were artists or friends of the artist performing—no surprise, given the organization's artist-first philosophy.

But McGinley also realized that the organization's survival was at issue. "If we really believed in this stuff, why were we hiding?" he remembers thinking. "If it was good, why did it have to be precious? And why was it just for the cognoscenti?"

He became convinced that On the Boards had to build a broader audience that was as knowledgeable and committed as the audiences developed by the opera or the establishment theater. Now, he says, "We have our own equivalent of that sophisticated audience, albeit ours is younger and the demographics are different. We realized that it was a matter of survival. We just couldn't afford to be complacent about our audience."

In the early years, McGinley and Wagner carried out the public relations, media and marketing work. Since 1985, Mark C. Murphy, who is now program director, has been responsible for developing and codifying the public relations and marketing approach. During his years at On the Boards, he has become sophisticated about the difference between marketing the established, and developing an audience for the unusual.

A recent study showed that forty percent of the adult population in Seattle attends a theater event at least once a year, Murphy says. With this kind of high interest, he feels that it makes sense to pursue the existing audience, particularly when it is so large. "We recognize that we are not for everybody, but we encourage as many people as possible to try us," he says. "We let them know that just because they might not be able to describe why they've responded so strongly to something doesn't mean that it has not moved them."

Murphy's marketing approach includes developing a vocabulary to describe contemporary performance work and establishing felicitous relationships with the media.

He believes it is counterproductive to oversimplify and categorize performance work. The audience's understanding is enhanced when a presenter collaborates with an artist or group to describe a work, Murphy says. The temptation, he adds, is to find a few key points about a work and blow them out of proportion. "My goal is to encourage the audience to look forward to the work and to create realistic expectations," he says. "At the same time, I try to enhance their vision of the work's role in the evolution of the art form, in relation to themselves and to what's happening around them."

Another challenging and crucial part of Murphy's job is developing a working relationship with the media. He was concerned that critics might not be interested in the curious work being presented by the organization, but he quickly saw that the nature of the work was actually a strength. Over time, he has built a rapport with the press and learned the interests of individual critics.

Credibility is the key, Murphy says. "I am always honest. If I know something will appeal to a specific reporter or cameraman, I'll press them on it. Otherwise, I won't. I have tried to nurture a relationship in which they respect On the Boards as a whole, not just a specific event."

To support its audience-building efforts, On the Boards has developed a graphic image that reflects its irreverent, avant-garde spirit and communicates the contemporary, lively quality of the work. With no budget to support a high-priced graphic designer, On the Boards has challenged Seattle's graphic design community to sign on for volunteer work.

The response has been excellent, Wagner says. The designers have the leeway to stretch their creative talents at On the Boards in the same way that performing artists have the opportunity to experiment. "We almost always have a waiting list of graphic designers dying to work for us for free," Wagner says, "just for the opportunity to do something more creative and unusual than they normally have a chance to do."

Invariably, On the Boards sells out its subscription series each year. Sales are purposely stopped at a certain point to allow for single-ticket sales, a policy maintained to help with cash flow and to encourage new people to "join the On the Boards family," Wagner says. Approximately 500 to 600 subscriptions are sold for the 1,000 seats available each season for each run of four performances in the 250-seat Washington Hall. She's satisfied with the 50 percent renewal rate. "I like the idea that there's a constantly rotating single-ticket audience," she says. "Our aim is to keep the New Performance subscriber base the same, and to expand the audience for local artists."

Seattle's Arts Ecology

"On the Boards has been instrumental in advising us and being a very vital organization in the cultural ecology of this region," says Vicki Lee of the King County Arts Commission. "Without them, there would really be a gap in our programming. In many communities, there is support only for arts institutions, and not for individual artists. Here, we have more of an ecology, a fabric, that makes Seattle an exciting area. On the Boards is a vital part of that ecology."

Richard M. Campbell, music and dance critic for the morning Seattle *Post-Intelligencer*, offers insight into the area's cultural ecology. "The cross-currents of cultural life in America don't automatically intersect through Seattle," he observes.

He credits On the Boards with enabling Seattle audiences to encounter avant-garde, cutting-edge work. He says the organization is willing to take risks on projects that sometimes succeed, and sometimes do not. "They bring almost anything to Seattle if they think it's good," he says.

Other Seattle arts organizations have benefited from On the Boards' pioneering work in audience development. In the summer of 1988, for example, the Seattle Opera abandoned its annual production of Richard Wagner's Ring Cycle in favor of a production of the Philip Glass opera, *Satyagraha*. Campbell says that On the Boards was indirectly responsible because it has worked hard to create the interest and the market for the avant-garde. As if to prove his point, the opera took out a full-page ad in On the Boards' program booklet, a tacit acknowledgement that a substantial part of On the Boards' audience would be potential ticket-buyers for the production of *Satyagraha*.

> "No community is really worth much unless it can produce really first-rate local art."

Campbell is enthusiastic about the audiences he has seen at the Washington Hall Performance Gallery. "They're the kinds of audiences I see in Los Angeles, New York, Chicago, or San Francisco," he says. He describes them as young, hip, eager to see what is going on in the world. They talk about the work, Campbell says, and they are interested in what they see.

"No community is really worth much unless it can produce really first-rate local art," Campbell says. "And art doesn't happen unless there is encouragement. On the Boards has also helped stimulate the notion that you have to have art from outside your city and inside your city. They've been better than anyone at defining that *that* is what a city is all about."

A "chicken or egg" question lurks: Is there an abundance of local generative artists because On the Boards is in Seattle, or is On the Boards there because of the rich contemporary artistic community?

On the Boards clearly has a symbiotic relationship with local artists, making the environment conducive to creative development. Many artists come to the city in response to the existing creative community, which in turn gives On the Boards a more fertile atmosphere in which to encourage the development of new and contemporary work.

Choreographer Pat Graney offers this observation: "On the Boards came out of a community of artists, and has maintained that connection. That is its strength."

The organization has not isolated itself in an effete way from any communities in Seattle and beyond. It has interacted with the city, county, state and federal arts structures. It has had a sustained and significant effect on the local arts scene, and in turn it has made that region of the country a better, more stimulating place to live and work.

It has dedicated itself to keeping artists in Seattle by making sure their work is seen by local audiences as well as by national and international presenters and producers, when feasible; that local artists see important contemporary work on tour in Seattle; and that they are supported in their own generative efforts.

On the Boards is equally concerned about its audience. Wagner says that it is set apart from other contemporary art organizations by its willingness to use traditional marketing techniques to draw an audience. "This is not an organization that's just for artists," she says. "It's just as much for the audience, not always an important constituency for other performance spaces. We have a specific artistic bias, and we're not trying to do something just to please an audience. We're trying to contribute to the field."

Roger Downey, arts writer for Seattle's *The Weekly*, has observed that "On the Boards has all but singlehandedly introduced Seattle to the best of new performance work nationwide. Clearly, the public has come to trust On the Boards, to expect that any performance they sponsor will be worthy of serious attention. There can be no greater proof of the success of an artistic institution than that."

The B-Boys

Photo by Pete Kuhns

Photo by Dona Ann McAdams

15 A Nesting Place, and Wings

For a graduate of the New York City public school system, it is a peculiar experience to enter Public School 122 in New York's East Village neighborhood. Sensory memories cascade back from a childhood spent in classrooms and hallways: the architecture, the fixtures and fittings, the distinctive smell of the steam heat, and the general ambience of surroundings designed to house throngs of children.

But what goes on inside of Performance Space 122, as this former public school is now called, and what transpired inside the elementary school of memory are as distinct as the 21st century is from the 19th.

P.S. 122 was founded in 1979 by artists Charlie Moulton, Charles Dennis and Tim Miller as an artist's space, a home for rehearsals and performances. It has evolved into a well-respected though reluctant institution for the introduction of emerging artists and new works. It also provides a safe haven for artists to return to after sojourns in more mainstream theater or dance spaces.

Typically, the artists who perform in P.S. 122 are "making work" that pushes the frontiers of the performing arts, work that does not fall neatly into the traditional discipline nomenclatures. The generic classification "performance" is convenient, because it encompasses a multitude of expressions, and makes it possible for anyone with an idea to try and express it.

Mark Russell, executive director since 1983, confirms the nomenclature of the work. "We call what we do performance—something that happens live. I don't see performance necessarily being a field. These are emerging artists. They don't know where their real cards are or what they're really best at doing. They come from a TV generation that changes the channels. They have Casios; they can make music. Anyone can be a band."

He says that from the beginning, a certain style of work began to come through P.S. 122: "Dancers trying to talk, theater people trying to move, filmmakers trying to make dance and theater, video makers trying to do something different, visual artists trying to play music, musicians trying to collaborate—all these moving forms. We were doing unclassifiable art. We classified it mostly by the artist's name, and it was whatever that artist wanted to do."

Co-founder and performance artist Tim Miller says the punk movement had an enormous effect on performance, dance, and music. "There was this feeling of 'let's do stuff,' in the same way that anyone could form a punk band with three chords." He says the work that has found a home and grown up at P.S. 122 was a reaction to the "cool of the preceding generation of artists." It represented a shift from the minimalist work fomenting in the 1970s in New York's Soho neighborhood, "to the East Village as a neighborhood for younger people, more connected to content, popular culture, expressivity, political content, autobiography. All of that heat went into the early years of P.S. 122. It's like radioactive material, and it has kept the space going for over a decade. Over time, the work has become this new hybrid of dance-based performance art, the pushy expressivity of the East Village of our time."

The founders felt they could transcend audience preconceptions. Miller says they decided to "just let a lot of things happen. Some of it will be good, and most of it will probably be terrible—which is probably the same ratio no matter how much programming you do. Our impulse was to allow artists to come in and do 'stuff'."

Russell says the people involved with P.S. 122 see it as a performance laboratory. "It started as a workplace, and it continues as a workplace. We just keep moving. It's about a process. It's not about big amazing events. It's about an ongoing thing." He says they have a core audience that knows that frequently "we hit the big gong and it works, or at least it's an interesting failure. And so they come in. We're not saying, 'This is the hottest thing.' Some of it is good old-fashioned entertainment. Some of it is lousy art. Some of it's film, or work that people are trying out.

"You've got to come for the adventure. That's what they're buying into. And we want them to be able to make their own judgments for that work, that way."

Grasping what P.S. 122 is about requires some sense of the range of ideas that encompasses the terms "performance art" or "performance." Interestingly, people close to it qualify their definitions. Mark Russell says the term "performance art" is "a real hot potato that we only use when it's convenient to us. I see it as one of the pots of paint that our people use to make what they do. Performance art to me is very action-oriented, very visual art-oriented, a bit more on the conceptual side, on the one-time side. Actions: It has a certain sense of the performer as shaman, as action person—not an actor, but *of* action. We've seen a lot of people scrub the floor and make us watch."

Ann Carlson, choreographer and performance artist who has been closely associated with P.S. 122 since 1985, chooses to define her work "by saying what my interests are, and that is I'm most interested in the art of performance, in the broadest sense of the word—mixing media, bringing sound, bringing theatrical elements, animals, whatever life has to offer, into the performance setting. And that doesn't mean forcing things into it. I see it as being part community event—something that happens within a community—and part ritual. It is something that contributes to the lives of those who are doing it and who are seeing it, but also even to the lives of people who aren't there."

Carlson first came to P.S. 122 shortly after her arrival in New York, and knew immediately she wanted to work there. "There was a spirit there that was really infectious, and there was a sense of exploration. I felt like it was in the walls. There was a lot of exploring and risk-taking going on, and I wanted to be a part of that. I wanted my work to be seen with that attitude in mind."

Carlson says she was seeking an opportunity for her work to be experienced not as a polished, finished product, but something attempting to be better than itself. "In a certain sense," she says, "P.S. 122 became both a nesting place and wings on some level. I was able to go and experiment there, and sometimes fall flat on my face. That's invaluable to a working artist. I also got a lot of encouragement there, in the form of, 'What are you doing next?' "

Eric Bogosian has recently gained wide recognition for co-writing and starring in a screen adaptation of his *Talk Radio*, which had been an off-Broadway play. But long before Hollywood, Bogosian began his career as an actor, author and performance artist. He became actively involved at P.S. 122 during the summer of 1981, when he was working on his piece, *Fun House*.

"I really liked the performing experience at P.S. 122," he recalls, "because the audiences treated the place like their own. I got the sense of a community involved with the space, and involved with coming there. The people in the audience could easily be the people on the stage at any given time. They were predominantly artists and performers themselves, and I trusted them."

Another aspect that appeals to Bogosian is that "The whole thing is based in community to begin with, and must stick there to get its energy. It seeks the energy from that community and gives it back. It is pleasurable to perform at P.S. 122. But I also go there to workshop the work, to find out what it is about in the first place." When he performs in front of larger and more diverse audiences off-Broadway, "in my mind, I'm allowing them to come and visit a place that I inhabit with my downtown audience, my P.S. 122 audience. It's as if they're tourists in another land."

The term and concept "community of artists" is familiar to an increasing number of performers and presenters. It has a particular currency among the generative artists who are part of the P.S. 122 scene, as well as of the other contemporary arts center spaces both within and outside of New York City. The notion of a community of artists extends beyond a commitment to artists; in the case of P.S. 122, it also extends to who comprises a significant part of its audience.

Lisa Frigand, corporate contributions associate at Con Edison, New York City's public utility, has been a strong supporter of P.S. 122. She recognizes that "the community of artists is a very valid community in New York City that needs to be supported to keep artists here." She sees P.S. 122 as an East Village community resource, and one of the first presenting organizations to attract artists who previously had no venue.

There are very few places even in the contemporary art world that give artists the chance to try out new things with audiences. Co-founder Tim Miller says, "There is no question that there is still a genuine community of artists around 122. It is still a place where the artist is king or queen."

In New York, the arts get classified and divided as "uptown" or "downtown," and that is more than solely a geographical reference. There was a time when the kind of work that is nurtured at downtown spaces like P.S. 122, Dance Theater Workshop or The Kitchen would not have a presence uptown at concert venues like Carnegie Hall or Lincoln Center.

But the lines between "uptown" and "downtown" are blurring. Lincoln Center, the most uptown of all uptown organizations, in 1987 initiated a summer program in its staid Alice Tully Hall, called "Serious Fun! a festival of contemporary performance art."

Nathan Leventhal, president of Lincoln Center, enthusiastically credits P.S. 122 for providing inspiration for the festival. "Clearly, were it not for the work of groups like P.S. 122, 'Serious Fun' would not have happened. There is no question about it."

Leventhal says he was impressed with the sincerity of the artists he saw perform at P.S. 122. "I'm also struck by the audience every time I've been there. They're knowledgeable. They're committed. They love it. It's always crowded, too. I have seen a lot of things there that I hate, as well as a lot of things I love. But they are truly at the cutting edge. They are real risk-takers—but they have fun."

In describing the difference between P.S. 122 and other downtown spaces like Dance Theater Workshop, it has been said that artists perform at DTW to find their audience, but they perform at P.S. 122 to find their work. Not surprisingly, the work that is seen at P.S. 122 generally is described as more raw, funkier, less polished than what is seen at other spaces.

Increasingly, however, many artists are making the rounds and performing at both spaces as well as at a number of others in the course of their developing careers. Miller recalls a phrase someone had written on the wall early on at P.S. 122 which spoke about its "ultimate nurturing of a warm chaos." "There is something about that chaotic mess that 122 has always taken to heart," he says, "and there is a fertile ground for artists to find their voice."

However P.S. 122 and DTW are compared, Con Edison's Lisa Frigand says both have provided a "feeding system" for some of the larger-scale presenters like the Brooklyn Academy of Music, City Center, Lincoln Center, American Dance Festival, Jacob's Pillow and some international venues.

Cultivating that "chaotic mess" but simultaneously forging a strong stable organization has fallen to P.S. 122's committed staff. Erica Bornstein, administrative director from 1987–89, characterizes the challenge of running P.S. 122 as "keeping the machine moving, and keeping it from being a machine."

No discussion or conversation about P.S. 122 takes place without mention of Executive Director Mark Russell. He earns high praise from artists, colleagues, staff, board, newspaper critics and funders alike. Miller specifically cites Russell's ability to take on the reins of the organization in 1983 directly from the hands of the co-founder artists. "I feel extremely pleased with what Mark has done," he says. "I think he has been a remarkable spirit at 122. We were incredibly lucky, because it is a very tricky transition at an artist-run space. We were fortunate to have someone with those smarts, and who had been involved in the project almost from the beginning as a creative presence."

Eric Bogosian says Russell has provided strong leadership, and has understood the appropriate priorities for a space such as P.S. 122. "Administrators must go into their job knowing why they do their job, and

> ## P.S. 122 is a place where the artist is king or queen.

why and what they love about it. There is a great deal of love that Mark puts into his work. He's not an empire builder. I don't think he sees an ever larger and larger space and organization as necessarily desirable. He remembers why he's there: for the artists and the audience."

Remembering why it's there in the first place has probably helped P.S. 122 to remain "what it purports to be," as Lisa Frigand expresses it, and to garner significant press attention. But this attention and growing respect in press and funding circles creates an inner tension at P.S. 122 that pits the drive for stability and institutionalization against the conception of itself as an offbeat, rough-and-tumble space where spontaneous expressions could emerge or explode.

Board member Tim McClimon, vice president for arts and cultural programs at the AT&T Foundation in New York, says P.S. 122's rapid growth is due to the artistic integrity and vitality for which Russell is largely responsible. "It's one thing when you're running this funky little space in the East Village, and you're the outlaw. It's another thing when you're being quoted in *The New York Times* every few weeks as an important organization. That carries a lot with it, and I think that Mark's having some trouble with that—fitting into his own mind where the organization should be and where he should be."

The continuing challenge facing Russell and his staff is to bring stability to P.S. 122 without compromising its mission in supporting artists. Too often in the brief history of artist's spaces, the drive to stabilization and institutionalization subverts the original idealistic, individual and artistically driven intent. The question for P.S. 122 has been, are the continued embrace of the original mission and the drive toward stability mutually exclusive?

This tension had been seen in many areas of its organizational functioning. Artistically, the scheduling of performances once needed only a six-week lead time; it now requires six to nine months. Some of the new projects being developed—commissioning and touring, for example—require that amount of time to conceive, fund and implement.

In terms of promotion, the internal debate was how far P.S. 122's public relations effort should go in trying to attract new and larger audiences. Any effort in this arena almost inevitably dilutes the artist-based audiences which were the original constituency.

On the fundraising and development side, P.S. 122's efforts have met with impressive success from governmental, foundation, and corporate sources. The development effort has been increasingly well-organized and carefully conceived. P.S. 122 received an advancement grant from the National Endowment for the Arts (NEA), an important recognition of its move toward stabilization. In 1986, it received a special *Village Voice* Obie Award; in 1988, it was honored by an Arts and Business Council Encore Award for its quality of work; and in 1989, it received the Manhattan Borough President's Citation for Excellence in the Arts.

Board member Tim McClimon articulates the artistic and managerial issues that have been of concern to the organization and its board. He explains that P.S. 122 was founded by the three choreographers primarily as a rehearsal space, and secondarily as a performance space on a rental basis. In the process, it was recognized that a more active role as a presenting organization would open it up to grant money and would help support artists. Now, its very active life as a presenting organization has severely limited access to rehearsal time for its founders, because what rehearsal time exists must be available to those artists who are performing there.

The board of directors originally consisted solely of its three artist/founders. Now, there also are five non-artist members, and one additional artist who was not one of the original founders. This change came as a result of recommendations from both funding and consulting organizations that an expansion of the size and type of the board was needed so P.S. 122 could survive as an institution rather than solely as a rehearsal space.

In 1988, Russell appeared to be torn by the drive to institutionalize, and the simultaneous need to remain on the edge. "I'm constantly trying to subvert our own institutionalization, and find a different way to do that," he said at the time. "It pushes the organization sometimes, almost to a point where it feels like it's going to break. There are healthier ways to run an organization, but part of what we do demands that we keep throwing it out there, and keep providing odd opportunities for people."

By 1990, however, many of the tensions were on the road to resolution. In large part, this was due to the process the organization went through as a result of the advancement grant it received from the NEA.

Halsey North of the North Group, consultant for the advancement program, says the program helps organizations of proven artistic excellence strengthen their administrative framework and operations so they can strengthen the art. The advancement process assists groups faced with internal conflict about how to take their original creative mission and formalize it, so that it does not get destroyed in the process. "Often we're faced with how you take that vision and sustain it without deadening it," North says. "We find that some of the best work that is done in advancement is helping artists and creative administrators make choices about the future without getting too formal in the planning process."

Russell says the advancement process was intense for the P.S. 122 staff and board. Simultaneous with the process, the organization was doing more programming than ever before. Russell and some of his key staff members were meeting with consultants two to three times a week, increasing the number of staff meetings and board meetings. They were writing and talking, writing and talking about the future. In the course of this, a number of issues were clarified.

Most important, the tension between the founding purposes of P.S. 122 and its broader purposes as a presenting organization were resolved. Russell indicates that the organization's larger aims have won out. "The original artists are still involved, but not in as primary a way," he says. "They are listening to the ground way farther out, then feeding back to me information about interesting work, ideas, perceptions of the organization as it progresses. I listen and set up ways to listen to the local artists, as well as conceive of ways those artists need to be challenged. I'm also addressing P.S. 122's place in the world of the presenter and the world's culture."

Whatever tensions existed between the co-founders and the non-artist members now is seen as a "good, healthy tension," Russell says. He feels that the advancement process helped everyone focus on what the organization is about. "We still have a schizo situation," he says. "We're a community space, an artist space, a high-art space, a high-profile presenter and a workshop. We have an audience to deal with, and yet we're a performance laboratory. It's coming down on that side."

P.S. 122 also has instituted a program which grew out of the advancement thinking: Con Artists—consultant artists. Russell calls it a way to involve the older, more experienced artists with the artists of the community. Performers working at P.S. 122 can select a consultant from a roster of artists. That person sees a rehearsal, discusses how the project is developing, and what needs more work. Discussion often focuses on aesthetics. The consulting artists are paid a fee by P.S. 122 of $25 per hour for up to six hours of service.

Russell says the Con Artists program was established to give artists performing at P.S. 122 the benefit of an outside, dispassionate eye to see their work in advance of performance. In the past, he says, many performers after their run of shows would come away wondering why no one had told them their piece would have worked better if part of it had been cut or changed. "Now, instead of imposing a director," Russell says, "we've offered them this fresh set of eyes so there's a dialog about their work."

The tension between the new institution and the old outlaw space in the East Village also has dissipated, Russell says. "We've been coming to terms with that. For a long time, it was like this nice bottom of the barrel, and now it's becoming more of an equal player—with just a different taste."

He says P.S. 122 is now perceived as an institution, and is receiving larger grants. "It's harder now to subvert that institutionalism. Now we try to run a very efficient institution and hope that it's close to the needs of the artists," he says. Curators in music and film have been hired, and another artist is now on the board.

"I'm pushing my board to constantly see work here. I devise programs like Con Artists to keep people involved."

Still, he pushes himself "to articulate the mission more and more, and louder and louder. The more it institutionalizes, the more we feel we've done it, that it is what it is and we can concentrate on the work and stop talking about what we're doing.

"But that's a common trap," he says. "I've been trying not to fall into it. People perceive us as having a lot of money, so I must tell them where that money is going and why we're doing these artists at this time. I got called on the carpet because a bunch of dance artists thought I had abandoned them and dance. They wanted me to hire a dance curator. I asked them if the curation over the last seven years had been so bad. They didn't have any real problem with it. Then I described why and how I've made these choices, which helped explain what was going on. I just hadn't taken that time to describe it. It used to be that people didn't care."

What has emerged is a finely focused commitment to deepening the ways P.S. 122 serves its constituency by being a performance laboratory. One aspect of that continues to be to provide the space for people to perform their first work or work in first form before an audience. If anything, Russell has opened up more time for performances in its two spaces, adding an 11:00 p.m. show to the 8:00 and 9:30 p.m. shows.

Now, he is finding ways to support artists who have grown up artistically at P.S. 122. The organization has received a commissioning grant from the the Ford Foundation, which is enabling three artists to create new pieces during a two year process. The artists—Ishmael Houston-Jones, Ann Carlson and David Rousseve— have been associated with P.S. 122 for some time. Their work has matured through its being seen again and again at the space, which has served in large measure like a home base for them.

"We'll be getting them real money, real time and space, and co-presentation," Russell says.

Russell says he is trying to broaden and deepen the organization's range of vision. In 1988, Erica Bornstein said of the organization, "We're here to support artists moving through and moving on. It's about movement and development, change and growth."

P.S. 122 is there not only for those artists just at the beginning of their career, but now also has something to offer for the longer haul. It is supporting those artists as their work matures. This may not have been a part of the original mission, but no one would argue but that it is an organic extension of it, particularly as the organization enters its second decade.

P.S. 122-Style Programming

One organizational trademark is shared programming in which a number of artists perform successively on one evening. The shared program concept has worked well for the organization, and has appeared in several guises since its beginning. The Avant-Garde-Arama is one program that was warmly received. It is a series of four, two-day mini-festivals, each featuring 14 artists in a variety of media.

The touring project is tersely but appealingly described in the promotional material: "The P.S. 122 Field Trips evening gives a twist to the great American tradition of vaudeville, Ed Sullivan *et al*. It takes the traditional 20 minutes or less format of vaudeville and applies it to experimental performance, putting difficult and challenging works in an informal theater context."

Another enlightening and engaging introduction to the artists of P.S. 122 is the benefit performances which annually take place on the first weekend of February. Promotional information has called the project "a season in a weekend." Indeed, if someone wanted a crash course on what's currently being done in the East Village and national performance scene, and attended the extended weekend of six benefit shows, he or she would see nearly 100 performers doing all manner of music, dance, theater, film and performance. A host leads the audience through each performances with hip banter, and gives important fundraising information. A raffle and other contests bring a light, spirited feeling to the proceedings.

> "All of the heat that went into the early years of P.S. 122 is like radioactive material; it has kept the space going for over a decade."

This concept for a quasi-vaudevillian variety show that covers a lot of ground is the model on which the organization's touring program, P.S. 122 Field Trips, is based. Russell says the founding artists benefitted by going on dates outside New York and on the touring circuit. "I found that when they came back from these tours and started making their next piece, it changed," he says. "The frame was a little wider, usually having more to do with the social context. Some of them made their work harder, sharper. [Touring] forced them to make changes, to talk, to start a dialog. I found that pretty interesting, especially as it deepened the work."

He says the P.S. 122 Field Trips grew out of the shared program format, and the desire to help artists discover and be discovered by new audiences. Russell felt this also would enable artists to meet presenters outside of New York. Yet, it would be a more limited commitment on the part of presenters who would be unlikely to devote an entire evening to a performance artist totally unknown to that community.

"I wish I had the resources to run five different Field Trips," Russell adds, "or start a whole Borscht Belt of Field Trips. I would love to reinvent a vaudeville circuit so that people would take these short-formed works and keep moving them around."

He is devoted to demystifying the work, and wants the Field Trips to build a larger national audience for performance. "I want to get it out to the lay audience, the stranger audience, not just the converted. That's going to mean more to my artists, and it's going to mean more to those communities."

The Field Trips project has enjoyed several seasons of successful touring to predictable and unpredictable places. Its first outing was a New England tour co-produced with the New England Foundation for the Arts and the Massachusetts Council on the Arts and Humanities. The tour included performances in many rural and small communities, a new experiences for artists and audiences both. The Field Trips also have toured to the West, where artists played at performance spaces similar to P.S. 122 and with similar audiences, as well as at more mainstream theaters.

Interestingly, another tour was right in P.S. 122's own borough of Manhattan. In the spring of 1990, the Manhattan Theater Club, a well-known resident city company responsible for producing *Ain't Misbehavin'*, *The Lisbon Traviata*, and *Eastern Standard*, invited P.S. 122 to appear for a week of performances on its new DOWNTOWN/UPTOWN series presented at Stage II at the City Center.

The program consisted of the work of five artists who have been regulars at P.S. 122: Guy Yarden, Ann Carlson, Ruth Peyser, Ishmael Houston-Jones and Terry Galloway. The range of work included Yarden's electric violin; Carlson's performance art; an improvised choreography to text by Houston-Jones in which he danced one piece in total darkness while providing commentary; an animated film by Peyser; and a shocking and touching monolog by Galloway in which she addresses her own deafness and psychological landscape.

The audience was invited to stay after the performance for discussion and exchange with the artists, producer Mark Russell, and technical director Lori E. Seid. It was not an audience accustomed to experiencing this kind of work. The exchange was particularly sharp; some people were totally baffled by what they had seen. They wanted the artists to clarify its meaning; the artists assiduously demurred. Significantly, this work was unfamiliar to a group of people who otherwise are experienced theater-goers. Even in New York, this work is breaking new ground with people outside of P.S. 122's intimate inner sanctum.

Running a Presenting Organization

Russell has done his job at P.S. 122 intuitively. He is pragmatic and down to earth, and so is his description of the role of presenting organizations. "They bring artists and audiences together," he says. "They animate situations, and that's a tricky science. I think the good ones are able to buffer and support artists' work. They allow them to fly and create great explosions between audience and artist, which makes both grow. It's not a one-way street. I was taught that theater really happened in the trenches between the audience and the stage, and that's a producer's art. They're right there. They're pulling the two together."

Even so, he says, the presenter's job is easier and less important than the work itself. "Artists have done very well for a long time without presenters, in many cases, and can create their own situations and grab their own audiences, or act as their own presenters. And in some ways, one thing we try to do here is to allow them to still feel like they're involved in their own presentation."

One way this happens is the manner in which performances are publicized.

Michael Sexton, the former director of press and publicity, says he tries to take his cues from the artist. There is a certain regimen of sending out the usual press releases, calendars, and programs, "but the shape and character of the press releases and programs is really up to the artists. I try to fit them to the artists' needs."

The organization also has developed its visual and conceptual image by exploiting its location in a former elementary school. It has developed clever school-like terminology for its programs, short of calling Mark Russell the principal, and the imagery seems to work very well in an appropriately irreverent way. There are the Field Trips, with a promotional brochure done in the black-and-white marble swirl cover stock of elementary school notebooks. The PTA—a friends group—has been described as a wonderful milk-and-cookie organization defined as either Parents, Teachers, and Artists, or People That Ask.

In a recurrent theme, Sexton says his greatest challenge is learning to talk about the work. He observes that the artists themselves have difficulty with it. "A lot of the work is about violating certain standards of procedure and form," he says, so there is a resulting struggle to describe it.

In another familiar theme, it is not enough for P.S. 122 to just get a lot of people in the seats. There is real concern that they comprise an appropriate audience for the work that is to be seen. There also is some concern that big audiences might signal that the exalted place of the artist at P.S. 122 is somehow diminished.

Characteristically, the organization's management style is relaxed and friendly. The box office is a stanchion covered with the unmistakable black-and-white notebook cover paper. This is not the place to put down a plastic credit card to pay for tickets. There are no advanced ticket sales, no reserved seats. "It's about as scuzzy as you're going to get," admits Alan Siege, former director of development, "but it lends itself to the simple idea that you're not coming here because you're going to get a comfortable chair and have your art fed to you."

Finding Funds to Support the Vision

Siege, who served P.S. 122 from 1986–89, says raising funds for the organization provided a substantial challenge. Russell previously had done all the development work on a catch-as-catch-can basis, in addition to his other duties as executive director. Given the circumstances—Russell was practically a one-man show from 1983–86—it is remarkable that he laid such a substantial foundation for the development work that followed.

Siege's opening move was to look carefully at similar types of organizations and see which individuals, foundations and corporations had given money to them. Approaching these groups to tell P.S. 122's story was the beginning of a more intensive and ultimately successful fundraising effort. P.S. 122 began to receive donations from people and organizations that had heard of the space due to the impressive press coverage, but who had never been approached for a contribution.

Siege and Russell have been successful in making the case for P.S. 122 based on its spirit and commitment to artists. They stress that P.S. 122 gives artists the opportunity to be seen before their work is finished, and that the organization has been successful in ferreting out significant talent.

The board of directors also is responsible for the growth in development activity. Its fundraising capabilities increased tremendously when it was expanded beyond its original three founders to include non-artist members. Kathy Spahn, president of the board, had worked at Dance Theater Workshop for many years and was savvy about the funding community. Then there was Tim McClimon, who had worked for the NEA and was appointed to the AT&T Foundation soon after joining the P.S. 122 board. Both of these two new board members were known in the funding community, and brought the organization additional legitimacy.

By 1988, Siege could report several triumphs, including a $50,000 grant over two years from the W. Alton Jones Foundation, and $25,000 from the Surdna Foundation. He points out that the size of these grants is atypical; P.S. 122 more often receives funds in the $5,000 to $10,000 range. Each contribution opened the doors to donations from other foundations and corporations. The ripple effect was really felt when Morgan Guaranty Bank and Chase Manhattan both wrote checks for P.S. 122.

The budget breaks down to 38 percent earned income, with foundations and corporations bringing in about 28 percent, individuals 1 percent, and government 35 percent. Its budget was $600,000 for the 1990–91 season.

Maintaining the Vision

Mark Russell keeps his ear to the ground and tries to be in touch with the thinking of the community of artists. He says he has become aware of an "arts deficit"—an artistic emotional exhaustion and resulting shortage of excellent work—which has developed because it has become more difficult to be an artist in New York City. "The rigors of life, and the rigors of dealing with AIDS, death, homelessness and censorship have very subtly but pervasively affected the work," he says.

"These people are really begging for protection," he says of the artists. "They're looking for P.S. 122 to protect them. There are fewer opportunities. The money is less. This is a very scary time to be an artist, just as it is a scary time to be an institution. The demands on the institution are so great that it's easy to forget that there are people in the smaller heap that are having a hell of a time getting their first concert up. There's lack of space, lack of resources. It's very tough right now, and that's reflected in the work."

Russell speaks of an arts deficit with great concern and reserve. "At first, I put it up to my own shortsightedness," he says. "but lately I've asked other producers, 'What have you seen that's exciting?' No one has anything to say. But maybe there is something. Maybe the artists are taking a rest, or looking around for something, or lost the groove.

"We were in a time of great wealth," he says of the club days in the East Village. "There was a strong performance every other week. There was a whole wave; it was like being a part of the '60s, when all the walls were coming down. It was very exciting. Now, the walls are coming down in other parts of the world, and it's hard to respond to those things. The problems here have grown so that they're not easy to respond to.

"I see an AIDS piece every week. This is shaping a generation. They are grappling with these larger, harder ideas. The troubles are not so abstract any more. I think it eventually will forge some very strong work and some very strong artists— just as the Vietnam war influenced and produced some very strong work. AIDS has killed more people than Vietnam, and it cuts closer. The shock of something cutting that close is hard to deal with, and it's hard to make art in the face of it. But it will come out. It may not even deal with the disease. But the way people look at life will change, and it will influence the next 10 years."

Anyone who has observed the development of this organization knows that as the work and the artists' concerns change, so too will P.S. 122, to remain as supportive and responsive as possible. For that reason, it is a nesting place that artists never need outgrow.

Sun Ra

Photo by Dave Buechner

16 Bringing the World to Atlanta

The music was passionate and vivid, as one tango after another pushed the limits of the form. Astor Piazzolla and the New Tango Quintet, fresh from Argentina in the first stop of a 1988 tour, gave the audience at Atlanta's intimate Peachtree Playhouse a rich feast of musical ideas and sensations; in turn, the musicians fed on the reaction. As the evening went on, musicians and audience reached that perfect state of communication, a seamless exchange of energy and captive attention.

Piazzolla calls the tango "a sad music, a passionate music. You have to play it this way. You have to sweat. If you could bleed, it would be better." He and his musicians were at a nearly ecstatic level of improvisation and performance that night, in a performance that eloquently demonstrated his lifelong achievement in elevating a concrete, popular, indigenous dance form to the level of poetry.

Piazzolla is the composer and inventor of the iconoclastic and provocative "nuevo tango" (new tango). So hot are the passions about the tango in Argentina that when he first began creating this new form he was called "the assassin and murderer of the tango." Piazzolla performs his work on the *bandoneon*, a squeezebox instrument that in the hands of this master can go from the lyrical tones of a harmonium in a church to the brash sound of a beer-hall serenade.

His performance was typical—if anything can said to be typical—of the work of Quantum Productions, a young organization that breaks new ground every time it invites musicians to perform on one of Atlanta's stages.

Since 1984, Quantum has presented a wide variety of jazz, contemporary, and world music to audiences throughout the area. Its presentations emphasize live music, and include concerts, workshops, lectures, films, and video. The goal is to have American jazz and other art music from around the world listened to seriously, and to emphasize what they have in common.

Quantum Productions is an example of personal enthusiasm and artistic vision made public. The person behind the vision is Rob Gibson, who founded the organization in 1984 with his wife, Caroline Howell. Gibson says he wants to present and produce quality programs that are enlightening, educational, and entertaining, all at once. He wants to interest as many people as he can in quality music. For the present, Quantum Productions is one of his vehicles.

It is a unique organization in a unique city. "It definitely fills a niche here," says Bill Anschell, jazz coordinator for the Southern Arts Federation, and himself a jazz pianist. "It is the only organization that is committed to world musics. If it weren't for Quantum, there would be little of this type of programming in Atlanta."

Says Astor Piazzolla: "These people are helping us be known in Atlanta, and in the entire world. That's the most important thing for an artist: that there are people in an audience listening to us, getting an idea of what we do in Argentina. If presenters like Quantum don't exist, we don't exist."

Atlanta has for some years been an increasingly diverse and international city. The demographics include a 70 percent African American population, as well as newer immigrant communities of Indians, Koreans and Africans. Gibson says Atlanta has the largest Gambian population in the U.S.

Consequently, Quantum's purpose springs organically from the nature of the city. It offers a stage and a shared forum, focusing on each discrete genre of musical/cultural expression. There is no one single Quantum audience. Rather, each presentation penetrates into another cultural community.

Quantum Mechanics and Music

Why call a presenting organization "quantum?"

Gibson explains that the discovery at the turn of this century of new, subatomic worlds made Isaac Newton's laws of physics outmoded.

"Quantum mechanics is the great connection theory that has tied the world together," he says. "I feel that is what our music does."

As Quantum explains in its newsletter, people in every culture are seeking the answers to the same questions about what it means to be a human being. One type of person intimately involved in this search is the 20th-century artist—and, of special interest to Quantum, the 20th-century musician.

"Because people are people no matter when or where they live," the article says, "and because quantum mechanics says interconnectedness is more powerful than isolation, and because Einstein says time and place aren't what we thought they are, we know that as we search for meaningful values today we can sift forward and backward in time and sideways to other cultures around us.

"We know that answers discovered by Ghanaian griots centuries ago, new data the Kronos Quartet is uncovering now, truths Johnny Griffin has articulated since the '40s, and new visions Astor Piazzolla shook from the tango tradition in Argentina—that all of these may help us in our own searchings in Atlanta."

Those at Quantum feel that the world is wide open for exploration and re-definition. "This is a pursuit artists are traditionally good at," the article continues, "and one which all the musicians Quantum brings to Atlanta have in common. Ornette Coleman, Ali Akbar Khan, Sheila Jordan, the McIntosh County Shouters: They and all the others invite us to journey with them into sometimes new, some-times old, always different territories."

Each season's programming reflects this all-encompassing mission to share the music of the world. As just one example, Quantum described its 1989–90 concert series, "Manifest Evidence," as a continuing attempt to point the way to a broader understanding of the development of musical cultures and of the meaning of sound.

The unique series presented music from India, South Africa, Zimbabwe, Brazil, Bulgaria, Austria, Germany, The Netherlands, and the United States. It united clas-sical European concepts of music and form, non-European folk and classical music, improvised music, and music with a social message. Performances included an evening of jazz from England featuring the Courtney Pine Quartet; Egberto Gismonti Quartet with Brazilian music; the Bulgarian State Radio and Television Female Vocal Choir; and Mahlathini and the Mahotella Queens with the Makgona Tsohle Band from South Africa.

"Any person in today's music scene knows that rock, classical, folk, and jazz are all yesterday's titles," says Ornette Coleman in Quantum's 1988–89 season brochure. "I feel that the music world is getting closer to being a singular expression, one with endless musical stories of mankind."

The Gibson-Quantum Story

Rob Gibson is a man with a mission, and it drives him in everything he does. He wants people to hear and appreciate the world's musics. And he wants them to understand that this music can show us what everyone, no matter what culture, has in common.

Gibson says he founded Quantum when he came to realize that New York City was the only place to hear and see a wide range of music from around the world. He felt a cultural void in Atlanta, and he wanted to fill it.

His unique artistic vision, and the missionary zeal that accompanies it, comes from an abiding love of the music. His knowledge is not superficial, limited to the names and groups alone. He not only knows about the many musics of many different countries, he is familiar with the masters of each musical form.

How did this unlikely odyssey begin? Gibson remembers that he was mostly interested in rock and roll as a youngster, especially bands based in the Southeast that played Southern rock, such as the Allman Brothers. "I thought Duane Allman was great, but then I began to learn that I liked him so much because he was coming out of the blues. And when I really began listening to the blues, especially urban Chicago blues, that led me into jazz. I started listening to jazz, and then I wanted to trace that back, too.

"Once you start tracing that back, you get into the roots of the African

American tradition. You can follow it through the Caribbean or down to South America and over to Africa. I discovered that music in Africa was this incredibly complicated and beautiful spiritual music."

He pursued his interest in world musics while studying political science at the University of Georgia in Athens, and produced a program for the student radio station. He also produced some concerts for the university, including Joni Mitchell and Peter Tosh. After graduation, he became the station manager for WRFG-FM in Atlanta's Little Five Points neighborhood. He went to work on the staff of the 1983 Atlanta Jazz Festival, presented by the city's Bureau of Cultural Affairs, but became disenchanted with the Festival when it started becoming commercial. He felt that the city was missing the perfect opportunity to expose people to the less commercial and more challenging side of jazz.

He decided to start his own presenting organization. Nonprofit status was granted in the summer of 1984, and Quantum Productions began presenting concerts. The first was presented on New Year's Eve, 1984. This concert, featuring Sun Ra and his Bible Belt Shakers/Cosmos Love Arkestra, is memorable to many.

Lil Friedlander, an Atlanta photographer and developer of a warehouse space for artists, recalls that she attended the concert, and wondered who was responsible for bringing such a unique experience to Atlanta. "Who is this person?" she recalls thinking. "I felt that this person is way beyond where the arts are in this city."

Gibson and Howell openly acknowledge that they were doing their work by the seat of their pants in these early years, using their own money to front expenses until the box office receipts came in. Gibson then began to write grants, and over time began to receive funding. For more than four years, he and Howell kept Quantum going while he maintained a full-time job, first as a salesman for an embossing business, and then marketing products for a software company.

Howell has been an integral part of the organization from its beginning. Gibson typically oversaw the backstage details while Howell took charge of the front-of-house operations, including box office and house management. She has consistently been involved in the business management side of Quantum. Her role began immediately when the couple returned from their honeymoon in 1984.

Although she is important to the operations and has a keen interest in the music, she admits that she might not be involved in the organization if Gibson were not part of it. "The impulse to start the organization definitely came from Rob," she says.

Gibson says he comes out of "a fairly bourgeois background as a white kid in suburban America, and many people say the same thing: 'We see you on stage and you don't look like the type, you don't act like the type that would be interested in this kind of music.' I'm a fairly typical American in other ways: married, two kids, house payment, car payment . . .

"My goal is to get good music heard by as many people as possible. I want to facilitate that however I can." He feels the technology and capitalism of the 20th century have mass-marketed a certain type of music, leaving behind so much that deserves to be heard. "Music is a very spiritual and very serious thing, and deserves a better kind of treatment," he says.

Gibson says he feels good about the organization and its continuing ability to attract more people—and new people—to its events. "We haven't made any artistic compromises yet. Right now, we want to present as many different kinds of music as we can. Five years is the first hump for an organization. If we're around 10 years, I'll feel like we really have been making a statement."

He has a very personal tie with his audiences, according to Ruby Lerner, executive director of Image Film/Video Center, a media arts organization in Atlanta. Lerner formerly was executive director of Alternate ROOTS (Regional Organization of Theaters South), as well as a consultant in community arts and marketing. She agrees with the notion that a presenter is, in a certain way, an artist. "There are a lot of ways to create," she says. "Creating an organization is creating a work of art. Rob is infinitely curious. That's what drives him. I never leave anything that he presents without feeling stimulated about it."

> Quantum Productions is a young organization that breaks new ground every time it invites musicians to perform.

Undeniably, Gibson is the core of the organization. Lerner says it's hard to imagine replacing him as head of Quantum Productions. "The organization is a function of the things he cares about," she says. "It is so personal that in effect there are no lines between the person and the organization. Can this organization survive beyond the founder? It's an irrelevant point. It may and it may not. It doesn't matter. The artistic impact on this community, whether or not Rob were to pack his bags and leave tomorrow, has been enormous."

But Gibson doesn't seem to have invested his own ego in the organization. His is a pure vision, a belief in the music rather than the organization. Quantum exists because he wants the music to be heard. He seldom introduces himself during his welcoming speeches on stage. He also doesn't identify himself on his weekly radio show. He says that if someone came onto the scene and met these same musical objectives in the community, he would be relieved of his need to do so.

Lil Friedlander says Gibson's vision is special because of his expansive knowledge of the music and the fact that he is making it available and accessible in the city. "Atlanta is very much a small town," she says. "Groups within the city are self-identified; they're most comfortable when they're surrounded by people who are like they are. But Rob's vision is much more all-encompassing, all-embracing: the fact that music unites us all.

"Art is important in its ability to give us access to the best parts of what it means to be human," she continues. "To be truly a human being means to be aware of what is divine in the biggest sense. Art, good or bad, has the ability to touch that in people. What Rob is doing is important, like world peace or brotherhood. For people of all colors to be sitting in an audience together, having a positive and powerful experience together . . . maybe people's hearts and minds are being changed just a little bit. Quantum is an enormous asset to this city."

That Gibson's work and Quantum's record have made a difference to Atlanta also is borne out in their receiving the 1988 *Creative Loafing* Award "for significant contributions to the cultural life of Atlanta." *Creative Loafing* is an Atlanta arts and entertainment weekly that annually bestows awards on people who have had an important impact on the community.

Singular Programming

What is so special about Quantum's programming?

Gibson's philosophy—that the music of a people is a window into their culture—informs his programming decisions. "We can better appreciate Zimbabwe if we know something about the political situation there," the 1988–89 season brochure says. "In turn, this provides us with a broader perspective on the culture of that country. Similarly, hearing Japanese music of the T'ang dynasty helps us understand the social changes which occurred during that time. Watching a New Orleans marching band stroll down Bourbon Street can make all the difference in our comprehension of jazz and the culture that produced it."

The 1988–89 season offered a wealth of diversity, as have all of Quantum's seasons. There were performances by Pandit Hariprasad Chaurasia and Sabir Khan, India's master flutist and tabla player; Grupo Aymara from Bolivia, playing the ancient melodies of the Andean highlands; jazz tenor saxophonist Courtney Pine from Great Britain; Cajun fiddler Dewey Balfa and Friends; and other music from Asia, Africa, South America, Europe (medieval and contemporary) and the Caribbean. "Music from North America" emphasized jazz and other music indigenous to the American South. Several film/lecture events looked at the history of the jazz trumpet, and paid tribute to John Coltrane and Gil Evans.

In other seasons, Quantum has presented the McIntosh County Shouters, performing the oldest African-American performance tradition surviving on the North American continent. It fuses call-and-response singing, percussive rhythm, and expressive and formalized dance-like movement. Quantum also programmed "The Asian Connection," a concert of the music of Japan, Korea, and India. There also have been more well-known performers such as the Kronos Quartet, Meredith Monk, the Art Ensemble of Chicago, and the World Saxophone Quartet.

From the beginning, Quantum has provided cogent and edifying information in its brochures and promotional materials, looking at each of the performers and the musical traditions being presented. The notes also explain the general philosophical approach, why it presents the artists it does.

In the introduction to "Sound Legacies," Quantum's fall 1986 series, the organization restated its commitment to present concerts featuring the music of cultures and continents around the world, each performed by a virtuoso performer or group steeped in their respective traditions.

"We find it impossible to understand very much about a music without knowing something about its cultural and historical background. At the same time, we feel the inverse is true: that one cannot really understand a culture without taking into account its music." In that series—featuring folk and classical music from

Japan, Korea, India, Gambia, and south Georgia, plus contemporary music rooted in both European and African traditions—"tradition becomes the focus as the single common denominator." The series of concerts, most of which were Atlanta debuts, drew more than 2,500 people to hear the traditional music.

Jazz as a world music has always been a focus for the organization. However, since the fall of 1988—when Gibson was offered a contract with Atlanta's Bureau of Cultural Affairs to program and produce the summertime Atlanta Jazz Series— the number of jazz events presented by Quantum has been reduced. Before then, however, Quantum's jazz events gave the city the opportunity to hear some of the most seminal and creative figures on the jazz scene today, as well as those with long-established reputations.

"Rob books a cross-section of the entire jazz tradition, although he shies away from traditional jazz music from before the 1940s," says Bill Anschell. "He touches on everything since then—bebop, hard bop, progressive or free jazz. He tends to deal with significant, contemporary figures and there seems to be no consideration for commerciality. I think he's booking strictly from his vision of what the most important music is."

"Now's the Time," Quantum's winter/spring 1987 series of seven programs, featured some of jazz's greatest talents who have worked in relative obscurity during their lives. The series was described as "a small scratch into the surface of a music that continues to beat the odds—and in Atlanta, a city with few jazz concerts and even fewer clubs, the odds are being beat more often these days."

Such elder statesmen as Jimmy Hamilton and Randy Weston were featured, along with young bandleaders David Murray (winner of Denmark's prestigious Jazzpar prize in 1990) and Bobby Watson. Other performers were the George Adams-Don Pullen Quartet; Lester Bowie's Brass Fantasy; Clarinet Summit with Jimmy Hamilton, Alvin Batiste, John Carter, and David Murray; the Robert Watson-Curtis Lundy Quartet; and Han Bennink and Ernst Reijseger from Holland.

Harriet Sanford, director of the city's Bureau of Cultural Affairs, says Quantum Productions has set a standard for itself, and goes out and pursues it. "It all just doesn't fall into their laps," she says. "They go out and they seek and they find."

She cites as just one example the Ed Blackwell Festival of three concerts held in 1987 to celebrate one of jazz music's master performers. The three-day tribute, which also raised funds for the ailing drummer, was co-sponsored with the High Museum of Art and Image Film and Video Center. It included workshops, speakers, and videos. Workshops included sessions with Blackwell himself, and bassist Charlie Haden. Film screenings featured rare footage of Blackwell in performance with Mal Waldron's Quintet and the Ornette Coleman quartet.

The festival included two reunion concerts as a tribute to Blackwell's musical beginnings in New Orleans with the Original American Jazz Quintette, and then later with the Ornette Coleman Quartet and Quintet from the late 1950s and '60s. The New Orleans group reunited Ellis Marsalis (respected and renowned teacher and father of Wynton and Branford), Alvin Batiste (another renowned teacher), and Harold Battiste, Richard Payne, and Blackwell. Joining in was another Crescent

City musician, Earl Turbinton. The final concert of the tribute reunited Coleman and members of his bands, including Don Cherry, Charlie Haden, Blackwell, and Dewey Redman.

Gibson created the tribute out of his deep commitment to the music and to Blackwell's importance in jazz history. It was a special, one-time performance which took place only in Atlanta. It did not go on tour, and was not replicated anywhere else in the U.S. The historic series of concerts was audio-recorded, and arrangements have been made to release the recordings.

"Ed Blackwell to me is one of the great drummers in the music known as jazz," Gibson says, explaining his motivation for doing such an unusual event. "He's a very important and influential drummer, although largely unrecognized by the populace and the media. This particular event celebrated his legacy to American music."

Bill Anschell adds, "Blackwell is what you would call a musician's musician, meaning his name has relatively little drawing power. But he is a very important drummer in the evolution of music. That shows me a real commitment to the art, as opposed to trying to sell a lot of seats and make a lot of money."

Although Blackwell is largely unrecognized by the mainstream jazz audience, Gibson reports that an impressive media contingent was in attendance in Atlanta that weekend. International journalists from England, France, and Canada attended, as did writers from *The New York Times, Wall Street Journal*, and *Village Voice*.

Another event of particular interest in 1987 was another unique-to-Atlanta event. It showcased the music of Alvin Singleton, then composer-in-residence at the Atlanta Symphony, and now composer-in-residence at Spelman College. Two performances of the same concert featured music prepared and performed by the combined forces of the music departments of Spelman College, Morehouse College, and Georgia State University. Two new works were composed and premiered as part of the project, one for each of the Morehouse and Spelman College choruses. In addition, Singleton's *Inside-Out* for piano four-hands was performed. The climax of the events came when the three choruses filed onstage to sing Singleton's *Mass*, representing the Southeastern premiere of the work, which had its official premiere at the Vatican in 1975.

The significance of these concerts was both musical and social. Musically, they focused on four important works by one of the country's important younger composers. Socially, the concerts showcased the work of a noted Black composer, and provided the opportunity for the music departments of two historically Black colleges and one traditionally white university to collaborate, Harriet Sanford says.

Sanford remembers that the Singleton concert was filled to capacity at Spelman College's Sisters Chapel. "I was five minutes late, and no seats were available. So, I stood for a few hours. They could have performed it 10 nights straight and still have sold out.

"What Rob did is bring Atlanta's two very different environments together," she continues. This resulted in a diverse audience that could experience original music performed by groups to which they might not otherwise have been exposed. They also could begin to appreciate the depth of what it takes to be a composer. "Here you had an international composer, who has lived in Europe for much of his life, come to Atlanta and understand that we can merge the differences that exist in our city, and have a beautiful result," Sanford says.

"It was an emotional opportunity, too. Atlanta is the center of civil rights activity. As we watch what happens around the country, sometimes we feel we're immune to it, but we're not. In a concert like this, we saw a merging of Atlanta's differences—and Singleton's music was the bridge."

In 1987, Quantum also commissioned Singleton to write a string quartet for the Kronos Quartet. This work was premiered in Atlanta; happily, it also was performed in San Francisco, and in New York on the Kronos' Tully Hall series presented by Lincoln Center.

> Those at Quantum feel that the world is wide open for exploration and redefinition.

Steve Rosen, a member of Quantum's board of directors and its legal officer, says he recognizes the riskiness of Quantum's programming. "There is a risk, but also nothing to lose except money. Quantum has a proven track record. There's always a risk if no one else has done it. But it also gives the the opportunity to find your own niche by doing things no one else is doing. Your neck is always on the line financially, but as an arts group, you've got to take that kind of risk. We're holding ourselves out to the public and to the IRS that we're doing something for the public good that no one else is."

Gibson maintains that just about every show Quantum presents is an artistic and financial risk. Relatively speaking, he says, the Astor Piazzolla performance was less so because his music is accessible to audiences. However, a concert by artists such as the World Saxophone Quartet or the David Murray Octet is more difficult to sell. "You have to sell the people on the connection of their music to the jazz tradition," Gibson says, "and that's an artistic risk."

Singleton, with whom Gibson has had a long friendship and professional association, says "The kind of programming Quantum does is unusual for anywhere, New York or anywhere else. When you visit Rob in his home or his studio, it's an experience. He always has something new on the tape recorder or the CD or the video. He's a novel guy."

Harriet Sanford describes Atlanta as a magnet for all kinds of people. "We're not an insulated Southern city that just has dogwoods and great weather. There's a cultural co-mingling. We really are changing. The cityscape is so different than before. Each of the buildings represents something new and different. And the people in them are new and different—and bring new and different interests. They may be Japanese or Chinese, or from somewhere in Europe, or they may be New Yorkers. They're not inclined to attend the same kinds of events or concerts that were interesting to people 20 years ago."

Sanford says Gibson never followed the old standard in the first place. "He always wanted to be on the edge, and he took us to a new level," she says. "Quantum is a model for other organizations. While you may not win on every event, you're creating a new following, or finding people who weren't interested before. Rob has shown us the edges. Other organizations are beginning to see that there are a lot more edges than we ever thought.

"I think the most important thing about Quantum is its vision, its willingness to take risk, and to do the work without government support. If the Bureau of Cultural Affairs didn't fund their grant proposals, they'd still be out there. This gives them more credibility than many other organizations."

In 1988, the bureau engaged Gibson to program a downtown brownbag lunchtime series of free concerts. "I knew he would find the very different groups, not the standard ones you'd expect to find," Sanford says. "He searched, and found talent from Georgia. That was more exciting because it helped us promote ourselves. If we don't, no one will.

"Rob understands the essence of that. So, while he brings us things from all over the world, he also brings us things that are very Southern. (He brings us) a sense of pride, and helps us put our role into perspective. He reminds us that there are great and wonderful things all over the world. But he also lets us see that what we have at home also is essential."

Marketing Diverse Programs to Diverse Communities

Ruby Lerner says that Quantum's strength as a unique organization also is its weakness when it comes to marketing. "The different work they do appeals to different constituencies," she says, and that calls for aggressive marketing for each concert to draw the appropriate segment of the Atlanta community.

Gibson reports that there is a core group of people who come to every Quantum event, but he would like it to grow much larger. That means he has to tap into the different cultural communities that might be interested in a particular event. "We have to start from scratch for each event," Gibson says. "We've got to interest the public every time, and our shows are wildly varied. We had Argentines for the first time at the Astor Piazzolla concert. You can market a jazz show to jazz lovers, but that market is not monolithic."

His zeal in presenting this music has made him aggressive when it comes to marketing. He says he has no qualms about selling the organization, because he believes in it so deeply. "My dad always tells me I'm preaching. He says I'm like his father, who was a Baptist preacher, except my message is different. I guess I sort of agree with that."

Frequently, Quantum's approach to marketing is educational, because the musical genres, forms, sources, or artists it presents are largely unfamiliar to the public. But even though the programming seems to lack continuity, and each event is apparently unique, Gibson says he still sees them all as connected. This is where the underlying foundation of quantum theory—the interconnectedness of all things—comes into play.

"It's a matter of educating the audience over time," Gibson says. "That's our basic role as an educational organization. We have to help them learn about the past history of the music and tie this music in with people like the World Saxophone Quartet or David Murray, who are right out on the edge. They have as much to do with jazz as any of the beboppers did, or those who came before."

Gibson has found the best way to market his concerts is to cultivate the arts writers at the Atlanta newspapers, and he spends much of his time sharing his knowledge of the music with them. He regularly provides them with tapes so they can develop an ear through active listening of various kinds of music. Frequently, the music on the tapes has nothing to do with an upcoming concert. "This keeps them listening to the music and learning," Gibson says. "What is a minimal investment for me helps educate thousands of readers."

He also continues to produce his own radio show, *Continental Drift*—a kind of 90-minute weekly Quantum Productions—as public service work. He has been doing the show on WREK-FM for the past five years. "It's one of the things you do to push the music," he says. It also helps to promote Quantum events—although he is careful to avoid the appearance of conflict of interest by not focusing solely on those artists who will be appearing on Quantum's series. He also cultivates people at the area's five public radio stations, who can play the music on their programs and can do interviews or make public service announcements.

Because of a limited budget, Quantum tries to market without spending much money. "I believe that you can sell anybody anything if you do it correctly," Gibson says. "I think we have a quality product, so it's easy to sell. You have to get articles written about you in the paper, get the music on the radio, and get your name out there in front of the people."

Quantum's graphics have always been arresting and of the highest quality. The organization has utilized the services of Atlanta artist George Davidson from the beginning. In 1986, after receiving a grant in marketing and audience development from the Fulton County Arts Council, Quantum determined that a high-profile brochure with seven commissioned linoleum block prints by Davidson was in order. The 1986 brochure for "Sound Legacies" was a work of art itself, including a series of essays about each type of music, graphically enhanced by the prints.

Quantum now also has a newsletter, appropriately called *LEAP!*, that is distributed to those on the mailing list. The newsletter keeps readers informed about upcoming events, and also explains the organization's philosophy.

Raising Funds

Financial difficulties continue to plague Quantum, and Gibson is continually frustrated by them. "I feel as if we're doing the best work we've ever done artistically, drawing the best crowds, with the best staff we've ever had working for us. We're doing our best marketing, but the funding seems to be tighter than it has ever been.

"We're doing better in terms of everything," he continues. "We've done larger programs and more expensive groups—Meredith Monk, Astor Piazzolla—and more programs in the Symphony Hall. But the struggle is harder than it has ever been. I just don't think it's meant to be easy. That's probably what makes it fun. It's a challenge."

He says he is driven to keep Quantum growing, because an organization can lose its impetus and edge once growth is contained. "I'd like to see Quantum become larger and more prolific, and influence lots of people. The quality has got to remain true, but the numbers of people have to become larger."

> "This music makes me feel whole, and I can only hope that other people out there will connect with it in the same way."

Based on certain criteria that are applied in evaluating grant applications, the Georgia Arts Council for three years has ranked Quantum as the number-one presenting organization in the state. This has resulted in a 50 percent increase in its grant allocation, to $18,000.

Quantum also is the first in terms of earned income—nearly 75 percent of its budget of nearly $400,000—of any group that has applied for funding from the state arts council. This has been both a blessing and a curse, bringing in much-needed monies but also indicating that the organization isn't as successful as it should be with fundraising.

In addition to its Georgia Arts Council grant, Quantum receives money from other governmental agencies, including the Fulton County Arts Council ($20,000) and the Bureau of Cultural Affairs ($7,500). It also has a contract to produce the Montreux-Atlanta International Music Festival.

The organization has received funding from the National Endowment for the Arts for a number of years, However, Gibson complains that the small allocation of $3,000 to $5,000 is not worth the trouble of providing the necessary documentation. He feels the grant amounts speak to the NEA's lack of interest in the kind of programming done by Quantum. Further, the NEA has not actively supported art and artists from abroad, and Gibson feels that Quantum's extensive international presentations work strongly against a more generous allocation.

Quantum is still a relatively unknown quantity in Atlanta as far as the corporate and foundation world is concerned, Gibson says. He says most of this money goes to the long-established arts institutions, just as in many other major cities. "Quantum is not a household world," he says. "I haven't found a person who can sell the organization better than I can, and I haven't got enough time. It's completely different than trying to sell the symphony. I'm trying to sell the music. I go in and talk to corporations, and it's hard to explain what we do."

He's expecting some organizational and developmental improvement as a result of Quantum's new three-year plan, based on a consultant's analysis of the organization's financial condition.

Looking Ahead

As the 1990 season ends, Gibson speaks of two setbacks. One is the resignation of Beth Judy, who since 1987 had the major share of Quantum's administrative responsibilities, built the membership rolls, and served as editor of *LEAP!*. Judy returned to the technical writing she had been doing for the Center for Disease Control in Atlanta. Gibson intends to fill the position, plus hire someone to do fundraising.

The other setback is the change of assignment of *Atlanta Constitution* arts writer Bo Emerson. Emerson covered many of Quantum's events, and wrote with great interest and acumen about the music. Gibson has mounted a campaign to make the newspaper administration change its mind. "It's in Quantum's interest for survival," Gibson explains, "because he is the most important music writer in the Southeast U.S."

Quantum's operations in 1990 and beyond also will be deeply influenced by two developments in 1988. That year, Atlanta's Bureau of Cultural Affairs engaged Gibson as the artistic director of the Atlanta Jazz Series. Quantum Productions also received the contract to take on the ailing Montreux-Atlanta International Music Festival (MAIMF), which was in danger of disintegrating in its inaugural year. Quantum took on the MAIMF on very short notice—but, according to public reaction and press reports, it managed to do a more than creditable job. Highlights included the Brazilian Martinho da Vila, the Bundu Boys from Zimbabwe, and the Cajun group John Delafose & the Eunice Playboys.

Gibson explains that the MAIMF runs six days, culminating on Labor Day. It is presented free of charge in sites all over Atlanta, including three performances in the parks. It incorporates jazz, zydeco, Cajun, blues, rock, reggae, folk music, world musics, symphony and opera. He says it is very much like what Quantum does during the regular year, but is broader and condensed into a short period of time. The events have drawn 40,000 people in a single day.

In contrast, Gibson says, "The great success of Quantum is the intimacy of the programming that we do. I feel as if I've got the best of both worlds."

A total of $750,000 is available to program and produce the Atlanta Jazz Series and the MAIMF. This is money that Quantum does not have to raise either by development efforts or by selling tickets. "Quantum can continue to do things that the Atlanta Jazz Series cannot," Gibson explains, "and the international music festival can do things that Quantum can't afford to do."

"I just want to get this music here. If somebody came tomorrow and offered a budget of $3 million to program jazz throughout the year in St. Louis, it would be very hard to turn down. Quantum could be around for the next 30 years—or if someone else fulfilled the need in Atlanta, it could close down in January. But I don't think that's going to happen."

Meanwhile, the organization continues to present unique events. In the 1990–92 seasons, Quantum will participate in the Festival of Indonesia tour of music and dance. It will be the first time that some of the classical forms of Indonesia have been performed outside of that country.

Characteristically, Gibson says he is as excited about the festival as he has been about anything Quantum has presented. "There will be some amazing programs," he says. "Even though Indonesia has been exposed to western culture for decades, these musics have not changed that much.

"Many of the world's musics have succumbed to the western influences of rock and pop," he adds. "Much of African music has become Afro-pop. But this music is still very much rooted in the classical and folk traditions of Indonesia, and not much exploited by the western tradition. I think that Indonesian musics are some of the highest art musics ever created by mankind."

Gibson has remained committed to his personal vision. "Because music changed my life the way it did and opened my views up to the world completely—opened me up politically, socially, morally, spiritually—I feel that it can do that to other people as well."

In an interview with *Creative Loafing*, Gibson said, "You've got to be in it for the long haul if you're going to make a lasting, meaningful statement. What do we hear in Sun Ra? We hear a whole history that reaches back beyond Egyptian culture, beyond downtown Lower East Village, and beyond Saturn. It's deep, spiritual communication with what some people would call God, what some people would call their soul, and what some other people consider pure entertainment or pleasure. Personally speaking, it makes me feel whole, and I can only hope that other people out there will connect with it in the same way."

Ornette Coleman

Photo by Jay Anderson

David Gordon/Pick Up Company

Photo by Andrew Eccles

17 Quiet Fanfare in San Francisco

"Ruth Felt is the kind of presenter who is extremely generous, extremely open, and faithful. It is heartening when someone invites you back several years in a row, comes and watches your work every night, seems to care about both the situation and the circumstances that surround it, and goes out on a limb to present your work in an entirely different way. Does one grow for being loved? I think probably one does."

So David Gordon—choreographer, dancer, and founder of the Pick Up Company—describes the founder, president, and executive director of San Francisco Performances.

The organization reflects the quiet determination of the woman who has nurtured it from modest but calculated beginnings. The institutional persona of San Francisco Performances is devoid of fanfare, reticent about singing its own praises. But despite its modesty, this quiet organization has had a remarkable impact on the arts in San Francisco. It is solid and stable, and it has grown significantly during the 11 seasons it has been presenting in the Bay area.

Ruth Felt had eminent mentors on her professional path to the founding of San Francisco Performances. As assistant concert manager of the UCLA Department of Fine Arts, she worked with Frances Inglis, one of the most influential presenters of the performing arts in the U.S. during the years when presenting was beginning to coalesce as a field.

Felt then joined the San Francisco Opera staff in 1971, rising to the position of company administrator. She worked with the late Kurt Herbert Adler, who was internationally renowned as one of the finest general directors of an opera company.

After eight years there, Felt began to think about starting a presenting organization in the city she loved.

From its inception, San Francisco Performances was designed to complement rather than compete with what was available in the performing arts. "San Francisco has an opera company, a symphony, a ballet, a repertory theater—all of great significance," Felt says. "But when it came to the major chamber music ensembles or to individual artists in recital, the offerings were erratic. San Francisco needed a presenter that would regularly bring in a variety of the best performing artists." Felt points out that colleges and universities usually do a large share of presenting because they can offer institutional support. But in San Francisco, she says, they had never been involved in presenting on the same scale as Cal Performances at the University of California at Berkeley, Stanford University, or UCLA.

Felt saw the need for an organization that would present in recital both world-class performers and emerging artists who were on their way to becoming world class. "I also believed it was important for the smaller dance companies to have an organization that would help them, showcase them, and take risks with them," she says. Eventually, she recognized another gap—in high-quality but somewhat lighter fare—and decided that this, too, was an area in which the public should experience the best.

To give such a presenting organization a chance to flourish, Felt knew she needed to develop a solid subscriber base and to assemble a strong board of trustees that would establish the organization's significance in the community. Since Felt had no family resources or financial connections of her own in San Francisco, she also needed a board to provide a financial base and raise money.

Felt began looking at organizations that might serve as models. She especially recalls the advice she received from Patrick Hayes and Douglas Wheeler of the Washington Performing Arts Society. She repeats it forcefully, as if it was indelibly inscribed on her mind: "Draw up a five-year plan and be prepared to stick with it. Say you're going to present seven programs your first season, announce it, budget for it, then do just that. Don't get seduced into doing another concert that is 'a sure thing,' because there is no such thing." Hayes, Wheeler, and other presenters confirmed Felt's inclination toward a fiscally conservative approach to ensure the organization's survival in its difficult first years.

She then formed a nonprofit organization, assembled an eight-member board, and drew up a five-year plan complete with fundraising goals, a schedule of events for the first season, and growth projections. She called it San Francisco Performances. "I was trying to establish an institution, not a vehicle for self-aggrandizement," she says. "That's why it's not called Ruth Felt Presents." She became its president, sitting on the board of trustees and its executive director.

The first season consisted of six events, all carefully chosen, Felt says, to address the gap she wanted to fill in the local cultural scene. San Francisco Performances opened with a recital by the eminent pianist André Watts, a longtime friend of hers, who donated his fee for the first concert. Watts also joined the board, adding his considerable artistic weight to help establish the organization's credibility.

The season also included Canada's Orford String Quartet, which had never performed in California; the Chicago Symphony Chamber Players; Swedish soprano Elisabeth Söderström, who had sung at the San Francisco Opera, but had never given a recital in the city; Martha Clarke's dance trio Crowsnest; and a duo recital by Ruth Laredo, piano, and Paula Robison, flute.

A Commitment to Artistic Vision

San Francisco Performances has grown in a steady, logical way, resisting the temptation to overextend itself or to do that one extra concert that is "a sure thing." From the six events in the 1980–81 opening year to the eighth season of 35 programs, from 300 subscribers to 1,750, from an opening season budget of slightly more than $100,000 to the 1987–88 season's $800,000 budget, San Francisco Performances has proven that deliberate and measured expansion can bring stability to an organization. And with controlled growth, artistic vision has been able to flourish.

Insights into Ruth Felt's artistic vision are better garnered from other people's comments than from any pronouncements she might make, for she is not given to the grandiose. In the view of those who have known her for years and observed how she began the organization, Felt has established consistently high artistic standards.

Jillian Steiner Sandrock, director of the arts and culture program at the L.J. and Mary C. Skaggs Foundation, has known Felt since the mid-1970s, when both worked at the San Francisco Opera. "Ruth started off with a global, top-notch view of the performing arts world that came naturally from working at the opera with Kurt Herbert Adler," Sandrock says. "From the beginning, she had the ability to cast the whole concept of San Francisco Performances in terms that would allow for experimentation and young artists and new artists—but only the best. Making those choices is a tough balance when local and national artists are knocking at your door constantly. You must have your own standards in front of you all the time. Ruth knows what will work and what won't. She has been absolutely unafraid to make artistic judgments as part of her job as an impresario."

Board Chairman Mary Falvey Fuller, vice president of finance for the Shaklee Company, says she has been most impressed with Felt's "total commitment to artistic quality." Fuller also has been impressed with Felt's managerial side, as she has ably projected costs and income, hedging the financial risks so the board always knows what it is facing.

San Francisco Performances derives its greatest psychic rewards from artists who are well served, and audiences that are growing both in size and in their ability to appreciate and understand the work and artists being presented.

Kary Schulman, director of grants for the arts at the Hotel Tax Fund, which is part of the city and county government, credits Felt with establishing a serious sense of purpose and valuing her artists' and audiences' contributions to the process of presenting. "Ruth is a beloved figure here in San Francisco," Schulman says. "Although she is not a high-profile person, people remember her fondly from her years at the opera. She has a reputation for fair dealing with the unions and with artists. People feel very well taken care of when they are presented by her."

Unique Programs

From the beginning, the organization's mission has been well defined: to "present outstanding artists and attractions, including emerging artists and experimental works; bring new and more diversified audiences to the performing arts in San Francisco; and serve and strengthen the local performing arts community."

> This quiet organization has had a remarkable impact on the arts in San Francisco.

Every year, San Francisco Performances presents instrumental and vocal series with four to six recitals each, a chamber music series with six events, a series of lighter fare with three to four events, and a series of three to four events with new, less-familiar performers.

Jillian Steiner Sandrock of the Skaggs Foundation comments on what the organization has meant to the Bay area. "We have supported San Francisco Performances every year because we feel that what Ruth is doing is critical to the Bay-area arts scene. Without Ruth's efforts, we simply would not have access to many East Coast-based artists like the Kalichstein, Laredo, Robinson Trio. We would not have the more intimate arts events, the recitalists, and the chamber music ensembles. We might hear the German lyric tenor Peter Schreier at the opera, but we would never hear him in recital singing Schubert's *Die Schöne Müllerin*. People are thirsty for this kind of thing because it exposes another side of the artist's capabilities and interpretive abilities. Ruth knew there was a niche here, and she knew she could fill it."

This commitment to the individual artist is one of the organization's unique qualities. At a time when the popularity, acceptance, and frequency of the solo recital is in serious decline all over the United States, it is a tribute to San Francisco Performances that its first concert was a solo recital, and that each season since then it has offered some of the finest musicians of the world in recital.

James Schwabacker—singer, longtime local arts supporter, and activist member of the symphony and opera boards—is one of the founding trustees of San Francisco Performances. "The recital field," he says, "is doing very badly. These days, people want entertainment. They don't want to listen in a quiet way to beautiful music."

If the instrumental recital is less available, then the vocal recital has become the musical equivalent of an endangered species. Unlike the spectacle of opera, the song recital is simply a singer and a pianist, music and words. The only theatricality is in the interpretation of the music being sung. The experience is subtle: no supertitles, no costumes, no dazzling stage effects. It requires commitment and interest by the audience, and some sophistication.

But while many presenters have given in to audience resistance to the weightiness of instrumental and vocal recitals, San Francisco Performances is one of the few that devotes a significant part of its season to this genre of musical expression. Certainly, it is one of the few recently founded, independent organizations that is making the effort. So unusual has been its commitment that in 1985, the organization was the first recipient of the Harold Shaw Award in recognition of high achievement in programming and presenting recitals. It was a great honor for such a young organization.

The Local Performing Arts Community

The "Performance at Six" series is further evidence of San Francisco Performances' dual commitment to artists and the public. The series, which began in 1981 with 12 concerts and now features more than 30 performances each season, has two objectives: to give Bay-area artists paid performance opportunities, and to build audiences for the performing arts.

The concerts take place in a restaurant called The Cultured Salad at the Embarcadero Center downtown. The audience is multifaceted—employees of companies in the financial district, senior citizens, families with children. Rudy Nathanberg, chief administrative officer of the City and County of San Francisco, regularly attends "Performances at Six." He describes the series as "very intimate and great fun. Ruth's enthusiasm infuses most of what she does. She has always presented a good variety of artists, and is very careful about maintaining high consistency and quality."

Admission is $5 and includes a glass of wine provided by various California wineries. The restaurant donates the space; as it is solely a lunchtime place, these events don't impinge on evening clientele. Attendance varies from 40 to standing-room-only crowds of 150. Since the series' inception, more than 150 Bay-area artists have been engaged and paid to appear. Part of the financial support for the series has come from corporations, including Chevron, Citicorp, IBM, Montgomery Securities and Pacific Gas Transmissions.

Mary Falvey Fuller says "Performances at Six" increases the audience for classical music by bringing it to people and "overcoming the natural barriers they face at certain stages of their lives—the logistics of getting a baby sitter, parking, the lack of money for a big ticket price, or lack of knowledge." It's also a way for people to attend without a companion and end up making friends.

The concerts are informal. The artists speak to the audience, describe the works that are to be performed, and talk about their instruments and the composers. "This is a way of bringing music to a public that otherwise might not find it," Fuller says.

Another example of the organization's commitment to the local performing arts community is the collaborative project it initiated in the 1985–86 season between the Kronos Quartet and ODC/San Francisco, two of the area's finest and best-known resident companies.

It was the first time the two groups had worked together. The plan was to commission a new string quartet from an American composer for the Kronos, and to have ODC choreograph a new piece to the music. Choosing the composer—

Jalalu-Kalvert Nelson—was a cooperative process. Also on the program were two new dances by ODC choreographers Katie Nelson and Kimi Okada, with music taken from the Kronos' extensive repertoire of contemporary music. The world premieres took place in May 1986.

Everyone benefited: The Kronos and ODC each added a newly commissioned work to their repertoires. The young Black composer received a commission from the premier exponent of contemporary music, whose concert schedule is full enough every year that multiple performances of the work were virtually assured. And the project formed an alliance among three outstanding San Francisco cultural groups, each of which brought to the project what it does best.

San Francisco Performances conceived the idea, initiated the project, and then found the way and the financial wherewithal to make it happen, giving it the attention an event of this magnitude requires.

The cost of undertaking such a collaborative project is not modest. The total budget was more than $70,000, of which only $26,000 (37 percent) was recouped at the box office. The remainder was raised from the public and private sector. The California Arts Council supported the project because it was the first collaboration among three California arts organizations with local and national standing, several new works would be created, and two performances would be open to the public. San Francisco Performances also received grants from six of the 10 foundations to which it applied—about double the usual response.

San Francisco and the Pacific Rim

Performing arts presenters are becoming more aware of the need to be responsive to their multicultural communities. For San Francisco Performances, this awareness has translated into presenting artists from the Pacific Rim.

In the 1987–88 season, two of the four pianists presented in recitals were Japanese artist Mitsuko Uchida and Korean artist Kun Woo Paik. Marketing and development director Laura McCrea says San Francisco Performances tried, for the first time, to reach the Korean community through special promotional efforts, including advertising in the area's Korean press. For the Paik recital, there was a full house composed almost entirely of Korean Americans. Some of the same promotional techniques were used to reach the Japanese community for several Japanese artists appearing in the in the 1988–89 season. Mailing lists from area Japanese organizations also were used to announce the performances.

David Gordon's *United States*

San Francisco Performances had twice presented David Gordon/Pick Up Company in a traditional environment, the 928-seat Herbst Theater for the San Francisco Performing Arts Center. But Gordon's *United States* project was a massive undertaking that ultimately would involve more than 20 co-commissioning presenters across the country.

In the 1987–88 season, Pick Up Company Managing Director Alyce Dissette had settled on the Walker Art Center and San Francisco Performances as the two organizations that could offer the special kind of participation the piece required. They were to be the anchor of a large nationwide tour in the 1988–89 season, when the project would move on to the other presenters and to the Brooklyn Academy of Music's Next Wave Festival.

Dissette realized that Gordon would need more than the two-night stand in San Francisco to realize the piece's full potential. She worked with Felt to develop a way of presenting the Pick Up Company to support Gordon's creative process. They decided to bring the company to San Francisco for 10 performances over a two-week period at the Theater Artaud, an alternative space in a converted warehouse south of Mission Street. In March 1988, "Sang and Sang," the San Francisco section of *United States*, premiered at the theater.

Although David Gordon/Pick Up Company had been developing a following in the Bay area, moving from a two-evening presentation to 10 performances was a leap. San Francisco Performances' involvement in the co-commissioning project also was a much bigger commitment than any Felt had made before.

"Ruth is one of the real gamblers," Dissette says. "She is a very responsible presenter in terms of the way she carries out her fiscal duties, but the truth is that she really likes the work that artists create. And she really likes working with artists. She likes to be invested in people. I think she is quite extraordinary that way."

> "I see presenters as one of the major—maybe *the* major—way artists are presented to the public."

Making the Case for a Presenting Organization

Presenters are usually adventurous out of a sense of personal curiosity and a desire to spread their enthusiasm for certain artists and repertoire. To develop an audience that willingly joins presenters on those odysseys requires a team of people, both within and outside the organization. The team must include a cooperative press that recognizes the merit of what is being presented, and public and private funding agencies that help make up the gap between earned income and total revenues needed.

San Francisco Performances represents most clearly the struggle many presenting organizations experience as they try to make the case to the public, funding sources and the press. Even in the face of impressive achievement, there is a sense of frustration. Some of it comes from the organization's status as the "new kid on the block," navigating a path long ago taken by other major performing arts groups in the city.

In San Francisco, the public has long supported major producing organizations like the San Francisco Symphony, San Francisco Opera, San Francisco Ballet, and American Conservatory Theater. The issue is not building a public that is aware of and willing to buy tickets for performing arts events, or even that will contribute money to support the shortfall between revenues and costs. The issue is making the case for supporting a presenting organization that does not own or maintain a facility, and does not have a highly visible operation; there is no huge physical plant, no company of musicians, singers, dancers or actors, and no production and technical staffs.

"The variety of what presenters present make it more difficult to establish a clear identity and to market the organization in the community," Felt explains. "Very often, the artists we present are the ones that receive the recognition. They certainly deserve it—but we do, too. If you were to ask the members of the audience, 'Who presented this concert?' not everyone would know. That poses a survival problem."

Laura McCrea, marketing and development director, talks about her frustration as she tries to establish the validity of presenting as an enterprise, so that corporations and others can understand the need for contributed income. "When you say 'symphony' or 'opera,' people know exactly what you mean. They see a big institution with a big staff, big productions with an orchestra and sometimes more than 100 people on stage, so they understand that it costs money to run this kind of enterprise.

"When you say 'presenting organization,' people don't have a clear definition. There are people who still think that when a concert by the Juilliard or Guarneri Quartet is sold out, the cost of the tickets pays for the performance. People—including people in the corporate world—think we make money on performances. Our job is to educate them to the contrary. The best way to do that is to get them to the concerts."

Kary Schulman of the San Francisco Hotel Tax Fund has been involved in funding and evaluating the local arts scene for many years. She describes the challenge for San Francisco Performances as a presenting organization making its case to the public: "There is not so much difficulty understanding what the organization does as much as building an emotional attachment to it. With the symphony, opera, ballet and theater, the audience experiences the resident artists interacting with the guest artists and developing and growing in their creative expression. But with a presenting organization, the variety of artists makes it more difficult to build that loyalty."

Another difficulty centers on the media's reluctance to help establish the organization's identity. Although the two San Francisco daily newspapers send their critics to cover the performances, the organization itself is rarely mentioned in the reviews. Under these circumstances, the public might think that the artists appear as if by magic. "Ruth plans a season so carefully so that the whole is more than the sum of its parts," Schulman says. "There is a pattern. We never get a sense of that in the press. It's always a discrete concert here, here and here."

Felt says the city's print media give extensive coverage to the city's ballet, opera and other major producing organizations. But the same press has been unreceptive to doing a feature article on San Francisco Performances or on Cal Performances, the other major presenting organization in the area. She says she has asked the morning paper to include in its reviews that San Francisco Performances is the presenting organization, but editors have refused. "Occasionally we are listed as the presenters," she says, "but very infrequently. If it weren't for us, an artist or ensemble simply wouldn't be here. But the press doesn't seem to feel that is important."

Then, there are the problems with general fundraising. San Francisco Performances must raise approximately 45 percent of its budget from contributed income. It taps the usual sources for project support—the National Endowment for the Arts, the California Arts Council and private foundations. The only organization that provides operating support is the San Francisco Hotel Tax Fund's Grants to the Arts Program. San Francisco Performances also conducts a direct-mail campaign involving its subscriber base. In the 1986–87 season, the organization realized $126,000, or 21 percent of its income, from individual contributors.

An annual campaign raises corporate and business donations. "Over and over, we have to answer the question, 'Why can't you make it at the box office?' " Felt says. "We cite statistics for presenters around the country, showing that it is considered healthy if earned income is 50 percent. Ours is more than 55 percent, so we compare quite favorably. Just showing the budget for an actual concert usually helps to explain the costs."

When prospective donors ask why she can't double ticket prices or the number of seats, Felt explains that San Francisco Performances is committed to keeping ticket prices affordable and to offering half-price rush tickets to students and seniors. "Often, corporations can be made to understand," she says, "although sometimes the reaction is, 'There has to be a better way.' " Felt listens to marketing ideas and tries to use them within the limits of their applicability and budgetary feasibility.

Although the staff handles government and foundation fundraising for specific projects, Felt says the board of trustees is instrumental in corporate fundraising. Board Chairman Mary Falvey Fuller in particular has many significant contacts in the city's corporate world.

Fuller makes the case to the corporate community by emphasizing two important points: the organization's track record of artistic quality, and the tangible benefit to the corporation. By understanding the corporation and its client base, Fuller says, the diversity of the San Francisco Performances' various programs affords many opportunities to "dovetail what we are doing with something the corporation might be doing, thereby giving the corporation a tangible benefit as well as visibility in community service."

But the number of major corporations in San Francisco is apparently dwindling, and it is more difficult for the organization now than it was in the corporate environment it first encountered in 1979. In response, the organization is broadening its business fundraising efforts to encourage commitment to an annual gift of $1,000 to $5,000 in a subscription-style concept. Through this mechanism—called the Business Circle—the board has begun to approach firms comprised of such professionals as lawyers, architects, accountants and physicians. Board members also continue to pursue large corporations to sponsor concerts or an entire series.

As a result of contacts by board members, Chevron Vice Chairman J. Dennis Bonney now serves on the organization's Business Advisory Council. This has set the stage for Chevron to take a pathfinding role in the corporate community on behalf of the organization. In 1987, Chevron became a charter member of the Business Circle, and placed an advertisement in the local Chamber of Commerce publication to speak proudly of its commitment and to encourage other corporations to join.

J.W. Rhodes, Jr., manager of corporate contributions, says Chevron has supported San Francisco Performances because it "is both a wonderful community arts organization and a meaningful part of San Francisco's arts community." R.C. Wooton, Chevron's arts liaison, says the organization has "filled a void in the performing arts scene. It has helped to establish emerging artists and groups, and has undertaken some very risky ventures like commissioning new works. I think they are a pioneer in that sense."

Future Challenges

"It's a constant challenge to continue doing what we're doing in the changing economy," Felt says. "But I hope we can keep taking new steps. It would be wonderful to make it possible for a composer or choreographer to create a new work—a major symphonic work or a major theatrical piece—and for us to produce it. I would like to see us do more in the area of community outreach, with the schools, for instance. This takes so much staff time. Our staff is very small, and working up to capacity."

Felt makes some penetrating conclusions about the presenter's role vis-à-vis the artist. In doing so, she reveals those qualities David Gordon has attributed to her. "I see presenters as one of the major—maybe *the* major—way artists are presented to the public," she says. "We should as a profession be more conscious of this responsibility and this power. Because of this power, we should engage in careful self-criticism and evaluation.

"Artists are unaware of the economic realities of being presented; even artists who perform a great deal don't have any idea what it costs for them to walk out on stage. I also suspect, on the other hand, that as presenters we are ignorant of many of the agonies an artist must endure to reach a place where we even know about them."

Members of ODC/San Francisco and the Kronos Quartet

Photo by Paul Latoures

Spoleto Festival Orchestra members

Photo by William Struhs

18 A Moving and Moveable Feast

Festivals are different. That's clear at the Spoleto Festival USA in Charleston, South Carolina. Each day begins with a sense of great anticipation, a hunger for what is to happen. Each day ends with a sense of fullness, similar to what's felt after a splendid banquet. It's a different kind of experience than attending a single event, or a series of events over time or over a season.

What is a festival, and how is it different from other forms of presenting? Festival authority Christopher Hunt was director of Pepsico Summerfare and has been associated with the Wolf Trap Festival, Australia's Adelaide Festival and the San Francisco Opera. The word "festival" has been casually tossed around by presenting and producing organizations, Hunt says, "with endless licentiousness." He says serious arts festivals have a number of characteristics which distinguish them from other forms of arts presentation:

—"A festival must do what other people are not doing. It must contrast with the regular pattern of entertainment of the area or city or town in which it is found;

—"It usually takes its character from a 'genius look-eye' person who in some ways is identified with the place in which it happens—Mozart at Salzburg, Britten at Aldeburgh, Rossini at Pesaro, Menotti at Spoleto;

—"The place itself should constitute the major reason for the festival to exist, and determine a great deal of its character. The place needs to encourage a particular kind of ambiance that is unusually sympathetic to performance, where people are put into an unusually good and receptive mood;

—"Festivals provide a special context for excellence—better rehearsal circumstances, a more receptive and better-prepared audience;

—"There is usually a particular artistic purpose to a festival, most often from the artistic person who dominates it;

—"Festivals very often constitute a crucial meeting point and melting pot for the artistic exchange of ideas, especially among performing artists."

In sum, Hunt says: "The most distinctive elements are the sense of preparation for a performance of special character, and the sense of doing something which is not done in the rest of the general repertoire. If I had to pick out a single characteristic that makes a festival the most important—which is not always the reason it is successful—it would be the catalytic effect among artists for future work."

Hunt's analysis embraces the Spoleto Festival USA. The Festival annually provides a set of joyful feast days that are a recess from life's ordinary routines; it offers celebration in a discrete period of time in one of the country's oldest and most lovely cities.

During 17 days in May and June of 1988, the 12th annual Spoleto Festival in Charleston presented 112 performances of 41 different events, held in 11 locations (including concert halls, theaters, churches, a park, an old plantation and an art museum), involving 568 artists from across the U.S. and the world. The multi-disciplinary events included opera, music, dance, theater, the visual arts—even a circus. Total attendance was 83,906, showing a high volume each day. The number of performances per day ranged from a low of three on opening day to 11 on the Sunday of Memorial Day weekend; a typical day contained between five and nine performances. Every day except opening day began at 11 a.m. with a chamber music concert; every day closed with at least one 9 p.m. performance.

The 1988 Festival was unusually rich and fascinating. The events included two operatic rarities, Dvorak's *Rusalka* and Graun's *Montezuma*; and two music-theater premieres, Martha Clarke's *Miracolo D'Amore*, and Lee Breuer and Bob Telson's *The Warrior Ant*. In dance, a ballet gala of American regional companies featured performances by the companies of Twyla Tharp, David Parsons, Danny Buraczeski's Jazz Dance, Yoshiko Chuma and the School of Hard Knocks and Dana Reitz. There were 32 performances of 11 different chamber music programs, including premieres by composers Lowell Liebermann, Ken Frazelle and Leon Kirchner; the U.S. debut of Brussels' RTBF Orchestra; Circus Flora; a major retrospective exhibit of works by painter Larry Rivers; jazz artists Les McCann, Eddie Harris, Carmen McRae, Michel Petrucciani, Roy Haynes and Gary Peacock; Mozart's *Thamos, King of Egypt*, Strauss's *Enoch Arden* and Convery's *The Blanket*; the 12th-century musical drama, *Herod and the Innocents*, performed by the Ensemble for Early Music . . . and the list goes on.

Nigel Redden, general manager of the Spoleto Festival USA since 1986, and American manager of the Italian Festival, says the distinguishing character of Spoleto is that "it is festive. It's a celebration. But that doesn't mean that it is fluffy. We are very serious about what we put on—and we put on very serious things, but in the context of a lovely city and a lot of parties." He says that Artistic Director and Festival founder Gian Carlo Menotti has set the tone: "There's a lot of work, and it should add up to something more than the individual productions. One should come here not for an individual production, but to see the Festival."

Redden refers repeatedly to the "tone" of the Festival. He says the 1988 Festival was very different from the 1987 Festival, which to him "is what makes a festival a festival." It is something more than just a lot of events put together at the same time.

"Next season will be at least as challenging as this year," he says, "but in a different way. I do not want to create a particular aesthetic that the Spoleto Festival espouses. It has always been about an eclectic vision." He worries about becoming too comfortable with a particular successful formula. "The strength of the Festival is that if there is a formula, it's a loose one."

Redden describes the triumvirate that makes the artistic decisions: Artistic Director Menotti; Greek-born, Cologne-based Music Director Spiros Agiris; and Redden. Menotti sets the tone, Agiris is primarily involved with the musical side of things, and Redden takes on all the other artistic aspects, excepting the chamber music series programmed by violist Scott Nickrenz.

Redden says the decision-making process is a constant artistic balancing act among the three. Discussions can go on for months while the program is being developed. "There's a lot of give-and-take," Redden says, "with everybody feeling passionate about the end product. Whatever ends up on stage must be worth 49½ weeks of work." He says the first criterion is that whatever is presented or produced must be intriguing to the triumvirate. Then, the Festival must be important to the people outside itself—the audience, critics, and funders.

Redden feels strongly about being a festival presenter. "It's being an artistic director of something that is much larger than a single dance company or a single theater company or a single opera company." He is quick to point out that this does not mean meddling with the artists. "It means believing in what an artist does enough so you don't have to meddle in his or her work."

Many people have begun to compare presenters to museum curators. But Redden feels that presenting is a more exciting job. A curator tries to "pigeonhole things" with individual exhibitions or collections. The performing arts are "more ragged," he says. "They are intractable human beings, not quiet, dead things that you can put in a crate."

Redden's background fits his tasks. In 1969, at age 18, he began working at the Festival dei Due Mondi (The Festival of Two Worlds) in Spoleto, Italy, the grandfather of the three Festivals worldwide. Although he is a U.S. citizen, he was brought up in Italy and England as the son of a diplomat. He worked at the Spoleto Festival in Italy for five years.

In his first year, he was assigned to the print shop. He then went to artist relations and met Arthur Mitchell, John Cage, Ezra Pound, Stephen Spender, Isamu Noguchi, Willem de Kooning, Merce Cunningham and Eliot Feld. "It was a time when everyone seemed to be interested in what young people were thinking," he says, "and I was a token young person. I was definitely the mailroom clerk who made good."

It took Redden a few years to make good as general manager of the American Festival. Before he took that post, he worked with La MaMa E.T.C., the Brooklyn Academy of Music, Jacob's Pillow Dance Festival, the Murray Louis Dance Company and the American Dance Festival. He also was director of performing arts at the Walker Art Center.

The Festival in Charleston

Spoleto Festival USA began its first season in Charleston in 1977, during the 19th anniversary season of the Festival dei Due Mondi. The idea to establish an American Festival had long been discussed in Italy. Redden offers a brief background:

From the start, American support was an important part of the financial base for the original Festival of Two Worlds, founded by Menotti in 1958. The Italian Festival was a place for young and emerging artists to be seen by European audiences. It made sense to have an American Festival at which productions could be built and shipped to Italy.

The prevailing wisdom held that the Americans would pay for the productions, which could be performed before they appeared in Italy. But, Redden adds, no one foresaw that whoever ran the American Festival would "find it to be his or her first allegiance." This is, in fact, what happened. In many ways, Redden says, the American Festival has been a liability to the Italian for this reason.

When the National Endowment for the Arts heard that Menotti was contemplating the establishment of an American Festival, then-chairman Nancy Hanks encouraged him to look for a site in the South.

Menotti went to Charleston first. He found an intimate, genteel, European-feeling, historic city, which had a tradition of arts activities dating back to colonial times.

He met Mayor Joseph P. Riley Jr., who recognized the importance of the arts for their power and value as a vehicle to revitalize his city. Several "old-line" Charlestonians also were interested. Redden says Mayor Riley continues to be the key to making the city's resources available to the Festival.

Another important figure at the founding of the Spoleto Festival USA was Dr. Theodore S. Stern, who was president of the College of Charleston. Mayor Riley asked Stern to take on the Festival as his personal project. Stern made the college's facilities—including theaters, office space, and some administrative personnel—available to Menotti.

In Charleston, Menotti found a beautiful city, which for its size has a number of different kinds of theaters, including the European-style Dock Street, whose history dates to 1736. The theaters were well-equipped and in good working condition, and could be accessed for several months in a concentrated period of time during the spring—just what Menotti needed.

Charlestonians have taken an active and passionate interest in preserving their buildings, homes, and landmarks. This city of approximately 70,000 has more than 10 theaters, concert halls and churches which are workable sites for music events, so that many performances can be run concurrently. Menotti also found a government and a populace that were more than eager to welcome an enterprise like the Spoleto Festival, with its world-class status, publicity, and glitter. It seemed like a marriage made in heaven.

In the 10th anniversary Festival program, Mayor Riley reflected on its impact on his city, and paid tribute to the ways Spoleto irrevocably changed it. He recalled that when the Festival began in 1977, he called it "one of the most significant days in our city's history—a rendezvous with our destiny."
In fact, the mayor says, the Spoleto Festival "has caused an explosion of interest in the arts that has enriched us all . . . The arts are no longer seen as elitist, but rather as necessities for the enjoyment and the enrichment of all citizens."

> The Festival provides a set of joyful feast days that are a recess from life's ordinary routine.

Mayor Riley is amazed at the effect the Festival also had on non-arts-related aspects of city life. Without question, he says, the Festival is one reason for the city's extraordinary redevelopment. He recalls his words at the opening ceremonies: "Mediocrity has no place in a community or society that admires a commitment to excellence, its artists, its musicians, dancers and poets." He believed that Spoleto's constant search for excellence would rub off on Charleston, and it did. "We have developed a belief that there is nothing worthwhile that we cannot do. This city, by straining and struggling to put on the world's most comprehensive arts festival, is now unwilling to settle for second best in anything."

Flutist Paula Robison, co-host of Spoleto's chamber music concerts, speaks of Charleston in glowing terms: "Charleston is perfect because of its historical importance. The city is a work of art. The place is an inspiration to the artists. The whole city is the Festival."

Menotti's Presence and Artistry

Undeniably, Gian Carlo Menotti has been the driving force behind the Spoleto Festivals in Italy, the U.S., and in Australia, which was founded in 1986 in Melbourne. As Christopher Hunt observes, Menotti provides the "genius look-eye" to make the Festival specific and unique. Menotti's presence has occasioned the production of no less than nine of his operas, and one for which he wrote the libretto (Samuel Barber's *Vanessa*). He has directed 13 operas there, as well as his own theater piece, *The Leper*. Other performances of his varied opuses include one for dance choreographed by the North Carolina Dance Theater's Salvatore Aiello, and innuerable concerts of instrumental and choral music.

The Festival's comprehensive programs are striking, not so much for the abundance of programming of Menotti works or for his stage directing, but rather that his work actually represents a small percentage of the overall program. This reveals his eclectic vision and willingness to share center stage.

Even so, Menotti's stamp, and the tone he sets, are everywhere. People speak about Menotti's apparent aversion to making timely decisions, waiting until the last possible minute to make programming decisions for each season. Redden feels most strongly the imperatives of selling tickets and raising money. Music Director Spiro Agiris has other, but equally pressing imperatives, since he auditions and casts singers for the opera productions.

Paula Robison, co-host of the chamber music concerts, comments on the impact this way of working has on the Festival's artistic tenor. She marvels that Menotti "likes taking chances and having a kind of chaotic situation which he engineers from the side." This makes for a fertile artistic environment, she says. "It's a real community of artists, who sometimes fight but get together and make things that are very interesting happen, that are not predictable."

This creates an appealing vision of a bubbling cauldron of creativity in which participants are kept on their creative toes. Clearly, it has its hazards for administering a well-run and well-publicized Festival. But Redden and his team have kept ahead of the challenges.

Redden's Influence

Redden has had a substantial impact on programming since his arrival in 1986. He brought with him a commitment to contemporary artists, to creating new works in theater, dance and music, and the points where these disciplines intersect.

In the 1988 season, two major music-theater works received world premieres at Spoleto Festival USA—Martha Clarke's *Miracolo D'Amore*; and *The Warrior Ant*, written and directed by Lee Breuer, and composed by Bob Telson. Redden was committed to both projects.

These works were complex to produce because of their technical challenges, as well as the fact that they were being rehearsed and performed for the first time. Both works also were co-produced with other arts organizations—Clarke's with Joseph Papp/New York Shakespeare Festival in association with the New York International Festival of the Arts; and *The Warrior Ant* with the American Music Theater Festival as well as Breuer's own production company, Colonus, Inc., in association with the Brooklyn Academy of Music and Yale School of Drama. Working cooperatively with production partners in ventures like these poses significant challenges.

Compounding the problems was *The Warrior Ant* venue at the outdoor Cistern of the College of Charleston, which necessitated hauling in everything that comes as standard equipment in a theater.

The Warrior Ant is a massive work. Breuer calls it "an epic narrative, a comic narrative." It includes a Trinidadian steel band, a Brazilian samba group, gospel singers, Afro-Cuban percussionists, a rock and roll band, actors, dancers and local Charleston young people to dance and serve as extras in the huge cast.

Breuer and Telson had only five rehearsal days in Charleston before the five performances. Two years of producing went into this rehearsal schedule at Spoleto, plus a few days in Philadelphia, a week in New Haven, and a few days before the

Next Wave Festival in Brooklyn. Altogether, creative time amounted to 10 or 12 days, because no more could be afforded. "To be absolutely frank," Breuer says, "for every day of creative time you get, you probably put in half a year hustling money."

He speaks of the wonderful relationship he enjoys with Nigel Redden, who has supported his work for many years, and who produced his *Sister Suzie Cinema* and an early version of *The Gospel*. He speaks similarly of Harvey Lichtenstein at BAM, giving him credit for the first full production of *The Gospel at Colonus*. "I believe that producers are artists," Breuer says, "but they just work with real time and real money and real people, instead of paint or music."

Telson adds a perspective on the opportunity to create this work. "Lee and I have been unbelievably lucky with the fact that nobody has forced us to deal with reality very seriously. (We essentially said) 'We have a steel band, a samba school, Afro-Cuban percussionists, 50 extras to dance and sing, two of the greatest gospel singers in America, some of the top musicians from New York . . . Let's put them together and do a piece about a giant ant.' I'm sure other people have crazy ideas, but we actually get to do these things."

For his part, Redden admits these new productions, these big deals, make immense demands. "*The Warrior Ant* is a total nightmare (due to its production demands). But we try to provide whatever it is that the company wants. We keep going until we hit some barrier, which is often financial." He calls Carmen Kovens, the Festival's director of operations, "the glue that keeps the place together." Another invaluable member of staff is Production Manager John Paull III, who can call on the very best technical support personnel and equipment.

The Warrior Ant was one of the most anticipated productions of the 1988 season. Since it was rehearsed outdoors, a casual stroller could easily hear the music being rehearsed, or slip in the unpatrolled gate to see a rehearsal in progress. Most of the technical work was done during the day, with rehearsals during the evening to see how the lights would work and what special effects needed adjustment.

Martha Clarke's *Miracolo D'Amore* was another demanding music-theater premiere for the 1988 season. Its path to the Festival began with Joseph Papp, who asked Clarke to create a new work for the first New York International Festival of the Arts (NYIF). The project came into being after all the commissioning money from the NYIF had been committed. In search of funds, Clarke gained Redden's interest and the piece ultimately received support through grants.

Clarke says one problem with co-productions is that "somehow, occasionally the artists get squeezed between the financial and political needs of the festivals." For instance, Spoleto Festival USA didn't want the Charleston run being viewed as an out-of-town tryout. Meanwhile, the NYIF wanted the major New York press coverage to wait until the work played in New York.

Miracolo D'Amore caused quite a stir in Charleston, and probably was the most controversial work of the season. The sources of Clarke's work are fairy tales, including inspirations from Grimm and Calvino, and the visual impetus she received from the drawings of J.J. Grandville and the paintings of Tiepolo. Female and male full-frontal nudity in sections of the piece shocked the audiences. Another topic for discussion was the way in which men are portrayed as hunchbacked clowns who treat the women violently; brutal images abound, including a gang rape. The work conveys a decidedly strong feminist point of view.

It was a bit too much for some members of the Festival audience. Critical response in Charleston was polarized. The morning paper characterized the piece as "a feminist revenge," while the afternoon paper raved about it.

Even with the controversy, Clarke has enjoyed the opportunity to work at the Spoleto Festival. Christopher Hunt's thoughts about the special attributes of artist-to-artist cross-fertilization resonate in her discussion of the project. "One of the nicest things about Spoleto is that I've had a chance to meet other artists, and to cross-pollinate," Clarke says. "Some of this may result in joint works in the future. This sort of thing does not happen in New York." Her contact with the Circus Flora troupe in Charleston has resulted in talks about a collaborative work. "I've thought about doing a circus piece for years," she says.

Meanwhile, Flora, the troupe's elephant, was to perform in Clarke's *Endangered Species*, due to open at the Brooklyn Academy of Music's Next Wave Festival in October 1990.

Continuing Festival Traditions

The chamber music concerts have been a mainstay of the Spoleto Festival. The two driving forces are Scott Nickrenz, artistic director and violist; and Paula Robison, flutist and co-host of the concerts with Charles Wadsworth.

"Our concerts are like the backbone of the Festival," Nickrenz says. "With us, every day there's something new. The main opera of the Festival might be a flop, something else a smash. What's expected of us is that every single concert should be played well and programmed in a very interesting and wonderful way. People have come to expect that. People come because they can count on the quality of the Spoleto chamber music. To be able to do a festival and repeat every concert three times and have full houses is a miracle in this day and age."

One aspect which promotes a sense of spontaneity and informality is that no programs are announced to the public in advance. When the audience arrives in the lobby of the Dock Street Theater, a blackboard lists the performers and program. No printed program is provided. Instead, each concert is hosted by either Paula Robison or Charles Wadsworth.

Each has a unique style of providing a roadmap into the program and players. Robison's is warm, gracious, informational, and serious. Wadsworth's is that of a hometown boy (he grew up in Newnan, Georgia) who, through his own discoveries, helps you fathom the mysteries of the music. He also tries to engage the audience in some homespun tale or occasional piece of gossip about the performers. Everybody feels like they're part of one big, happy family.

This sense of family is no coincidence. Nickrenz and Robison are husband and wife, and have worked together since before their marriage. This collaboration, originally as co-directors of Spoleto's chamber music concerts, has existed for more than 10 years. They must agree on repertoire, programming, and artists. They confirm that it never could have worked without similar tastes and points of view. In fact, they cannot give an example of a case in which they seriously disagreed.

"That's a miracle," Nickrenz says. "I think our example of mutual affection and respect is a good example for younger people which sets a family tone for this particular festival. When musicians are invited to this festival, they're invited into a family."

Charles Wadsworth founded the chamber music concerts, but Nickrenz and Robison took over as co-directors in 1978, one year into the American Festival. Since 1988, Nickrenz has been the sole director, with Robison moving into the host position. Nickrenz explains that they always split the duties when putting together the concerts. "Paula took over more of the high-profile activities, and it became limited to that. Increasingly, I took over the year-'round things—finding the artists, picking the programs, putting things together. She's the glamour, and I'm the glue."

> "The Spoleto Festival has caused an explosion of interest in the arts that has enriched us all."

Of her hosting duties, Robison says, "It's part of the informality, part of the tradition: that it can be as close as possible to being in a home among people making music with friends. This is what chamber music is supposed to be. Some of the audience is extremely knowledgeable, some not at all. But the latter have, bit by bit, become informed followers of the series."

Robison says they have always felt Menotti's support, without his looking over everything they do. He allows them autonomy, which they consider crucial to their knowing that they are trusted, and promotes their taking chances.

In turn, Nickrenz transfers Menotti's trust to the musicians. He doesn't attend their every rehearsal, allowing each ensemble to formulate and execute its own interpretation of the works. He does, however, attend every dress rehearsal to make sure they have what they need, and to listen for balance. He sets rehearsal schedules, and assigns the 15 players to each of the works performed.

Although there is no organized program of commissioning for the chamber music concerts, Redden supports them whenever Nickrenz is moved enough by a composer's work to want to commission a piece. "I don't want to commission an American composer every year just because it might look good to the NEA," Nickrenz says. "I'd rather wait until we find someone we're excited about—then we might commission that person three years in a row."

Redden met Nickrenz and Robison when the pair began playing at the Italian Festival in the early 1970s; Redden was a young assistant at the time. Says Robison: "Nigel understands the quality in Menotti by which he encourages, or at least allows, chaos—the type of artistic, vivacious, inflamed kind of wonderful thing that Gian Carlo wants to see happen. Because of Nigel, everything is in balance."

Risk and its Relationship to the Financial Picture

"I don't think there's such a thing as artistic risk," Redden says. "I think there's artistic foolishness." He is clear and concise about this, as he is about many other subjects. "You can risk finances and audience, but no reasonable organization would take artistic risks." He says that asking Martha Clarke to do a new work is not an artistic risk, because she's a known quantity. "I'd be taking artistic risks if I started programming people who I thought would be lousy. The risk is that your audience will be offended."

The Warrior Ant, he says, was a financial risk. "It had to have a minimum audience to be a financial success, and we didn't know we would get them—but we did. Marketing skills help you avoid total disaster. It was a hot ticket!" In fact, an extra performance was added to meet the demand.

Redden says he rarely loses sleep about whether things are going to work out on stage. "But the things that I am sleepless about are money and audiences. We must break even, because of some bad periods haunting us from the past. I don't like going to a performance where you're alone. It's not a fun party if there's no one there."

How does the Festival meet the challenges of such an ambitious program year after year? Redden reports that each year's budget is realized from a ratio of about 50 percent earned, and the rest from contributed income. In the 1987 season, tickets reached record sales of 77 percent of capacity. He says ticket sales have been growing, and climbed by 10 percent in the last few seasons.

He wants to avoid too high a dependency on box office income, suggesting that artistic success and box office success are not always related. Thus, there is an on-going search for contributed income from individuals, foundations, government and corporations.

Redden acknowledges that Charleston is not a wealthy area, and has no significant corporate headquarters. Unlike other arts festivals, there is no "angel" behind Spoleto Festival USA. No one person picks up the annual deficit. The largest individual gift in Charleston is $50,000, and the next is $40,000. After that, it drops. The Festival raises more money from outside than from inside Charleston.

The Festival has begun to come into its own with national foundations and corporations, creating projects that are of significant enough interest to receive funding from a Who's Who of American foundations and corporations. The Rockefeller Foundation's director of Arts and Humanities, Dr. Alberta Arthurs, says: "We funded the Spoleto Festival USA because they were not only presenting, but helping to shape, in its formative phases, Lee Breuer's *The Warrior Ant*. The work interests us because it speaks to our intercultural designs, and Spoleto was one of several presenters working together to try and give that piece the room it needed, the space it needed and the audiences it needed as it evolves and develops."

The NEA provides funding for different projects from a variety of its programs. In addition, a challenge grant has spurred a growth in local donations to the Festival because of the grant's three-to-one matching requirements.

Other government money comes from the state, which has a line-item allocation for the Festival in the budget of the South Carolina Arts Commission. The city provides a cash donation in addition to its in-kind services and other supportive assistance. Spoleto Festival USA Board Chairman Charles S. Way, Jr. says this relationship goes beyond money. "It's the most wonderful relationship in the world," he says. "The city administration has bent over backwards from the inception."

Way says the Festival's successful track record has helped to establish a sense of stability and liveliness which is attractive to government and larger corporations. When making the case for the Festival during his fundraising calls, Way also stresses its philosophy of doing unfamiliar work, as well as the new and innovative.

Making the Case for the Festival

Getting the word out to the public is crucial to a festival's success. But, Redden says, "You must first figure out what you want to do and then how you're going to get an audience for it, not the reverse. It's wrong to analyze the audience's taste and then try to accommodate it."

Redden says the Festival spends no money on paid advertising, depending instead on marketing efforts targeted to its mailing list of 60,000 to 80,000, and does not buy additional mailing lists.

"My strong feeling is that we shouldn't try to convert the world," he says. He thinks the way to build and maintain an audience is by selling to the easiest people first, as cheaply as possible, and by maximizing ticket orders from each of them. He converts people by letting them see the events, by offering free tickets to children and certain limited groups, by providing an educational component for teenagers, and by getting positive news coverage.

"We want to have many, many bodies in the seats, and we will push like mad, but we have to get our message out as cheaply as we can. Rather than spending money on advertising or mailing lists, my sense is that we will get a larger audience by doing another production. Adding something to the program will have a greater impact on the overall audience than sending out another brochure." The Festival's events must be critically important, he says. And to engage the artists it needs for very little money, they must feel that the Spoleto Festival is a place where it is important to be seen. "If critics don't come down here, we die," he says.

Tom Kerrigan has been the national press representative for the Festival since 1981, and has directed the process from his office in Brooklyn, New York. He maintains a press mailing list of 5,000, including both print and electronic media outlets. In a typical year, it is not unusual for the Festival to have 500 members of the media attend some part of the Festival, which results in 2,000 to 3,000 stories, items, pictures or reviews in the U.S. media. In a typical year, each press visitor attends an average of five performances, often receiving two tickets per performance. About 5,000 press tickets are distributed in a single season.

Kerrigan says the press effort contributes in two important ways. One is as a fundraising tool; the other is in building the mailing list for long-term ticket sales.

He says reviews or articles may not create a demand for tickets in the same season. Rather, press coverage creates long-term interest in the Festival, influencing the box office a year or two down the road.

Story reprints help to establish the case for the Festival with potential funders. Redden calls this the single most important result of national and regional press coverage.

To eschew paid advertising, the Festival has an extremely well-developed relationship with national and international press outlets. Over the years, Kerrigan has cultivated members of the arts and travel press, and values their role in disseminating information about the Festival. He also provides them with access to the people and stories they consider newsworthy.

The Festival has received many wonderful breaks on network shows. One *Today* show segment featuring Menotti and actor Fritz Weaver resulted in a line forming at the box office within 20 minutes after the broadcast.

Kerrigan says that Menotti has long fascinated the press. Indeed, Kerrigan reports that eight out of 10 requests for interviews are for Menotti.

"He provides a focus locally, nationally and internationally. To have Menotti at the head of this festival has been crucial for publicity. He does *The New York Times* interview, he goes on the *Today* show, he speaks to *CBS Evening News*."

But just because Menotti provides the entree does not guarantee the amount and quality of press coverage. If there were not more events, works, or personalities of interest to the press, the coverage would begin and end with Menotti, Kerrigan says.

The City of Charleston is another focus for the press, and travel stories also showcase the Festival. Therefore, Kerrigan has extensive interaction with the travel media as well as the arts press.

Kerrigan never can assume that any publication or network will cover the Festival. Frequently, he must deal with new critics, new assignment editors, new policies. So while each year is not a brand-new beginning, it is a fresh start.

Kerrigan encourages critics who travel to Charleston, no matter what their customary beat, to see events outside of their fields. "Spoleto is not about attending a play, or an opera. It's going to all of them and seeing how Menotti has mixed it up. That's what makes Spoleto work: the mix."

All local press is handled from Charleston by a marketing and public relations consulting company. Still, Kerrigan says, "I do think that publicity on this level, no matter how or where you do it, boils down to a cottage industry. It takes a great deal of care to spoon-feed all of this stuff and craft it to the individual editor, critic, or reporter. It can get extremely time-consuming, but if you don't give it that, you lose it."

The Spirit that is Spoleto

No matter how well planned a festival, certain things cannot be controlled. One is the spirit of the audience. Observing this is often as interesting and telling as what is happening on stage.

The Spoleto Festival USA offers a unique experience. There is an air of informality, even if audience members are in elegant evening dress. People are incredibly friendly, whether it is day or night. They introduce themselves to one another, make friends with their neighbors. Before performances, the halls buzz with people talking about what they've seen, and what is on their agenda for the next day. They voice their opinions about the productions and performances. They trade restaurant tips, and talk about where they come from and with whom they're travelling.

The Festival has had a profound effect on the tourism industry of the city and state. Scott Sanders, executive director of the South Carolina Arts Commission since 1980, says the Festival has shown what the arts can do for tourism. In a study completed in 1988, it was demonstrated that the arts had a $127 million per year direct economic impact on the state, plus an additional $230 million indirect impact. She says the Festival has set a compelling example of artistic excellence for South Carolina, with much growth of performing arts organizations as a result.

> The Festival has had a profound effect on the tourism industry of the city and state.

In addition, many professional organizations now hold their meetings in Charleston during the Festival. Groups view it as a place for their people to congregate, do their business, and enjoy the events. The State Development Board also has invited chief executive officers from corporations that it is courting to move headquarters to South Carolina, an approach that has proven a success in at least one case.

Piccolo Spoleto

Piccolo Spoleto was established in 1979 by the city's Department of Cultural Affairs as a complement to the Spoleto Festival USA and to showcase local, state, and regional artists. It includes more than 600 events during the 17-day period. Typically, admission is free; donations sometimes are solicited by passing the hat. The events draw very heavily on the Charleston community, since what is presented is often family-oriented.

Piccolo Spoleto encourages grass-roots participation and volunteerism, according to Wilfred Delphin, who with his duo-pianist partner, Edwin Romain, served as the director of Piccolo Spoleto's "Musica da Camera" series. He says Piccolo "brings the Festival to the people of Charleston. It makes Charlestonians feel that the Festival is theirs." Delphin feels that neither festival could work without the other.

This mixture of the international flavor of Spoleto Festival USA, and the uniquely American/regional/community flavor of Piccolo Spoleto offers a richness and range of events for visitors and residents alike. The city is experienced as festival just by walking on the streets of Charleston and enjoying the Piccolo Spoleto programming of street performers, for example.

Charleston and Spoleto after Hurricane Hugo

In September 1989, Hurricane Hugo roared into Charleston, leaving horrendous devastation in its wake. Eighty percent of the city's roofs were damaged, many of them on buildings crucial to the Festival. Gaillard Municipal Auditorium sustained damages which required reconstruction work estimated at between $5 million and $7 million; the roof of the Festival offices was damaged, and extensive damage was done to the computer system. One theater was condemned due to serious structural damage; miraculously, the historic Dock Street Theater was untouched.

There was much more damage to contend with. Still, cleanup efforts moved quickly, and both Mayor Riley and Maestro Menotti declared that the Festival would open its 14th annual program on time in May 1990. Seven days after Hugo, a press release with that information went out.

Redden insisted that the Festival could not cut back on its offerings. Outside of Charleston, people would have forgotten about the storm and would not understand an abridged program. Plans went ahead for a "bigger and better" 1990 Festival, with an increased budget of $4 million. Redden felt that the circumstances dictated that bold measures be taken.

Even before Hurricane Hugo, Redden was passionate about his work. "If the art does not come first, you're not an arts festival. If the city comes first, then you're a city festival. I feel that arts festival organizers must keep their eyes firmly on their rationale. I am paid by Spoleto Festival USA, but my purpose is to run something that is important to the arts. Our purpose transcends the organization, but embodies the organization. Menotti has set that tone. One has to be convinced that this is not simply a job and not simply a city. One must be convinced that this is a crusade in the best place to hold a crusade."

For Redden, perhaps there is no higher calling than to be one of the knights of the crusade to help restore normalcy to hurricane-ravaged Charleston—and to continue to present artistically engaging and exciting Spoleto festivals in this beautiful setting.

The Joffrey Ballet with Iowa schoolchildren

19 A Modern-Day de Medici

Different images may come to mind when thinking about patrons of the arts. One is of the doges of Renaissance Venice or the kings and queens of 18th-century Austria, who nurtured the musical, operatic and plastic arts. The other is evoked when sitting in a theater and reading in that evening's program the names of everyone who has made donations to a performing arts organization.

The university as an arts patron has seldom been a powerful image. But in Iowa City, the University of Iowa has taken on that role. Its committed and enlightened position vis-a-vis the arts has figured substantially in the way they have flourished in the fertile ground of that state. The university's largess has been directed not only to its academic arts programs, but also to Virgil Hancher Auditorium, which opened in 1972. Poised on the west bank of the Iowa River, it is an immense structure that physically dominates the arts campus.

Wallace Chappell, the director of Hancher Auditorium, is quick to acknowledge the depth of the university's commitment. "The university is a remarkably effective patron," he says. "I could not wish for a better de Medici!" He also points to another aspect that is just as important to a successful presenting program: "Iowans are a remarkably supportive audience."

The University of Iowa's commitment to the arts began in 1916, when the university added the responsibility of community and public service to its mission of teaching and research. Teachers and students would be involved and productive for the benefit of the Iowa public. In the context of the fine and performing arts, this signaled two guiding principles: faculty members would be practicing artists, and creative work would be accepted for academic credit. Iowa was among the first universities in the country to establish these precedents.

Jim Wockenfuss was the founding director of Hancher Auditorium. He was hired to oversee its construction in 1970, when he moved to Iowa City from Louisiana State University in Baton Rouge, where he had opened another auditorium. During the next 16 years, he created and directed Hancher's substantive, highly successful programs and developed and managed its efficient operations.

Wockenfuss credits the University of Iowa with establishing the context for Hancher. Then-president Willard "Sandy" Boyd encouraged him to think of the auditorium as serving the entire state. Boyd often said, "This is not the University of Iowa City; it is the University of Iowa." This concept is true to the Big Ten tradition, Wockenfuss adds. "Big Ten universities tend to have a real affinity for the people in their area and to provide many services." This strong community relationship seems to transfer easily to the arts.

When Wockenfuss arrived in Iowa City, the world-famous Writer's Workshop was already four decades old. There was a strong following for the School of Music's orchestra, chorus, and opera programs. The theater program was strong, and the dance program was in its infancy. "It was a very positive, very receptive environment," Wockenfuss says. "I recognized this and tried to involve people in Hancher as much as I could."

He built a tradition of high artistic and operational standards. He inaugurated programs that brought world-class performers to Iowa City. In dance, he initiated an active presence that included a relationship with the Joffrey Ballet. He created Hancher Loft to present smaller dance companies and musical ensembles that required a more intimate setting than the monumental 2,700-seat auditorium. In music, Wockenfuss brought to Iowa such eminent international recitalists as guitarist Andres Segovia and pianist Vladimir Horowitz, as well as emerging artists such as pianist Emanuel Ax and violinists Ani and Ida Kavafian.

Wockenfuss also began to challenge the Hancher audience by presenting new contemporary repertoire pieces like *The Photographer*, a collaboration among composer Philip Glass, choreographer David Gordon and director JoAnne Akalaitis. In Wockenfuss' estimation, it was a box office calamity. But the experience convinced him that unless he developed sources of contributed income to support programs that had not yet found their audience, he would be consigned to programming only the safe, familiar and unchallenging. A well of contributed income would enable him to keep the presenting program growing, conceptually and artistically. It would effectively guarantee artistic freedom from the box office.

Wockenfuss began to forge a path to financial stability so he could advance his artistic concept for Hancher's programs. He energetically pursued contributions while trying to maintain an increasing level of earned income. He built a base of ticket income with an aggressive and consistent series of marketing campaigns to sell series subscriptions and single tickets. He also established income-producing centers at Hancher, such as a cafe and a volunteer-run gift shop.

Under his direction, Hancher was awarded a challenge grant from the National Endowment for the Arts to create an endowment fund. This led to an annual giving campaign to build an endowment that would subsidize ventures that might not have huge box office appeal. It also catalyzed the effort to organize a guild of volunteers to serve as community liaisons.

In 1986, Wockenfuss left Iowa for the University of California at Davis, leaving a legacy of excellence. When Wally Chappell was tapped for the position after serving as Hancher's acting director, he was a faculty member in the Theater Department in charge of the acting and directing program. Chappell had been an actor, then a stage manager and director, then exclusively a director in theaters in Honolulu, Atlanta, Los Angeles and St. Louis.

When asked how it felt to step into Wockenfuss' shoes, Chappell's reflexive response is, "Oh, boy!" He credits Wockenfuss with being the "architect" of the Hancher program and having an enormous influence on the field of presenting. He says his predecessor had a "very sure hand at balancing events. The only thing I have done is to take it farther, doing a few more experimental events, and at times getting a bit more commercial in order to pay for the experimental. I have benefited from Jim's understanding of where you meet your audiences and where you take them."

> The University of Iowa's enlightened position toward the arts has figured substantially in the way the arts have flourished in that state.

Chappell's 1988–89 season consisted of 44 events in 11 different series. It showed great diversity, including the Moscow State Symphony, *1,000 Airplanes on the Roof*, the Peking Opera, the Acting Company, and a production of *Camelot*. Chappell also featured four emerging artists from Young Concert Artists, plus university-generated events.

Chappell has followed Wockenfuss' approach, which strongly emphasized the quality and content of the artistic director's ideas. Says Wockenfuss, "Programmers and operators of facilities should literally play their facilities as an artist would an instrument. When you know your facility, you know its potentials and capabilities. You then stretch those capabilities with programming that enhances them."

Chappell also sees himself as the artistic director at Hancher. "I see no difference between my function as an artistic director for a regional theater, and my function here. I worry about the presenting process in this country, because it seems to me that a lot of people who are working as presenters are technocrats. They're usually running scared to balance their budget at the box office, very afraid to take chances. I've heard people say in our profession that you've got to take yourself out of it when you make a choice to present a particular artist or work of art. I don't believe that for a second. The more I put my own personality and taste into it, the more I am able to bring a program to the public with success."

University and audience support enable Chappell to take chances as an artistic director. "I am very proud that 60 to 70 percent of our income is earned at the box office," he says, "but I benefit very much from the university's desire to take that gamble, whether it's with an expensive, big-name event like the Royal Philharmonic with André Previn or an unknown experimental event. I couldn't do without the other 30 to 40 percent coming from somewhere. The other important part of this mix is the audience that has the courage to try things."

Chappell says it's a quick death to present the same things year in and year out just to sell tickets. "You've got to keep the bubbles coming out of the champagne bottle all the time. Hancher's success is based on the wide-ranging diversity of what we do, from the commercial to the experimental, including everything in between. Through the diversity, you bring people in for one reason and then they cross over to different events. We really go after them once we get them in here to see something."

He says he's devoted to new works and new ways of working. He feels that Iowa is an ideal place to present new works because the state was settled by people who were utopians or wanted to start religious colonies. The positive effects of that heritage are still felt.

When communicating with Hancher's audience and contributors, Chappell stresses that they are supporting the artists they come to see. Their ticket purchases have "a direct relationship to the continuation of the performing arts in this country," he says. "Often, they have never thought of themselves in that way. They just thought they were buying a ticket to an event. Now they feel part of a movement."

Chappell becomes an activist whenever he can to shape programs and ideas. He has created opportunities for several companies to realize important projects. He says the artists and companies with which he has worked—Mabou Mines, Joffrey Ballet, Laura Dean, Kronos Quartet, David Gordon, Carolyn Carlson—"are all realizing what we can do for them. We are partners in crime; we're in league together."

In the 1989–90 season, Chappell involved Hancher in commissioning, co-commissioning, or presenting the world premieres of six new works from a variety of musical, dance and experimental theater ensembles. They were a new work choreographed by David Parsons; *Power Failure*, a collaboration by Paul Dresher and Rinde Eckert; Kronos Quartet's *The Songlines*, by composer Kevin Volans; the Joffrey Ballet's revival of *The Nutcracker*; and the St. Paul Chamber Orchestra performing a new work by Paul Dresher.

The Hancher Loft is one reason the more experimental, less accessible performances and commissions of new works are possible. Wockenfuss created this space in 1983 when he realized that some of the most interesting new work was being created for small spaces. To overcome the daunting obstacle of Hancher's gargantuan stage, Wockenfuss developed a "loft space" within the auditorium, using the stage for both the performers and the audience. To maximize sightlines, the audience sits on gym bleachers and folding chairs on the stage floor and on platforms. The loft provides an intimate space for the audience without making technical compromises, since Hancher is one of the best-equipped halls in the country.

Companies such as David Gordon/Pick Up Company, Molissa Fenley and Jim

Self were first introduced at the Hancher Loft. The space is used for other companies whose work—whether for lack of public familiarity or because of a highly experimental approach—is best presented in an intimate setting.

The Joffrey Ballet

"They came. We saw. They conquered." With those six words, Larry E. Eckholt describes the genesis of the 17-year relationship between Hancher Auditorium and the Joffrey Ballet. Eckholt was the university foundation's director of development for the Iowa Center for the Arts, of which Hancher is a constituent member.

The Hancher-Joffrey relationship began in 1974, a mere two years after Hancher opened its doors, when the Mid-America Arts Alliance organized a midwestern tour for the company. The partnership achieved its highest degree of expression when Hancher commissioned the Joffrey's first production of *The Nutcracker*. The world premiere performances of the new work in December 1987, just six months before Robert Joffrey died, were given at Hancher Auditorium. The production moved on to the Kennedy Center in Washington, D.C., and then to the City Center in New York. It was billed as "Iowa's holiday gift to the nation."

Every few years, it seems, a new and special tale is added to the annals of the Joffrey-Hancher relationship. One wonders if the telling of the stories by Iowa "Joffrey junkies"—as Eckholt calls himself and others who have been drawn to the company—has not reached heroic proportions.

In 1978, a blizzard halted the Joffrey's five semitrailer trucks on the interstate in Ohio. The repertoire for the Hancher performances featured works with elaborate sets and costumes, all of which were stranded on the road. Since the dancers and artistic staff already had arrived, Joffrey revamped the program and had the company perform works that focused simply on dance and dancers, with a setless stage and classic black velour curtains. The three sold-out performances were a triumph.

In 1980, the company was on sabbatical for the season to solve chronic financial problems, and was not available for its customary performances at Hancher. Jim Wockenfuss did not want to lose the momentum of support in Iowa for the Joffrey, so he engaged the Joffrey II—the "farm team," but a fine young professional company in its own right—to fill the gap.

Wockenfuss had an idea. Joffrey II was more modest in size and cost than the main company, so an extended residency that moved throughout Iowa might be feasible. By the summer of 1982, the first major residency was under way. "Iowa: A Place to Dance!" consisted of five weeks of activities that were held in the university's Dance Department and in communities across the state. The activities outside the university included informal performances, lecture-demonstrations and social events with local citizens. The grand finale was an invitation to participants and audiences from the neighboring communities to come to Iowa City for the culminating performance.

Wockenfuss reminisces about the experience: "During the first year of the residency, the lobby before a performance was absolutely electric, just like a small-town high school basketball team playing the championship game. That kind of electric feeling literally propelled those young dancers to perform light years beyond their capabilities. We had 2,500 people turn out to see this very young dance company because they knew them, and there was a strong personal interest in the members."

The residency brought the Joffrey and Hancher even closer. By 1984, Hancher began negotiations to commission a new work for the company. The result was the 1986 world premiere performance of James Kudelka's *The Heart of the Matter*. The work received significant positive critical attention and gave the Joffrey-Hancher connection national visibility. By the time the Kudelka work was premiered, Wockenfuss had left and Chappell was in charge of Hancher.

> "The university is a remarkably effective patron. Iowans are a remarkably supportive audience."

In 1986, Chappell and Eckholt met in New York with Penelope Curry, Joffrey Ballet's former executive director. She spoke about the company's desire to mount a production of *The Nutcracker*. Chappell saw it as a perfect event that Iowans could back with enthusiasm. The production offered great promise for extensive community participation. Iowans also would be able to observe the process of creation: They would see the finished production, but they also would learn what and how long it takes to create, build, rehearse and coalesce ideas and efforts around a new work, even one based on tradition.

With Eckholt's support, Chappell went about selling the project to James O. Freedman, then president of the university, and to Darrell E. Wyrick, president of the University of Iowa Foundation. Both were cautious about giving the go-ahead for such an immense undertaking, which would require a considerable fundraising effort. The budget for the production and presentation at Hancher was more than $750,000, a hefty figure by anyone's calculation. It was clear that this sum would have to be assembled from box office ticket sales, Hancher endowment income and general operating funds and grants, as well as from an unprecedented major fundraising campaign aimed at individuals.

Of the $750,000, $214,000 came from ticket sales while $407,000 represented grants and donations, including contributions specifically for the project from more than 600 individuals and businesses who gave between $25 and $25,000 each. The university carried the deficit of $129,000 as a loan to Hancher, a concrete example of the university's active involvement as an art patron. Chappell acknowledges that the project required a huge subsidy—about 72 percent—because the local and statewide market could sustain only six performances.

There was a great deal of local, regional and national press coverage of the commission and the events that surrounded it. Robert Joffrey created an appealing local angle by transferring the environment of the ballet from its traditional European setting to a Victorian American setting, circa 1850. There also was much excitement over the involvement of 44 Iowa children chosen by the Joffrey through auditions to perform in the production. Thirty-three of them were brought to Washington, D.C., to appear in the Kennedy Center performances.

No one would deny the tremendous impact the project had on the community and the state, as well as the extensive national attention it brought the university. Describing the gala world premiere, Richard Remington, who was interim president of the university when the event took place, commented, "For one night, the town came alive. It sparkled and glittered and filled us with the notion that, 'By golly, we can do it.' There were an awful lot of excited Iowans in Hancher Auditorium that night."

Reaching Out

Having invested substantial resources in the arts, the University of Iowa has not left to chance the delivery of benefits to the statewide community. In 1978, at the behest of then-president Willard Boyd, the Arts Outreach Program was established as part of the Iowa Center for the Arts, the combined forces of the university's schools and services for the arts.

The program has three major components. The first, academic activities, includes Performance Plus, through which faculty artists and ensembles participate in events for schools, community organizations, arts councils, arts centers, or concert associations in Iowa. Through Artconnection, graduate students in the university's arts programs and the Writer's Workshop are available for performances and to participate in arts development projects that help communities realize specific projects.

A second component, public programs, typically features events tied to the professional touring performances being presented in Hancher Auditorium and often involving the principal creative forces. Sometimes these programs are simply pre-performance lectures to give audience members a context for the evening. Or, they can be elaborate symposiums or series that extend over a semester and involve university faculty or staff as resources. A third component, programs for young audiences, involves special student matinees of evening events scheduled at Hancher or at other university theaters.

Mary Louise Plautz has been the director of the Arts Outreach Program since its founding in 1978. She describes the program's four objectives: to send out artists to raise the credibility of arts activity on campus; to motivate and encourage people to go to the campus and become involved in the arts either as consumers or participants; to develop the center's own student artists; and to encourage talented high school students to enroll in arts programs at the university.

Plautz calls Hancher the "flagship" of all the outreach programs. "Hancher has provided the avenues through which we really speak about the arts," she says. This happens through residencies, lectures, informal chats with artists and major conferences and symposiums. One particularly potent example was a one-day symposium called "The Subject is Suicide," planned for the presentation of the touring production of Marsha Norman's Pulitzer Prize-winning play, 'night Mother.

"I knew there were tons of young people dealing with this issue," Plautz says, "so I set up a conference using social service and health professions from our campus as speakers. People came from as far away as 120 miles to participate in that conference prior to the performance.

"This symposium was an indication that the arts are the language of our lives, and through them, in a non-threatening way, we can open up ideas and difficult subjects and discuss them meaningfully. When 500 people register for a conference on suicide with very little promotion other than a simple flyer, the need is pretty clear." After the symposium and performance, satellite symposiums were held in high schools and hospitals in surrounding communities.

"The Subject is Suicide" took a broad approach that used a Hancher event as a point of departure. Other examples are more directly based in the arts. In collaboration with the dance program and Hancher, Plautz created "Discover Dance," a one-time, three-month program in which participants were invited to eight different lecture-demonstrations by university faculty members or choreographers. Registrants were encouraged to attend the seven spring dance events at Hancher, and were offered ticket discounts.

Plautz has a modest budget to produce these events, but she never appears to be at a loss for ideas. The enthusiasm, even passion, she has for her work more than compensates for whatever is wanting in the size of her budget.

Building Interest and Support

Part of Hancher's concept of reaching out involves marketing: informing and gathering the widest audience from the community and the state that might be interested in particular events, and building student interest and enthusiasm to develop a life-long theater-going habit.

Judith Hurtig, marketing director for the auditorium, takes an active approach. Rather than orienting her efforts solely to regular performing arts attenders, she has instituted a multi-layered strategy. She recognizes that focusing on the serious content of some events attracts certain people and drives others away. Instead, she varies the messages and disseminates them to different people in different ways.

To reach students and faculty, she pairs familiar techniques like direct mail with personal appearances to bring the message home. Attracting new people to Hancher is a high priority—25 percent of Iowa City's population turns over every two years. With the help of Welcome Wagon and real estate agents, Hurtig supplies brochures about the current season and offers two free tickets to an event selected by Hancher. Similar efforts focus on new faculty and staff.

Drawing students is a challenge, as it is for most college and university presenters, even with the incentive of student discounts. But each season, the staff goes beyond the passive flier, poster, or ad in the student newspaper. Students are welcomed to Hancher from the beginning of their college careers. They are invited to tour the auditorium, and offered special freshman convocation week programs. Hancher's group sales coordinator identifies what classes might be interested in particular events. The staff visits classrooms and offers discounts to students at their dorms, fraternities and sororities. Despite the labor-intensive nature of this effort, it has been very successful. "It's a way of bringing Hancher Auditorium directly into their classrooms," Hurtig says.

Administrative Structure

Mary Louise Plautz and several other university employees are not actually members of the Hancher staff. Rather, they're "feeder staff." Their responsibilities extend beyond Hancher into the Iowa Center for the Arts, of which the auditorium is just one component. Interestingly, the people who work on behalf of Hancher in private fundraising, public relations, and outreach officially report not to Chappell, but to other department heads.

> "The arts are the language of our lives, and through them, we can open up ideas about difficult subjects."

This is a way for the administration to have oversight on the components of the university, to control costs, to avoid the duplication of services and to prevent fiefdoms from developing. Chappell's challenge is to forge a team from the Hancher staff, who report directly to him, and the feeder staff, who report to others but are essential to Chappell's program.

Winston Barcklay of the Arts Center Relations Office, who has Hancher as his beat, describes the attitude of Chappell and other Hancher staffers. "They have always treated us as one of their team. We're in on the planning and marketing meetings, for example. They're very concerned that what they do is coordinated with what we do."

Larry Eckholt uses "we" as opposed to "they" when speaking about his former relationship with Hancher, communicating his strong sense of alliance even though he was based in another university office and administrative structure. He is particularly clear about the balancing act. "There has been controversy on campus that Hancher is too prominent, that we spent too much time and money pushing it and positioning it. So, I had to be very careful to maintain balance. I called myself the Averell Harriman of the arts here. I had to find out what all the issues were and make sure I would be part of the solution rather than the problem, so I would be able to get my job done."

Fundraising

Eckholt got his job done through the University of Iowa Foundation, established in the late 1950s. Many consider it to be on a par with foundations at major private universities such as Harvard and Stanford. This is due in large part to the impressive fundraising machinery that foundation President Darrell E. Wyrick and his staff have assembled.

Eckholt describes the evolution of the fundraising process for Hancher. In 1977, he and Jim Wockenfuss established the Hancher Circle, a friends support group. It was the classic example of fundamental pyramid fundraising: "We get that base as large as we can, and then figure out all of the ways to get more people to give larger sums," Eckholt says.

Before Hancher's box office was computerized, the mailing list consisted of former audience members who had subscribed, bought single tickets, or asked to be on the mailing list. There was no profile information to indicate whether the names were good prospects. Eckholt says their first mailing went to approximately 15,000 people, with a return of only 300 contributions, some of which were at the $500 level. At that point, he says, they began to "massage" those contributors, using the group as a sounding board to test ideas for expanding the level and number of contributions.

As the Hancher Circle effort began to grow, large projects needed contributed income. There were several ways that potential contributors could become involved. If a corporation contributed to a major project, for instance, it was fair game to be approached for a donation to the annual campaign. Eckholt says that a $250,000 challenge grant from the National Endowment for the Arts enabled Hancher's fundraisers to successfully mobilize their forces. "It took a lot of determination and patience," he says. "Luckily, the University of Iowa Foundation primed the pump by underwriting the fundraising costs, and enabled the concept of a support group for Hancher to get off the ground. Now, most fundraising costs are assessed directly against what is raised."

The full fundraising machinery was put into action on the campaign for the Joffrey *Nutcracker*. Chappell and Eckholt set a goal of $200,000 to $250,000, and exceeded it by raising $254,000 with 599 contributions. Three of the donations were for $25,000.

The annual giving drive in anticipation of the 1989–90 season eloquently picked up the theme Chappell has been driving home to his audience: Being a member of the audience is more than simply being a ticket buyer. Chappell has tried to make audience members recognize their supporting role in enabling artists to create new work.

The campaign was direct in its appeal. One set of printed materials included a postcard with a striking black-and-white action shot of the young choreographer David Parsons. Small red letters proclaimed, "I make dance." The flip side of the card read: "You make the opportunities." A brief note signed by Parsons said, "Hancher Auditorium is giving me an opportunity to create a new ballet in 1990, and I'm grateful to the Hancher Circle contributors who made that commission possible. You'll be hearing from me soon about how important it is for that circle of collaborators to keep growing so that Hancher can continue its crucial mission: supporting and presenting the arts. Thanks." The follow-up was a personal letter from Parsons on his own letterhead, with a well-designed brochure that made the pitch in full color.

Surely, it was one of the most sophisticated fundraising campaigns produced by a presenter. It sent a potent and important message to the public, declaring loudly its commitment to emerging artists and new works. It trumpeted the public's potential role in making a difference to a presenting program. And it expressed the organization's accomplishments and dreams for the future.

The Presenter as Community Leader

Wally Chappell is a quiet, contemplative man, not a flamboyant type. But he realized early on that to keep Hancher Auditorium and its program in his community's consciousness, he would have to go public. This means being in the lobby to greet the audience. It means participating in community organizations like the Chamber of Commerce, and chairing its arts committee. It means cultivating and nurturing productive relationships with the university faculty and administration, particularly in the fine and performing arts departments.

Chappell has articulated his vision for Hancher and its programs so clearly that people can understand the vision, embrace it, and be committed to realizing it. Richard Remington, who was interim president of the university during the early part of Chappell's tenure, notes Chappell's "can do" mentality. "He communicates that nothing is impossible to achieve until you've tried it," Remington says. "Don't let the price tag turn off a good idea." Remington says Chappell "really proves you don't have to give up everything worthwhile when you become an administrator. You have to keep in mind that administration and management are only tracks on which this train runs."

Can this kind of creative center continue to exist at Hancher, or is it a passing phenomenon? Says Remington: "More than being a shell into which things are put, when you look at commissioning works, when you look at the development of the arts, and when you look at building an informed and—if you will—a demanding community audience, then Hancher itself becomes an integral part of the creative experience. It's not passive; it's not a receptacle. It's a part of the overall creative drive. That will keep it alive."

In his inaugural address in 1989, president Hunter R. Rawlings III put forth his priorities for the University of Iowa in the next decade. Developmental programs at the Iowa Center for the Arts were second on his list, after the College of Medicine. Key to his remarks was Hancher Auditorium. He exhorted the university community to "interrelate the arts so that we have a true academic and cultural center."

To these comments, there is Chappell's terse statement: "We are powerful as presenters if we do our work well. We're not if we don't."

20 An Iconoclastic Pillar of the Community

It is an arresting sight in the dead of a biting Minneapolis winter—an enormous, bright-red cherry balanced on the tip of a gigantic spoon poised above a frozen pond. It draws attention, not only to itself, but to its surroundings—the 7½-acre Minneapolis Sculpture Garden which is part of the Walker Art Center/Guthrie Theater complex.

The sculpture, the work of Claes Oldenburg and Coosje van Bruggen, is but one piece in the magnificent new garden, which represents a remarkable cooperative project by the Walker Art Center with the Minneapolis Park and Recreation Board, in association with the Minnesota Landscape Arboretum of the University of Minnesota.

The sculpture garden, including the Sage and John Cowles Conservatory, is a public art space within an urban environment. It is free and open to the public. There are no fences, no granite walls to keep people out. Directly across the street from the Walker, the sculpture garden is linked to the downtown business district by a walking bridge designed by Minneapolis-based artist Siah Armajani. The bridge, which spans a busy interstate highway, was commissioned by the Walker to make the complex more accessible to people in the downtown area.

The sculpture garden is a tangible expression of the Twin Cities community. John Killacky, director of the Walker's Performing Arts Program since 1988, says he is moved by the commitment and spirit that it illustrates.

"This community values its art," he says. "It is a necessity, not a luxury. Outside my window is an outdoor sculpture garden that cost $12.5 million, funded from this community to display this work, which is vandal free. Not too many cities

cities could have open, unguarded sculpture worth millions of dollars and not have some kind of angry reaction to it."

A programmatic philosophy is evident in the sculpture garden. It combines the works of major international sculptors with equally large-scale and fine work from Twin Cities sculptors and designers.

Not surprisingly, this same philosophy is evident in the Walker's Performing Arts Program. The program presents major works—many of them commissioned by the Walker alone, or in collaboration with other commissioning partners—as well as an extensive series of performances with music, dance, and theater institutions from the Twin Cities.

A Performing Arts Program Within a Visual Arts Institution

The Walker Arts Center is a thoroughly visual arts-oriented institution. What role does the Performing Arts Program play in the mix?

A full 85 percent of the Walker's annual budget is allocated for building its visual arts collection; for organizing, presenting, and touring exhibitions; and for maintaining the physical facility. Five percent is for programming in education and film. The remaining 10 percent of the budget allocated to the performing arts fuels a very active, stimulating, and fascinating program.

Martin Friedman, executive director of the Walker for more than 30 years, casts light on the role of the performing arts within a visual arts institution. It is not uncommon for museums to have performing arts presenting programs, he says, citing many examples of sublime relationships between the visual arts and performing arts in general—and, in particular, the visual arts in combination with music, dance, theater, and literature.

"Contemporary art, particularly 20th century art," Friedman says, "is filled with examples of collaborative activities between painters and sculptors on the one hand, and musicians, theater, and film people on the other. Many of these collaborations have produced some of the most energetic and radical manifestations of 20th century art."

He cites the classic case of Diaghilev bringing together Picasso, Massine, Cocteau, and Satie for *Parade*. Later examples include Martha Graham and Isamu Noguchi; then, there is Merce Cunningham's work with Robert Rauchenberg, Jasper Johns, and John Cage.

Within this context, and given this tradition, he says it is not so surprising that an institution like the Walker would serve as a host for interdisciplinary activities which characterize the history of modernism.

With Friedman setting the tone of the institution for more than three decades, certain approaches naturally followed. Robert Stearns, who served as director of the performing arts from 1982-88, feels that he pursued certain artistic paths because the Walker is a visual arts institution devoted to the contemporary world. The Walker's exhibitions are almost always committed to the works of living, creative artists; it therefore makes sense that the works of living, creative artists be presented in the Walker's performing arts program.

Today this philosophy, which was established at the inception of the Performing Arts Program in 1961, is carried on by John Killacky. Killacky came to the Walker with a 20-year career in the arts—first as a dancer, then as an administrator—behind him. He had been company manager and executive director for the Laura Dean Dance Company, and executive director for the Trisha Brown Dance Company. He also was general manager for artistic director Christopher Hunt of the now-defunct Pepsico Summerfare, and directed the cultural programs of the Pew Charitable Trusts. Killacky was very familiar with the Walker because it had commissioned works from the Dean and Brown companies during his tenures with them.

Killacky points to the differences between being a presenter in a museum environment and being a presenter in other environments. "Two things make this unique," he says. "One is that the audience knows (a program) is under the aegis of the Walker Art Center. They know you walk into a museum to learn something. You don't always walk in to have a good time. The audiences here have learned that art isn't just entertainment—that art *can* be entertainment, but that it is not just entertainment. They come in with a sense of investigation."

The other, he says, is that the Walker shows a range of an artist's work, not just the great paintings, so the audiences are used to staying with an artist and understanding the process of art.

Cynthia Gehrig, President of the Twin Cities' Jerome Foundation, points out that the performing arts program of the Walker has an inherent advantage because of the strength of the visual arts program.

"The Walker has prepared an audience for whatever it mounts," she says. "People go to the Walker to be surprised or to see something different or challenging."

Killacky credits his predecessors Suzanne Weil, Nigel Redden and Robert Stearns for the quality of the artists they presented. "Right from the beginning, Sue brought in Twyla Tharp in a residency. We are bringing artists to a community, not just their productions. Some things were commissioned that maybe weren't ready or maybe weren't successful, and found their legs later on. Others became great hits."

Killacky points to the Lee Breuer/Bob Telson work *Gospel at Colonus* as having started out at the Walker in 1982 as a small workshop production. The team's *The Warrior Ant* began as a radio program and was later done as a workshop production at the Walker before it was further developed.

Killacky says his audiences are used to seeing things on an intimate level, and at a beginning level. But not everything that the Walker presents is in a nascent form, he adds. *Gospel at Colonus* was brought back after it had evolved into its full production. And, since 1987, the Walker Art Center has had a shared series with the University of Minnesota's 4,800-seat Northrop Auditorium. They have jointly presented large-scale, fully-produced contemporary work by such artists as Martha Clarke, Merce Cunningham and Philip Glass.

"People are not coming into the theater necessarily demanding to be entertained," Killacky says. "They want to be challenged." He says part of their willingness can be attributed to the fact that contemporary performing art is being presented in the environment of a contemporary art center.

But another crucial part of this receptive environment is the Twin Cities' highly educated and literate population. The area reportedly has the highest number of bookstores per capita in the U.S. A reading, thinking community is, not surprisingly, receptive to the untried, the unfamiliar and the challenging.

Killacky says the Walker audiences understand the process of creativity. He points to a 1989 appearance by Rachel Rosenthal. Rosenthal is a feminist, political performance artist from Los Angeles. Her work, *Rachel's Brain*, is a 95-minute-long, "very strident, very political, very harsh" piece, Killacky says. Still, he had to add a matinee performance because the other performances had sold out—as did the matinee.

Rosenthal came out to answer audience questions after the Saturday evening performance. A full two-thirds of the audience stayed, Killacky says, which amazed him. "They didn't ask about the work, didn't ask, 'Why did you do that?' They wanted to know about her as a person, and what she thought about, what informed her as an artist. Audiences here look at the context."

The Presenting Process

The Performing Arts Program has a distinguished history. Each of its directors brought a unique vision to the mix and put his or her special stamp on the program. Each moved on to other significant positions in the arts.

John Ludwig, the first director, became the executive director of the American Music Theater Institute in Washington, D.C. Suzanne Weil is the managing director of the Sundance Institute, after stints as vice president for programming at the Corporation for Public Broadcasting, and as director of the Dance Program at the National Endowment for the Arts. Nigel Redden also directed the NEA's Dance Program before becoming general manager of the Spoleto Festival USA. Robert Stearns moved from the Walker to the Wexner Center for the Arts at Ohio State University.

Killacky offers a litany of the unique contributions made by his last three predecessors. He says that Weil started as a volunteer and did her work "by the seat of her pants." She found artists she was interested in—Patti Smith and Twyla Tharp among them—and followed her instincts. "Looking back," he says, "her intuitions were really right on."

He says that Redden also had an incredible capacity for finding new talent. "He found artists that were really seminal at the time, and will be remembered. He knew who the really important young ones were."

For his part, Stearns was talented at putting together commissions and partnerships with artists, Killacky says. He put together the commission for the Robert Wilson-David Byrne collaboration, *The Knee Plays*, which was part of the massive and problematic Wilson opera, *The CIVIL warS*.

Stearns also brought in the Trisha Brown company while Killacky was still its executive director. "Then, he went to her and said, 'Well, what do you want to do next?' Not, 'When do you want to come back?' but 'What do you want to do as an artist?' Robert was very good about that."

Brown told Stearns that she needed a theater for a month to build her next piece with painter and sculptor Nancy Graves. Stearns found them a theater in the Twin Cities for a month to create *Lateral Pass*, a new work in collaboration with lighting designer Beverly Emmons.

"If we were doing that in a house in New York," Killacky says, "it would be $1,500 per hour. There would be no time for experimentation. Robert Stearns allowed experimentation to happen. He funded the process, found a way to do it. I think the Walker throughout its history has done that—gone to artists and asked them what they would like to do. I've inherited an extraordinary mantle with these predecessors."

> The Walker serves as a host for interdisciplinary activities that characterize the history of modernism.

Killacky debunks the idea that he is a tastemaker for the Twin Cities. However, he admits that the idea of being a curator—a word well-suited to the museum context—interests him. "I hope my particular aesthetic focus and preferences will inform the programming," he says, "so that people can look back at the years that I'm here and say, 'Well, that was his point of view.' But I'm not programming just for myself. I'm programming for a community under the framework of contemporary work."

The word "curator" is apt, he says. "You're really showing a range of work, a range of disciplines, and different points of view" in the presenting program, he says. But unlike many presenters, Killacky feels he doesn't have to like everything he presents. "I hope I can respect something. I hope I can dislike a lot of stuff, too. If we're inviting artists in to develop work in progress, it is important to find that dialog. If I was only bringing in things I liked, then there would be no way to risk anything."

He acknowledges the need for a well-managed and well-administered program, and for detached intellectual pursuit in curating the performing arts. But he also has a notion of presenter as social provocateur. In this role, the presenter challenges his audiences' basic assumptions and forces them to examine their personal and social beliefs, and how they view a work of art.

If anything marks Killacky's singular vision early in his tenure at the Walker, it is his wish to build a program with a strong foundation in two interdependent areas: He is reaffirming a commitment to the generative artist, and to community in the Twin Cities. "Community" is broadly defined, but includes the local arts community, and others who can be affected by the Walker's performing arts offerings.

Killacky says that when he approaches artists, "a key thing to me is, 'What would you like to do in *our* community?' '' He has been talking to Trisha Brown about coming back. He also has a six-year commitment with Merce Cunningham to do several commissions. "But I want to make sure that these are not just touchdowns from Mars. They must create some kind of relative relationship with the artists and audiences in our community," he says.

This integration with local artists is not new to the Walker. When Breuer and Telson needed singers for their *Gospel at Colonus*, Nigel Redden arranged for local gospel choirs to work on the production. When auditions were being held for dancers and musicians in *The Knee Plays*, Robert Stearns urged Wilson and Byrne to schedule auditions in Minneapolis in addition to New York and Los Angeles.

Killacky is continuing a well-established tradition in advocating links between the visiting artists and local artists and community. But he reveals a much more sweeping conception of community than ever before. "I'm here to really empower artists," he says. "I think presenters are like a service organization, but we have two constituencies: our artists and our audiences."

He says he is developing programs so that the visiting artists form a counterpoint for Twin Cities artists who are working in the same genre. Killacky also is actively seeking pockets in the community that will respond to the style and content of the work being performed at the Walker.

For example, Killacky planned a two-week performance art festival in 1989 in partnership with the Southern Theater in Minneapolis. It featured Rachel Rosenthal in *Rachel's Brain*, and David Cale in *Smooch Music*.

The program could have been complete with just these two important names, but Killacky chose to do more. He and Jeff Bartlett of the Southern Theater decided to present late-night showcases of local performance artists. Killacky says that no other institution in the Twin Cities at that time had recognized the genre of performance art. The local artists were chosen through an open audition process, in keeping with the mission to open doors to the community.

The same festival presented Alex Alexander, a local woman who had been unsuccessfully trying to make a career as a stand-up comedian. A feature article previewing the festival, which appeared in the *Minneapolis Star-Tribune*, quoted Alexander as saying, "Well, I never thought of myself as a performance artist, but why not?" Killacky says Alexander's work is quite eccentric and hadn't fared well in comedy clubs. He was pleased to realize that the Walker had given her a context in which she could feel she had as much validity as any other artist. "(That quote was) one of the nicest presents I'll ever get," Killacky says. "I'm really interested in making opportunities for artists."

The Walker works with artists to builds linkages with the Twin Cities community in a number of ways. For example, audiences were captivated by choreographer Ann Carlson after her appearance at the Walker as part of New York's P.S. 122 Field Trips touring program and Killacky wanted to ask her back to create a new work.

When he asked her the crucial question—"What do you want to do?"—she replied that she would like to do a piece for 65 people and a horse. Killacky decided it would be a perfect outdoor event. He says Carlson's *Dead* made an excellent first-year anniversary event for the Minneapolis Sculpture Garden in 1989, with the audience ignited by the vision of the artist lying face down in her nightgown on a magnificent Arabian horse.

"That really works for me, that I respond to an artist, the community responds to an artist, and we find something unique and site-specific to bring into the community. That leaves something behind—some kind of after-image on our retinas—so that we feel something unique has happened for the Twin Cities and the Walker audiences."

The audiences are very important, Killacky says. "They are key for me, and I think for the museum. What's important to me is that I feel an artist has a window here, and that the audience—whoever they are and how many there might be in numbers—know about the work, and that we find the appropriate audience."

He cites Rachel Rosenthal as a case in point. Although she has been a leading feminist and environmentalist for years on the West Coast, she still is not well known nationally. "It's important for me that the feminist community, the political community, the animal rights people know that this artist is making work about the things that they care about, too." The audiences for her shows at the Walker included people from those special interest groups, due to extra efforts by Killacky and his staff.

In view of the density of activity in the performing arts program— more than 100 performances per year—the Walker has a comparatively tiny staff. Three people—Killacky, an assistant director, and a secretary—curate, market, fundraise, and produce the program.

The Walker tries to draw audiences by starting with the tried and tested methods, especially the 13,000-member mailing list for the monthly calendar of museum events.

This takes care of only one segment of the audience, however. Killacky then moves on to a more personalized approach that he says is essential. He is becoming convinced of the impact of going personally into each of the communities. For Rosenthal's performances, Killacky approached Amazon Books, a popular woman's bookstore, as well as groups involved in animal rights.

"This is introducing me to different segments of the community," he says. "I really felt that Amazon Books appreciated the presenter in town feeling that they are important, and that their audiences should feel welcome. I went back the next week, and there was Rachel's poster with a big circle around it. It's all about community relations."

When performance artist Danny Mydlack came to the Walker on a P.S. 122 Field Trips tour, Killacky promoted the event as more than a dance or a theater event. Mydlack is "kind of this wild, crazy performance artist from Boston who plays an accordion and tells jokes," Killacky says. "I thought, 'His work is so off the wall that we really should find a rock audience for this.' " He approached a local club called First Avenue, which is owned by the musician Prince. The young people who go to that club ordinarily don't feel comfortable walking into a museum auditorium, Killacky says.

Killacky arranged for First Avenue to present Mydlack as the opening act for the Red Hot Chili Peppers, a local rock band. "For the first 20 minutes, I thought they were going to throw beer at him. But then they were transformed, and they fell in love with him. After that, people were coming up to the Walker and saying, 'Is that crazy man performing this weekend?' That was successful. We found a way to get to these kids and make them feel that what is happening in the Walker is relevant to their lives, too."

Killacky says he is most interested in finding a mix of compelling artists and projects. "If there has to be a balance, I want to make sure that we present really interesting finished work, from the small-scale to the large."

The work Walker presents covers vast territory. Its music programs in a single season have included chamber music concerts by members of the Minnesota Orchestra as well as the Kronos Quartet, the Minneapolis-based contemporary music ensemble Zeitgeist with guest artist-composer Terry Riley, the latest hot local rock band, and the female vocal choir from Bulgaria's state radio and television system.

In dance, the fare has been equally diverse. Choreographers' evenings are held in conjunction with the Minnesota Dance Alliance; then, there are the eclectic offerings of the P.S. 122 Field Trips, and residencies by such artists as Bebe Miller and Eiko & Koma.

In the role of presenter as social provocateur, Killacky in his second season organized "Cultural Infidels: Film and Performance for Consenting Adults." The festival, which ran for the entire month of January 1990, featured artists who "probe terrain once perceived as forbidden, taking us on journeys through the subconscious and into the realm of present-day social and psychological realities." The series carried a warning label: "This series contains adult language and subject matter. Audience discretion is advised."

In addition to 11 of Andy Warhol's films, the festival showcased work from a new generation of filmmakers, including John Greyson, Isaac Julien, and Mary Hestand. There were provocative works by such performance artists and musicians as Karen Finley, Shelly Hirsch, John Kelly and Guillermo Gomez-Peña.

The festival placed the work into the context of the history of modernism, looking back to the Dadaists of the early 20th century, the surrealist poets and painters of the 1920s and '30s, playwrights and composers like Bertolt Brecht and Kurt Weill, and the pop statements of the 1960s.

"By presenting the work of these emerging artists to the community," the program brochure explained, "and by recalling their aesthetic predecessors, this series offers a look at an area of creativity that, while at times controversial and confrontational, has historically provided art with some of its most important themes and forms."

Killacky says the program was meant to usher in the final decade of the 20th century. He feels it was a wonderful joint project, something the Walker is uniquely capable of doing well by combining the resources of the performing arts, film, and education departments.

Cynthia Mayeda, Chair of the Dayton-Hudson Foundation, speaks of the "rather delicious dialog that goes on from one part of the Walker to the other." This seems to be a good case in point.

The program was unusually risky, challenging, and provocative—especially in the wake of the Robert Mapplethorpe and Andres Serrano controversies, and in light of the growing drive to censor artistic expression. On the one hand, it dared people to come forward and object to what was being presented. On the other, it offered the artists a context which meaningfully placed their work in a continuum of historical and artistic development.

Killacky remembers that advance publicity and discussion generated strong public reaction to some of the work—especially that of Karen Finley—even before the opening.

> "This community values its art. It is a necessity, not a luxury."

Finley's piece, *We Keep Our Victims Ready*, forcefully—some would say stridently—addresses rape, alcoholism, AIDS, censorship, and oppression of and violence against women. She appears both costumed and unclad during the work. At times, she smears her almost-nude body with various foods—bean sprouts, chocolate, Jell-O—to make her points.

According to the *St. Paul Pioneer Press Dispatch*, that which a year before "might have been an esoteric endeavor suddenly became the province of a radio talk-show host and the Minneapolis vice squad." A radio host condemned Finley's program and urged members of the Walker to cancel their membership. In rebuttal, Walker Executive Director Martin Friedman appeared on the radio show and chastised the host for calling for censorship of something he hadn't seen. Friedman warned that the same thing could happen with the airwaves.

Three plainclothes Minneapolis policemen from the vice squad attended Finley's first performance to determine if the piece violated city obscenity codes. Two of them stayed for an hour, and the third stayed to the end. Killacky figures that they found "there was nothing to fear in Karen Finley," since no further action was taken.

"It was an incredible catharsis for this community," Killacky remembers. "The Walker was totally supportive of the issues these artists were dealing with. The community came out of it well. The media handled it well. The audiences were very strong, very supportive. Karen got wonderful reviews." He hopes to continue to present other controversial artists, but will integrate them into the regular programming.

As if this were not enough controversy, the Walker, in collaboration with Northrop Auditorium, that same season presented the Bill T. Jones/Arnie Zane Dance Company in a performance of "The Promised Land," the final section of *The Last Supper at Uncle Tom's Cabin*.

The project involved the Jones/Zane Company dancers, plus local dancers from the Zenon Dance Company, the New Dance Ensemble, independent dancers affiliated with the Minnesota Dance Alliance and the student University Repertory Company.

The *Minnesota Daily* called the project "the biggest local dance event in years." It also was a very controversial work in which Jones—whose choreographic work has become increasingly politicized since his creative and personal partner, Zane, died of AIDS—explores issues of race, religion, sex and the AIDS epidemic. In addition, the final scene involved nudity for the more than 60 dancers on stage. This precipitated much controversy, and the university refused to let any of its students appear nude in the work. The work also was controversial because of its treatment of racism and homophobia. "When people began thinking and talking about it," Killacky says, "they really got nervous. But Bill kept talking to the press, and 2,700 people came to see the performance. In the final moments of the piece, there was an incredibly beautiful, innocent tableau of 60 people on stage—45 of them completely nude."

Jones was in residence in the Twin Cities for one month to create the piece. The process, Killacky says, "allowed the community to have its own perceptions and fears. It allowed all of us at the institution to deal with our own perceptions and fears, and then allowed the artist to have his work seen as he wanted to have it seen."

The Walker's performing arts program routinely presents many unknown artists performing unknown or unfamiliar work. It also frequently presents the work of now well-known artists who are unveiling new work that has been commissioned or co-commissioned by the Walker. Much of what it does would be considered risky by many presenters.

"Risk is an interesting word," Killacky says, "because one gets a sense of reckless abandon. Risk isn't a word I use. I think it's all about the process of discovering and investigating and exploring. For me, it's about mixing with great respect and integrity, that mix of interesting artists with our audiences with our mission of presenting contemporary work. Is that a risk? I don't think so. It's a wonderful exploration. Do I take chances? Yes. Do I follow my intuitions? I hope so, but in an informed way."

Presenting such provocative events as "Cultural Infidels" and "The Promised Land" requires great courage in the wake of the assault on the National Endowment for the Arts. But the Walker, being a thoroughly contemporary institution, has not shied away from controversial work.

"This institution under Martin Friedman has questioned aesthetic values in the 31 years he has been here," Killacky says. In fact, he adds, the Walker has stood for and encouraged examination, controversy, and intelligent exploration of even the fringes of contemporary art.

The "Cultural Infidels" series was large-scale in conception, but small-scale in production. It utilized, for the most part, the 344-seat Walker auditorium. The Walker also presents large-scale works that require large-scale production, providing an important part of the mix that is intrinsic to its artistic mission.

Since the 1987–88 season, the Walker and Northrop Auditorium at the University of Minnesota have teamed up to offer "Discover," a four-event series of performances. Robert Stearns described it as bringing to the Twin Cities "a set of work which is sufficiently established, significantly scaled, and awesome enough to be of interest to those people who might otherwise be skeptical. This is no longer experimental work, but rather completed work, intentionally contemporary works which could and should be interesting to a sizable audience."

"Discover" enters its fourth season in 1990–91. The series continues to enable Killacky and Dale Schatzlein, director of concerts and lectures at Northrop, to merge their strengths and those of their respective institutions.

Schatzlein traces the first "Discover" series to Nigel Redden's New Dance USA Festival in 1981. The final performance presented Lucinda Childs' dance company at Northrop Auditorium. A new work commissioned by the Walker for Merce Cunningham's company also was presented there.

The collaborative efforts afford the opportunity to "make the new work that is being created in this country and internationally accessible for a larger number of people," Schatzlein says. He says the Twin Cities public often perceives the Walker's offerings as avant-garde, perhaps because they are presented in smaller spaces. There also is a perception that the Walker's presentations might not be accessible, or that the public simply won't like them. Audiences have tended to be young and on the cutting edge.

By contrast, Northrop has presented more familiar, big-draw companies like the American Ballet Theater, New York City Ballet, Paul Taylor Dance Company and the Joffrey Ballet. The community is much less resistant to attending events by big, established companies. By joining forces, both organizations are giving the works a larger scale and context, showing how important the work is, that it is accessible and that it needs an audience's attention.

The artists presented in the first year of the "Discover" series included the Japanese Butoh company Sankai Juku, the Philip Glass Ensemble's live appearance with the film *Koyaanisquatsi*, Martha Clarke's *Garden of Earthly Delights* and the Mark Morris Dance Company. Season two included Michael Moschen *In Motion*, Nina Wiener Dance Company, Merce Cunningham Dance Company and Astor Piazzolla and the New Tango Quintet. The third season program included Paul Dresher's *Power Failure*, Bill T. Jones/Arnie Zane and Company's *The Last Supper at Uncle Tom's Cabin*, the Lyon Opera Ballet in Maguy Marin's *Cendrillon* and the Grand Kabuki Theater of Japan.

The partners in the "Discover" series have unsuccessfully tried to build a subscription base to reduce the financial risk of this type of large-scale venture. Part of the reason for this failure is due to the fact that those who are interested in these artists and works are not long-standing subscription-oriented people.

(Fortunately, the Dayton-Hudson Foundation has chosen to support the Walker's performing arts programs through the "Discover" series. Mayeda reports that a grant is allocated to support the general concept of the series rather than any specific program. She expresses a significant measure of the foundation's trust in the Walker when she says that "we support 'Discover' because it's good and it aspires to be better." The grant is made to advance a certain point of view, to advance a mission in general, not artists in the specific." The NEA Inter-Arts Program also has supported "Discover" from its beginning.)

Also, Killacky says the subscriptions have been promoted primarily through direct mail, which is no longer effective. He plans to shift the focus from direct mail and the season brochure to a general announcement followed by more specific event-oriented marketing.

He says radio appearances by artists and Walker staff members have been an effective way to publicize his overall program. When artists speak about their work, it personalizes it for many listeners. He says editorial coverage in the print media also is important and effectively informs the public.

However, Killacky feels that dialog with the community is the most effective marketing tool, and that is exactly what he has done in his role as social provocateur. The Twin Cities print media were unusually responsive to the "Cultural Infidels" festival and to the Bill T. Jones residency. In-depth articles featured the artists and their work, and examined the controversies in the context of the NEA politicization. Writers from the dailies as well as weekly papers and the gay and lesbian press covered the events in articles, columns and analysis pieces, in addition to reviews.

Fundraising

The Walker's performing arts program budget was $572,000 for the 1990/91 season. The museum administration provides the cost of the department's overhead and salaries for the three-member staff. Killacky must raise all the program monies. Approximately 35–40 percent of the budget is earned from the box office. The rest is raised from the typical mix of funding sources.

Killacky says that the Twin Cities are blessed to have an impressive complement of local foundations to provide philanthropy to the area. Just as Minneapolis-St. Paul is a community that values its art, it also is a place in which there is a strong and enlightened commitment to philanthropy. The most well-known supporters of the arts are the St. Paul Foundation, the Jerome Foundation, the Dayton Hudson Foundation, the Northwest Area Foundation and the St. Paul Companies.

Cynthia Gehrig of the Jerome Foundation points to the fact that the state of Minnesota was settled heavily by northern European immigrants, who brought with them a strong tradition of allocating resources for culture.

Cynthia Mayeda of the Dayton-Hudson Foundation, which has long been a leader in local and national philanthropy, points to the large proportion of corporate headquarters relative to the population in the Twin Cities. She says that the founding families of the city had a good deal of interest in developing and cultivating a rich cultural climate. This has fostered a sense of the adventurous and curious, she says, and has created "a terrific environment" in which organizations like the Walker can flourish.

John Killacky says that the Dayton-Hudson Corporation years ago asserted a leadership role in committing its company, and challenging other companies, to establish generous policies of corporate giving.

Not surprisingly, the Walker Art Center has been the recipient of the largess of these policies, with the Minneapolis Sculpture Garden only the most recent example of the Twin Cities' commitment to the arts.

The Walker also is well known to other major national foundations. Martin Friedman's long-time tenure as executive director has brought stability, coherence, and a consistently high artistic purpose to the institution. And if the performing arts component is any indication, the Walker has drawn committed, innovative, and visionary people to the staff.

Killacky knows the ways of foundations, what they look for in funding a program and who the players are at all the national foundations. Having this knowledge, he knows he must create fascinating, substantive programs to garner the needed philanthropic support. "Each of those funders or individuals won't be funding just me or the Walker," he says. "They will be funding the programs that I develop and want to present here."

The Andrew W. Mellon Foundation represents one of those private funding organizations that became responsive to a proposal of the Walker soon after Killacky arrived on the scene. Rachel Newton Bellow, Program Associate for the Arts for the foundation, speaks with excitement about the Mellon grant that provides funds for a commissioning consortium among the Spoleto Festival/USA, the American Music Theater

> "We follow the artists, follow their leads, and make it possible for them to continue making work."

Festival in Philadelphia and the Walker. Mellon instituted a leadership grant to provide seed money for a pool of funds from which those three organizations could draw to commission new work.

"The grant is for the concept in general," Bellow says. She speaks of trusting these three institutions to be astute in working with the artists most willing to take risks in the creation of new work.

The Jerome Foundation has also provided money for commissioning projects. Cynthia Gehrig says, "We're interested in presenters who see themselves as artistic producers, not just as passive presenters; in people who take an interest in how a work is created, as well as how it is presented."

Killacky feels his ability to keep listening has served him well in the foundation world and as a presenter. "I have found that the hardest thing is to listen to people. I think one of the keys is that we remain listeners. I think our best presenters in America are those who listen to artists. They follow artists. The Diaghilevs of our time are the ones who are listening and really empowering artists to make their work happen."

It is a continuing challenge to keep the edge in the performing arts program at the Walker. Most significantly, the challenge is to find the balance in the programming of artists at different points in their careers. Some of the artists who were first presented in the Walker's auditorium have now become a part of what can only be called the establishment avant-garde.

How can balance be maintained between those artists who were once totally unknown and are now celebrities, and those who are today's unknowns? What does it take to maintain a commitment to those who are developing and emerging today, and still maintain consistency and a record of excellence?

Killacky says he is trying to accomplish this in a number of ways. "We don't try to become the flavor of the month, don't try to find the mega-moment artist of the day and (present them) because everyone else is. It's really looking back at Nigel and Sue and Robert and listening to those artists who interested them and interest me, and saying 'What would you like to do?'

"Artists are there creating. Every day, they are risking something really extraordinary. They are the soul of our society. They are pushing the limits and finding something from their inner depths and making it concrete. They are taking the risks.

"That's where the risk is. We follow them, follow their leads, and make it possible for them to continue making work. Then, it becomes exciting."

The Gospel at Colonus

Sophie Corriveau, Theatre Ballet of Canada

Photo by Richard Desmarais

21 The Little Town That Could

Jackie Torrance casts a spell the instant she begins to ply her specialized art of storytelling. An ample African-American woman with graceful, expressive hands, brightly-painted long fingernails, a collection of butterfly jewelry, a hypnotic voice, and a storehouse of stories, she quiets all murmuring in a classroom of young children, or in a Rotary Club luncheon filled with business people, or in a theater filled with expectant families as she spins the tales she has lovingly collected from her grandparents, other family members, and friends in North Carolina and beyond.

Torrance brought her captivating persona and her enchanted world of Appalachian Jack stories, ghost stories, African American animal tales and old-time Southern stories to the Yreka Community Theater for the first time in 1988, at the end of the theater's 12th year of existence. During that visit, she opened up the world of storytelling to Yrekans, and even may have inspired nascent local storytellers to take up the long-forgotten legacy of ancestors who settled the area more than 100 years ago. Her presence in the community for several days is a perfect example of the kinds of unique experiences that the theater has provided since 1976 for the citizens of Yreka and Siskiyou County in northernmost California. Torrance came to Yreka in 1988 through the Performing Arts for Siskiyou Schools (PASS) program, a cooperative effort between the theater and the county school system. The 307-seat Yreka Community Theater was half-filled for Torrance's appearance that time. When she returned two years later, tickets were sold out, with a waiting list of 80 people. Those who had seen her before wanted to experience the magic again; those who had heard about her from friends didn't want to miss her this time around.

The range of Yreka's program—which has built audiences for performances as intimate as Torrance's, as large and highly-produced as the Western Opera Theater or the Oakland Ballet and as unique as U-ZULU Dance Theater from South Africa—is amazing. In the past six years especially, each season has brought a multidisciplinary mix of events from the traditional to the challenging.

The story of the Yreka Community Theater itself is amazing, and unlikely. The opening of such a facility in a metropolitan center anywhere in the U.S. would probably be noted by many, attended by some, and fervently appreciated by a few. But in a rural town with a population of 6,000, what goes on in this theater has positively affected the lives of a large number of Siskiyou County citizens.

Yreka is the county seat of Siskiyou, whose sparse population of 40,000 is spread over a land area equal to Connecticut and Rhode Island combined. The area also is very isolated. Yreka is almost exactly in between San Francisco and Portland, Oregon, and is a six-hour drive on Interstate 5 to either one of them. It is not unusual for Yreka audiences to drive more than 30 miles over narrow mountain roads to attend performances. Even assuming that a sold-out audience on any given night comes from within the town, the people in the theater represent an astounding 5 percent of Yreka's population.

Robert Marshall, who has managed the theater since 1977, describes Yreka as a fairly conservative community that generally votes Republican; its population is well-balanced between older people and younger families with children, and it has a large proportion of professional people, plus retirees and younger residents who have retreated from urban areas to change their lifestyles. "There's no guarantee of a job here," Marshall says, "and no industry. But some living costs are lower, and there are things you don't need—like security systems on your home."

Yreka was once a gold camp site that later boomed as a lumber town. The timber industry has been in decline in recent years, and the area's major employer now is the Klamath National Forest, the local outpost of the U.S. Forest Service. Another cadre of professional people works in county management, administration and support services. This is followed by the timber industry, and then by agriculture.

Everyone who speaks about life in Yreka and environs comments on its isolation. Ada Dodd, educational consultant to the county school system, explains just how vast the county is, and how far-flung the settlements. She says that one school for which she is responsible is 100 miles from Yreka. She spends the better part of a day travelling on mountain roads to reach it, and stays overnight with a friend in order to visit the school the next morning.

But the same people who describe Yreka's isolation also say that the existence of the Yreka Community Theater somehow vitiates the feeling of isolation. Dodd describes it as a hub for people in Siskiyou County. In fact, there seems to be a universally strong sense of ownership and civic pride.

Jerry Willis, director of public events at the California Institute of Technology, relates an incident that illustrates how widespread is that sense of ownership. It happened when Willis made an unplanned visit to Yreka after driving 400 miles from Los Angeles on his way to Seattle.

"I had known Bob Marshall for a number of years," Willis says, "and had listened to him spin stories about the mythical kingdom of Yreka. On the freeway, I saw a sign for Yreka. I thought, this is my chance to go look at Bob's palace." He sought the help of a gas station attendant to direct him to the theater. "I didn't think the pump jockey would be able to help me. But he turned around and he gave me directions, and he said, 'Yeah, we're pretty proud of that around here.' It was as if I had asked him for directions to the local shrine. He invited me back and said I should stop by any time, as if inviting me to his home."

> What goes on in the Yreka Community Theater has positively affected the lives of many people in the town.

This sense of ownership is well-founded. In fact, the citizens of Yreka *do* own the Community Theater. It is an identified department within the city's administrative structure. All income from the facility flows into—and all expenses come out of—the city's general fund.

The saga of the building of the Yreka Community Theater combines a groundswell of grass-roots feeling and need with a city government's determination and tenacity. That the theater was built at all is a tribute to the citizens of Yreka, and to the government that found a way to make it happen. In a sense, this is the story of the little town that could.

Building a Dream

For many years, the state of the performing arts in Yreka had been similar to that of many other small, rural American communities. Local drama groups and students had enthusiastically mounted productions in the high school gymnasium.

Norman Berryhill, drama instructor at the high school for more than 20 years, says the productions always had strong support, and tickets were hard to come by. Through his dedication and influence, people had developed an awareness, respect, and interest in theater.

There also were cultural events at the local junior college, College of the Siskiyous, and theater productions at the 85-seat Siskiyou Performing Arts Center. But touring artists from outside the community could not perform in Yreka because it lacked an appropriate facility.

In the early 1970s, Yreka was a small community with a population of about 3,500 and an unemployment rate of more than 20 percent—high enough to qualify it for a public works grant from the federal government. The City Council sent out a survey to everyone within the city limits. It contained a list of 12 projects that the city might build, and asked people to rate them according to importance.

More than 70 percent of the respondents rated a theater as their first choice. One of the important reasons for this interest surely was a result of so many Yreka citizens having participated in or or attended performances by Norman Berryhill's drama classes.

Thomas Sieber, Yreka's mayor from 1988–90, says he remembers being surprised by the results. "I had no idea there were so many people here who wanted theater in their community," he says. "Support for the theater came from everywhere—the ranches, the valleys, everywhere!"

Ethel Berryhill, Norman's wife and founding member of the Yreka Community Theater Guild, says "We were all surprised at how many people said they wanted a theater and not a senior citizen center—or a bowling alley!"

Don Carey, county assessor since 1978, is credited with being the driving force behind the city government's efforts to make the theater a reality. Carey brings with him an oral history about the theater's beginnings, as well as his scrapbook of photographs of the site, its ground-breaking, the early stages of construction and the building's dedication. He shows and comments on the photographs as if they were pictures in a treasured family album. It is clear this is his own personal album, not some official document kept by the city.

Carey was elected to the City Council in 1970. He recalls that economic development monies were available at that time. Public hearings were held to find out if people were serious about a theater. "There was very little opposition voiced about the project," he says. "I think the general perception was that these grants were made up of taxpayer money that already had been allocated for building things. Some people felt that if Yreka didn't get the grant, someone else would. And they wanted the jobs here."

Still, the question gnaws: Why were people so interested in a theater? Carey ventures that it was the lack of a good place to hold plays by the community groups and the high school. The community took pride in its school plays, he says, "but the kids couldn't give their best. We wanted a good theater with a sloped floor, decent seating . . . And extra-wide aisles were a requirement so you wouldn't be stepping on people's toes. People just rallied around the idea."

Between 1972 and 1975, the city did all the preparatory work of receiving public input, establishing a center commission, selecting a site, and—with the help of Bizz Johnson, its U.S. congressman—researching the availability of federal monies to fund the project.

Yreka's first application, directed to the Department of Housing and Urban Development under the Community Development Act, was turned down. The city persevered. With Johnson's help, it found another federal program that made money available for community projects. Yreka's application was accepted in 1975, and a grant of $500,000 to build the theater was made from the Public Works and Economic Development Act.

The city put the project out to bid. No one bid on it, because the proposed specifications far exceeded the funds available. Plans were revised and put out to bid again. Four bids came in—but even the lowest exceeded the budget by $65,000.

A groundswell of citizen activism ensued. Carey says people responded immediately, even though it was just before Christmas, in the middle of a recession and with unemployment in the area at more than 20 percent.

They pledged enough money to cover about one-half of the shortfall, most of it in pledges of $25 and $50. Groups organized bake sales; service clubs took money out of their treasuries; businesses contributed, as did employees of the Forest Service. In all—and in the space of two week's time—the townspeople raised $30,000 from private donations. The city covered the remaining shortfall with some of the revenue-sharing funds it had received that year.

Ground was broken in December 1975, and construction began in January 1976. The completed project was accepted by the city 10 months later.

During construction, Berryhill was often pulled out of his classes at the high school when he was needed at the site, which was just next door. Another teacher covered for him while he was gone. "I feel very fortunate," he says, "because very few high school drama teachers get to build a theater."

But it wasn't easy, he says. "It's a special kind of facility. The City Council knew it wanted a theater, but didn't know what should be in it. The architect had never designed one before, either." Berryhill drew on his academic experience, and on Richard Turner, owner of the local music store, who had worked in professional theater. "It was a good relationship," Berryhill says. "The architect was very open to our suggestions, and kept bringing us problems and asking us questions. We talked to an acoustical engineer, and visited other theaters of a comparable size on the coast. Our ideas made a difference."

Three months before the theater was completed, Richard Turner was hired as a part-time employee. Activity in the completed building began immediately. The opening week brought two performances by jazz pianist Randy Weston, a gospel concert, and performances by groups from Yreka schools and the Siskiyou Performing Arts Center.

In 1977, Turner needed to return to his thriving music store full time. He was replaced by freelance musician Robert Marshall, who had just moved to the area with his wife and two children.

As a newcomer to the area, Marshall's first order of business was to get to know the people and how they did business. It took time for him to integrate himself into the community. "There are certain rules, unspoken policies and contacts," he says. He occasionally "butted heads and had to back-pedal," but he quickly developed a feel for the community.

Marshall has brought special qualities to his job, says Peter Pennekamp, vice president for cultural programming and program services at National Public Radio, and former director of the NEA's Inter-Arts Program. Pennekamp is familiar with presenting in Northern California; until 1987, he was director of CenterArts at Humboldt State University in Arcata, Calif.

"Bob has been the key ingredient in what has created a real revolution in the support of performance in that area," Pennekamp says. Marshall shares the community's values, he adds, and doesn't act as a missionary from the outside who thinks his own taste is better than that of the local residents. "He has none of that pretense. Even though he's from a different state and different area, he fits the people. He is relatively conservative in his behavior and in his sense of what's right and wrong in the world."

Pennekamp also thinks that as an artist himself, Marshall has a real love for performance. "He's able to provide the linkage between the people and the things they would not normally experience. I think people trust Bob."

Many communities in America built theaters in the 1960s and 1970s. But building a facility doesn't guarantee it will be well used. Once built, communities often have had no idea how to use their theaters imaginatively and constructively. Even in Yreka, the first few years of operation faced a skeptical segment of the population that considered the building over on Oregon Street to be little more than a white elephant.

At first, the city wasn't sure what it wanted to do with the theater, other than use it for rentals and high school drama productions and concerts. But Marshall wanted to take a more active role. He started slowly and modestly, self-producing some concerts, and collaborating on several musicals with local theater companies.

But since he was new to the job, he wasn't in touch with the presenting field. "I kept plugging away at it," he remembers, "and tried to become better informed about who was doing what."

He instinctively knew that the theater should become a part of a professional network, both for his own professional growth and for the theater to flourish. He contacted the Western States Arts Foundation and joined the Western Alliance of Arts Administrators. He also attended a workshop on marketing the performing arts, and then went to his first Western booking conference in Seattle.

He didn't know anyone at that first conference, but Peter Pennekamp introduced himself and other colleagues. They welcomed Marshall. Eleven years later, he became president of the California Presenters Network, an organization that fosters cooperative projects among performing arts presenters in the state. "Meeting people is the whole thing," Marshall says. "The more people in the field you meet, the more people know about you and your program. That's the way it builds."

At the beginning of his tenure on the job, Marshall also had no presenting experience. But while training as a musician, he had worked with symphonies, been in shows and had pit orchestra experience. He had some idea of the operational scope of a facility. The other aspects of the job would have to be a learn-as-you-go affair.

One thing was clear: There was only Marshall to take care of everything. He literally was a one-man band, taking on every aspect of the new theater's operations and program development. Former Yreka Mayor Thomas Sieber notes how Marshall has developed the theater's potential. Sieber, a bona fide colorful character who makes his living as the postmaster of nearby Greenview, has a very engaged interest in the theater, not just as the City Council's presiding officer, but also as a dedicated comedic actor.

"Somebody else could have got by very easily," he says, "just sitting in the office and making up schedules for the high school and other groups. But Bob wasn't the type of person to be satisfied doing that.

"There's no guaranteed audience for the things he works so hard to bring in," Sieber continues. "It would be easy just to stick with country and western and other crowd-pleasers; that would make his job a lot less frustrating. But his vision is to expose as many people to as many different kinds of performing arts as possible. He's brought in things that people don't like—and to me, that's great."

Sieber says he has never received any complaint about the theater. "I think this and our volunteer fire department are the only two areas in the community where there has never been a complaint," he says.

Radio station owner Gary Hawke also supports Marshall's variety of programming. "Many people in Bob's position would tend to gravitate toward their own likes and dislikes," he says. "But over the years, Bob has brought in such a wide spectrum of the performing arts that sometimes people will attend events even when they've never heard of the artist or the particular style of music. He takes chances. He gives us a taste of everything."

> "A presenter can be an interpreter, an explainer, a definer of the arts in the community."

Hawke explains that Yreka doesn't have a large arts budget, so the city fathers cannot tolerate a lack of some return on the city investment. Some of the programs are risky, requiring special fundraising and matching funds and grants. "If nobody goes or nobody likes what is done," he says, "you can cut yourself off really quickly."

People in town like Marshall as a person, and he has built a track record as a presenter. Hawke, who is a former president of the local Rotary Club, says the club has supported arts activities at the theater, even though many of the members may not attend every event. "Whether they go to one event per year, or one every week, the members of the Rotary feel that the theater contributes to the community," he says. "We have something that other communities our size and in our region don't have. Good performing arts give a different spirit to a community."

J.J. Lewis-Nichols, actress, theater teacher, and director of Shasta Starcraft Theater, says that Marshall crosses over between the business and artistic ends of the theater. "As an employee of the city, he must pass inspection by the city fathers as well as answer to the artistic needs of the community. His uniqueness is that he's a total businessman and a total artist."

As a professional artist who had spent much of her career acting on the New York stage, she says she's grateful for the resources Marshall has offered the local artistic community. She arrived in the area in 1982, and wondered how she would be able to continue in theater. "He made it possible for me to work, and introduced me to the people who would be part of the group I work with. The theater really provides a focal point (for artists) to be seen and heard in this community."

Educational consultant Ada Dodd says the key to Marshall's success is his ability to blend informality with a professional air. "I don't know how he does it," she says, "but he makes the farmer feel as welcome and as comfortable as the pharmacist in town. He has blended very nicely with the community."

City Manager James Dillon says he's noticed a positive change in the area.

"We've dramatically upgraded our cultural attitudes and atmosphere," he says. "We haven't grown that much in population, but we've sure grown in attitudes and quality of life."

Although he has been referred to as "Yreka's Mr. Theater" by Karl Barron of the *Siskiyou Daily News*, Marshall is more modest when evaluating the magnitude of his own star. He says his condition as a one-man band got an assist in 1988 with the appointment of a part-time assistant, whose salary was provided with a grant from the California Arts Council.

Since 1978, Marshall also has managed the Community Center, built on a piece of land adjacent to the theater. The center was built with the same type of economic development grant that made the theater a reality. It houses a weekday senior citizen program, and is rented out for classes by the junior college and the Yreka Recreation Department. The community also can rent it for social functions, since it is equipped with a professional kitchen. Marshall makes the center available for community projects, and works with representatives to help them make arrangements.

He draws heavily from his long-time experience as musician in describing his life as a presenter, the other very important part of what he does. He likens a good presenter to a clarinet player who learns the mechanics but also has the innate talent for the art of playing. Some clarinetists are incredible technicians who can play with great facility—but they lack the ability to express the heart and soul of the music. Marshall says that type of clarinetist is analogous to presenters who see themselves as organizational whizzes, but cannot breathe any life or excitement into their programming.

He says today's presenter is significantly more than someone with a telephone, a calculator, and a calendar, "although I have all of the above," he says with a smile. "[But those tools are] only part of the image that we are working to expand; that's the way the job has always been defined. But in the last couple of years, presenters have been standing up and demanding to be viewed differently. The telephone and the calculator are only the mechanics of it.

"A presenter is an artistic person, which is a pretty grandiose thing to say." A presenter has an artistic direction, he adds, and a vision of how the arts are important in the community. He or she can be "an interpreter, an explainer, a definer of the arts in the community."

"AT LAST!"

The Yreka Community Theater hosted several major events each year from 1978 to 1984, each offered separately and never as a series. In the first few years, the Yreka Community Theater Guild provided the financial wherewithal and the volunteer staff of ushers for the programming of events. Ethel Berryhill explains that the guild was formed from the nucleus of people who had spearheaded the emergency fundraising for the theater in 1976.

The guild presented the Oakland Ballet in 1977, and the first appearance in Yreka of the Western Opera Theater in a 1978 production of Donizetti's *Don Pasquale*.

In 1984, having brought some stability to the theater and its early programs, Marshall put together an official season series. He called it, "AT LAST!" It consisted of nine events and included the Western Opera Theater's production of Rossini's *La Cenerentola*, chamber music, jazz, dance, children's theater and a country string band. (Over the years, the Western Opera Theater has been the common thread in an annually evolving presenting program sometimes brought in by the guild, sometimes co-presented with the city, and more recently presented by the city alone.)

Marshall says it was important to him to offer the programs as a series. It provided the opportunity to convey a sense of structure and direction, along with the chance to create a printed brochure that was mailed and handed out across the area. Approximately 80 season tickets were sold in the first season, and the number grew steadily to 183 for the 1989–90 season—almost 60 percent of the theater's capacity.

Each season since has brought a multidisciplinary mix of events, which has traditionally and steadfastly included the Western Opera Theater. The opera company has made an appearance in Yreka every autumn since 1978. The company celebrates its own 25th anniversary in the 1990–91 season, and a special anniversary celebration was planned to acknowledge the mutually supportive relationship between the opera group and the theater.

Marshall says he has been careful to include in his mix several events that are sure to be crowd-pleasers, along with performances to challenge the community. In Yreka, this could mean presenting Los Angeles' Back Alley Theater in a production of Eric Bentley's politically-charged *Are You Now or Have You Ever Been*, a dramatization of the House Un-American Activities Committee investigation of the show business industry.

Or, it could mean the presentation of artists and companies grounded in cultures of color. Yreka is 92.9 percent Caucasian. Marshall has presented U-ZULU Dance Theater, a South African Zulu company that focuses on elements of its cultural tradition and illuminates its country's political conflicts. He acknowledges that U-ZULU was a bit of a stretch for his community.

"Obviously, what is risk-taking in Yreka is not necessarily risk-taking in Berkeley," he says. "We all understand that. Presenting contemporary dance is risk-taking for me, because I haven't built a big, solid audience. My audience is basically conservative, and Yreka is not a real free, open, liberal community that's ready for anything you'd find in urban areas."

He says presenting a group like U-ZULU means taking a risk, because its message is very political, and the dancing might be perceived as erotic. "But I will sell it, in the series, as exactly what it is: 'Get ready for this one! It's controversial!' They'll come, they'll want to see it. So, I think risk-taking is important, but in a rural area I have to go a little more slowly, a little bit at a time."

He has worked hard to develop his audiences' trust by being completely honest, sometimes noting that a particular program might seem shocking to some viewers, and that it's all right to react that way.

Norman Berryhill says Yreka has hosted some modern dance groups which may be standard for an urban area, "but for rural America, they're a little shocking. They were never on the Carol Burnett show. But the type of comment I hear now is, 'Well, they were certainly quite good, but I didn't like them.' I think people are at the point where they can appreciate the artistry, even when they don't care for the work."

> Support for the theater came from everywhere —the ranches, the valleys, every-where.

Former Mayor Sieber says he's all for risk-taking in scheduling events. "People have accepted more than they thought they would accept," he says. "If you talk to people before certain shows, some already have their minds made up not to like them. But bingo—by the end of the show, they want to see it again!"

In addition to the "AT LAST!" season and additional programs throughout the year, the number of events presented by the theater itself has risen to about 17 per year since 1984. The series holds steady each season with seven events. The rest of the time, the theater continues to be available for rentals at a nominal charge for community organizations.

Then, there is the Performing Arts for Siskiyou Schools (PASS) program, the cooperative effort between the theater and the county school system that twice brought Jackie Torrance to Yreka. In the 1990 season, 5,000 students took part in the program, which Marshall created with educational consultant Ada Dodd. Marshall also presents an increasingly popular four-part Youth and Family Series, featuring the same artists and companies presented in the school program.

As the theater has become more of an established part of the community, Marshall has presented a mini-series of Monday night performances in May of each year. One year featured classical music; the others ethnic music and dance.

Putting Out the Word

It is a challenge to keep the community informed about what is happening at the theater, Marshall says. He publishes a season brochure which is mailed out late in the summer. The mailing list for the city has approximately 2,500 names and is sent out to everyone who pays a water bill in Yreka. He also puts together a mailing list of nearly 3,000 to cover the rest of the county, and additional mailings are made for programs of special interest. A monthly newsletter, *ArtBeat of Siskiyou County*, lists the theater events as well as other arts and cultural events in the county.

Marshall says the local media have been very supportive. Mary Ann Potter, the lifestyles editor of the *Siskiyou Daily News*, says she appreciates the material that Marshall brings in to her, and uses much of it on the Friday entertainment page. She also has run frequent in-depth feature articles about the theater and Bob Marshall.

In addition, Gary Hawke's two radio stations help air public service an-

nouncements on theater events. PSAs are also often aired by stations as far away
as Redding, 90 miles from Yreka.

Financing the Arts

In building the Yreka Community Theater, the city has made a commitment to support Marshall's increasingly ambitious programming. Marshall has
kept ticket prices low so the performances will be financially accessible. The series
ticket for the 1989–90 season was $48, less than $7 per event. Senior and student
series tickets are even lower, at $44. Single tickets range in price from $6 to $11.
Marshall reports increasing numbers of sold-out houses each season.

His expense budget for 1989–90 was $157,917, with about 70 percent al-
located to operations, maintenance, and salaries. The presenting budget of $47,290
represents about 30 percent of the total.

Since 1988, Marshall has launched an annual membership campaign for individual and business contributions. At the end of the 1989–90 season, he raised
some $1,350 toward his budget. Other sources of income were generated from
rentals (9 percent), ticket sales (21 percent), and grants/subsidies (15 percent)—
totaling 45 percent of the revenue. The other 55 percent, or $85,115, comes from
the city's general fund.

He says it's natural that money comes from the general fund, "just as the city
pays for its police department and fire department." He's always concerned about
theater profits and losses, but they are not his primary focus. He says the city
doesn't look upon the theater as a money-making venture but as a community
service that demonstrates its commitment to presenting the performing arts. "I've
always told them they can't expect to make money from the performing arts,"
Marshall says.

Indeed, City Manager Jim Dillon says the city is "in up to our ears" in expenses
for the theater. "And we have made monetary commitments that—to tell you the
truth—I never thought we'd make. We really roll the money. But it's surprising how
close we come to breaking even, not on building maintenance, but on the performances."

It hasn't been easy to generate corporate contributions for the theater, primarily because there is a paucity of companies in the county. There also are very
few foundations. Marshall has applied to one of the few foundations in the area
for a $50,000 capital grant to upgrade the theater lighting system and computerize
the box office system.

Plans for the Future

Marshall's vision has grown exponentially in the 13 years he has been
manager of the Yreka Community Theater, beginning with his first efforts to join
presenters networks and professional organizations. Now, as outgoing president of
the California Presenters Network, he believes he is still developing his professional
skills.

"Serving as president has allowed me to become a little more global in my thinking," he says. "It has helped me personally, because it has put me very much in touch with what's going on in the arts, not just in presenting. It has enabled me to become a lot more sophisticated in how I do and perceive things. This has helped me on the local level very much. I haven't lost that grass-roots ability to know this community and what it wants; I'm just able to present it to them better."

At the same time, he says, he has been able to advance the rural agenda, bringing smaller presenters into the organization and developing a camaraderie among presenters all over California. Rural presenters have become more comfortable with their urban counterparts; presenters from the metropolitan areas are more sensitive to the unique problems and issues of presenters from rural and small communities.

"The issues, concerns, and needs of the presenters and artists in rural areas are totally different than those in the suburban and metropolitan areas," Marshall says. Physical location and a lack of resources often make it difficult for an artist or presenter to meet the guidelines for grant programs coming from the California Arts Council or the NEA. In addition, he says, grant criteria or reports are too often written from the context of a metropolitan area. "We choose to be *here*," he adds. "I'm not complaining, but it's very difficult."

Marshall's increasing exposure and broadened awareness have led him to think that events cannot be presented purely to build a spectator audience. He is equally committed to the idea that the city must provide opportunities for grass-roots participation in hands-on arts activities.

He has turned his mind to thinking about how he can establish participatory arts programs. He now is actively developing plans, all of which will require City Council approval, to form a community band and choir, and to provide classes in visual arts, music, drama, and dance. He also hopes to implement conversational language courses in French and Spanish, a lecture series, and a community artists series.

Despite this wealth of responsibilities, decisions to be made and deadlines to meet, Marshall manages to maintain a relaxed, friendly, and informal style. He enthusiastically engages an audience with his pre-curtain comments, or while chatting in the lobby during intermission.

That one-on-one style is thoroughly appropriate to the mission and style of the institution.

Since the beginning, the Yreka Community Theater has sought to make the performing arts a part of every age group. Norman Berryhill is now able to teach his high school students more about theater. They sometimes fill slots in the stage crew or are ushers for some events, joining with volunteer members of the Community Theater Guild.

Poignantly, the theater's mission statement now speaks of providing the space and the opportunity for citizens to experience, enjoy, and participate in the arts: "to promote, encourage, and support the idea that the arts are an integral part of man's spirit and that the cultural and artistic well-being of our communities begins and sustains with this premise."

The theater's success stems from the community's knowledge of its ownership and participation, and from the feeling of trust Marshall has carefully built over the years. "I think the theater is an integral part of the community now," he says. "People know about us and support us. They don't necessarily come to all the performances—and some don't come to any—but they talk about the theater, and they're proud of it." Ask the attendant at that gas station.

It's said that Marshall is always on the soap box about the arts, particularly at Rotary Club meetings. He doesn't mind that characterization. It's probably why the theater has come from being considered the white elephant on Oregon Street to a well-loved, successful part of city government.

Final Notes

Arts presenters often feel isolated in their daily work lives. They struggle to get the show up, the word out. They covet time to reflect on their future directions and to stay current with the worlds of artists and the needs of the community. It's easy to forget that there are many others dreaming the same dreams and struggling with the same problems.

As I traveled from one arts presenter to another, I felt the continuity among presenting organizations all over the country. I observed the qualities that are common to all, and those that make each organization singular. Few people are accorded the opportunity I had, to see the kinship among organizations that represent the ever-widening range of the field. The commonalities and the differences now bring the field much strength and vigor.

Throughout the research and writing of *21 Voices*, I was also engaged by the National Task Force on Presenting and Touring the Performing Arts as a co-consultant and co-writer. The Task Force project, which was designed to explore the future of performing arts presenting in the United States and to develop a philosophical framework for action, dovetailed with this one seamlessly. Many of the ideas that emerged from the discussions of Task Force members powerfully influenced my thoughts in writing this book.

The field of presenting is undergoing a significant progression from the once widely-held view of presenters as agents of a distribution network, with art as the product. The emerging view of the field focuses on presenting organizations as arts organizations with artistic missions and purposes. Presenters now have an active relationship with artists and their work, and with the communities they serve. Through vision, passion, commitment and understanding—as well as through administrative acumen—presenters have the opportunity to nurture artistic endeavor and lay the groundwork for a future in which the performing arts are a vital part of their communities.

The organizations profiled here eloquently illustrate the art of presenting the performing arts.

Talking with the presenters you have met in these pages was revelatory for me. They shared with me the sources of their ideas, traced the ways in which they became engaged with certain artforms and artists, and set forth the philosophical bases for their organizations.

Time and again I observed the power and force of people who worked to realize a particular vision for their organizations. Especially remarkable were the individuals who created organizations out of their own sense of what was missing from the fabric of their communities, whether those communities were major cities or isolated rural areas.

Phyllis Brzozowska's need to hear Celtic music gave rise to CITYFOLK; Marta Moreno Vega's drive to document the cultural roots of the people of the African diaspora, and to celebrate their living traditions, was the foundation for the Franklin

H. Williams Caribbean Cultural Center/African Diaspora Institute. Ruth Felt's love for vocal and instrumental recitals, and her realization that there was a gap in the arts offerings in her city, brought forth San Francisco Performances. Small groups of generative artists who wanted to find space to develop and show their work created artist-run spaces like On the Boards in Seattle, and Dance Theater Workshop and P.S. 122 in New York. A group of young people in Appalachia who wanted to hold on to a disappearing culture founded Appalshop. Out of Harvey Lichtenstein's deep devotion to a growing body of large-scale contemporary work evolved the Next Wave Festival at the Brooklyn Academy of Music; out of a small group of individuals concerned about the political and cultural situation in Chile grew La Peña Cultural Center.

But though these organizations may have begun with the vision of an individual or a small group of people, they have gone on to grow and survive as thriving institutions with ever-broadening missions. Their bases of support extend to their members, their contributors, their boards of directors and—most importantly—their communities. In several stirring instances, the communities they serve are the organizations' *raison d'être*. One presenter spoke eloquently about how humbled he felt as more and more people embraced the vision for the organization he founded and still directs.

These organizations work because they have each found what is organic to them, whether it is a particular kind of artform or artist or a deep commitment to the arts as one component of a broader cultural picture. These organizations have each found a voice of their own. That voice is always unique to the physical and cultural space in which the organization grows. It would be impossible to transplant any of these organizations into another community. They have gone through a process of organizational self-discovery unique to themselves and the place in which they grow. There is significance in each organization's journey; without the journey of organizational self-discovery, the destination becomes meaningless.

21 Voices is meant to encourage presenting organizations to begin listening to their own—and their communities'—voices and impulses. Part of finding a voice of one's own lies in developing the courage, confidence and means to express it in programmatic terms—to go public.

Many, if not all, of these 21 organizations have advisors whom they consult regularly. These people may offer advice about artistic matters, or about community needs, about traditional approaches or about scholarly insights—or about a combination of these things. The essence for the organization is always to strike a balance between listening and responding, leading and following. These organizations nourish and are nourished by their communities; they simultaneously follow their communities' leads and lead their followers.

The odyssey of discovery from which *21 Voices* grew is, as much as anything else, a story of the United States and its diverse and unique communities. It is about the richness of the people, and the depth of their desire to coalesce around mutual interests. I found community in every region, in rural and isolated areas like Whitesburg, Kentucky, Yreka, California and Helena, Montana; and in megalopoli like New York, Atlanta and Chicago. I found people who wanted to commune with something deeply meaningful in their lives. I found stories of passion, commitment, dedication, vision and activism.

I also saw commitment to a mission and a demonstration of the kind of selflessness that once was a familiar part of the personal and professional landscape, but that seemed to lose ground in the 1980s as self-interest took center stage. Many of the directors of the 21 organizations hold on to an idealism and commitment familiar from times gone by. Their contribution to the field, the arts world, and their own communities is that much richer.

My own odyssey of discovery has come to an end. I have been greatly enriched by the experience. I think differently, see differently and hear differently than I did before. I have confidence that the field of presenting is primed to proceed in richer and more expansive ways toward the goal of treating what it does as an art. Life in the best of all possible worlds is within reach. We must all embark on the journey.

PHOTO CREDITS

American Dance Festival
Page 6: The African American Dance Ensemble in Donald McKayle's *Games*, performed as part of "The Black Tradition in American Modern Dance." Photo by Jay Anderson.
Page 21: Students dancing outdoors on the Duke University campus. Photo by Jay Anderson.

Appalshop
Page 22: The staff of Appalshop Festival, fall of 1988. Photo by Scot Oliver.

Baltimore Theatre Project
Page 32: Robert Sherman in performance. Photo by Gerry Goodstein.

Brooklyn Academy of Music
Page 48: Members of the international cast of *The Mahabharata* in the first section of the work, entitled "The Game of Dice." Photo by Marc Enguerand.

Caribbean Cultural Center
Page 66: Roots of Brasil in the tribute to Oya and Yemanja. Photo by Tony Bennia.

Chamber Music Chicago
Page 82: The Vermeer Quartet. Photo courtesy of ICM Artists.
Page 95: Keith Jarrett. Photo by Susanne Stevens.

CITYFOLK
Page 96: Andy M. Stewart and Johnny Cunningham of Silly Wizard, performing in "The Celtic Series 1988." Photo by Stephen Matyi.

Dance Theater Workshop
Page 108: LA LA LA Human Steps. Photo by Edouard Lock.
Page 123: David Parsons. Photo by Lois Greenfield.

Dartmouth College, Hopkins Center
Page 124: The Hopkins Center Community Dance Program in a 1988 performance of *Carmina Burana*.
Page 137: Students participating in a program sponsored by the Hopkins Center's Arts Education Services.

Helena Film Society/Series for the Performing Arts
Page 138: The old Lewis and Clark County Jail—now the Myrna Loy Theater—circa 1920. Photo by Ed. Reinig.

La Peña Cultural Center
Page 152: The Big Small Theater of Philadelphia. Photo by Adam B. Lairson.
Page 165: Grupo Huachalal from Guatemala performing on an outdoor stage during the La Peña Block Party in June 1988. Photo by Laura Ruiz.

Madison Civic Center
Page 166: Sankai Juku in performance. Photo by Jack Vartoogian.
Page 179: Mikhail Baryshnikov.

92nd Street Y
Page 180: Gerard Schwarz, Music Director and Principal Conductor, conducting the New York Chamber Symphony of the 92nd Street Y in Kaufman Concert Hall. Photo by Jonathan Atkin.

On the Boards
Page 194: Debbie Poulsen and choreographer Wade Madsen in *Men and Women*, a work performed during the 1988 "Northwest New Works Festival." Photo by John Klicker.
Page 207: The B-Boys—Elija Muied, Steve Wesley and Shawn Miller—in a scene from *Boys Will B-Boys*. Photo by Pete Kuhns.

P.S. 122
Page 208: P.S. 122. Photo by Dona Ann McAdams.

Quantum Productions
Page 222: Sun Ra. Photo by Dave Buechner.
Page 237: Ornette Coleman. Photo by Jay Anderson.

San Francisco Performances
Page 238: The David Gordon/Pick Up Company performing *United States*. Photo by Andrew Eccles.
Page 249: Kronos Quartet and ODC/San Francisco. Photo by Paul Latoures.

Spoleto Festival USA
Page 250: Spoleto Festival Orchestra members rehearsing before an outdoor concert. Photo by William Struhs.
Page 265: Fireworks following an outdoor concert at Middleton Place, a former plantation near Charleston, S.C. Photo by William Struhs.

University of Iowa, Hancher Auditorium
Page 266: The Joffrey Ballet in rehearsal with Iowa schoolchildren for the company's new production of *The Nutcracker*. Photo by Jon Van Allen.

Walker Art Center
Page 278: Trisha Brown Company in *Lateral Pass*, created during a residency in the Twin Cities.
Page 293: Early workshop performance of *The Gospel at Colonus*.
Photos courtesy of the Walker Art Center.

Yreka Community Theatre
Page 294: Sophie Corriveau of Theatre Ballet of Canada in *Tribute*. Photo by Richard Desmarais.

DATE DUE